LAURENCE GARDNER is an internationally known sovereign
genealogist and historical lecturer. Distinguished as
the Chevalier Labhràn de St. Germain, he is Presidential
Attaché to the European Council of Princes, a constitutional
advisory body established in 1946. He is also Prior of
the Sacred Kindred of St. Columba and a Fellow of the Society
of Antiquaries of Scotland. Formally attached to the Noble Order
of the Guard of St. Germain, founded by King James VII of
Scots in 1692 and ratified by King Louis XIV of France,
he is the appointed Jacobite Historiographer Royal.

BLOODLINE
⊙ OF THE
HOLY GRAIL
THE HIDDEN LINEAGE OF JESUS REVEALED

LAURENCE GARDNER

THE CHEVALIER LABHRÀN DE SAINT GERMAIN

BARNES & NOBLE BOOKS

NEW YORK

This edition published by Barnes & Noble, Inc.,
by arrangement with Fair Winds Press.

2004 Barnes & Noble Books
M 10 9 8 7 6 5 4 3 2 1
ISBN: 0-7607-6259-7

Produced and packaged by The Book Laboratory® Inc.

Printed in Singapore by CS Graphics

CONTENTS

Bible references are from
AUTHORIZED KING JAMES VERSION
Oxford Edition

LIST OF MAPS

LIST OF CHARTS

FOREWORD

Bloodline of the Holy Grail is a remarkable achievement in the field of genealogical research. Rare is the historian acquainted with such compelling facts as are gathered in this work. The revelations are entirely fascinating and will surely be appreciated by many as real treasures of enlightenment. Herein is the vital story of those fundamental issues which helped to shape the Christian Church in Europe and the Crusader States.

To some, aspects of this book will perhaps appear heretical in nature. It is the right of any individual to take this view since the inherent disclosures are somewhat removed from the orthodox tradition. However, the fact remains that Chevalier Labhràn has penetrated the very depths of available manuscripts and archival data concerning the subject, moving far beyond the bounds of any conventional domain. The resultant unveiled knowledge is presented in a very articulate, interesting and tantalizing manner.

This work offers an incredible insight into centuries of strategic governmental alignments, together with their associated deceits and intrigues. For around two thousand years, the destinies of millions of people have been manipulated by unique, though often whimsical, personalities, who have perverted the spiritual aspirations of our civilization. With marvelous detail, the author has removed the constraints of vested interest to relate numerous suppressed accounts of our heritage. In so doing, he resurrects the politically silenced history of a resolute royal dynasty which the Church has long sought to vanquish in order to further its own ends. Now, in this new age of understanding, may the truth prevail, and may the Phoenix rise once again.

HRH Prince Michael of Albany
Head of the Royal House of Stewart

ACKNOWLEDGMENTS

For their valued assistance in the preparation of this work, I am indebted to the good offices of the Celtic Church of the Sacred Kindred of Saint Columba, the Royal House of Stewart, the European Council of Princes and the Order of Knights Templars of Jerusalem. I would similarly like to thank all the archivists and librarians who have aided my quest, especially those at The British Library, Bibliothèque Nationale de France, Bibliothèque de Bordeaux, Somerset County Library, Birmingham Central Library, Glasgow Mitchell Library and the National Library of Scotland.

Since this book is very much a synthesis of interrelated subject matter, I am greatly beholden to those specialist authors whose individual mastery in their respective fields has facilitated the coverage of specific aspects. Their personal research, expertise and pre-eminent published works have been invaluable. Apart from a comprehensive Bibliography, selected reading material is identified within the Notes and References and attention is drawn to certain writers in the general text.

My utmost gratitude is due to HRH Prince Michael of Albany for affording me privileged access to Household and Chivalric papers. I am also thankful to my wife, Angela, and son, James, for their forbearance during my time-consuming endeavor.

To those many friends who have smoothed the path of this venture in one way or another I offer my appreciation. In particular, I am grateful to John Baldock, Chev. David Roy Stewart, Chev. Jack Robertson, Rev. David Cuthbert Stalker, Karen Lyster, Michael Deering, Leo van de Pas, Chris Rosling and Dr. A. R. Kittermaster.

Inestimable thanks are due to Michael Mann, Sue Hook, Jeff Landis, Greg Brandenburgh and all my colleagues at Element Books UK and USA, together with Philip Dunn of The Book Laboratory and Julie Foakes for their professional design of this illustrated volume.

For their generous support in aiding my work internationally, my special thanks to JZ Knight and all at Ramtha's School of Enlightenment, to Nancy Simms of Entropic Fine Art, to Christina Zohs of *The Golden Thread* and to Duncan Roads, Ruth Parnell and Marcus Allen of *Nexus*. Also to the directors and staff of MediaQuest International for their production of the *Bloodline* lecture recordings, together with Reg Presley and Phamie MacDonald of Four Corners Vision for their enthusiasm concerning the proposed *Bloodline* TV series.

My thankful recognition is due to Sir Peter Robson for his artistic liaison by way of the specially conceived painting, *Bloodline of the Holy Grail*. Similarly, to the musical composer, Adrian Wagner, who, in the family tradition of such masterworks as *Lohengrin* and *Parsifal*, has endorsed this book with the release of his album, *Holy Spirit and the Holy Grail* <www.mediaquest.co.uk/lgardner.html>.

Finally, I must convey my gratitude to all those readers who have supported and encouraged my work since the publication of the first edition of *Bloodline*. Especially to those many thousands who have written to me with so many useful comments and contributions, which have helped to pave the way towards this special Millennium Edition.

Laurence Gardner

On page 397 in Appendix IV of the 1996 first edition of *Bloodline of the Holy Grail*, I inadvertently credited a *Sinclair Genealogist* article concerning Christopher Columbus to its publisher, H. S. 'Pete' Cummings, Jnr, instead of to its author. With my apologies, the credit in this regard should have been to Ian F. Brown.

Here is the Book of thy descent.

Here begins the Book of the Sangraél.

The Perlesvaus

Also by the same Author:
GENESIS OF THE GRAIL KINGS

Recommended in conjunction with this work:
THE FORGOTTEN MONARCHY OF SCOTLAND
by HRH Prince Michael of Albany

Frontispiece:
The red-caped priestess Mary Magdalene in Provence.
Netherlandish, 16th century

I

ORIGINS OF THE BLOODLINE

WHOM DOES THE GRAIL SERVE?

Following the Jewish Revolt in Jerusalem during the first century C.E., the Roman overlords were reputed to have destroyed all records concerning the Davidic legacy of Jesus the Messiah's family. The destruction was far from complete, however, and relevant documents were retained by Jesus's heirs, who brought the Messianic heritage from the Near East to the West. As confirmed by the *Ecclesiastical History* of Eusebius, the fourth-century Bishop of Caesarea,[1] these heirs were called the Desposyni (ancient Greek for 'of the Master'),[2] a hallowed style reserved exclusively for those in the same family descent as Jesus.[3] Theirs was the sacred legacy of the Royal House of Judah—a dynastic bloodline that lives on today.

During the course of this book, we shall study the compelling story of this sovereign lineage by unfolding a detailed genealogical account of the Messianic Blood Royal (the *Sangréal*) in direct descent from Jesus and his brother James. However, in order to cover this ground, it will first be necessary to consider the Old and New Testament Bible stories from a different perspective to that normally conveyed. This will not be a rewriting of history, but a reshaping of familiar accounts—bringing history back to its original base, rather than perpetuating the myths of strategic restyling by those with otherwise vested interests.

Throughout the centuries, an ongoing Church and governmental conspiracy has prevailed against the Messianic inheritance. This heightened when Imperial Rome diverted the course of Christianity to suit an alternative ideal and has continued to the present day.

Many apparently unconnected events of history have in fact been chapters of that same continuing suppression of the line. From the Jewish Wars of the first century through to the eighteenth-century American Revolution and beyond, the machinations have been perpetuated by English and European governments in collaboration with the Anglican and Roman Catholic Churches. In their attempts to constrain the royal birthright of Judah, the High Christian movements have installed various figurehead regimes, including Britain's own House of Hanover-Saxe-Coburg-Gotha. Such administrations have been compelled to uphold specific religious doctrines, while others have been deposed for preaching religious forbearance.

Now, at the turn of a new Millennium, this is a time for reflection and reform in the civilized world—and to accomplish such reform it is appropriate to consider the errors and successes of the past. For this purpose there is no better record than that which exists within the chronicles of the Sangréal.

The definition, *Holy Grail*, first appeared in the Middle Ages as a literary concept, based (as will be later discussed) on a series of scribal misinterpretations. It derived immediately as a translation from *Saint Grail* and from the earlier

1

The Roman Conquest of Jerusalem
by Nicolas Poussin, 1594-1665

forms, *San Graal* and *Sangréal*. The Ancient Order the Sangréal, a dynastic Order of the Scots Royal House of Stewart, was directly allied to the continental European Order of the Realm of Sion[4] and of the knights of both Orders were adherents of the Sangréal, which defines the true Blood Royal (the Sang Réal) of Judah: the *Bloodline of the Holy Grail*.

Quite apart from its dynastic physical aspect, the Holy Grail also has a spiritual dimension. It has been symbolized by many things, but as a material item it is most commonly perceived as a chalice, especially a chalice that contains, or once contained, the life-blood of Jesus. The Grail has additionally been portrayed as a vine, weaving its way through the annals of time. The fruit of the vine is the grape—and from the grape comes wine. In this respect, the symbolic elements of the chalice and the vine coincide, for wine has long been equated with the blood of Jesus. Indeed, this tradition sits at the very heart of the Eucharist (Holy Communion) sacrament, and the perpetual blood of the Grail chalice represents no less than the enduring Messianic bloodline.

In esoteric Grail lore, the chalice and vine support the ideal of 'service', whereas the blood and wine correspond to the eternal spirit of 'fulfillment'. The spiritual Quest of the Grail is, therefore, a desire for fulfillment through giving and receiving service. That which is called the Grail Code is itself a parable for the human condition, in that it is the quest of us all to achieve through service. The problem is that the precept of the Code has been overwhelmed by an avaricious society complex, based on the notion of the 'survival of the fittest'. Today, it is plain that wealth, rather than health, is a major stepping-stone towards being socially fit, whilst another criterion is obedience to the law.

Above such considerations, however, there is a further requirement: the requirement to toe the party line while paying homage to the demigods of power. This prerequisite has nothing to do with obeying the law or with behaving properly—it relies totally on not rocking the boat and on withholding opinions that do not conform. Those who break ranks are declared heretics, meddlers and troublemakers, and as such are deemed socially unfit by their governing establishment. Perceived social fitness is consequently attained by submitting to indoctrination and forsaking personal individuality in order to preserve the administrative status quo. By any standard of reckoning, this can hardly be described as a democratic way of life.

The democratic ideal is expressed as 'government *by* the people *for* the people'. To facilitate the process, democracies are organized on an electoral basis whereby the few represent the many. The representatives are chosen *by* the people to govern *for* the people—but the paradoxical result is generally their government *of* the people. This is contrary to all the principles of democratic community and has nothing whatever to do with *service*. It is, therefore, in direct opposition to the Grail Code.

At a national and local level, elected representatives have long managed to reverse the harmonious ideal by setting themselves upon pedestals above their electorate. By virtue of this, individual rights, liberties and welfare are controlled by political dictate, and such dictates determine who is socially fit and who is socially unfit at any given time. In many cases this even corresponds to decisions on who shall survive and who shall not. To this end, there are many who seek positions of influence for the sheer sake of gaining power over others. Serving their own interests, they become manipulators of society, causing the disempowerment of the majority. The result is that, instead of being rightly served, that same majority is reduced to a state of servitude.

Accordingly, *Bloodline of the Holy Grail* is not restricted in content to genealogies and tales of political intrigue, but its pages hold the key to the essential Grail Code—the key not only to a historical mystery but to a way of life. It is a book about good government and bad government. It tells how the patriarchal kingship of people was supplanted by dogmatic tyranny and the dictatorial overlordship of land. It is a journey of discovery through past ages, with its eye set firmly upon the future.

Whom does the Grail serve? It serves those who quest despite the odds—for they are the champions of enlightenment.

THE PAGAN IDOLS OF CHRISTENDOM

In the course of our journey we shall confront a number of assertions which may at first seem startling, but this is often the case when setting historical matters to rights, for most of us have been conditioned to accept certain interpretations of history as matters of fact. To a large extent we have all learned history by way of strategic propaganda, whether Church or politically motivated. It is all part of the control process; it separates the masters from the servants and the fit from the unfit. Political history has, of course, long been written by its masters—the few who decide the fate and fortunes of the many. Religious history is no different, for it is designed to implement control through fear of the unknown. In this way the religious masters have retained their supremacy at the expense of devotees who genuinely seek enlightenment and salvation.

In biblical terms our Grail quest begins with the Creation, as defined in the book of Genesis. A little more than two centuries ago, in 1779, a consortium of London booksellers issued the mammoth

42-volume *Universal History*, a work that came to be much revered and which stated with considered assurance that God's work of Creation began on August 21, 4004 B.C.E.[5] A debate ensued over the precise month, for some theologians reckoned that March 21 was the more likely date. All agreed, however, that the year was accurate and everyone accepted that there were only six days between cosmic nothingness and the emergence of Adam.

At the time of publication, Britain was in the grip of the Industrial Revolution. It was an unsettled period of extraordinary change and development but, as with today's rapid rate of advancement, there were social prices to pay. The prized skills and crafts of yesteryear became obsolete in the face of mass production and society was regrouped to accommodate an economically based community structure. A new breed of 'winners' emerged, while the majority floundered in an unfamiliar environment that bore no relation to the customs and standards of their upbringing. Rightly or wrongly, this phenomenon is called 'progress' and the relentless criterion of progress is that very precept propounded by the English naturalist Charles Darwin: the 'survival of the fittest'.[6] The problem is that people's chances of survival are often diminished because they are ignored or exploited by their masters—those same pioneers who forge the route to progress, aiding (if not guaranteeing) their own survival.

It is easy now to appreciate that the 1779 *Universal History* was wrong. We know that the world was not created in 4004 B.C.E. We also know that Adam was not the first man on Earth.[7] Such archaic notions have been outgrown—but to the people of the late eighteenth century this impressive *History* was the product of men more learned than most and it was, naturally, presumed correct. It is therefore worth posing ourselves a question at this stage: How many of today's accepted facts of science and history will also be outgrown in the light of future discoveries?

Dogma is not necessarily truth; it is simply a fervently promoted interpretation of truth based on available facts. When new influential facts are presented, scientific dogma changes as a matter of course—but this is rarely the case with religious dogma. In this book we are particularly concerned with the attitudes and teachings of a Christian Church which pays no heed to discoveries and revelations, and which still upholds much of the incongruous dogma that dates from medieval times. As H. G. Wells so astutely observed during the early 1900s, the religious life of Western nations is 'going on in a house of history built upon sand'.

Traditional concept of the Creation.
19th-century engraving
from a painting by N. Blakey

**Imperial Britannia receives
the Riches of the East**

Charles Darwin's theory of evolution in *The Descent of Man* in 1871[8] caused no personal harm to Adam, but any thought of his being the first living human was naturally discredited. Like all the organic life forms on the planet, humans had evolved by genetic mutation and natural selection through hundreds of thousands of years. The announcement of this fact struck religious minded society with horror. Some simply refused to accept the new doctrine, but many fell into despair. If Adam and Eve were not the primal parents, there was no Original Sin and the very reason for atonement was, therefore, without foundation!

The majority completely misunderstood the concept of Natural Selection. They deduced that if survival was restricted to the fittest then success must be dependent on outdoing one's neighbor! Thus, a new skeptical and ruthless generation was born. Egotistical nationalism flourished as never before and domestic deities were venerated as were the pagan gods of old. Symbols of national identity—such as Britannia and Hibernia—became the new idols of Christendom.

From this unhealthy base was generated an imperialist disease and the stronger, advanced countries claimed the right to exploit less developed nations. The new age of empire building began with an undignified scramble for territorial domain. The German Reich was founded in 1871 through the amalgamation of hitherto separate states. Other states combined to form the Austro-Hungarian Empire. The Russian Empire expanded considerably and, by the 1890s, the British Empire occupied no less than one-fifth of the entire global land mass. This was the impassioned era of resolute Christian missionaries, many of them dispatched from Queen Victoria's Britain. With the religious fabric sorely rent at home, the Church sought a revised justification abroad. The missionaries were especially busy in such places as India and Africa, where the people already had their own beliefs and had never heard of Adam. More importantly, though, they had never heard of Charles Darwin!

In Britain, a new intermediate stratum in society had emerged from the employers of the Industrial Revolution. This burgeoning middle class set the true aristocracy and the governing establishment far beyond the reach of people at large, effectively creating a positive class structure—a system of divisions in which everyone had a designated place. The chieftains wallowed in Arcadian pursuits, while the merchant opportunists competed for station through conspicuous consumption. The workingman accepted his serfdom with songs of allegiance, a dream of Hope and Glory, and a portrait of the tribal priestess Britannia above his mantelshelf.

Students of history knew it would not be long before empires set their sights against each other, and they forecast a day when competing powers would meet in mighty opposition. The conflict began when France endeavored to recover Alsace-Lorraine from German occupation, while the pair battled over the territory's iron and coal reserves. Russia and Austria-Hungary locked horns in a struggle for dominion of the Balkans and there were disputes resulting from colonial ambitions in Africa and elsewhere. The fuse was lit in June 1914 when a Serbian nationalist murdered Archduke Francis Ferdinand, the heir to the Austrian throne. At this, Europe exploded into a great war, largely instigated by Germany. Hostilities were commenced against Serbia, Russia, France and Belgium, and the counter-offensive was led by Britain. The struggle lasted for more than four years, coming to an end when a revolt erupted in Germany and Emperor (Kaiser) William II fled the country.

Following all the technological advancements of a manufacturing age, history had made little progress in social terms. Engineering achievements had led to unprecedented martial ability, while Christianity had become so fragmented as to be barely recognizable. Britain's pride emerged intact, but the German Reich was not of a mind to take its losses lightly. With the

**Assassination of Archduke Ferdinand
at Sarajevo on June 28, 1914**

old regime overthrown, a fervent new party rose to dominance. Its despotic Führer (leader), Adolf Hitler, annexed Austria in 1937 and swept into Poland two years later. The second great war—truly a World War—had begun: the fiercest territorial struggle to date. It was waged through six years and was centered upon the very core beliefs of religion itself: the rights of everyone in a civilized environment.

Quite suddenly, the Church and the people realized that religion was not, and never had been, about patriarchs and miracles. It was about belief in a neighborly way of life, an application of moral standards and ethical values, of faith and charity, along with the constant quest for freedom and deliverance. At last any continuing general dispute about the evolutionary nature of human descent was put aside; that was the province of scientists and the majority relaxed in acceptance of the fact.

The Church emerged as a far less fearful opponent of scholars, and the new environment was more agreeable to all concerned. For many, the text of the Bible had no longer to be regarded as inviolable dogma and venerated for its own sake. Religion was embodied in its precepts and principles, not in the paper on which it was printed.

This new perspective gave rise to endless speculative possibilities. If Eve had truly been the only woman in existence and her only offspring were three sons, then with whom did her son Seth unite to father the tribes of Israel? If Adam was not the first man on Earth, what actually was his significance? Who or what were the angels? The New Testament also had its share of mysteries. Who were the apostles? Did the miracles really happen? And most importantly, did the Virgin Birth and the Resurrection genuinely take place as described?

We shall consider all of these questions before we embark on the trail of the Grail Bloodline itself. In fact, it is imperative to understand Jesus's historical and environmental background, in order to comprehend the facts of his marriage and parental fatherhood. As we progress, many readers will find themselves treading wholly new ground—but it is simply the ground that existed before it was carpeted and concealed by those whose motives were to suppress the truth for the sake of retaining control. Only by rolling back the carpet of strategic concealment can we succeed in our Quest for the Holy Grail.

BLOODLINE OF THE KINGS

It is now generally acknowledged that the opening chapters of the Old Testament do not represent the early history of the world as they appear to suggest.[9] More precisely, they tell the story of a family: a family that became a race comprising various tribes—a race that in turn became the Hebrew nation. If Adam was the first of a type, then he was certainly a progenitor of the Hebrews and the tribes of Israel.[10] Indeed, as described in this book's companion volume, *Genesis of the Grail Kings*, he was actually the first of a predestined line of priestly governors.

Two of the most intriguing Old Testament characters are Joseph and Moses. Each played an important role in the formation of the Hebrew nation and both have historical identities that can be examined quite independently of the Bible.

Genesis 41:39-43 tells how Joseph was made Governor of Egypt:

> And Pharaoh said unto Joseph ... Thou shalt be over my house and according unto thy word shall all my people be ruled: only in the throne will I be greater than thou ... and he made him ruler over all the land of Egypt.

Referring to Moses, Exodus 11:3 informs us similarly that:

> Moses was very great in the land of Egypt, in the sight of the Pharaoh's servants, and in the sight of the people.

Yet for all this status and prominence, neither Joseph nor Moses appear in any Egyptian record under their given biblical names.

The annals of Ramesses II (c.1304-1237 B.C.E.) specify that Semitic people were settled in the land of Goshen and it is further explained that they went there from Canaan for want of food. But why should Ramesses' scribes mention this Nile delta settlement at Goshen? According to standard Bible chronology, the Hebrews went to Egypt some three centuries before the time of Ramesses and made their exodus in about 1491 B.C.E., long before he came to the throne. So, by virtue of this first-hand scribal record, the standard Bible chronology as generally promoted is seen to be incorrect.

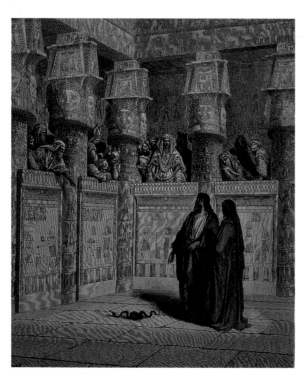

**Moses negotiates the Israelites'
freedom with the Pharaoh of Egypt
by Gustave Doré, 1832-83**

**Statue of Pharaoh Ramesses II
(c.1304-1237 BC) at Luxor, Egypt**

It is traditionally presumed that Joseph was sold into slavery in Egypt in the 1720s B.C.E. and was made Governor by the Pharaoh a decade or so later. Afterwards, his father Jacob (whose name was changed to Israel)[11] and seventy family members followed him into Goshen to escape the famine in Canaan. Notwithstanding this, Genesis 47:11, Exodus 1:11 and Numbers 33:30 all refer to 'the land of Ramesses' (Egyptian: 'the house of Ramesses')[12]—but this was a complex of grain storehouses built by the Israelites for Ramesses II in Goshen some 300 years after they were supposedly there!

It transpires, therefore, that the alternative Jewish Reckoning is more accurate than the Standard Chronology: Joseph was in Egypt not in the early eighteenth century B.C.E., but in the early fifteenth century B.C.E. There he was appointed Chief Minister to Tuthmosis IV (c. 1413-1405 B.C.E.) To the Egyptians, however, Joseph (Yusuf the Vizier) was known as Yuya and his story is particularly revealing—not just in relation to the biblical account of Joseph, but also in respect of Moses. The Cairo-born historian and linguist Ahmed Osman has made an in-depth study of these personalities in their contemporary Egyptian environment and his findings are of great significance.[13]

When Pharaoh Tuthmosis died, his son married his sibling sister Sitamun (as was the pharaonic tradition) so that he could inherit the throne as Pharaoh Amenhotep III. Shortly afterwards he also married Tiye, daughter of the Chief Minister (Joseph/Yuya). It was decreed, however, that no son born to Tiye could inherit the throne and, because of the overall length of her father Joseph's governorship, there was a general fear that the Israelites were gaining too much power in Egypt. So when Tiye became pregnant, the edict was given that her child should be killed at birth if a son. Tiye's Israelite relatives lived at Goshen and she owned a summer palace a little upstream at Zarw,

Pharaoh Amenhotep III (c.1405-1367 BC)
and the Egyptian crocodile god Sobek,
the great Messeh

where she went to have her baby. She did indeed bear a son, but the royal midwives conspired with Tiye to float the child downstream in a reed basket to the house of her father's half-brother Levi.

The boy, Aminadab (born c. 1394 B.C.E.), was duly educated in the eastern delta country by the Egyptian priests of Ra. Then, in his teenage years he went to live at Thebes. By that time, his mother had acquired more influence than the senior queen, Sitamun, who had never borne a son and heir to the Pharaoh, only a daughter who was called Nefertiti. In Thebes, Aminadab could not accept the Egyptian deities with their myriad idols and so he introduced the notion of Aten, an omnipotent God who had no image. Aten was thus an equivalent of the Hebrews' Adon—a title borrowed from the Phoenician and meaning 'Lord'—in line with Israelite teachings. At that time Aminadab (the Hebrew equivalent of Amenhotep: 'Amun is pleased') changed his name to Akhenaten (servant of Aten).

Pharaoh Amenhotep then suffered a period of ill health and, since there was no direct male heir to the royal house, Akhenaten married his half-sister Nefertiti in order to rule as co-regent during this difficult time. In due course, however, when Amenhotep III died, Akhenaten was able to succeed as Pharaoh, gaining the official style of Amenhotep IV. He and Nefertiti had six daughters and a son called Tutankhaten.

The Pharaoh's daughter finding the baby Moses
by Paolo Veronese, c.1575

Pharaoh Akhenaten closed all the temples of the Egyptian gods and built new temples to Aten. He also ran a household that was distinctly domestic—quite different from the kingly norm in ancient Egypt. On many fronts he became unpopular, particularly with the priests of the former national deity Amun (or Amen) and of the sun god Ra (or Re), as a result of which, plots against his life proliferated. Loud were the threats of armed insurrection if he did not allow the traditional gods to be worshipped alongside the faceless Aten. But Akhenaten refused and was eventually forced to abdicate in short-term favor of his cousin Smenkhkare, who was succeeded by Akhenaten's son Tutankhaten. But, on taking the throne at the age of about eleven, Tutankhaten was obliged to change his name to Tutankhamen. He, in turn, was only to live and reign for a further nine or ten years, meeting his death while still comparatively young.

Akhenaten, meanwhile, was banished from Egypt. He fled with some retainers to the remote safety of Sinai, taking with him his royal scepter topped with a brass serpent. To his supporters he remained very much the rightful monarch—the heir to the throne from which he had been ousted—and he was still regarded by them as the *Mose*, *Meses* or *Mosis*, meaning 'heir' or 'born of'—as in Tuthmosis ('born of Tuth') and Ramesses ('fashioned of Ra').

Evidence from Egypt indicates that Moses (Akhenaten) led his people from Pi-Ramesses (near modern Kantra) southward, through Sinai, towards Lake Timash.[14] This was extremely marshy territory and, although it was manageable on foot with some difficulty, any pursuing horses and chariots would have foundered disastrously.

Pharaoh Akhenaten, the Mose of Egypt
(Amenhotep IV), c.1367-1361 BC

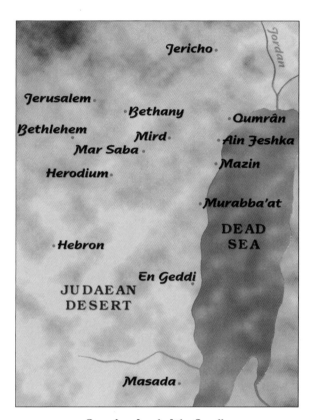

Qumrân—Land of the Scrolls

Among the retainers who fled with Moses were the families of Jacob (Israel): the Israelites. Then, at the instigation of their leader, they constructed the Tabernacle[15] and the Ark of the Covenant at the foot of Mount Sinai. Once Moses had died, they began their invasion of the country left by their forefathers so long before, but Canaan (Palestine) had changed considerably in the meantime, having been infiltrated by waves of Philistines and Phoenicians. The records tell of great sea battles and of massive armies marching to war. At length, the Israelites (under their new leader, Joshua) were successful and, once across the Jordan, they took Jericho from the Canaanites, gaining a real foothold in their traditional Promised Land.

Following Joshua's death, the ensuing period of rule by appointed Judges was a catalogue of disaster until the disparate Hebrew and Israelite tribes united under their first king, Saul, in about 1048 B.C.E.. Eventually, however, with the conquest of Canaan as complete as possible, David of Bethlehem married Saul's daughter to become King of Judah (corresponding to half the Palestinian territory) in around 1008 B.C.E.. Subsequently, he also acquired Israel (the balance of the territory) to become overall King of the Jews—and the reigning Bloodline of the Holy Grail had begun.

IN THE BEGINNING

JEHOVAH AND THE GODDESS

Together with the military exploits of the Israelites, the Old Testament describes the evolution of the Jewish faith from the time of Abraham. The story is not that of a unified nation devoted to the God Jehovah, but tells of a tenacious sect who fought against all odds to contrive the dominant religion of Israel. In their opinion, Jehovah was male, but this was a sectarian concept that gave rise to severe and manifold problems.

On the wider contemporary stage, it was generally understood that the creation of life must emanate from both male and female sources. Other religions—whether in Egypt, Mesopotamia or elsewhere—accordingly had deities of both sexes. The primary male god was generally associated with the sun or the sky, while the primary goddess had her roots in the earth, the sea and fertility. The sun gave its force to the earth and waters, from which sprang life: a very natural and logical interpretation.

In relation to such theistic ideas, one of the more flexible characters mentioned in biblical texts is King David's son, Solomon, celebrated not just for the magnificence and splendor of his reign, but for the wisdom of the man himself. Much later, Solomon's legacy was crucial to emergent Grail lore because he was the true advocate of religious toleration. Solomon was king centuries before the period of the Israelites' captivity in Babylon and he was very much a part of the old environment.

During Solomon's era, Jehovah was afforded considerable importance, but other gods were acknowledged as well. It was a spiritually uncertain age in which it was not uncommon for individuals to hedge their bets in respect to alternative deities. After all, with such a plethora of different gods and goddesses receiving homage in the region, it might have been shortsighted to decry all but one—for who was to say that the devout Hebrews had got it right!

In this regard, Solomon's renowned wisdom was based on considered judgment. Even though he worshipped Jehovah, the God of a minority sect, he had no reason to deny his subjects their

**A presentation to King Solomon of Israel
by Denise Bourbonnais**

PATRIARCHS AND TRIBES OF ISRAEL

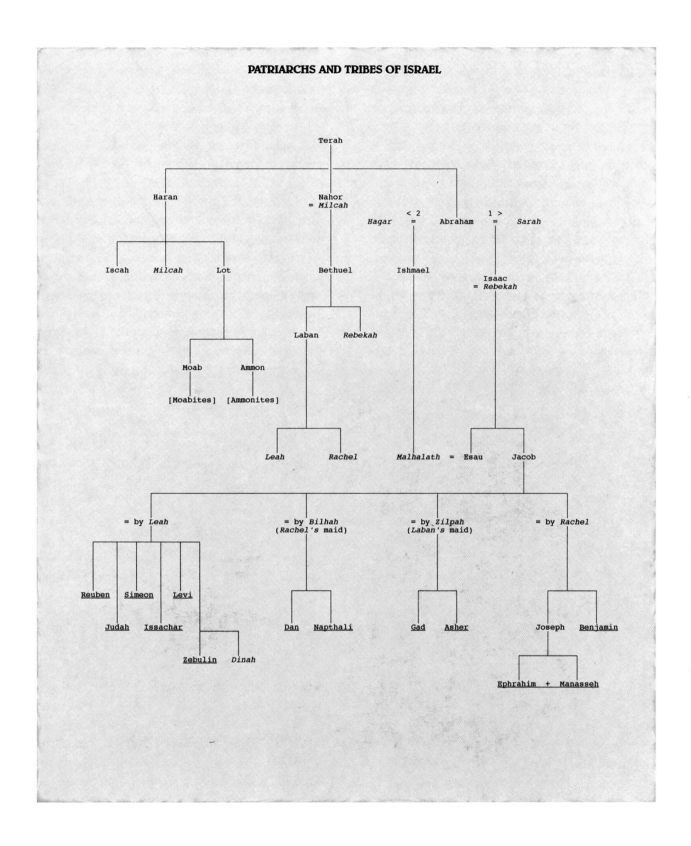

own gods (1 Kings 11:4-10). He even retained his own beliefs in the divine forces of nature, no matter who or what was at the head of them.

Veneration of the primary female deity was of long standing in Canaan, where she took the form of the goddess Ashtoreth. She was equivalent to Ishtar, the major goddess of the Babylonians. As Inanna, her Sumerian temple was at Uruk (the biblical Erech, modern Warka) in southern Mesopotamia, while in nearby Syria and Phoenicia she was reported by the ancient Greeks to have been called Astarte.

The Holy of Holies, or Inner Sanctum of Solomon's Temple, was deemed to represent the womb of Ashtoreth (alternatively called Asherah, as mentioned several times in the Old Testament). Ashtoreth was openly worshipped by the Israelites until the sixth century B.C.E.. As the Lady Asherah, she was the supernal wife of El, the supreme male

King Solomon
by Simeon Solomon, c.1854

deity, and they were together the Divine Couple. Their daughter was Anath, Queen of the Heavens, and their son, the King of the Heavens, was called He. As time progressed, the separate characters of El and He were merged to become Jehovah. Asherah and Anath were then similarly conjoined to become Jehovah's female consort, known as the Shekinah or Matronit.

The name Jehovah is a late and somewhat Anglicized transliteration of Yahweh, which is itself a form of the four-consonantal Hebrew stem YHWH into which two vowels have been rightly or wrongly interpolated.[1] Originally, these four consonants (which later became a sort of acronym for the One God) represented the four members of the Heavenly Family: Y represented El the *Father*; H was Asherah the *Mother*; W corresponded to He the *Son*, and H was the *Daughter*, Anath. In accordance with the royal traditions of the time and region, God's mysterious bride, the Shekinah, was also reckoned to be his sister. In the Jewish cult of the Kabbalah (an esoteric discipline that reached its height in medieval times) God's dual male-female image was perpetuated. Meanwhile other sects perceived the Shekinah (or Matronit) as the female presence of God on Earth. The divine marital chamber was the Sanctuary of the Jerusalem Temple but, from the moment the Temple was destroyed, the Shekinah was destined to roam the Earth while the male aspect of Jehovah was left to rule the heavens alone.

In practical terms, the cementing of the Hebrew ideal of the one male God did not actually occur until after their fifty years of captivity in Babylon (c.586-536 B.C.E.). When the Israelites were first deported there by Nebuchadnezzar, they were effectively disparate tribes belonging to at least two major ethnic streams (Israel and Judah), but they returned to the Holy Land with a common national purpose as Jehovah's 'chosen people'.

Much of what we now know as the Old Testament (the Hebrew Bible) was first written down in Babylon.[2] It is hardly surprising, therefore, that Sumerian and Mesopotamian stories were grafted onto the early Jewish cultural tradition—including accounts of the Garden of Eden (the Paradise of Eridu[3]), the Flood[4] and the Tower of Babel.[5] The patriarch Abraham had migrated to Canaan from Ur of the Chaldees (in Mesopotamia), so the cultural grafting was justifiable, but the fact remains that stories such as that of Adam and Eve were by no means restricted to Hebrew tradition. In this regard, their lives and historical relevance are discussed at length in *Genesis of the Grail Kings*.

Alternatives to the Bible's version of the Adam and Eve story may be found in the writings of Greeks, Syrians, Egyptians, Sumerians and Abyssinians (ancient Ethiopians). Some accounts tell of Adam's first consort, Lilith, before he was enchanted by Eve. Lilith was handmaiden to the Shekinah and she left Adam because he tried to dominate her. Escaping to the Red Sea, she cried 'Why should I lie beneath you? I am your equal!' A Sumerian terra-cotta relief depicting Lilith (dating from around 2000 B.C.E.) shows her naked and winged, standing on the backs of two lions and holding the rods and rings of divine rulership and wisdom. Although not a goddess in the traditional sense,

Israelites in chains before Nebuchadnezzar of Babylon.

13th-century manuscript illustration

**Sumerian terra-cotta relief of Lilith,
with the rods and rings
of divine justice, c.2000 BC**

her incarnate spirit was said to flourish in Solomon's most renowned lover, the Queen of Sheba. Lilith is described in the sacred book of the esoteric Mandaeans of Iraq as the Daughter of the Underworld[6] and, throughout history to the present day, she has represented the fundamental ethic of female opportunity.

When the Israelites returned from Babylon to Jerusalem, the first five Books of Moses[7] were collated into the Jewish Torah (the Law). The rest of the Old Testament was, however, kept separate. For a number of centuries, it was regarded with varying degrees of veneration and suspicion but, in time, the Books of the Prophets[8] became especially significant in stabilizing the Jewish heritage.[9] The

main reason for hesitation was that, although the Jews were understood to be God's 'chosen people', Jehovah had not actually treated them very kindly. He was their all-powerful tribal Lord and had promised the patriarch, Abraham, to exalt their race above all others. And yet, for all that, they had faced only wars, famines, deportation and captivity! To counter the nation's growing disenchantment, the Books of the Prophets reinforced Jehovah's promise by announcing the Coming of a Messiah, an anointed King or Priest who would serve the people by leading them to salvation.[10]

This prophecy was sufficient to ensure the rebuilding of Solomon's Temple and the Wall of Jerusalem, but no Messianic savior appeared. The Old Testament ends at this point in the fourth century B.C.E.. Meanwhile, the bloodline of David continued, although not actively reigning. Then, more than 300 years later, a whole new chapter of sovereign history began when the revolutionary heir of Judah stepped boldly into the public domain. He was Jesus the Nazarene, the King de jure of Jerusalem.

SCROLLS AND TRACTATES

The Dead Sea Scrolls are now the most useful aids to understanding the Judean culture of the pre-Gospel era,[11] but they were discovered by pure chance as recently as 1947. A Bedouin shepherd boy, Mohammed ed-Di'b, was searching for a lost goat in the cliff-hill caves of Qumrân, near Jericho, when he found a number of tall earthenware jars. Professional archaeologists were called in and excavations were subsequently undertaken—not only at Qumrân but at nearby Murabba'at and Mird in the

THE HOUSE OF HEROD
37 BC - AD 99

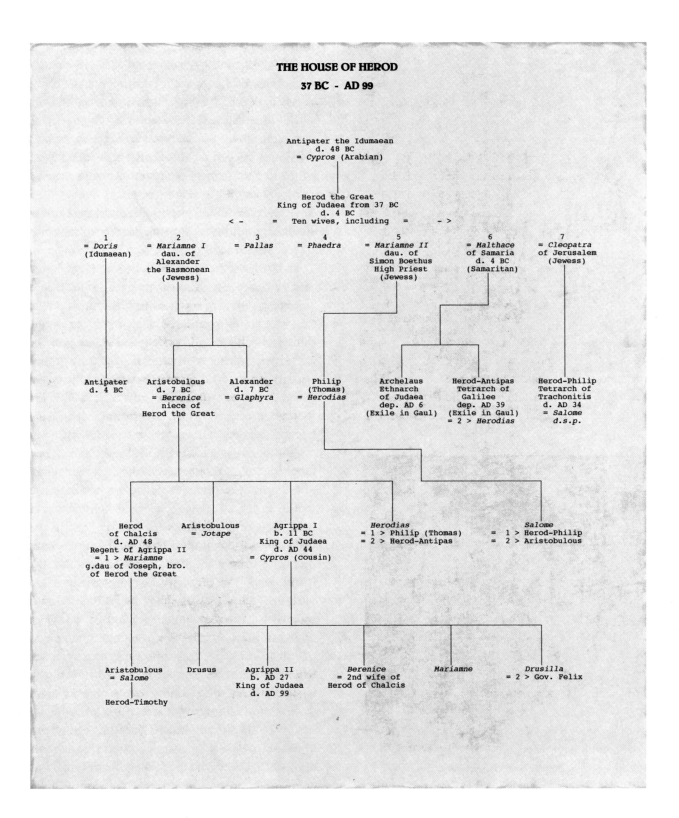

Antipater the Idumaean
d. 48 BC
= *Cypros* (Arabian)

Herod the Great
King of Judaea from 37 BC
d. 4 BC
< - = Ten wives, including = - >

1	2	3	4	5	6	7
= *Doris* (Idumaean)	= *Mariamne I* dau. of Alexander the Hasmonean (Jewess)	= *Pallas*	= *Phaedra*	= *Mariamne II* dau. of Simon Boethus High Priest (Jewess)	= *Malthace* of Samaria d. 4 BC (Samaritan)	= *Cleopatra* of Jerusalem (Jewess)

Antipater
d. 4 BC

Aristobulous
d. 7 BC
= *Berenice*
niece of
Herod the Great

Alexander
d. 7 BC
= *Glaphyra*

Philip
(Thomas)
= *Herodias*

Archelaus
Ethnarch
of Judaea
dep. AD 6
(Exile in Gaul)

Herod-Antipas
Tetrarch of
Galilee
dep. AD 39
(Exile in Gaul)
= 2 > *Herodias*

Herod-Philip
Tetrarch of
Trachonitis
d. AD 34
= *Salome*
d.s.p.

Herod
of Chalcis
d. AD 48
Regent of Agrippa II
= 1 > *Mariamne*
g.dau of Joseph, bro.
of Herod the Great

Aristobulous
= *Jotape*

Agrippa I
b. 11 BC
King of Judaea
d. AD 44
= *Cypros* (cousin)

Herodias
= 1 > Philip (Thomas)
= 2 > Herod-Antipas

Salome
= 1 > Herod-Philip
= 2 > Aristobulous

Aristobulous
= *Salome*

Herod-Timothy

Drusus

Agrippa II
b. AD 27
King of Judaea
d. AD 99

Berenice
= 2nd wife of
Herod of Chalcis

Mariamne

Drusilla
= 2 > Gov. Felix

Wilderness of Judea.[12] Many more jars were discovered in 11 different caves. Altogether the jars contained around 500 Hebrew and Aramaic manuscripts—among them Old Testament writings and numerous documents of community record, with some of their traditions dating back to about 250 B.C.E. The Scrolls had been hidden during the Jewish Revolt against the Romans (between 66 and 70 C.E.) and were never retrieved. The Old Testament book of Jeremiah (32:14) states prophetically, 'Thus saith the Lord of Hosts ... Take these evidences ... and put them in an earthen vessel, that they may continue many days'.[13]

Among the more important manuscript texts, the *Copper Scroll* lists an inventory and gives the locations for the treasures of Jerusalem and the Kedron Valley cemetery. The *War Scroll* contains a full account of military tactics and strategy. The *Manual of Discipline* details law and legal practice along with customary ritual and describes the importance of a designated Council of Twelve to preserve the faith of the land. The fascinating *Habakkuk Pesher* gives a commentary on the contemporary personalities and important developments of the era. Also in the collection is a complete draft of Isaiah which, at more than 30 feet (around 9 meters) in length, is the longest scroll and is centuries older than any other known copy of that Old Testament book.

To complement these discoveries, another significant find relating to the post-Gospel era had been made in Egypt two years earlier. In December 1945 two peasant brothers, Mohammed and Khalifah Ali, were digging for fertilizer in a cemetery near the town of Nag Hammadi when they came upon a large sealed jar containing thirteen leather-bound books. The books' papyrus leaves contained an assortment of scriptures, written in the tradition that was later to be called Gnostic (esoteric insight). Inherently Christian works, but with Jewish overtones, they have become known as the *Nag Hammadi Library*.[14]

The books were written in the ancient Coptic language of Egypt during early Christian times. The Coptic Museum in Cairo ascertained that they were, in fact, copies of much older works originally composed in Greek. Indeed, some of the texts were discovered to have very early origins, incorporating traditions from before 50 C.E. Included in the fifty-two separate tractates are various religious texts and certain hitherto unknown Gospels. They tend to portray an environment very different from that described in the Bible. The cities of Sodom and Gomorrah, for example, are not presented as centers of wickedness and debauchery, but as cities of great wisdom and learning. More to our purpose, they describe a world in which Jesus gives his own account of the Crucifixion, and in which his relationship with Mary Magdalene reaches enlightening new proportions.

**Cliff-hill cave at Qumrân,
land of the Scrolls**

Secret Codes of the New Testament

The excavations at Qumrân have produced relics dating from about 3500 B.C.E., at which time (during the Bronze Age) the settlement was a Bedouin[15] camp. The period of formal occupation seems to have commenced in about 130 B.C.E.. Jewish chronicles describe a violent Judean earthquake in 31 B.C.E.[16] and this is confirmed at Qumrân by a break between two distinct times of habitation.[17] According to the *Copper Scroll*, old Qumrân was called Sekhakha.

The second residential period began during the reign of Herod the Great (c. 37-4 B.C.E.). Herod was an Idumaean Arab, installed as King of Judea by the Roman authorities who had first taken control of the region under Julius Caesar. Apart from the evidence of the Scrolls, a collection of coins has also been amassed from the Qumrân settlement,[18] relating to a time-span from the Hasmonaean ruler John Hyrcanus (135-104 B.C.E.) to the Jewish Revolt of 66-70 C.E.

The uprising in 168 B.C.E., in which the priestly caste of Hasmonaean Maccabees came to prominence, was prompted largely by the action of King Antiochus IV Epiphanes of Syria, who had foisted a system of Greek worship upon the Jewish community. The Maccabees later reconsecrated the Temple but, successful as the Jews were against Antiochus, internal social damage had been done because the campaign had necessitated fighting on the Sabbath. A core of ultra-strict Jewish devotees known as the Hasidim (Pious Ones) strongly objected to this and, when the triumphant House of Maccabaeus took control and set up their own King and High Priest in Jerusalem, the Hasidim not only voiced their opposition but marched en masse out of the city in order to establish their own 'pure' community in the nearby Wilderness of Qumrân. Building work started in around 130 B.C.E..

Horsemen of the Hasmonaean Maccabees, who secured Judaean independence from Syria in 163 B.C.E.

Many relics of the time have since been discovered and, during the 1950s, more than a thousand graves were unearthed at Qumrân. A vast monastery complex from the second habitation was also revealed, with meeting rooms, plaster benches, a huge water cistern and a maze of water conduits. In the Scribes' room were inkwells and the remains of the tables on which the Scrolls had been laid out—some more than 17 feet (c. 5 meters) in length.[19] It was confirmed, by archaeologists and scholars, that the original settlement had been damaged in the earthquake and rebuilt by the incoming Essenes in the later Herodian era. The Essenes were one of three main philosophical Jewish sects (the other two being the Pharisees and the Sadducees).

Many biblical manuscripts have been found at Qumrân, relating to such books as Genesis,

Exodus, Deuteronomy, Isaiah, Job and others. There are, in addition, commentaries on selected texts and various documents of law and record. Among these ancient books are some of the oldest writings ever found—predating anything from which the traditional Bible was translated. Of particular interest are certain biblical commentaries compiled by the Scribes in such a way as to relate the Old Testament texts to the historical events of their own time.[20] Such a correlation is especially manifest in the Scribes' commentary on the Psalms and on such prophetical books as Nahum, Habakkuk and Hosea. The technique applied to link Old Testament writings like these with the New Testament era was based on the use of 'eschatological knowledge'[21]—a form of coded representation that used traditional words and passages to which were attributed special meanings relevant to contemporary understanding. These meanings were designed to be understood only by those who knew the code.

The Essenes were trained in the use of this allegorical code, which occurs in the Gospel texts in particular relation to those parables heralded by the words 'for those with ears to hear'. When the Scribes referred to the Romans, for example, they wrote of the Kittim—ostensibly a name for Mediterranean coastal people, which was also used to denote the ancient Chaldeans, whom the Old Testament describes as 'that bitter and hasty nation which shall march through the breadth of the land to possess dwelling places that are not theirs' (Habakkuk 1:6). The Essenes resurrected the old word for use in their own time and enlightened readers knew that Kittim always stood for Romans.[22]

In order that the Gospels should be beyond Roman understanding, they were largely constructed with dual layers of meaning—evangelical scripture on the surface and political information beneath—and the carefully directed messages were generally based on the substitution codes

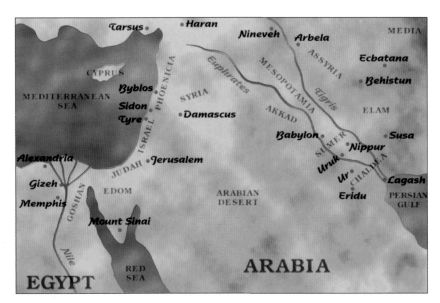

Old Testament Bible Lands

laid down by the Scribes. However, a working knowledge of the code was not available until some of the Dead Sea Scrolls were recently published. Only since then has an appreciation of the cryptic technique facilitated a much greater awareness of the political intelligence that was veiled within the Gospel texts. The most extensive work in this field has been conducted by the noted theologian Dr. Barbara Thiering, a lecturer at Sydney University from 1967.

Dr. Thiering explains the code in very straightforward terms. Jesus, for example, was referred to as 'the word of God'. Thus, a superficially routine passage—such as that in 2 Timothy 2:9, 'The word of God is not bound'—would be apprehended at once to concern Jesus, in this case meaning that Jesus was not confined. Similarly, the Roman Emperor was called 'the lion'. Being 'rescued from the lion's mouth', therefore, meant escaping the clutches of the Emperor or his officers.

Study of the Scrolls—particularly the *Pesharim*,[23] *the Manual of Discipline*, the *Community Rule* and the *Angelic Liturgy*—reveals a number of such coded definitions and pseudonyms[24] that were previously misunderstood or considered of no particular importance. For instance, the 'poor' were not poverty-stricken, under-privileged citizens; they were those who had been initiated into the higher echelons of the community and who, on that account, had been obliged to give up their property and worldly possessions. The 'many' was a title used for the head of the celibate community, whereas the 'crowd' was a designation of the regional Tetrarch (Governor) and a 'multitude' was a governing council. Novices within the religious establishment were called 'children'. The doctrinal theme of the community was known as the 'Way' and those who followed the principles of the Way were known as the 'Children of Light'.

The term 'lepers' was often used to denote those who had not been initiated into the higher community, or who had been denounced by it. The 'blind' were those who were not party to the Way and could therefore not see the Light. In these respects, texts mentioning 'healing the blind' or 'healing a leper' refer more specifically to the process of conversion to the Way. Release from excommunication was described as being 'raised from the dead' (a term that is of particular importance and will be returned to later). The definition 'unclean' related · mostly to uncircumcised Gentiles, while the description 'sick' denoted those in public or clerical disgrace.

Such information, hidden in the New Testament, was of considerable relevance when written and it remains very important today. Methods of disguising the true meanings included allegory, symbolism, metaphor, simile, sectarian definition and pseudonyms. The meanings were fully apparent, though, to 'those with ears to hear'.

There are, in fact, very similar forms of jargon in modern English. Those of other countries would have difficulty understanding such common English expressions as 'the Speaker addressed the Cabinet', 'the silk prepared his brief', or 'the chair opposed the board'. So too was there an esoteric language of New Testament times—a language that included clouds, sheep, fishes, loaves, ravens, doves and camels. All of these classifications were pertinent, for they were all people—just as are today's screws, fences, sharks, bulls and bears. Currently, we call our top entertainers 'stars', while entertainment investors are called 'angels'. What, then, might an unenlightened reader 2000 years from now make of the statement, 'The angels talked to the stars?'

Additionally, some of the esoteric terms in the New Testament were not merely descriptive of people's social status, but were titles which had special relevance to Old Testament tradition. The doctrine which the community regarded as its guiding message was the 'Light' and this was represented by a high-ranking triarchy (corresponding, respectively, to Priest, King and Prophet) who held the symbolic titles of Power, Kingdom and Glory. In the clerical patriarchy the *Father* was supreme and his two immediate deputies were designated his *Son* and his *Spirit*.[25] (Once again, this is crucial to our story and we shall return to it.)

ARMAGEDDON

Some of the most important non-biblical records of the New Testament era have been preserved in the writings of Flavius Josephus, whose *Antiquities of the Jews* and *Wars of the Jews* were written from a personal standpoint, for he was the military commander in the defense of Galilee during the Jewish Revolt in the first century C.E..

Josephus explains that the Essenes were very practiced in the art of healing and received their therapeutic knowledge of roots and stones from the ancients.[26] Indeed, the term 'Essene' may well refer to this expertise, for the Aramaic word *asayya* meant physician and corresponded to the Greek word *essenoi*.

A fundamental belief of the Essenes was that the universe contained the two cardinal spirits of Light and Darkness. Light represented truth and righteousness, whereas Darkness depicted perversion and evil. The balance of one against the other in the cosmos was settled by celestial movement and people were individually apportioned with degrees of each spirit, as defined by their planetary circumstances of birth. The cosmic battle between Light and Darkness was thus perpetuated within humankind and between one person and another: some contained proportionately more Light, others proportionately more Dark.

God was held to be the supreme ruler over the two cardinal spirits, but to find the Way to the Light required following a long and arduous path of conflict. Such a path culminated in a final weighing of one force against the other at a Time of Justification, later called the Day of Judgment. It was thought that, as the time drew near, the forces of Darkness would gather in strength during a Period of Temptation. Those who followed the Way of Light sought to avoid the impending evaluation with the plea, 'Lead us not into Temptation, but deliver us from evil'.

By tradition, the Spirit of Darkness was identified with Belial (Worthless), whose children (Deuteronomy 13:13) worshipped gods other than Jehovah. The Spirit of Light was upheld by the hierarchy and was symbolized by a seven-branched candlestick, the 'Menorah'. In the time of the Davidic kings, the Zadokite priest was considered the foremost proponent of the Light.

Apocalyptic representation of the War in Heaven by Albrecht Dürer, 1471-1528

But just as the Spirit of Light had its representative on Earth, so too did the Spirit of Darkness. It was an appointment held by the Chief of the Scribes, whose purpose was to provide a formal opposition within the hierarchical structure.[27] A primary responsibility of the designated Prince of Darkness was to test female initiates within the celibacy, in which capacity he held the Hebrew title of 'Satan' (Accuser). The equivalent title in Greek was *Diabolos* (Aggressor), being the origin of the English word 'Devil'. (The Satan's office was not unlike that of the Devil's Advocate, who probes the background of potential candidates for canonization in the Roman Catholic Church.)

In the book of Revelation (16:16), the great final war between Light and Darkness—between good and evil—is forecast to take place at Armageddon (*Har Megiddo*: the Heights of Megiddo), a historically important Palestinian battlefield where a military fortress guarded the plains of Jezreel, south of the Galilean hills. *The War Scroll* describes in detail the forthcoming struggle between the Children of Light and the Sons of Darkness.[28] The tribes of Israel were to be on one side, with the Kittim (Romans) and various factions on the other. In the context of this climactic war, however, there is no mention of an omnipotent Satan—such mythical imagery played no part in the community's perception of the Final Judgment. The conflict was to be a purely mortal affair between the Light that was Israel and the Darkness of Imperial Rome.

Much later, the fundamental notion behind this ancient concept was purloined and adapted by the emergent Church of Rome. The symbolic battle of Har Megiddo was removed from its specific location and reapplied on a world scale, with Rome (the hitherto 'Darkness') usurping the 'Light' in its own favor. In order that the rule of the Catholic bishops should prevail, it was strategically decreed that the Day of Judgment had not yet

Doctrinal concept of the Last Judgment.
Spanish Church altarpiece, c.1486

come. Those who, thereafter, obeyed the revised principles of the Roman Catholic Church were promised the right of entry to the Kingdom of Heaven, as sanctified by the bishops. The one-time hill-fort of Har Megiddo was thereby invested with supernatural overtones, so that the very word Armageddon took on the hideous ring of apocalyptic terror. It implied the fearsome ending of all things, from which the only sure route to salvation was absolute compliance with the rule of Rome. In this regard, it has proved to be one of the most ingenious political maneuvers of all time.

3

JESUS, SON OF MAN

THE VIRGIN BIRTH

The Gospels of the New Testament are written in a manner not common to other forms of literature. However, their method of construction was no accident, for they had a common purpose and were not intended to relate history. The aim of the Gospels was to convey an evangelical message (Greek: *eu-aggelos*—'bringing good news'). The English word 'Gospel' is an Anglo-Saxon translation from the Greek, meaning precisely the same thing.

The original Gospel of Mark was written in Rome in around 66 C.E. Clement of Alexandria, the second-century churchman, confirmed that it was issued at a time when the Jews of Judea were in revolt against the Roman occupiers and were being crucified in their thousands. The Gospel writer, therefore, had his own safety to consider and could hardly present a document that was overtly anti-Roman; his mission was to spread the Good News, not to give cause for its condemnation. Mark's Gospel was a message of brotherly support, a promise of independent salvation for those subject to the overwhelming domination of Rome. Such a forecast of deliverance eased the people's minds and took some pressure off the governors whose subjugation was felt throughout the growing Empire.

The Gospel of Mark subsequently became a reference source for those of Matthew and Luke, whose authors severally expanded upon the theme. For this reason, the three are known together as the Synoptic Gospels (Greek: *synoptikos*—'[seeing] with the same eye'), even though they do not concur in many respects.

The Gospel of John differs from the others in content, style and concept, being influenced by the traditions of a particular community sect. It is, nevertheless, far from naive in its account of Jesus's story and, consequently, has its own adherents, who preserve its distinction from the Synoptic Gospels. John also includes countless small details which do not appear elsewhere—a factor that has led many scholars to conclude that it is a more accurate testimony in general terms.

The first published Gospel, that of Mark, makes no mention of the Virgin Birth. The Gospels of Matthew and Luke bring it into play

The Adoration of the Magi
by Domenico Ghirlandaio, 1449-94

with varying degrees of emphasis, but it is totally ignored in John. In the past, as now, clerics, scholars and teachers have thus been faced with the difficulty of analyzing the variant material, as a result of which they have made choices of belief from a set of documents that are very sketchy in places. In consequence, bits and pieces have been extracted from each Gospel, to the extent that a whole new pseudo Gospel has been concocted. Students are simply told that 'the Bible says' this, or 'the Bible says' that. When being taught about the Virgin Birth they are directed to Matthew and Luke. When being taught about other aspects they are directed to the Gospel or Gospels concerned, as if they were all intended to be constituent chapters of the same overall work which, of course, they were not.

Over many centuries, various speculations about biblical content have become interpretations and these have been established by the Church as dogma. The emergent doctrines have been integrated into society as if they were positive facts. Pupils in schools and churches are rarely told that Matthew says Mary was a virgin but that Mark does not; or that Luke mentions the manger in which Jesus was placed whereas the other Gospels do not; or that not one Gospel makes even the vaguest reference to the stable which has become such an integral part of popular tradition. Selective teaching of this kind applies not only to the Bethlehem Nativity, but to any number of incidents in Jesus's recorded life. Instead, Christian children are taught a tale that has been altogether smoothed over; a tale that extracts the most entertaining features from each Gospel and merges them into a single embellished story that was never written by anyone.

The concept of the Virgin Birth of Jesus sits at the very heart of the orthodox Christian tradition. Even so, it is mentioned in only two of the four Gospels and nowhere else in the New Testament. Matthew 1:18-25 reads:

**12th-century French stained glass depiction
of Joseph and the Archangel Gabriel**

Now the birth of Jesus Christ was on this wise: When as his mother Mary was espoused to Joseph, before they came together, she was found with child of the Holy Ghost.

Then Joseph her husband, being a just man, and not willing to make her a public example, was minded to put her away privily.

But while he thought on these things, behold, the angel of the Lord appeared unto him in a dream, saying, Joseph, thou son of David, fear not to take unto thee Mary thy wife: for that which is conceived in her is of the Holy Ghost. And she shall bring forth a son, and thou shalt call his name Jesus: for he shall save his people from their sins.

Now all this was done, that it might be fulfilled, which was spoken of the Lord by the prophet, saying, Behold, a virgin shall be with child, and shall bring forth a son, and they shall call his name Emmanuel, which being interpreted is, God with us.

The prophet referred to is Isaiah who, in 735 B.C.E., when Jerusalem was under threat from Syria, proclaimed to the troubled King Ahaz, 'Hear ye now, O house of David ... Behold, a virgin shall conceive, and bear a son, and shall call his name Immanuel' (Isaiah 7:13-14).[1] But there is nothing in this to suggest that Isaiah was predicting the birth of Jesus more than 700 years later. Such an anachronistic revelation would actually have been of little use to Ahaz in his hour of need! Like so many instances in the New Testament, this illustrates how events of the Gospels were often interpreted to conform with ambiguous prophecies.

That apart, popular understanding of the Gospel text is based on numerous other misconceptions. The Semitic word translated as 'virgin' was *almah*, which actually meant no more than 'a young woman'.[2] The Hebrew word denoting a physical virgin was *bethulah*. In Latin, the word *virgo* means, quite simply, 'unmarried' and, to imply the modern English connotation of 'virgin', the Latin noun would have to be qualified by the adjective *intacta* (i.e., *virgo intacta*), denoting sexual inexperience.[3]

The physical virginity attributed to Mary becomes even less credible in relation to the dogmatic Catholic assertion that she was a 'virgin forever'.[4] It is no secret that Mary had other offspring, as confirmed in each of the Gospels: 'Is this not the carpenter's son? Is not his mother called Mary and his brethren, James, and Joses, and Simon, and Judas?' (Matthew 13:55). In both Luke 2:7 and Matthew 1:25, Jesus is cited as Mary's 'first-born son'. The above quotation from Matthew, furthermore, describes Jesus as 'the carpenter's son'

Jesus and the Supper at Emmaus
by Caravaggio, 1601

(that is, the son of Joseph) and Luke 2:27 clearly refers to Joseph and Mary as Jesus's 'parents'. Matthew 13:56 and Mark 6:3 both indicate that Jesus also had sisters.

The portrayal of Jesus as the son of a carpenter is yet another example of how a later language misinterpreted an original meaning. It is not necessarily a deliberate mistranslation, but it does show how some old Hebrew and Aramaic root words, enveloped within the Greek texts, have no direct counterparts in other tongues. The term translated into English as 'carpenter' represents the much wider sense of the ancient Greek, *ho tekton*, which is a rendition of the Semitic word *naggar*.[5] As pointed out by the Semitic scholar Dr. Geza Vermes, this descriptive word could perhaps be applied to a trade craftsman, but would more likely define a scholar or teacher. It certainly did not identify Jesus and Joseph as woodworkers. More precisely it defined them as men with skills—learned men, who were masters of what they did. Indeed, better translations of the Greek, *ho tekton*, relate to a Master Craftsman or a Master of the Craft, as might be applicable to modern Freemasonry.

In much the same way, the mention in Luke of the baby Jesus's being placed in a manger has given rise to the whole concept of the Nativity being set in a stable, complete with its familiar cast of attentive animals. But, there is no basis whatever for this image; no stable is mentioned in any original or authorized Gospel. In fact, Matthew 2:11 states quite clearly that the baby Jesus lay within a house: 'And when they were come into the house, they saw the young child with Mary his mother, and fell down, and worshipped him'.[6]

It is also worth noting that the precise words used in Luke 2:7 relate that Jesus was laid in a manger because there was no room '*in* the inn',

not '*at* the inn',[7] as is so frequently misquoted. The author and biographer A. N. Wilson specifies, however, that the original Greek (from which the New Testament was translated into English) actually states that there was 'no *topos* in the *kataluma*'— denoting that there was 'no *place* in the *room*'.[8] In reality, it was quite common for mangers (animal feeding boxes) to be taken indoors and used as substitute cradles.

DYNASTIC WEDLOCK

According to Hebrews 7:14, Jesus was of the tribe of Judah. It is evident, therefore, that he was of the family line of King David. The scriptures also say that Jesus was a 'Nazarene', but this does not mean that he came from the town of Nazareth. Although Luke 2:39 implies that Joseph's family came from Nazareth, the term 'Nazarene' (or Nazarite) was strictly sectarian and had nothing whatever to do with the settlement.

In Acts 24:5, St. Paul is brought on a charge of religious sedition before the Governor of Caesarea: 'For we have found this man a pestilent fellow, and a mover of sedition among all the Jews throughout the world, and a ringleader of the sect of the Nazarenes'. The Arabic term for Christians is *Nasrani* and the Islamic Koran refers to Christians as *Nasara* or *Nazara*. These variants ultimately derive from the Hebrew, *Nozrim*, a plural noun stemming from the description *Nazrie ha-Brit* (Keepers of the Covenant), a designation of the Essene community at Qumrân the Dead Sea.[9]

It is actually a point of contention whether the settlement of Nazareth existed at all during Jesus's lifetime, for it does not appear on contemporary maps, neither in any books, documents, chronicles or military records of the period, whether of Roman or local compilation.[10] Even St. Paul, who relates many of Jesus's activities in his letters, makes no allusion to Nazareth. This being the case, every reference to Nazareth in English translations of the Gospels must be regarded as incorrect—stemming from a misunderstanding of the word 'Nazarene'. As far as has been ascertained, Nazareth (which does not feature in the Hebrew Talmud) was of no significance before the Roman destruction of Jerusalem in 70 C.E., long after the crucifixion of Jesus.

John the Baptist and Jesus's brother James were both Nazarenes, but the older, equivalent sectarian term, 'Nazarite', can be traced back to the Old Testament figures of Samson and Samuel. Nazarites were ascetic individuals bound by strict vows through predetermined periods, as related in Numbers 6:2-21. In the Gospel era, Nazarites were associated with the Essene community of Qumrân—the environment of Joseph and Mary.

St. Paul at Ephesus
by Eustache Le Sueur, c.1648

The community observed some highly regulated disciplines in relation to dynastic betrothal and matrimony, so we should refer the question of Mary's said virginity to this specific context.

Both Matthew 1:18 and Luke 2:5 state that Mary was 'espoused' to Joseph and she is thereafter referred to as his 'wife'. As determined in this regard, the word 'espoused' does not mean betrothed or engaged—it refers to contractual wedlock. But, in what circumstance would a married woman also be virginal? To answer this question we must refer to the original Semitic word *almah*, the word that has been translated as 'virgin' (*virgo*) and incorrectly thought to mean *virgo intacta*.

As we have seen, the real meaning of *almah* was 'young woman' (and it had no sexual connotation). It was quite feasible, therefore, for Mary to be both an *almah* and Joseph's wife. Let us look again at how Matthew describes that, when Joseph learned of Mary's pregnancy, he had to decide whether or not to hide her away. It is of course perfectly normal for a wife to become pregnant, but this was not the case for Mary.

As the wife of a dynastic husband, Mary would have been governed by the regulations applicable to Messianic (anointed) lines such as those of King David and Zadok the Priest. In fact, Mary was serving a statutory probationary period as a married woman of the dynastic hierarchy—a period of espousal during which sexual relations were forbidden—and Joseph would have had just cause for personal embarrassment when Mary was discovered to have conceived. The situation was resolved only when the high-ranking Abiathar priest (the designated Gabriel)[11] granted approval for the confinement.

From the time of King David, the dynasty of Abiathar (2 Samuel 20:25) was established in the hierarchy of senior priests. The line of Zadok was the primary priestly heritage and the line of

The Marriage of Mary and Joseph

by Ludovicio Carracci, c.1589

Abiathar was second in seniority. In addition to the traditional priestly styles, the Essenes also preserved the names of the Old Testament archangels within their governing structure.[12] Hence, the Zadok priest was also the archangel Michael, while the Abiathar priest (whatever his personal name) was also the angel Gabriel.[13] Being subordinate to the Zadok/Michael (the Lord—'like unto God'), the Abiathar/Gabriel was the designated 'Angel of the Lord' (the ambassador of the Michael-Zadok). This angelic system is detailed in the Book of 1 Enoch 4:9, whilst the *War Scroll* 9:15-17 identifies the angels' order of priestly ranking during the Gospel era.

In the Luke account, it was through the mediation of the angel Gabriel that Mary's pregnancy was granted approval, being of holy consequence. This is known as the Annunciation, but it was not so much a matter of announcing as one of sanctioning.

Prior to Jesus's birth, the High Zadok (the Michael) was Zacharias. His wife was Mary's cousin Elizabeth,[14] and his deputy, the Abiathar (the Gabriel), was Simeon the Essene.[15] It was he who gave the formal consent for Mary's confinement, even though she and Joseph had disobeyed the rules of dynastic wedlock.

It is evident, then, that these dynastic rules were no ordinary matter and were quite unlike the Jewish marital norm.[16] Parameters of operation were explicitly defined, dictating a celibate lifestyle except for the procreation of children and only then at set intervals. Three months after a betrothal ceremony, a 'First Marriage' was formalized to begin the espousal in the month of September. Physical relations were allowed after that, but only in the first half of December. This was to ensure that any resultant Messianic birth occurred in the Atonement month of September. If the bride did not conceive, intimate relations were suspended until the next December, and so on.[17]

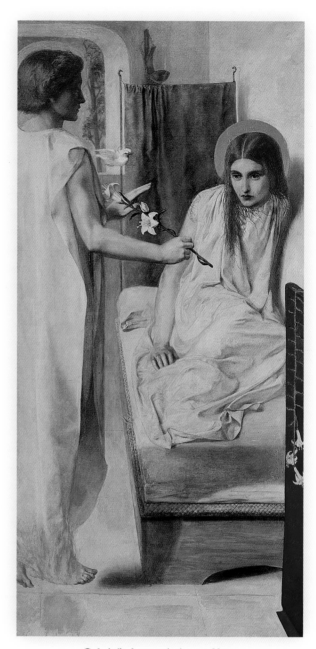

Gabriel's Annunciation to Mary
by Dante Gabriel Rossetti, c.1849

Once a probationary wife had conceived, a 'Second Marriage' was performed to legalize the wedlock. However, the bride was still regarded as an *almah* (young woman) until completion of the Second Marriage which, as qualified by Flavius Josephus, was never celebrated until she was three months pregnant.[18] The purpose of this delay was to allow for the possibility of a miscarriage. Second Marriages thus took place in the month of March. The reason that full wedlock was not achieved until pregnancy had been firmly established was to accommodate the dynastic husband's legal change of wife if the first should prove barren.

In the case of Joseph and Mary, it is apparent that the rules of dynastic wedlock were infringed, since Mary gave birth to Jesus at the wrong time of year (Sunday, March 1, 7 B.C.E.)[19] Sexual union must therefore have taken place six months before the designated December, in June, 8 B.C.E.—at about the time of their initial betrothal—some three months before their First Marriage in the September. And so it was that Mary not only conceived as an *almah*, but also gave birth as an *almah* before her Second Marriage.

Once Mary's unauthorized pregnancy had been confirmed, Joseph would have been granted the choice of not going through with the Second Marriage ceremony. To save embarrassment he could have placed Mary in monastic custody ('put her away privily', as in Matthew 1:19), where the eventual child would be raised by the priests.

But if the child were a boy, he would be Joseph's firstborn descendant in the Davidic succession. It would have made little sense to bring him up as an unidentified orphan, leaving a possible younger brother to become his substitute in the kingly line. Joseph and Mary's unborn child was plainly a significant prospect and demanded special treatment as an exception to the general

rule. The angel Gabriel would, therefore, have advised that, since a sacred legacy was at stake, Joseph should go ahead with the Second Marriage ceremony: 'for that which is conceived in her is of the Holy Ghost' (Matthew 1:20).

Following this dispensation, the normal rules would have been applied once more—the first being that no physical contact was allowed between man and wife until some while after the child had been born: 'Then Joseph being raised from his sleep did as the angel of the Lord had bidden him, and took unto him his wife: And knew her not till she had brought forth her firstborn son: and he called his name Jesus' (Matthew 1:24-25). All that remained was for the Gospel writers to wrap the whole sequence in a blanket of enigma, and this was made possible by the Old Testament prophecy of Isaiah.

DESCENT FROM KING DAVID

Strange as it may seem, the Gospel of Mark—from which both Matthew and Luke took their leads—makes no mention of the Nativity. John 7:42 does allude to the birth at Bethlehem, but not as a mysterious event. Neither does John suggest that Mary's conception was virginal. In fact, the Gospel refers only to Jesus's Davidic descent: 'Hath not the scripture said, that Christ cometh of the seed of David, and out of the town of Bethlehem, where David was?' Even the Gospel of Matthew, which implies the notion of Virgin Birth, opens with the statement, 'The book of the generation of Jesus Christ, the son of David, the son of Abraham'.

Paul's Epistle to the Romans 1:3-4 refers to 'Jesus Christ our Lord, which was made of the seed of David according to the flesh; And declared to be the Son of God'. Again, in Mark 10:47 and Matthew

**18th-century carved Spanish altarpiece
denoting the genealogical tree of Jesus**

22:42 Jesus is called the 'Son of David'. In Acts 2:30, Peter, referring to King David, calls Jesus the 'fruit of his loins, according to the flesh'.

All things considered, the divinity of Jesus is figuratively portrayed, whereas his human descent from David ('in accordance with the flesh') is consistently stated as a matter of fact.[20] Indeed, Jesus generally referred to himself as the 'Son of Man' (as for instance in Matthew 16:13). When asked by the High Priest whether he was in truth the Son of God, Jesus replied, 'Thou hast said'—implying that the priest had said it, not he (Matthew 26:63-64). In Luke 22:70, Jesus answered in virtually identical terms: 'Then said they all, Art thou then the Son of God? And he said unto them, Ye say that I am'.

THE MESSIANIC DISPUTE

One of Jesus's foremost problems was that he had been born into an environment of controversy over whether or not he was legitimate. It was for that very reason that Mary and Joseph took him to Simeon the Gabriel for legitimizing under the Law (Luke 2:25-35). Despite this endeavor by his parents, Jesus evoked a mixed response and the Jews were polarized in two opposing camps on the subject of his lawful status in the kingly line. He had been conceived at the wrong time of year and had been born before Joseph and Mary's wedlock was formalized by their Second Marriage. Six years later his brother James was born within all the rules of dynastic wedlock and there was no disputing his legitimacy. Hence, the opposing factions each had a prospective Messiah to support.

The Hellenists (westernized Jews) claimed that Jesus was the rightful Christ (Greek: *Christos*— King), whereas the orthodox Hebrews contended that the kingly entitlement lay with James. The argument persisted for many years but, in 23 C.E., Joseph—the father of both candidates—died and it became imperative to resolve the dispute one way or the other.

Through long prevailing custom, the Davidic kings were allied to the dynastic Zadokite priests and the prevailing Zadok was Jesus's own kinsman, John the Baptist.[21] He had risen to prominence in 26 C.E. upon the arrival of the Roman governor, Pontius Pilate. John the Baptist was very much of the Hebrew persuasion, but Jesus was a Hellenist. John therefore supported James, even though he acknowledged Jesus as legitimate and baptized him in the Jordan. It was because of the Baptist's attitude that Jesus realized he must make a stand for, if the prospect of a revived Jewish kingdom were to gain momentum, he would undoubtedly lose out to his brother James. In view of this, he decided to create his own organized party of supporters: a party that would not follow any conventional social policy. His vision was straightforward, based upon the logic that a split Jewish nation could never defeat the might of Rome. But he perceived too that the Jews could not accomplish their mission if they continued to hold themselves separate from the Gentiles (native non-Jews). Jesus's ambition for the Kingdom of Israel was one of harmonious, integrated society, but he was more than frustrated by the unbending Jews of rigid Hebrew principle.

And so, at length, Jesus stepped into the public domain, resolving to give the people their long-awaited Messiah. After all, he was the firstborn son of his father, no matter what the wrangling priests and politicians had to say on the subject. In a short while he gathered his disciples, appointed his twelve Apostles (delegates) and began his ministry. In this, he sought acceptance in a world where he perceived no selection by class, conviction or fortune—promoting an ideal of princely service that was to carve its mark in time.

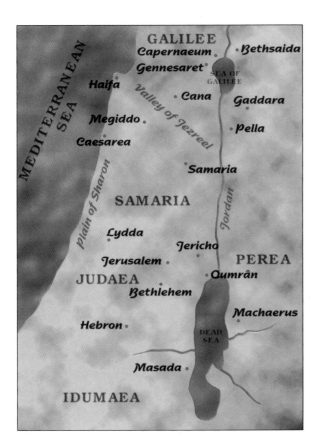

Gospel Locations

THE EARLY MISSION

WHO WERE THE APOSTLES?

For all his apparent humility, there is very little to suggest anything faint-hearted or pacifist about Jesus. He knew full well that his task would make him unpopular with the authorities. Not only would the Romans be at his heels, but so too would the Jews' own governing body of legal elders, the powerful Sanhedrin Council. Regardless, Jesus made his entry in due accord, stating at the outset, 'Think not that I am come to send peace on earth: I came not to send peace, but a sword' (Matthew 10:34).

**Jesus and the Apostles
by William Hole, c.1890**

Under those circumstances, it seems rather odd that a group of everyday working men would give up their livelihoods for a leader who announced, 'Ye shall be hated of all men for my name's sake' (Matthew 10:22). There was no formal Christianity to preach in those early times and Jesus promised neither earnings nor public status. However, the Gospels appear to indicate that his envoys forsook their various employments and followed blindly into the unknown to become 'fishers of men'. Who, then, were these mysterious Apostles? Can anything of the Qumrân scribal codes be applied to the texts, in order to make their identities and purpose more understandable?

Luke (6:13 and 10:1) tells that Jesus appointed eighty-two followers in all; seventy he sent out to preach and twelve were designated his immediate circle, his Apostles. It is no secret to Bible readers that the Apostles were armed, even though Sunday school tradition would have it otherwise. Indeed, Jesus made sure of their martial ability at the very start of his campaign, saying, 'He that hath no sword, let him sell his garment, and buy one' (Luke 22:36).

All four Gospels agree that Simon was the first recruit; three Gospels also mention his brother Andrew. But there is some disagreement between John and the Synoptic Gospels as to precisely where this recruitment took place. It was either at the Sea of Galilee (the Lake of Gennesaret), where the pair were mending their nets, or at a baptism ritual at Bethabara, beyond Jordan. Moreover, the

**The Sermon on the Mount
by William Hole, c.1890**

accounts differ again as to who was present at the time. John 1:28-43 states that John the Baptist was there, whereas Mark 1:14-18 claims that it all happened while the Baptist was in prison.

The account in John's Gospel is undoubtedly the more correct, for the first disciples were recruited in March 29 C.E. In *The Antiquities of the Jews*, Flavius Josephus of Galilee (born 37 C.E.) indicates that Jesus began his ministry in the fifteenth year of the rule of Tiberius Caesar—that is 29 C.E. John the Baptist was not discredited until a year later in March 30 C.E. (as confirmed in John 3:24). He was executed by Herod the Great's successor, Herod-Antipas of Galilee, in September 31, C.E.

Luke 5:11 relates the story of Simon's enlistment as told in the Mark account, but makes no mention of Andrew. Next on the scene are James and John, the sons of Zebedee. Mark and Luke then declare that Jesus enrolled Levi. In Matthew, however, the next disciple is not called Levi, but Matthew. In John, an early recruit is Philip, who is said to come from Bethsaida, the hometown of Simon and Andrew. Philip, in turn, brought Nathanael of Cana into the fold and, from that point, no more is told of individual appointments.

Instead, it is next explained that Jesus gathered all his disciples together and from them chose his twelve personal delegates. Certain anomalies then become apparent. Levi disappears, as does Nathanael, but Matthew then appears in all listings. The Gospels of Matthew and Mark both name Lebbaeus Thaddaeus as one of the twelve, whereas the other Gospels do not, but Luke and Acts list Judas, the brother of James, in the twelve, whereas he does not appear in this context elsewhere. In Matthew and Mark we are also introduced to Simon the Canaanite, described in Luke and Acts as Simon Zelotes.

Mark narrates how Jesus gave Andrew's brother Simon the name of Peter sometime after their meeting, but Matthew and Luke indicate that he had this other name already. From John we learn that Simon and Andrew were the sons of Jona and that Jesus referred to James and John (the sons of Zebedee) as *Boanerges* or 'Sons of Thunder'. In Mark and Luke, Levi the publican is described as a 'son of Alphaeus', while listed among the final recruits is James, another son of Alphaeus. Thomas, a constant Apostle throughout the Gospels, is referred to in John and Acts as Didymus (the Twin). This leaves only Philip, Bartholomew and Judas Iscariot, each of whom is listed by all the Gospel writers.

It is plain that the Apostles were not a group of sheep-like altruists, who abandoned all to join a charismatic faith healer (even if he was of kingly descent). Jesus's prospects were unknown and, at that stage, he had not gained any divine reputation. It is, therefore, evident that something vital is missing from the Gospels. However, since they were compiled so as not to arouse the suspicions of the Roman overlords, much of their content was phrased in esoteric language for an audience who would understand what was written between the lines.

On many occasions our attention is drawn to specific textual passages by the words, 'He that hath ears to hear, let him hear' (as for instance Mark 4:9). In this regard, we now enter the enlightening world of the New Testament scribal codes—and there is no greater exponent of the ancient translatory art than Dr. Barbara Thiering, whose work is essential reading in this regard. For more than twenty-eight years Dr. Thiering has been concerned with research into the Dead Sea Scrolls and has paved the way to a wealth of new Gospel awareness. We shall now open the door to the Apostles and, in so doing, gain insight into the politically formidable role of Jesus as the Messianic descendant of King David.

JAMES AND JOHN

Jesus referred to James and John (the sons of Zebedee) by the descriptive Greek name of *Boanerges*: the 'Sons of Thunder' (Mark 3:17).This is a positive example of cryptic information aimed at initiates. 'Thunder' and 'Lightning' were the titles of two high-ranking ministers of the Sanctuary. The symbolic titles derived from references to the phenomena at Mount Sinai,[1] described in Exodus 19:16, when thunder and lightning enveloped the mountain and Moses went up from the camp to meet with Jehovah. The Sanctuary was emblematic of the Tabernacle (Exodus 25:8) and the Essene Sanctuary was at the Monastery of Mird, nine miles southeast of Jerusalem—once the site of a Hasmonaean fortress.

The man known to Jesus as 'Thunder' was Jonathan Annas, the son of Ananus, the Sadducee High Priest from 6 to 15 C.E. Jonathan (which means 'Jehovah gave') was alternatively called Nathanael ('Gift of God'), being essentially the same name. His counterpart and political rival, known as 'Lightning', was Simon Magus (also called Zebedee or Zebadiah: 'Jehovah hath given'), the influential head of the Samaritan Magi. He is better known in the Gospels as Simon the Canaanite or Simon Zelotes.

So, were James and John the sons of Thunder (Jonathan Annas) or the sons of Lightning/Zebedee (Simon Magus)? The answer is that they were both—not by birth, but by distinction. As *Boanerges*, James and John were spiritual sons (deputies) of the Ananus priests; they were also under instruction from Simon, who was destined to hold the highest patriarchal office—that of the community Father.

At once we are presented with a very different picture of the Apostles' social prestige. Even James and John, who are identified as 'fishers', turn out to be prominent in Hellenist society. But why were they depicted (along with Simon-Peter and Andrew) in an environment of fishing boats? This is where the alternative account of John comes into its own, for symbolic fishing was a traditional part of the ritual of baptism.[2]

Gentiles who sought affiliation with the Jewish tribes could take part in the baptism, but could not be baptized in the water. Although they joined the Jewish baptismal candidates in the sea, they were permitted only to receive priestly blessings after they had been hauled aboard ships in large nets. The priests who performed the baptism were called 'fishers'. James and John were both ordained fishers, but Simon-Peter and Andrew were among the lay net-haulers (fishermen). It was in allusion to his own more liberal ministry that Jesus promised them canonical promotion, saying, 'I will make you to become fishers of men' (Mark 1:17).

The Apostles were clearly no ragtag band of righteous devotees, but an influential Council of Twelve under their supreme leader Jesus the Christ. Only much later did his royal style, 'Jesus Christ' (King Jesus), become misconstrued as if it were a proper name in its own right.[3] It is worth reminding ourselves here that the Qumrân *Manual of Discipline* details the importance of a Council of Twelve to preserve the faith of the land.

SIMON ZELOTES

Simon Magus (or Zebedee) was head of the West Manasseh Magi,[4] a priestly caste of Samaritan philosophers who supported the legitimacy of Jesus. It was their ambassadors (the Magi, or wise men) who honored the baby Jesus at Bethlehem. Simon was a master showman and manuscripts of his life deal with matters of cosmology, natural magnetism, levitation and psychokinesis.[5] He was a confirmed advocate of war with Rome and was accordingly known as Simon *Kananites* (Greek: 'the fanatic'). This was later mistranslated as Simon the Canaanite.

As an Apostle of Jesus, Simon was undoubtedly the most prominent in terms of social status, but he was also a keen Zealot commander and was often called Simon *Zelotes* (the Zealot). The Zealots were militant freedom fighters set on vengeance against the Romans who had usurped their heritage and their territory. To the Roman authorities, however, the Zealots were simply *lestai* (bandits).

Already, the Apostles have assumed a more daunting identity than their familiar image, but their purpose remains the same: to support and defend the oppressed of their homeland, being themselves of the elite class. The majority were

Familiar conniving image of Judas Iscariot

trained priests, therapeutics and teachers; they would have displayed merciful skills in healing and been able to expound as orators of great wisdom and goodwill.

JUDAS ISCARIOT

Another well-born nationalist leader of renown was Judas, Chief of the Scribes.[6] The Dead Sea Scrolls were produced under his tutelage and that of his predecessor, the fierce Judas of Galilee, founder of the Zealot movement.[7] Apart from his academic scholarship, Judas the Apostle was the tribal head of East Manasseh and a warlord of Qumrân. The Romans had a nickname for him: to them he was Judas *Sicarius* (a *sica* was a deadly, curved dagger). The Greek form of the nickname was *Sikariotes* and its corruption to *Sicariote* was, in due course, further corrupted to become 'Iscariot'.[8] Although always placed at the end of the Apostolic lists, Judas Sicariote would have been second in seniority only to Simon Zelotes.

THADDAEUS, JAMES AND MATTHEW

Lebbaeus Thaddaeus is described as a 'son of Alphaeus' and is also called Judas (Theudas) in two of the Gospels. He was an influential leader of the community and yet another Zealot commander. For more than fifty years, from 9 B.C.E., Thaddaeus was head of the Therapeutate, an ascetic order that had evolved during the Egyptian occupation of Qumrân. Thaddaeus was a confederate of Jesus's father, Joseph, and took part in the people's rising against Pontius Pilate in 32 C.E.

James, said to be another 'son of Alphaeus', was actually Jonathan Annas, leader of the Thunder Party. The name 'James' is an English variant of the name 'Jacob',[9] and the nominal style of 'Jacob' was Jonathan's patriarchal entitlement. Just as the names of the angels and archangels were preserved within the higher priesthood, so too were the Jewish patriarchal names preserved by the community elders. They were led by a tri-umvirate of appointed officials to whom were applied the titular names Abraham, Isaac and Jacob. In this regard, Jonathan Annas was the Jacob patriarch for a time (the English equivalent being James).

As for Matthew (also called Levi), he too is described as a 'son of Alphaeus'. He was, in fact, Matthew Annas (the brother of Jonathan)—later to succeed as High Priest from 42 C.E. until deposed by Herod-Agrippa I. Matthew was intimately concerned with the promotion of Jesus's work and actively sponsored the Gospel issued under his name. As Jonathan's successor, he was the chief Levite priest and held the nominal title of 'Levi'. He was also an appointed publican (a Jerusalem tax official), responsible for the collection of public revenues from the Jews who had settled outside their homeland, but were still liable to taxation.[10] Income from Asia Minor was collected by the Levites and deposited at the Treasury in Jerusalem: 'And as Jesus passed forth from thence, he saw a man, named Matthew, sitting at the receipt of custom' (Matthew 9:9). Similarly, in reference to the same event, 'He went forth, and saw a publican, named Levi, sitting at the receipt of custom' (Luke 5:27).

Thaddaeus, James and Matthew (Levi) are all described as 'sons of Alphaeus', but they were not all brothers. As elsewhere, the word 'son' is used to denote a deputy position. The style 'of Alphaeus' did not imply relation to a person or a place, for it meant, quite simply, 'of the Succession'.

Jesus meets with Levi the publican
by William Hole, c.1890

The body of St. Thomas carried by
Portuguese at Mylapore

PHILIP, BARTHOLOMEW AND THOMAS

As John 1:45-49 indicates, Philip was an associate of Jonathan Annas (alternatively known as Nathanael). An uncircumcised Gentile Proselyte,[11] Philip was head of the Order of Shem.[12] The Coptic Gospel of Philip was written in his name. Bartholomew (also known as John Mark) was Philip's evangelical and political companion. He was chief of the Proselytes and an official of the influential Egyptian Therapeutate (the healing community) at Qumrân.[13]

The Gospels say little about Thomas, but he was among the most influential of Christian evangelists, known to have preached in Syria, Persia and India. He was eventually lanced to death at Mylapore, near Madras. Thomas—originally Crown Prince Philip—was born into the Herod family,[14] but lost his inheritance when his mother, Mariamne II, was divorced by King Herod after she tried to assassinate him. Philip's half-brother, Herod-Antipas, later became Tetrarch of Galilee. In ridicule, the local people likened Prince Philip to Esau—the son of Isaac who lost both his birthright and his father's blessing to his twin brother Jacob (Genesis 25-27)—and they called him *Teoma* (Aramaic for 'twin'): in Greek this name became Thomas and was sometimes translated as Didymus (similarly meaning 'twin').

SIMON-PETER AND ANDREW

We are dealing here with the two Apostles who are often thought to have been the most prominent—yet in this sequence they are placed last. Indeed, the order in which the Apostles have been listed in this section pretty much represents the reverse of that followed in the Gospel lists. That is because such characters as Simon Zelotes, Judas Sicariote and Thaddaeus were far more powerful than their traditional end-of-list positions indicate. But, it was by no accident that the Gospel writers arranged the names as they did for, by this means, they diverted Roman attention from those Apostles in the very forefront of public life.

Hence, the Apostolic tables usually begin with the least influential members, Simon-Peter and Andrew, who were ordinary village Essenes and held no public office. In the context of their being 'fishermen' and not 'fishers', their role at the baptism ritual was strictly as laymen: they were in charge of the nets, but performed no priestly function (such as the bestowing of blessings) as did the ordained 'fishers' James and John.

For all that, Simon-Peter and Andrew's lack of public station was of great value to Jesus. It made the two brothers more readily available to him than others who had ministerial or legislative work to accomplish. The result was that Simon-Peter became Jesus's right-hand man and he was evidently a fellow of some solidity, being nicknamed Cephas (the Stone). In the Nag Hammadi Gospel of Thomas, Jesus refers to Simon-Peter as his 'guardian' and he was, presumably, Jesus's chief bodyguard. After losing his wife, Simon-Peter

became a prominent evangelist and, despite the occasional disagreement with Jesus, was largely responsible for perpetuating the Gospel in Rome. He was, eventually, martyred by crucifixion during Emperor Nero's persecution of the Christians.

PRIESTS AND ANGELS

We have already encountered the fact the that angelic structure was maintained within the priestly hierarchy of the Qumrân community—so that the highest ranking priest was not only the Zadok dynast but was also the archangel Michael. Thus, he was the Michael-Zadok (the Melchizedek). Second in ranking was the Abiathar, who was also the angel Gabriel. It is now worth taking a closer look at the angelic order, for it will shed even more light on the Apostles' social status. In this context, various

6th-century mosaic depicting
the fishermen Peter and Andrew

**St. Michael from the 15th-century
Sforza Book of Hours**

The Old Testament describes two types of angel, the great majority of whom acted like normal human beings—as for example in Genesis 19:1-3, when two angels visited Lot's house, 'and (he) did bake unleavened bread, and they did eat'. Most Old Testament angels belong to this uncomplicated category, such as the angel who met Abraham's wife Hagar by the water fountain,[15] the angel who stopped Balaam's ass in its tracks,[16] the angel who spoke with Manoah and his wife[17] and the angel who sat under the oak with Gideon.[18]

Another class of angel seems to have been rather more than a messenger, possessing fearsome powers of destruction. This type of avenging angel features in 1 Chronicles 21:14-16: 'And God sent an angel unto Jerusalem to destroy it ... having a sword drawn in his hand stretched out over Jerusalem'. Quite a few angels are described as wielding swords, but they are never described as divine and there is no hint in the text of the graceful wings that are so often portrayed. The now familiar wings were devised by artists and sculptors to symbolize the angels' spiritual transcendence above the mundane environment.

Notwithstanding the angelic portrayals of the Old Testament, the angels of the New Testament were, without exception, all men and their appointments to angelic office were strictly dynastic. The Book of Enoch (representing the patriarch sixth in line from Adam) was written in the second century B.C.E.. It forecast a restoration of the Messianic dynasties and laid down ground-rules for the structure of the priestly hierarchy.[19] Included was the premise that successive dynastic heads should carry the names of the traditional angels and archangels to denote their rank and position.

In the Old Testament days of King David, the senior priests were Zadok, Abiathar and Levi (in that order of precedence). The Essenes of Qumrân

customary practices—both priestly and patriarchal—will become apparent, leading the way, quite naturally, to a whole new understanding of Jesus's miracles.

The first thing to note is that there is nothing spiritual or ethereal about the word 'angel'. In the original Greek, *aggelos* (more usually transliterated as *angelos*—Latin: *angelus*) meant no more than 'messenger'. Modern English derives the word *angel* from this via Church Latin, but the Anglo-Saxon word *engel* came originally from the old French *angele*. An 'angel of the Lord' was, thus, a 'messenger of the Lord' or, more correctly, an 'ambassador of the Lord'. An 'archangel' was a priestly ambassador of the highest rank (the prefix 'arch' meaning 'chief', as in archduke and archbishop).

duly preserved their priestly heritage using those names as titles: Zadok, Abiathar and Levi, as we have seen. Also, in accordance with the Book of Enoch, the archangelic names were retained, under vow, as badges of priestly rank,[20] with the Zadok dynast being also the Michael; the Abiathar being the Gabriel and the Levi being the Sariel.[21]

We should, therefore, understand that the archangel Michael's battle with the dragon, in Revelation 12:7, corresponds to the conflict between the Zadokite succession and 'the beast of blasphemy' —Imperial Rome. The 'second beast' was that of the rigidly strict regime of the Pharisees, who thwarted the ambitions of the Hellenist Jews by segregating Jews from Gentiles. This was the beast to which was attributed the number 666 (Revelation 13:8)—the numerically evaluated polar opposite to the spiritual energy of water in the solar force.[22]

Outside the dynastic families (the heads of kingly and priestly successions who were expressly required to marry in order to perpetuate their lines), those of the high orders were generally required to remain celibate, as detailed in the *Temple Scroll*. Trainee priests were, therefore, in limited supply and were often raised within a monastic system from the community's illegitimate sons. Jesus might well have become one of those trainee priests, whose mother had been 'put away privily', were it not for the considered intervention of the angel Gabriel.

When procreation was embarked upon, a priestly dynast (such as the Zadok) had, temporarily, to suspend himself from his ordained role and pass his religious duties to another. When physical relations with his wife were completed, he would once more live apart from her and resume his celibate existence.

The Zadok/Michael of the early Gospel era was Zacharias (the husband of Mary's cousin, Elizabeth). His priestly deputy, the Abiathar/Gabriel, was Simeon. The story of Zacharias' procreational leave is very veiled in Luke 1:15-23, but his being rendered 'speechless in the Temple' actually means that he was prevented from speaking in his usual ordained capacity. Being concerned about his advancing age, Zacharias the Zadok transferred his priestly authority to Simeon the Abiathar so that Elizabeth could bear a son. That son was John the Baptist who, in time, succeeded as the Zadokite head.

At the time of Jesus's early ministry, the head of the Levi priests was Jonathan Annas. As chief of the Levite dynasty he held the third archangelic rank of Sariel, in which capacity he was the nominated King's Priest. Along with these three supreme archangels (chief ambassadors), Michael (the Zadok), Gabriel (the Abiathar) and Sariel (the Levi), there were also others with pre-eminent titles. These positions, however, were not dynastic and were denoted by the representative styles, *Father*, *Son* and *Spirit*. The *Father* was the equivalent of the Roman Pope of later times (Pope = Papa = Father)—the Roman style having been purloined directly from the original Jewish source. In essence, the *Son* and *Spirit* were his physical and spiritual deputies. The position of Father was elective and precluded its holder from certain other duties. For example, when Jonathan Annas became the *Father*, his brother Matthew (the Apostle) became his successor as the head of the Levi priests of the Succession. Hence, Matthew then became the 'Levi of Alphaeus'.

The Levi priests (Levites) operated as subordinates of the archangels. At their head, but junior to the Levi dynast, was a Chief Priest (as distinct from

Jesus washing Peter's feet at the Last Supper
by Ford Maddox Brown, c.1865

a High Priest). He was angelically designated Raphael. His senior priests were styled in accordance with the original sons of Levi (as given in Genesis 29:34) and they were called Kohath, Gershon and Merari. The next priest in seniority was Amram (the Old Testament son of Kohath), followed by Aaron, Moses and the priestess, Miriam. They, in turn, were senior to Nadab, Abihu, Eleazar and Ithmar—the representative sons of Aaron.

It is at this stage that the primary aspect of the Grail Code begins to emerge, for the heir to the Davidic kingly succession held no angelic title and was not in priestly service. The King was obliged to serve the people and it was his express duty to champion them against establishment injustice. The very name David means 'beloved' and, as an upholder of this distinction, Jesus would have made a very fine king. It was this royal concept of humble 'service' that the lay disciples found so hard to comprehend in their Messianic leader. This is well demonstrated in John 13:4-11, when Jesus washed the Apostles' feet. Peter queried the action, saying, 'Thou shalt never wash my feet', but Jesus was insistent, replying with finality, 'I have given you an example, that ye should do as I have done to you'. Such a charitable action is not the mark of a power-seeking dynast, but is emblematic of common fatherhood in the nature of true Grail kingship.

5

THE MESSIAH

WATER AND WINE

Although not considered to be history in the traditional sense, the Gospels relate the story of Jesus by way of a continuous narrative. Sometimes they are in agreement; sometimes they are not but, at all times, their purpose was to convey an imperative social message with Jesus as the focal catalyst. Not all of that message was delivered in an overt fashion, however. Jesus is often said to have spoken in the form of parables, thereby simplifying his message with allegorical discourse. To some, these moralistic tales would appear superficial, but their undertones were frequently political, being based upon actual people and real situations.

The Gospels were constructed in a similar manner and it is important to recognize that many of the stories about Jesus are themselves the equivalent of parables for the benefit of 'those with ears to hear'. This has often led to some perfectly straightforward events being dubbed with supernatural overtones. A good example occurs in John 2:1-10: the story of Jesus substituting the water for wine at the Cana wedding feast. This well-known event was the first of many presumptuous actions by which Jesus made known his intention to circumvent tradition.

Although raised within a strict regime that was influenced by customs and ancient laws, Jesus recognized that Rome could never be defeated while extremes of competitive doctrine

**Ruler of the Feast and the betrothal at Cana
by Paolo Veronese, c.1560**

existed within the Jewish community itself. There was no such thing as Christianity in those days—the religion of Jesus was Judaism and the Jews all worshipped one God, but even they were split into various factions, each with a different set of community rules. It was generally perceived, however, that Jehovah 'belonged' to the Jews, but Jesus aspired to share Jehovah with the Gentiles in a way that did not require them to take on all the trappings of orthodox Judaism.

Jesus had little patience with the rigorous creeds of Jewish groups like the Pharisees, and he knew the people could not be freed from oppression until they had forsaken their own uncompromising sectarianism. He was also aware that a Messiah had long been anticipated—a savior who was expected to introduce a new era of deliverance. He would, therefore, be revolutionary in outlook and would set himself apart from customary practice. As the heir to the Davidic royal house, Jesus knew that he was qualified to be that Messiah and that, if he should emerge as such, few would be unduly surprised.

What Jesus did not have was any designated social authority—he was neither a reigning King nor a High Priest. However, he paid little heed to such technicalities and proceeded to implement ritualistic changes regardless of his titular deficiency. On his first opportunity at the Cana wedding, he hesitated, claiming, 'Mine hour is not yet come'. But his mother waved aside his lack of entitlement and directed the servants, saying, 'Whatsoever he saith unto you, do it'.

The only account of this appears in John's Gospel, where the incident of the water and wine is described as the first of Jesus's miracles. But, it is not stated that they 'ran out of wine', as is so often misquoted. The text actually says, 'And when they wanted wine, the mother of Jesus saith unto him, They have no wine'. According to the ritual described in the Dead Sea Scrolls, the relevance of this is plain. At the equivalent of Communion, only fully initiated celibates were allowed to partake of wine.[1] All others present were regarded as unsanctified and were restricted to a purifying ritual with water; these included married men, novices, Gentiles and all lay Jews.

The Gospel text continues: 'There were set there six water-pots of stone, after the manner of the purifying of the Jews'. The significance of Jesus's action is that he took it upon himself to break with tradition when he abandoned the water

and allowed the 'unclean' guests to take the sacred wine. The ruler of the feast (Greek: *architriclinos*) 'knew not whence it was (but the servants which drew the water knew)'. He did not comment on any marvelous transformation, but simply remarked that he was surprised the good wine had made its appearance at that stage. As Mary declared, when instructing the servants to obey Jesus, the episode 'manifested forth his glory and his disciples believed on him'.

THE KING AND HIS DONKEY

Shortly after Jesus began his mission, John the Baptist was arrested because he had angered Herod-Antipas, the Governor of Galilee. Antipas had married Herodias, the divorced wife of his half-brother, Philip, and the Baptist repeatedly condemned the marriage, declaring that it was sinful. As a result, he was imprisoned for a year and then beheaded. On his ignoble demise, many of his followers turned their allegiance toward Jesus. Some had thought that John was the expected Messiah, but a number of his prophecies had not been fulfilled[2] and so he was discounted in this regard. One of the reasons why John's prophecies proved inaccurate was because of the differences between the commonly used solar and lunar calendars, further complicated by the Julian calendar introduced from Rome.

The Essenes were advocates of the Greek philosopher Pythagoras (c. 570-500 B.C.E.), who in his great study of arithmetical ratios searched for meaning both in the physical and metaphysical worlds through mathematical proportions. Over the centuries, using his methodology, world events were foretold with surprising accuracy. One particular event so forecast was the beginning of a new World Order, an occurrence that was in many quarters determined to be the advent of the Savior Messiah.

The years (which we now designate B.C.E.) were thus already on a predetermined count-down long before Jesus was born. As things turned out, the Messianic forecast was actually seven years astray when applied to Jesus—which explains why he was (as far as we may be concerned) born in the year 7 B.C.E. and not in the notional year 0 (754 A.U.C.)[3] But, his brother James was actually born in the right year, as a result of which many considered James to be the legitimate heir. Much later, by way of a new Roman dating system, the notional year 0 was designated 1 C.E.

In 32 C.E., Simon Zelotes fell foul of the authorities, having led an unsuccessful revolt against the Governor of Judea, Pontius Pilate. The reason for the revolt was that Pilate had been using public funds to have his personal water supply improved. A formal complaint was lodged against him in court,[4] whereupon Pilate's soldiers murdered the known complainants. Armed insurrection immediately ensued, led by the prominent Zealots, Simon Zelotes, Judas Sicariote and Thaddaeus. Perhaps inevitably, the revolt failed and Simon was excommunicated by edict of King Herod-Agrippa. Simon's political opponent, Jonathan Annas, was thus enabled to accede to the supreme office of the Father.

Under the Law, excommunication (to be regarded as spiritual execution, or death by decree) took four days for complete implementation. In the meantime, the excommunicatee was dressed in a shroud, shut away and held to be 'sick unto death'. In view of his patriarchal rank up to that point, Simon was incarcerated in the patrimonial burial chamber at Qumrân known as the Bosom of Abraham.[5] His devotional 'sisters', Martha and Mary, knew that his soul would be forever condemned if he were not reprieved (raised)

by the third day and so they sent word to Jesus that Simon was 'sick' (John 11:3).

At first Jesus was powerless to act, for only the Father or the High Priest could perform such a raising (resurrection) and Jesus held no priestly office. It happened, however, that Herod-Agrippa fell into an argument with the Roman governors, losing his jurisdiction to the short-term benefit of his uncle, Herod-Antipas, who had supported the Zealot action against Pilate. Seizing his opportunity, Antipas countermanded the order of excommunication and instructed that Simon should be 'raised from the dead'. Jesus was, therefore, in something of a quandary. He was heir to the kingly line, yet with no formal entitlement, but he wished to come to the aid of his friend and loyal supporter—and so he did. Although the time of spiritual death (the fourth day following excommunication) for Simon had arrived, Jesus decided to presume a priestly function and perform the release. In so doing, he confirmed the spiritually dead Simon's rank as that of Abraham's Steward, Eliezer (corrupted in the Gospels to Lazarus) and summoned him, under that distinguished name, to 'come forth' from Abraham's Bosom.

And so it was that Lazarus was raised from the dead without official sanction from the new Father, neither from the High Priest, nor from the Sanhedrin Council. Jesus had blatantly flouted the rules, but Herod-Antipas then obliged Jonathan Annas to acquiesce in the *fait accompli* and, to the people at large, the unprecedented event was indeed a miracle.

Jesus had effected exactly what he wanted and, with this impressive action behind him, it remained only for him to be formally anointed and to appear before the people as their rightful Messiah in a way that would leave little room for

The Raising of Lazarus
by Sebastiano del Piombo, 1485-1547

dispute. How the Savior Messiah was to achieve such recognition was long established for it had been prophesied in the Old Testament book of Zechariah (9:9): 'Rejoice greatly, O daughter of Zion; shout O daughter of Jerusalem: behold, thy King cometh unto thee: he is just, and having salvation; lowly, and riding upon an ass'.

The arrangements were made when Jesus and his disciples were in Bethany during the week before Passover, March 33 C.E. First (as related in Matthew 26:6-7 and Mark 14:3) Jesus was anointed by Mary of Bethany, who poured a precious box of spikenard[6] over his head. A suitable beast of burden was found and, in accordance with Zechariah's prophecy, Jesus rode into Jerusalem.[7]

THE BRIDEGROOM AND THE BRIDE

It has often been said that the New Testament does not state in any forthright manner that Jesus was married. By the same token and more importantly, however, nowhere does it state that he was unmarried. In fact, the Gospels actually contain a number of specific pointers to his married status and it would have been very surprising if he had remained single, for the dynastic regulations were quite clear in this regard.

As we have seen, the rules of dynastic wedlock were no ordinary affair. Explicitly defined parameters dictated a celibate lifestyle except for the procreation of children at regulated intervals. A lengthy period of betrothal was followed by a First Marriage in September, after which physical relationship was allowed in December. If conception took place, a Second Marriage ceremony was then celebrated in March to legalize the wedlock. During that trial period, and until the Second Marriage, whether pregnant or not, the bride was regarded in law as an *almah*

('young woman' or, as so often erroneously cited, 'virgin').

Among the more colorful books of the Old Testament is *The Song of Solomon*—a series of love canticles between a sovereign bride and her bridegroom. The *Song* identifies the potion symbolic of espousal as the aromatic ointment called spikenard.[8] It was the same very expensive spikenard that was used by Mary of Bethany to anoint Jesus's head at the house of Lazarus (Simon Zelotes) and a similar incident (narrated in Luke 7:37-38) had occurred some time earlier, when a woman anointed Jesus's feet with ointment, wiping them afterwards with her hair.

**Mary Magdalene anoints the feet of Jesus
by Tintoretto, 1519-94**

John 11:1-2 also mentions this earlier event, then explains how the ritual of anointing Jesus's feet was performed yet again by the same woman at Bethany. When Jesus was seated at the table, Mary took 'a pound of ointment of spikenard, very costly, and anointed the feet of Jesus, and wiped his feet with her hair: and the house was filled with the odor of the ointment' (John 12:3).

In *The Song of Solomon* (1:12) is the bridal refrain, 'While the king sitteth at his table, my spikenard sendeth forth the smell thereof'. Not only did Mary anoint Jesus's head at Simon's house (Matthew 26:6-7 and Mark 14:3), but she also anointed his feet and wiped them afterwards with her hair in March 33 C.E. Two and a half years earlier, in September 30 C.E., she had performed this same ritual three months after the Cana wedding feast.

On both occasions the anointing was carried out while Jesus was seated at the table (as defined in *The Song of Solomon*). This was an allusion to the ancient rite by which a royal bride prepared her bridegroom's table. To perform the rite with spikenard was the express privilege of a Messianic bride and was performed solely at the First and Second Marriage ceremonies. Only as the wife of Jesus and as a priestess in her own right could Mary have anointed both his head and his feet with the sacred ointment.

Psalm 23 depicts God, in the male-female imagery of the era, as both the shepherd and the bride. Of the bride, the words say 'Thou preparest a table before me ... thou anointest my head with oil'.[9] According to the sacred marriage rite of ancient Mesopotamia (the land of Noah and Abraham), the Great Goddess, Inanna, took as her bridegroom the shepherd Dumuzi (or Tammuz)[10] and it was from this union that the concept of the Shekinah-and-Jehovah evolved in Canaan through the intermediate deities Asherah and El Elohim.

Pope Gregory I,
590-604

In Egypt, the anointing of the king was the privileged duty of the pharaohs' semi-divine sister-brides. Crocodile fat was the substance used in the anointing because it was associated with sexual prowess—and the word for 'crocodile' in Egyptian was *messeh*, which corresponds to the Hebrew *Messiah*: 'Anointed One'.[11]

Just as the men who were appointed to various patriarchal positions took on names that represented their ancestors—such as Isaac, Jacob and Joseph—so too were the women styled according to their genealogy and rank. Their nominal styles included Rachel, Rebecca and Sarah.[12] Wives of the Zadok and David male lines held the ranks of Elisheba (Elizabeth) and Miriam (Mary) respectively. That is why John the Baptist's mother is called Elizabeth in the Gospels and why Jesus's mother was Mary. It is also why Jesus's own wife would have been a Mary. These women underwent the ceremony of their Second Marriage only once they were three months pregnant, at which time the bride ceased being an *almah* and became a designated *mother*.

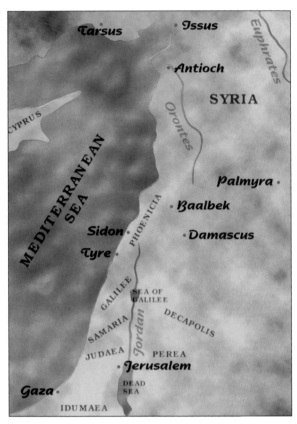

New Testament—The Wider Scene

As we have seen, sexual relations were permitted only in December; husbands and wives lived apart for the rest of the year. At the outset of a period of separation, the wife was classified as a *widow* and was required to weep for her husband. This is described in Luke 7:38, when Mary of Bethany, on the first occasion, is said to have 'stood at his feet behind him weeping, and began to wash his feet with tears'. Once the period of symbolic widowhood had been established, and during these lengthy periods of separation, the wife was given the conventual designation *sister*, just as a modern nun might be. So who exactly was Mary of Bethany—the woman who twice anointed Jesus with spikenard in accordance with Messianic tradition?

To be precise, she is never called 'Mary of Bethany' in the Bible. She and Martha are only ever referred to as 'sisters' at the house of Lazarus of Bethany. Mary's full title was Sister Miriam Magdala or, as she is better known, Mary Magdalene. Gregory I, Bishop of Rome 590-604, and St. Bernard, the Cistercian Abbot of Clairvaux 1090-1153, both confirmed that Mary of Bethany was synonymous with Mary Magdalene.

On the second occasion that Jesus was anointed with spikenard, Judas Sicariote declared his dissatisfaction at the way things were going. He stated his opposition (John 12:4-5) and, thus, paved the way for his betrayal of Jesus. Following the failed revolt by the Zealots against Pilate, Judas had become a fugitive. Jesus was of little political use to him, for he carried no influence with the Sanhedrin Council,[13] so Judas threw in his lot with Jesus's uncontroversial brother James, who was actually a member of that Council. Consequently, Judas not only had no interest in seeing Jesus anointed as a Messiah, but his new allegiance to James caused him to resent it once it had happened. Jesus, nevertheless, was adamant about the significance of his anointing by Mary (Mark 14:9): 'Verily I say unto you, Wheresoever this gospel shall be preached throughout the whole world, this also that she hath done shall be spoken of for a memorial of her'.

Apart from the fact that Jesus was said to love Mary Magdalene, there is not much in the Gospels to indicate their intimate closeness until Mary appears with Jesus's mother and Salome (the consort of Simon Zelotes[14]) at the Crucifixion. Not so, however, in the Nag Hammadi Gospel of Philip, where the relationship between Jesus and Mary is openly discussed:

And the companion of the Savior is Mary Magdalene. But Christ loved her more than all the disciples, and used to kiss her often on the mouth. The rest of the disciples were offended by it and expressed disapproval. They said unto him, Why do you love her more than all of us? The Savior answered and said to them, Why do I not love you like her? ... Great is the mystery of marriage, for without it the world would not have existed. Now the existence of the world depends on man, and the existence of man on marriage.

There is no talk in John's Gospel of any marriage service at Cana, only of a wedding feast and of the water and wine. The disciples were there, as were various guests including Gentiles and others who were technically 'unclean'. This, then, was not the ceremony of the marriage itself but the sacred meal that preceded the betrothal. The custom was for there to be a formal host (as appears in the account); he would be in full charge as the 'ruler of the feast'. Secondary authority rested only in the bridegroom and his mother— and this is entirely relevant for, when the matter of the communion wine arose, Jesus's mother said to the servants (John 2:5), 'Whatsoever he saith unto you, do it'. No invited guest would have had any such right of command and it is plain, therefore, that Jesus and the bridegroom were one and the same.

This betrothal communion (June 6, 30 C.E.) took place three months before Mary first anointed Jesus's feet at Simon's house (September 3, 30 C.E.). The rules were strictly defined: only as Jesus's bride would Mary have been permitted to perform this act. With her First Marriage duly completed in the September, she would also have wept for her husband (as in Luke 7:38) before they were parted for their statutory separation. Prior to this, as a betrothed *almah*, she would have been classified as a *sinner* and ranked as a *crippled woman*.[15] The couple would then not have come together for any physical union until the following December.

SUPPRESSION OF THE MARRIAGE EVIDENCE

One of the reasons why there is no obvious mention of Jesus's marital status in the New Testament is that the evidence was deliberately removed by Church decree. This was revealed as recently as 1958, when a manuscript of the Ecumenical Patriarch of Constantinople was discovered in a monastery at Mar Saba, east of Jerusalem, by Morton Smith, Professor of Ancient History at Columbia University, New York. The extracts quoted below are from his subsequent writings.[16]

Within a book of the works of St. Ignatius of Antioch was a transcription of a letter by Bishop Clement of Alexandria (c. 150-215 C.E.) It was addressed to his colleague, Theodore, and included a generally unknown section from the Gospel of Mark. Clement's letter decreed that some of the original content of Mark was to be suppressed because it did not conform with Church requirement. The letter reads:

For even if they should say something true, one who loves the Truth should not, even so, agree with them. For not all true things are the Truth; nor should that truth which seems true according to human opinions be preferred to the true Truth—that according to the faith.

To them one must never give way; nor, when they put forward their falsifications, should one concede that the secret Gospel is by Mark—but should deny it on oath. For not all true things are to be said to all men.

In the removed section of the Gospel is an account of the raising of Lazarus—but an account that has Lazarus (Simon Zelotes) calling to Jesus from within the tomb even before the stone was rolled back.[17] This makes it quite clear that the man was not dead in the physical sense—which, of course, defeated the Church's insistence that the raising should be accepted as a supernatural miracle. Moreover, the original Gospel of Mark did not include any details of the events of the Resurrection and its aftermath; it ended simply with the women fleeing from an empty sepulchre. The concluding twelve verses of Mark 16, as generally published today, were spuriously attached at a later date.[18]

The relevance of this is that the Lazarus incident was part of that same sequence of events which climaxed when Mary Magdalene anointed Jesus at Bethany. The Synoptic Gospels do not say what happened on Jesus's arrival at Simon's house, for the raising of Lazarus is not included in them, but in John 11:20-29, it is described:

> Then Martha, as soon as she heard that Jesus was coming, went and met him: but Mary sat still in the house ...
>
> [Martha] called Mary her sister secretly, saying, The Master is come, and calleth for thee.
>
> As soon as she heard that, she arose quickly and came unto him.

No reason is ventured for Mary's hesitant behavior although, apart from that, the passage seems straightforward enough. But the incident is described in much greater detail in the portion of Mark that was officially suppressed. It explains that Mary did come out of the house with Martha on the first occasion, but was then chastised by the disciples and sent back indoors to await her Master's instruction. The fact is that, as Jesus's wife, Mary was bound by a strict code of bridal practice. She was not permitted to leave the house and greet her husband until she had received his express consent to do so.[19] John's account leaves Mary in her rightful place without explanation, but the more detailed Mark text was strategically withheld from publication.

The suppression of the Lazarus story is why the accounts of anointing in the Gospels of Mark and Matthew are located at the house of Simon the leper, instead of at the house of Lazarus as in John. But the description 'Simon the leper' is simply another more guarded way of referring to Simon Zelotes (Lazarus); he was classified as a 'leper' because he was rendered hideously unclean by his excommunication. This, in turn, explains the anomalous account of a leper entertaining prestigious friends at his fine house and the symbolic description of 'leper' was used to veil the truth of the situation. However, the fact was that, with his wife three months into her pregnancy, Jesus was not only a formally anointed Messianic Christ when he rode into Jerusalem on the donkey; he was also a father-to-be.

BETRAYAL

POLITICS AND THE PASSOVER

Jesus rode into Jerusalem in style; coats and palm branches were scattered in this path and crowds cheered, 'Hosanna to the son of David' (Matthew 21:9). It has to be said, however, that this frenetic activity was mainly that of the disciples (as described in Luke 19:36-39). The strewing of the palm fronds was intended to remind the people of the triumphant entry into Jerusalem of Simon Maccabaeus, the deliverer of Palestine from the yoke of Syrian oppression in 142 B.C.E. But Jesus's face was not well known in the city; his familiar territory was Galilee and the land around. Indeed, Matthew 21:10 states: 'And when he was come into Jerusalem, all the city was moved, saying, Who is this?'

A prophecy of John the Baptist[1] had determined that March 33 C.E. would see the proclamation of the Savior Messiah and the restoration of the true King. Many things had been carefully prepared for this time—the anointing, the donkey, the palm leaves and so forth—but nothing of consequence happened! According to Mark 11:11, Jesus entered the Temple, 'and when he had looked round and about upon all things, and now eventide was come, he went out unto Bethany'. Luke 19:40 tells that the Pharisees ordered the disciples to be rebuked for creating a disturbance. Matthew 21:12 adds, 'Jesus went into the temple

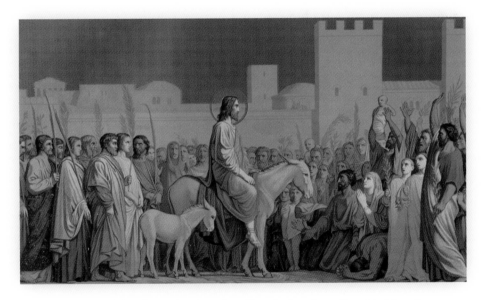

Jesus rode into Jerusalem in style, with palm fronds scattered in his path
by Hippolyte Flandrin, 1809-64

of God, and cast out all them that sold and bought in the temple, and overthrew the tables of the money changers, and the seats of them that sold doves'. He then returned to Bethany.

All things considered, the visit to Jerusalem was an unfortunate non-event. Jesus did not receive the acclaim he expected and he realized that his days were numbered, especially since he was a known associate of the Zealot commanders, Simon Zelotes, Judas Sicariote and Thaddaeus, who had led the revolt against Pilate. The Scribes and priests 'sought how they might take him by craft, and put him to death' (Mark 14:1). His plan to create an idyllic Judaea, free from the Roman oppression, had failed because his dream of unifying the people was not shared by his sectarian countrymen—in particular the stalwart Pharisees and Sadducees.

Also at that time, a serious rift occurred within the Apostolic group. Simon Zelotes had long been at odds with Jonathan Annas (James of Alphaeus) and their political rivalry came to a head. In their respective party roles they were styled Lightning and Thunder, and they were both contenders for the supreme position of Father. Simon was the Father from March 31 C.E., but lost his supremacy to Jonathan by default through his excommunication. Jonathan had been obliged to endorse the raising of Lazarus (by which Simon was restored to political and social life), but he was in no mood to relinquish the power he had only just gained, especially when Simon had been resurrected against the established rules.

Soon afterwards, it was time for the Jewish celebration of the Passover, when hordes of pilgrims joined the Jerusalem residents for the ritual of the Paschal Lamb in accordance with Exodus 12:3-11. In the course of this, we are told that Jesus and his Apostles made their way to that

**Judas leaves the Last Supper
by William Hole, c.1890**

legendary upper room where they were to eat the sacred Last Supper. But there are some questionable features about this. How was it that, at such a time when all the temporary accommodation in the city was full to bursting, the Apostles were so easily able to obtain a room of some considerable size for themselves? How also could the fugitive Zealots, Simon, Judas and Thaddaeus, possibly afford to move openly in Jerusalem, while being sought for leading the recent revolt?

The answer to these questions may be found in the Dead Sea Scrolls, wherein it is evident that the Last Supper did not take place in Jerusalem at all, but at Qumrân. Indeed, Josephus explains in

The Antiquities of the Jews that the Essenes did not observe the traditional Jewish festivals in Jerusalem[2] and did not, therefore, uphold the ritual of the Paschal Lamb at the Passover.

More than 160 years earlier, when the pious Hasidim vacated Jerusalem for Qumrân in around 130 B.C.E., their new environment became a substitute Holy City. The custom was continued by the later Essenes and, in this context, they often referred to Qumrân as 'Jerusalem' (*Yuru-salem*: City of peace). As evidenced by one of the Dead Sea Scrolls known as the *Community Rule*, the famous Last Supper corresponds, in fact, to the Messianic Banquet (the Lord's Supper). That it occurred at the same time as the Passover celebration in Jerusalem was entirely coincidental, for the Messianic Banquet had a quite different significance. The primary hosts of the Banquet were the High Priest and the Messiah of Israel.[3] The people of the community were represented by appointed officers who together formed the Council of Delegate Apostles. The *Rule* lays down the correct order of precedence for the seating and details the ritual to be observed at the meal. It concludes:

> And when they gather for the community table ... and mix the wine for drinking, let no man stretch forth his hand on the first of the bread or the wine before the Priest, for it is he who will bless the first fruits of the bread and wine ... And afterwards, the Messiah of Israel shall stretch out his hands upon the bread, and afterwards all the congregation of the community will give blessings, each according to his rank.[4]

When the time came for communion, Judas left the room, ostensibly to offer alms to the poor (John 13:28-30). Actually, he went to make the final arrangements for Jesus's betrayal, while Jesus—who perceived his intention—said, 'That thou doest, do quickly' (John 13:27). There was, however, still time for the Baptist's prophecy concerning the restoration of the true Christ to be fulfilled—but the final deadline was that very night, the vernal equinox of March 20, 33 C.E.[5] Jesus knew that if this passed with no proclamation being made in his favor, then his ambition was over. From that night there would be no hope of satisfying the Messianic prediction and he would be denounced as a fraud. When Judas left the room, the time was already fast approaching midnight.

Following the banquet, Jesus and the remaining Apostles went to the old monastery at Qumrân, customarily known as the Mount of Olives. There is some disagreement at this point between John's Gospel and the Synoptic Gospels on the precise course of events but, one way or another, Jesus foretold his fate and outlined to his companions what their reactions would be. He declared that even Peter would deny him in the face of the unfulfilled prophecy. While some of Jesus's disciples slept in the monastery

Jesus proclaims that he will be denied by Edward Deanes (19th century)

The Arrest at Gethsemane
by Friedrich Overbeck, c.1845

garden, Jesus walked among them (Matthew 26:36-45), agonizing that his bid to be recognized as the Savior Messiah might have failed. Midnight passed—then Judas Sicariote arrived with the soldiers.

The ultimate success of Judas's plan relied on retaining favor with the Father, Jonathan Annas. Whether Judas took a calculated gamble or whether he and Jonathan had come to some agreement beforehand is uncertain. But when the moment of seizure came, Jonathan certainly ranged himself alongside Judas. This is not really surprising, for Jonathan's daughter was married to the Pharisee High Priest, Joseph Caiaphas, while both Jonathan and Judas were politically opposed to Jesus's close friend Simon Zelotes. With the Gethsemane arrest duly made, 'the captain and officers of the Jews took Jesus, and bound him, and led him away to Annas first; for he was father-in-law to Caiaphas, which was the high priest that same year' (John 18:12-13).

It seems rather strange that Simon Zelotes, who must surely have been present at these events, is not mentioned in any of the Gospel accounts. Yet in Mark 14:51-52 there is a peculiar veiled reference to a person who might very well have been Simon: 'And there followed him a certain young man, having a linen cloth cast about his naked body ... and he left the linen cloth and fled from them naked'. Fleeing 'naked' could well have been symbolic of Simon's having been 'unfrocked' from his previous high ecclesiastical rank, while for him to be described as a 'young man' indeed relegates him to his newly demoted status as a Community novice following his excommunication.

CRUCIFY HIM!

Jesus's trial was hardly a trial at all and the scenario, as presented in the Gospels, is full of ambiguities. Matthew 26:57-59 describes matters thus: 'They that had laid hold on Jesus led him away to Caiaphas the high priest, where the scribes and the elders were assembled ... Now the chief priests, and elders, and all the council, sought false witness against Jesus'.

Even if all these priests, scribes and elders were somehow conveniently gathered together in the early hours at a moment's notice, the fact remains that it was quite outside the law for the Jewish Council to sit at night. Luke 22:66 indicates that although Jesus was taken firstly to Caiaphas, the Sanhedrin did not meet until it was day. But the meeting would still have been illegal because the Sanhedrin Council was not allowed to sit during the Passover.[6]

The Gospels all state that Peter followed Jesus to the house in which Caiaphas was located, where he denied his master three times as predicted. The house was not in the city of Jerusalem, though; it was the Vestry House at Qumrân.[7] In his capacity as the prevailing High Priest, Caiaphas would necessarily have been at the Messianic Banquet (as laid down in the *Community Rule*) and would, therefore, have been resident in the community along with other officials of the Sanhedrin on the night before the Passover Friday.

All accounts agree that Caiaphas passed Jesus over to the Roman Governor, Pontius Pilate, whose presence facilitated the immediate interrogation. This is confirmed in John 18:28-31, only for a further anomaly to emerge:

Then led they Jesus from Caiaphas unto the hall of judgment: and it was early; and they themselves went not into the judgment hall, lest they should be defiled; but that they might eat the Passover.

Pilate then went out unto them, and said, What accusation bring ye against this man?

They answered and said unto him, If he were not a malefactor, we would not have delivered him up unto thee.

Then said Pilate unto them, Take ye him, and judge him according to your law. The Jews therefore said unto him, It is not lawful for us to put any man to death ...

In this regard, the truth is that the Sanhedrin was fully empowered not only to condemn criminals but to pass and implement the death sentence if necessary. The Gospels also claim that Pilate offered to reprieve Jesus because 'it was customary for the Governor to release a prisoner at the

Jesus appears before Pontius Pilate
by William Hole, c.1890

feast of the Passover'. Again this is simply not true—there never was such a custom.[8]

Although the Zealots, Simon (Lazarus) and Judas, feature in the events leading to Jesus's arrest, it would appear that Thaddaeus—the third of the key revolutionaries—is not mentioned after the Last Supper. But he does actually come into the story at the trial. Thaddaeus was a deputy of the Succession ('of Alphaeus'), a deputy to the Father and thus a devotional 'son of the Father'. In Hebrew, the expression 'son of the Father' would incorporate the elements *bar* (son) and *abba* (father)—so Thaddaeus might be described as 'Bar-abba' and a man called Barabbas is intimately concerned with the possibility of Jesus's reprieve by Pontius Pilate.

Barabbas is described in Matthew 27:16 as 'a notable prisoner'; in Mark 15:7 as one who had 'committed murder in the insurrection'; in Luke 23:19 as a man who 'for murder had been cast into prison' and in John 18:40 as 'a robber'. The

John description is rather too vague, for everyday robbers were not customarily sentenced to crucifixion. However, the English translated word does not truly reflect the original Greek implication, for *léstés* does not mean 'robber' so much as 'outlaw'. Mark's words point far more specifically to the insurgent role of Barabbas in the recent revolt.

What seems to have happened is that when the three prisoners Simon, Thaddaeus and Jesus were brought before Pilate, the cases against Simon and Thaddaeus were clear cut; they were known Zealot leaders and had been condemned men since the uprising. On the other hand, Pilate found it extremely difficult to prove a case against Jesus. Indeed, he was only there because the Jewish contingent had passed him over to Pilate for sentencing with the others. Pilate asked the Jewish hierarchy to provide him, at least, with a pretext— 'What accusation bring ye against this man?'—but received no satisfactory answer. In

'Behold the man'. Pilate offers to spare Jesus.
Antonio Ciseri, 1821-91

desperation Pilate suggested they should take him and 'judge him according to your law', at which the Jews are said to have given the untrue excuse that 'It is not lawful for us to put any man to death'.

So Pilate then turned to Jesus himself. 'Art thou the King of the Jews?' he asked, to which Jesus replied, 'Sayest thou this thing of thyself, or did others tell it thee of me?' Confused by this, Pilate continued, 'Thine own nation and the chief priests have delivered thee unto me: what hast thou done?' The questioning progressed until, eventually, Pilate 'went out again unto the Jews, and saith unto them, I find in him no fault at all' (John 18:38).

At this point, Herod-Antipas of Galilee arrived on the scene (Luke 23:7-12). He was no friend of the Annas priests and it suited his purpose for Jesus to be released in order to provoke his nephew King Herod-Agrippa. Antipas therefore struck a deal with Pilate to secure the release of Jesus. The pact between Judas Sicariote and Jonathan Annas was thus superseded, without involving either of them, by way of an agreement between the Herodian Tetrarch and the Roman Governor. From that moment, Judas lost any chance of a pardon for his Zealot activities and his days were numbered.

In accordance with the new arrangement, Pilate said to the Jewish elders (Luke 23:14-16):

> Ye have brought this man unto me, as one that perverteth the people: and, behold, I, having examined him before you, have found no fault in this man touching those things whereof ye accuse him: No, nor yet Herod: for I sent you to him; and lo, nothing worthy of death is done unto him. I will therefore chastise him, and release him.

Had the members of the Sanhedrin waited until after the Passover, they could have conducted their own trial of Jesus in perfect legality. But they had strategically passed the responsibility over to Pilate because they knew there was no true charge to substantiate. They had certainly not bargained for Pilate's sense of justice, nor for the intervention of Herod-Antipas. But Pilate managed to defeat his own objective. He tried to reconcile his decision to free Jesus with the notion that it might be regarded as a Passover dispensation and, in so doing, he opened the door to a Jewish choice: Jesus or Barabbas? At this, 'they cried out all at once, saying, Away with this man, and release unto us Barabbas' (Luke 23:18).

Pilate pursued his course in favor of Jesus, but the Jews cried 'Crucify him!' Yet again Pilate asked, 'Why, what evil hath he done? I have found no cause of death in him'. But the odds were stacked against him and, giving way to his misguided commitment, Pilate released Barabbas (Thaddaeus). The Roman soldiers placed a crown of thorns on Jesus's head and wrapped a purple robe around him. Pilate then handed him back to the priests, saying, 'Behold, I bring him forth to you, that ye may know that I find no fault in him' (John 19:4).

TO GOLGOTHA

At that stage, things were going well for the Jewish elders; their plan had all but succeeded. The ageing Thaddaeus may have been released, but both Simon and Jesus were in custody along with Judas Sicariote. Undoubtedly, the greatest betrayer of all was the prevailing Father, Jonathan Annas, the one-time Apostle known as James of Alphaeus (or Nathanael). The three crosses were duly erected in the 'Place of a Skull' (Golgotha) and were set to bear Jesus and the two Zealot guerrilla leaders, Simon Zelotes and Judas Sicariote.

Veronica and the Cyrene come to Jesus's aid.
Engraved from an original by M. Bertinot

On the way to the Crucifixion at Golgotha a significant event occurred when a mysterious character named Simon the Cyrene offered to carry Jesus's cross (Matthew 27:32). Many theories have been put forward about who the Cyrene might have been, but his real identity does not matter too much. What matters is that he was there at all. There is an interesting reference to him in an early Coptic tractate called *The Second Treatise of the Great Seth*, discovered among the books of Nag Hammadi. Explaining that there was a substitution made for at least one of the three victims of the Crucifixion, it mentions the Cyrene in this connection. The substitution apparently succeeded, for the tractate declares that Jesus did not die on the Cross as presumed. Jesus is himself quoted as saying after the event, 'As for my death—which was real enough to them—it was real to them because of their own incomprehension and blindness'.

The Islamic Koran (chapter 4, entitled 'Women') specifies that Jesus did not die on the cross, stating: 'Yet they slew him not, neither crucified him, but he was represented by one in his likeness ... They did not really kill him'. Also, the second-century historian, Basilides of Alexandria,

wrote that the Crucifixion was stage-managed (with Simon the Cyrene used as a substitute) and the gnostic leader, Mani (born near Baghdad in 214 C.E.), made precisely the same assertion.

In the event, however, Simon the Cyrene was a substitute for Simon Zelotes, not for Jesus. Clearly, the execution of two such men as Jesus and Simon could not go unchallenged and so a strategy was implemented to outwit the Jewish authorities (even though Pilate's men may well have been party to the subterfuge). It hinged upon the use of a comatosing poison and the performance of a physical deception.

If any man could mastermind such an illusion, that man was Simon Zelotes, Head of the Samaritan Magi and renowned as the greatest magician of his day. Both *The Acts of Peter* and *The Apostolic Constitutions*[9] recount the story of how, some years later, Simon levitated himself above the Roman Forum. At Golgotha, however, things were very different: Simon was under guard and on his way to be crucified.

In the first instance it was necessary to extricate Simon from his predicament—and so a substitution was organized in the person of the Cyrene, who would have been in league with the released Thaddaeus (Barabbas). The deception began on the way to Golgotha when, by accepting Jesus's burden, the Cyrene was able to incorporate himself in the midst of the assembly. The switch itself was made at the Crucifixion site, under cover of the general preparatory confusion. Amid this bustle of erecting the crosses, the Cyrene seemingly disappeared—but actually took Simon's place.[10] In the Gospels, the following sequence of events is carefully veiled by giving very few details about the men crucified alongside Jesus, other than describing them as 'thieves'.

And so the scene was set—Simon (Zelotes) Magus had achieved his freedom and could successfully handle the proceedings from then on.

7

CRUCIFIXION

PLACE OF A SKULL

𝕬lthough the Crucifixion is generally portrayed as a relatively public affair, the Gospels affirm (for instance in Luke 23:49) that onlookers were obliged to watch the proceedings 'from afar off'. In Matthew, Mark and John, the site is named as Golgotha, whereas in Luke it is Calvary. However, both names (Hebrew: *Gulgoleth*, Aramaic: *Gulgolta*, Latin: *Calvaria*) derive from words that mean 'skull' and the meaning of 'Golgotha', as given in the Gospels, is straightforward: a 'place of a skull'.

Three centuries later, as the Christian faith spread its influence, various sites in and around Jerusalem were dubbed with supposed New Testament significance. On many occasions it was simply a case of finding a suitable place to hang a name—such were the demands of pilgrims and the tourist market. A suitable Calvary site was identified; a route along which Jesus carried his cross was mapped out and a convenient sepulchre was earmarked to represent the legendary tomb.

In the context of all this creativity, Golgotha (Calvary) was said to have been located outside Herod's wall, northwest of Jerusalem. It was a

The Last Supper
by Jean-Baptiste de Champaigne, 1631-81

61

barren hill and was selected because it was roughly skull-shaped. Later tradition romanticised the place as 'a green hill far away'—a theme on which many artists have produced variations. Yet for all of this fanciful idealism, not one of the Gospels makes any mention at all of a hill. According to John 19:41, the location was a 'garden' in which there was a private sepulchre owned by Joseph of Arimathea (Matthew 27:59-60). Heeding the evidence of the Gospels instead of pandering to popular folklore, it is apparent that the Crucifixion was no hilltop spectacle with enormous crosses against the skyline and an epic cast of spectators. On the contrary, it was a small-scale affair on controlled land—an exclusive garden that was, in one way or another, the 'place of a skull' (John 19:17).

The Gospels have little more to say on the subject, but Hebrews 13:11-13 provides some very important clues to the location:

> For the bodies of those beasts, whose blood is brought into the sanctuary by the high priest for sin, are burned without the camp. Wherefore Jesus also, that he might sanctify the people with his own blood, suffered without the gate. Let us go forth therefore unto him without the camp, bearing his reproach.

From this we gather that Jesus suffered 'outside the gate' and 'outside the camp'. Also there is some association with a place where the bodies of sacrificed animals were burned. This reference is particularly important because the sites at which animal remains were burned were regarded as unclean. According to Deuteronomy 23:10-14, 'without the camp' described areas set aside as cesspits, middens and public latrines which were both physically and ritually unclean. By the same token, 'without the gate' defined various other unclean places, including ordinary cemeteries.[1]

Furthermore, the Dead Sea Scrolls make it clear that, because it constituted an act of defilement to walk over the dead, human graveyards were identified with the sign of a skull. It follows, quite naturally, that the 'place of a skull' (Golgotha/Calvary) was a cemetery—a restricted cemetery garden that contained an empty sepulchre in the charge of Joseph of Arimathea.

A further clue comes from Revelation 11:8, which states that Jesus was crucified in 'the great city which spiritually is called Sodom and Egypt'. This positively identifies the cemetery location as Qumrân, which was designated Egypt by the

**(left) Mary Magdalene attends
to Jesus after the Crucifixion
by Andrea Busalti, c.1512**

**(above) 19th-century German allegory
of the Crucifixion**

Therapeutate[2] and was geographically associated with the Old Testament center of Sodom.

Who, then, was Joseph of Arimathea? In the Gospels, he is described as an 'honorable counsellor (a member of the Sanhedrin), which also waited for the kingdom of God' (Mark 15:43). He was also 'a disciple of Jesus, but secretly, for fear of the Jews' (John 19:38). But although Joseph's allegiance to Jesus was a secret from the Jewish elders, it came as no surprise to Pontius Pilate, who accepted the man's involvement in Jesus's affairs without question. That same involvement was no surprise either to Jesus's mother Mary, or to Mary Magdalene, Mary Cleophas, or Salome. They all went along quite happily with Joseph's arrangements, accepting his authority without comment or demur.

Sometimes presumed to relate to the village of Arimeh on the plain of Gennesareth, Arimathea was, in fact, a descriptive title like so many others in the New Testament. It represented a particularly high status. Just as Matthew Annas held the priestly distinction 'Levi of Alphaeus' (Levi of the Succession), so Joseph was 'of Arimathea'. However (as with Matthew's style of Levi), Joseph was not his true baptismal name. Arimathea derived (like Alphaeus) from a combination of Hebrew and Greek elements—in this case, the Hebrew: *ha ram* or *ha rama* (of the height or top) and the Greek: *theo* (relating to God), together meaning 'of the Highest of God' and, as a personal distinction, 'Divine Highness'.

Meanwhile, we know that Jesus was the heir to the throne of David. The patriarchal title of 'Joseph' was applied to the next in succession[3] and, in this respect, with Jesus regarded as the 'David', then his eldest brother, James, was the designated 'Joseph'. Hence, Joseph of Arimathea emerges as none other than Jesus's own brother James. It, therefore, comes as no surprise that Jesus was entombed in a sepulchre that belonged to his own royal family.

**Jesus is nailed to the cross
by William Hole, c.1890**

Neither is it surprising that Pilate should allow Jesus's brother to take charge; nor that the women of Jesus's family should accept the arrangements made by Joseph (James) without question. The reason that Joseph kept his personal support for Jesus a secret from the Sanhedrin is self-evident, for he had his own separate following amid all ranks of the Hebrew community.

From the time the Dead Sea Scrolls were first discovered at Qumrân in 1947, digs and excavations went on well into the 1950s. During this period important finds were made in a number of different caves. The archaeologists discovered that one cave in particular had two chambers and two separate entrances quite a way apart. The access to the main chamber was through a hole in the roof path, whereas the adjoining hollow was approached from the side.[4] From the roof entrance, steps had been constructed down into the chamber and, to seal the entrance against rainfall, a large stone had to be rolled across the opening. According to the *Copper Scroll*, this sepulchre was used as a Treasury deposit and as such it has been dubbed the 'Rich Man's Cave'. This, the sepulchre of the Joseph Crown Prince, was sited directly opposite the Bosom of Abraham.

The prophecy that the Messiah would ride into Jerusalem on an ass was not the only prediction made concerning the Messiah in the Old Testament book of Zechariah. Two other prophecies— Zechariah 12:10 and 13:6—stated that he would be pierced and mourned in death by all Jerusalem and that he would be wounded in the hands as a result of his friends. Jesus realized that by being crucified he would qualify in all of these respects. He might have missed the deadline as far as John the Baptist's prophecy was concerned, but the Crucifixion offered him another chance. So, as John 19:36 states in relation to Zechariah, 'These things were done, that the scripture should be fulfilled'.

Crucifixion was both punishment and execution: death by torturous ordeal extended over a number of days. First the victim's outstretched arms were strapped by the wrists to a beam which was then hoisted into place horizontally across an upright post. Sometimes the hands were transfixed by nails as well, but nails alone would have been useless. Suspended with all his weight on his arms, a man's lungs would be compressed and he would die fairly quickly through suffocation. To prolong the agony, chest pressure was relieved by fixing the victim's feet to the upright post. Supported in this manner a man could live for many days, possibly even a week or more. After a while, in order to free up the crosses, the executioners would sometimes break the legs of the victims so as to increase the hanging weight and accelerate death.

On that Friday, March 20, 33 C.E., there was no reason for any of the three men crucified to have died within the day. Nevertheless, Jesus was given some vinegar and, having taken it, he 'gave up the ghost' (John 19:30). Soon afterwards, a centurion pierced Jesus's side with a spear and the fact that he bled (identified as blood and water) has been held to indicate that he was dead (John 19:34). In reality, vascular bleeding indicates that a body is alive, not dead. Dr. A. R. Kittermaster, in his 1979 report entitled *A Medical View of Calvary*, confirmed that, 'dead or alive, the flow of water is difficult to explain, but blood does not flow from a stab wound which is inflicted after death'. At that stage, Judas and the Cyrene were still very much alive, so their legs were broken.

Allegory of the Rosi-crucis,
by Evelyn de Morgan, c.1916

The Gospels do not say who gave the vinegar to Jesus on the cross, but John 19:29 specifies that the vessel was ready and waiting. A little earlier in the same sequence (Matthew 27:34), the potion was said to be 'vinegar mingled with gall'—that is soured wine mixed with snake venom. Dependent on the proportions, such a mixture could induce unconsciousness or even cause death. In this case, the poison was fed to Jesus not from a cup, but from a sponge and by measured application from a reed. The person who administered it was undoubtedly Simon Zelotes, who was meant to be upon one of the crosses himself.

Meanwhile, Joseph of Arimathea was negotiating with Pilate to remove Jesus's body before the Sabbath and place it in his sepulchre. Pilate was amazed that Jesus had died in so short a time (Mark 15:44): 'And Pilate marvelled if he were already dead: and calling unto him the centurion, he asked him whether he had been any while dead'. To speed matters up further, Joseph quoted to Pilate a Jewish rule based on Deuteronomy 21:22-23 and confirmed in the Qumrân *Temple Scroll*: 'And if a man have committed a sin worthy of death, and he be put to death, and thou hang him on a tree: His body shall not remain all night upon the tree, but thou shalt in any wise bury him that day'. Pilate therefore sanctioned the change of procedure from hanging (as manifest in crucifixion) to the old custom of burial alive. He then returned to Jerusalem leaving Joseph in control. (It is perhaps significant that in Acts 5:30, 10:39 and 13:29, the references to Jesus's torture all relate to his being 'hanged on a tree'.)

With Jesus in a seemingly lifeless coma and with the legs of Judas and the Cyrene newly broken, the three were brought down, having been on their respective crosses for less than half a day. The account does not state that the men were dead; it simply refers to the removal of their bodies—that is live bodies as against corpses.

THREE HOURS OF DARKNESS

The next day was the Sabbath, about which the Gospels have little to tell. Only Matthew 27:62-66 makes any mention of this Saturday, but refers simply to a conversation between Pilate and the Jewish elders in Jerusalem, following which Pilate arranged for two guards to watch Jesus's tomb. Apart from that, all four Gospels continue their story from the Sunday morning thereafter.

Yet, if any day was important to the ongoing course of events, that day was the Saturday— the Sabbath day we are told so little about. This respected day of rest and worship was the key to everything that happened. It was what occurred on the Saturday that caused the women such amazement when they found the stone rolled from its position at daybreak on the Sunday. In practical terms, there was nothing startling about the

Jesus appearing to Mary Magdalene at the tomb by Rembrandt, 1638

**The women arrive at the tomb of Jesus
by Robert Leinweber (20th century)**

displacement of the stone—anyone could have moved it. Indeed, the women would have rolled it away themselves, for they had no reason to anticipate a prevention of access. What was so unthinkable was that the stone had been moved on the Sabbath, a sacred day on which it was utterly forbidden to shift a burden. The mystery was not in the 'act' of removal, but in the 'day' of removal. For the stone to have been moved on the Sabbath was quite impossible!

There is some variation between the Gospels over what actually happened on the third day—the Sunday. Matthew 28:1 tells that Mary and Mary Magdalene made their way to the tomb, while Mark 16:1 includes Salome as well. Luke 24:10 introduces Joanna, but omits Salome, whereas John 20:1 has Mary Magdalene arriving entirely alone. Mark, Luke and John claim that when the woman/women arrived, the stone had already been displaced. In Matthew, however, the two sentries were on guard and the stone was still in

position. Then, to the astonishment of the women and the sentries, 'the angel of the Lord descended ... and rolled back the stone'.

It subsequently became apparent that Jesus was not in the tomb where he had been laid. According to Matthew 28:5-6, the angel led the women into the cave. In Mark 16:4-5, they went in by themselves and were confronted by a young man in a white robe. Luke 24:3-4, however, describes two men standing inside. And John 20:2-12 tells how Mary Magdalene went to fetch Peter and another disciple before entering the cave with them. Then, after her companions had departed, Mary found two angels sitting within the sepulchre.

In the final analysis, it is not clear whether the guards existed or not. The number of women was either one, two, or three. Perhaps Peter was around; perhaps he was not. There was either an angel outside or a young man inside; conversely, there were two angels inside, who might have been sitting, or might have been standing. As for the

Leap of Faith. Allegory of the Crucifixion

by Sir Peter Robson

stone, it was possibly still in position at daybreak, or maybe it had already been moved.

There is only one potential common denominator in all of this: Jesus was no longer there—but even that is not certain. According to John 20:14-15, Mary Magdalene turned away from the angels to find Jesus standing there, whereupon she took him to be the gardener. She moved towards him, but Jesus prevented her approach, saying, 'Touch me not' (John 20:17).

These are the four accounts on which the entire tradition of the Resurrection is based—and yet they conflict in almost every detail. Because of this, centuries of argument have ensued over whether it was Mary Magdalene or Peter who first saw the reappeared Jesus. But can we trace what actually happened after Joseph (James) left Jesus in the tomb on the previous Friday?

Initially, the Cyrene and Judas Sicariote—with their legs broken, but still very much alive—had been placed in the second chamber of the tomb. Jesus's body occupied the main chamber. Within the confines of the double-hollow, Simon Zelotes had already taken up his station, along with lamps and everything else required for the operation. (Interestingly, a lamp was among the items found within the cave during the 1950s.)

Then, according to John 19:39, Nicodemus arrived, bringing with him 'a mixture of myrrh and aloes, about an hundred pound weight'.[5] Extract of myrrh was a form of sedative commonly used in contemporary medical practice—but why such a vast quantity of aloes? The juice of aloes, as modern pharmacopoeias explain, is a strong and fast-acting purgative—precisely what would have been needed by Simon to expel the poisonous gall (venom) from Jesus's body.

It was of great significance that the day after the Crucifixion was the Sabbath day. Indeed, the timing of the whole operation to 'raise Jesus from the dead' (release him from excommunication) relied on the critical timing of the precise hour at which the Sabbath might be considered to begin. In those days, there was no concept of any fixed duration for hours and minutes. The recording and measurement of time was one of the official functions of the Levites who programed the course of hours by ground-shadows on measured areas. Also, since about 6 B.C.E., they had been able to make use of sundials. However, neither ground markings nor sundials were of any use when there were no shadows. Hence, there were twelve designated 'hours of day' (daylight) and, similarly, twelve 'hours of night' (darkness). The latter were measured by Levitical prayer sessions (like the canonical hours of the Catholic Church today. Indeed, the prevailing *Angelus* devotion—held at morning, noon and sunset—derives from the practice of the early Levite angels). The problem was however that, as the days and nights became longer or shorter, adjustments were necessary where hours overlapped.

On that particular Friday of the Crucifixion, a forward adjustment of a full three hours was required and, because of this, there is a noticeable discrepancy between the accounts of Mark and John over the timing of events on that day. Mark 15:24 states that Jesus was crucified at the third hour, whereas John 19:14-16 claims that Jesus was delivered for crucifixion at about the sixth hour. This anomaly occurs because Mark's Gospel relies on time as measured by Hellenist reckoning, whereas John's Gospel uses Hebrew time. The result of the time-change was (as Mark 15:33 describes) that 'When the sixth hour was come, there was a darkness over the whole land until the ninth hour'. These three hours of darkness were symbolic only; they occurred within a split second (as do changes in time today when we cross between different time-zones, or when we put clocks forward or backward for daylight saving). So, on this occasion, the end of the fifth hour was followed immediately by the ninth hour.

The key to the Resurrection story lies in these three missing hours (the daytime hours that became night-time hours), for the newly defined start of the Sabbath began three hours before the old twelfth hour—that is at the old ninth hour, which was then renamed the twelfth hour. But the Samaritan Magi of Simon Zelotes worked on an astronomical time-frame and did not formally implement the three-hour change until the original twelfth hour. This meant that, without breaking any of the rules against laboring on the Sabbath, Simon had a full three hours in which he could do what he had to do, even while others had begun their sacred period of rest. This was time enough to administer the medications to Jesus and to attend to the bone fractures of the Cyrene. Judas Sicariote was dealt with none too mercifully and was thrown over a cliff to his death (as obliquely related in Acts 1:16-18). The earlier reference in Matthew 27:5, which indicates that Judas hanged himself, refers more precisely to the fact that, at that stage, he set the scene for his own downfall.

THE EMPTY TOMB

When the Sabbath began by Magian time (three hours after the standard Jewish Sabbath), there were still a full three night hours before Mary Magdalene arrived on the first dawn of the new week. Whether or not there were sentries on guard that night is quite irrelevant; any coming and going by Simon and his colleagues would have been effected by way of the second entrance which was some distance away. Whether or not the stone was moved is equally irrelevant. The important thing is that when Jesus appeared, he was alive and well.

Concerning the angel who moved the stone for the women, Matthew 28:3 reads, 'His countenance was like lightning, and his raiment white as snow'. As we have seen, Simon (Magus) Zelotes was politically styled 'Lightning'; his vestment was white and in rank he was indeed an angel. The sentence might thus be interpreted more literally as 'His countenance was like that of Simon Zelotes in his priestly vestment'. But why should this have been such a surprise to the women? Because as far as they knew, Simon had been crucified and entombed with his legs broken.

Not only was Simon present, but so too was Thaddaeus: 'There was a great earthquake, and an angel appeared' (Matthew 28:2). Just as Simon Zelotes was styled 'Lightning' (with Jonathan Annas being 'Thunder'), Thaddaeus was, in turn, designated 'Earthquake' (in similar imagery concerning Mount Sinai, as in Judges 5:5). Simon and Thaddaeus were, therefore, the two angels encountered by Mary (John 20:11-12). Simon was also the 'young man' in the white robe (Mark 16:5), the youthful description indicating his newly demoted status as a 'novice' subsequent to the Lazarus excommunication.

The garden in which Jesus was crucified was under the jurisdiction of Joseph of Arimathea (Jesus's brother James). It was a consecrated area symbolizing the Garden of Eden, in relation to which James was identified with Adam, the man of the Garden. Thus, when Mary first saw Jesus and thought he was the gardener, the inference is that she believed she was looking at James. The reason that Jesus stopped Mary from touching him was that Mary was pregnant and, according to the rules for dynastic brides, she was allowed no physical contact with her husband at that time.

It is evident that Mary and most of the disciples were not party to the subterfuge of that Friday and Saturday. Indeed, it was in Simon's own interest to remain mysterious; escaping from the burial cave alive and with his legs unbroken could only add to his already great reputation. It was also in Jesus's own favor that his reappearance should be astounding to all. In the event, their joint effort—with the support of Thaddaeus, the Cyrene and brother James (Joseph)—held the mission together after its near collapse, enabling the Apostles to continue their work. If Jesus had truly died, his disciples would have scattered in fear and dismay, whereupon his cause would have died with him.[6] As it was, the mission received a whole new lease of life—the result of which was the birth of Christianity.

RAISED FROM THE DEAD

But if there be no resurrection of the dead, then is Christ not risen: And if Christ be not risen, then is our preaching vain, and your faith is also vain ... For if the dead rise not, then is not Christ raised ...

This is the case for the Resurrection as presented as an item of faith by St. Paul in 1 Corinthians 15:13-16. It has to be said that it does not constitute much of an argument for something that is apparently so fundamental to the Christian belief. In fact, if anything it is fully self-defeating. Had Paul been speaking in spiritual terms, his contemporaries might have accepted his claim more readily, but he was not. He was talking literally, referring to the notion of corpses returning to life in accordance with the prophecy in the book of Isaiah (26:19): 'Thy dead men shall live, together with my dead body shall they arise'.

Immortality of the soul (rather than of the body) was around as a concept long before Jesus's time. In the ancient Greek world it was promoted by the followers of the Athenian philosopher Socrates (c.469-399 B.C.E.) Plato maintained in the

fourth century B.C.E. that mind, not matter, was the root of reality. Even earlier, Pythagoras (c.570-500 B.C.E.) expounded the doctrine of reincarnation: the idea that, upon death in one life, the soul enters another body and begins life anew. Indeed, belief in reincarnation is common to many religions deriving from around the same time, including Hinduism and Buddhism.

However, Paul was not referring to the transmigration of souls; he was expressing a belief in which Christianity stands alone as a major religion—the notion that a dead person came back to life 'in the flesh'. The Apostles' Creed states that Jesus was 'crucified, dead and buried; ... The third day he rose again from the dead'. Scholars have long challenged the literal interpretation of this

Peter and John arrive at the empty tomb
by William Hole, c.1890

**Buddhist wheel of the
Rebirth of the Soul**

statement and, in recent years, many churchmen have queried it too. But, old doctrines die hard and many feel that to dispense with the concept would be to dispense with the intrinsic ethic of Christianity itself.

Yet, if Christianity has a worthwhile base —which it surely has—then that base must rest upon the moral codes and teachings of Jesus himself. Indeed, these social standards and their associated teachings are what the Gospels are all about.

It has often been pointed out that, after nearly 2000 years, some three-quarters of the world's population does not subscribe to the idea of bodily resurrection. Many actually find the idea more disturbing than uplifting, as a result of which the Christian message is severely repressed. Few

(of any religion or none) would dispute the inspiring neighborly motive of Jesus's own ideal—an ideal of harmony, unity and service in a fraternal society. In fact, there is no better basis for a religion; yet the wrap of a constraining dogma prevails— along with a constant wrangling about matters of interpretation and ritual. While such disputes continue, there can be no true harmony and a divided Church society can provide no more than a limited service to itself and to others.

One of the main problems associated with the acceptance of Jesus's bodily resurrection from physical death is that its premise is supported by little, if anything, in the Gospels. We have already seen that verses 9 to 20 of Mark 16 were spuriously attached long after the Gospel was completed and published. And if Mark's was the first of the Synoptic Gospels, forming a base for the others, then legitimate doubt is cast on the authenticity of the final verses of Matthew and Luke. But, if we ignore all of this, to accept the four Gospels as they are presented, we are faced with a very vague picture in which many details are not only confusing but conflicting. At first Mary Magdalene thought Jesus was someone else. Then Peter and Cleophas talked with him for several hours thinking he was a complete stranger. Not until Jesus sat down to eat with his Apostles did they recognize him—at which point he vanished from their sight.

What emerges is that the concept of the Resurrection as we know it today was completely unknown to those of the time. Apart from those directly concerned with the overall Crucifixion scenario, the disciples were kept in the dark. They truly believed their master had died and would have been totally bewildered at his reappearance. These were not the high-ranking priests such as Simon, Levi and Thaddaeus, but the less sophisticated Apostles such as Peter and Andrew. Nonetheless, they would certainly have appreciated that Jesus's own forecast of how his temple would be raised in three days (John 2:19) had nothing to do with a later European interpretation that completely missed the point of the death symbolism.

As apparent in the story of 'Lazarus',[7] a man was regarded as dead when excommunicated—a form of spiritual death by decree. The process took four days for implementation, during which period the excommunicatee was held to be sick unto death. In this regard, Jesus had been formally denounced by the Sanhedrin Council of legal elders, by the High Priest, Joseph Caiaphas, and by the new Father, Jonathan Annas. His excommunication was absolute and, from the early hours of the Crucifixion Friday, he was officially 'sick'. The only way to escape 'death' on the fourth day was to be previously released (raised) from the denouncement by the Father or the High Priest, which is why Jesus made such a point of being raised on the third day. In any other context, the period of three days had no significance whatever. But with the establishment set so firmly against him, who was there to perform the raising?

The only man who might presume to undertake the rite was the deposed Father, the loyal Simon Zelotes. Irrespective of the machinations in Jerusalem, Simon's rank as the Father was still upheld by many, but Simon had been crucified along with Jesus, or so most of the disciples believed. As it transpired, though, Simon emerged fit and well along with Jesus, whom he had 'raised from the dead' in the early hours of the Sunday morning. To those who were not party to the scheme, the raising of Jesus was indeed a miracle and, as the Gospel states, 'When therefore he was risen from the dead, his disciples ... believed the scripture, and the word which Jesus had said' (John 2:22).

It was Paul (a later Hebrew convert to Hellenist ways) who established the blood and bones Resurrection doctrine, but even his enthusiasm was short-lived. However, since he had expressed himself so excitedly on the subject and had backed his

The Resurrection
by Gaudenzio Ferrari, 1471-1546

fervor with such clinching non-arguments as we saw earlier ('if there be no resurrection from the dead, then is Christ not risen ...' and so forth), Paul was regarded as a fanatic[8] by Jesus's brother James, whose Nazarenes never preached the Resurrection. Indeed, from those times of initial Pauline exaltation, the Resurrection diminished as a factor of fundamental concern. This is fully apparent in the later Epistles (letters) of Paul and in other New Testament books, where it hardly features at all.

More important was the fact that Jesus had seen fit to suffer for the sake of his ideals and Paul eventually sought to find a more explanatory basis for his earlier doctrine, declaring,

> There is a natural body, and there is a spiritual body. Flesh and blood cannot inherit the kingdom of God; neither doth corruption inherit incorruption. Behold, I shew you a mystery.
>
> (1 Corinthians 15:44, 50-51)

It is essential to remember that Jesus was neither a Gentile nor a Christian. He was a Hellenist Jew whose religion was radical Judaism. In time, however, his original mission was usurped and taken over by a religious movement that was named after him in order to obscure his true heirs. That movement centered upon Rome and based its self-proclaimed authority on the statement of Matthew 16:18-19, in which Jesus supposedly said 'Thou art Peter, and upon this rock I will build my church'. Unfortunately, the Greek word *petra* (rock), relating to 'the Rock of Israel', was mistranslated as if it had been *petros* (stone), referring to Peter[9] (who was indeed dubbed *Cephas*—a stone, as in John 1:42). Jesus was actually affirming that his mission was to be founded upon the Rock of Israel, not upon Peter. Irrespective of this, the new movement then decreed that only those who had received authority handed down directly from Peter could be leaders of the Christian Church. It

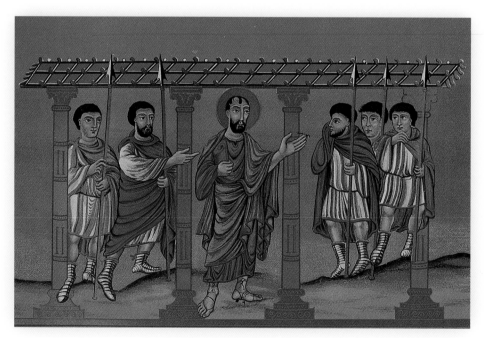

9th-century French depiction of St. Paul
preaching the Gospel

was an ingenious concept which, as was intended, restricted overall control to a select, self-promoting fraternity. The Gnostic[10] disciples of Simon (Magus) Zelotes called it 'the faith of fools'.

The Gospel of Mary Magdalene confirms that, for a short time after Jesus had been 'raised from the dead', some of the Apostles knew nothing about it and went on believing that their Christ had been crucified. The Apostles 'wept copiously, saying, How can we possibly go to the Gentiles and preach the gospel of the kingdom of the Son of Man? If they were ruthless to him, won't they be ruthless to us?' Having already spoken with Jesus at the tomb, Mary Magdalene was able to reply: 'Stop weeping. There is no need for grief. Take courage instead, for his grace will be with you and around you, and will protect you'.

Peter then said to Mary, 'Sister, we know that the Savior loved you more than other women. Tell us all that you can remember of what the Savior said to you alone—everything that you know of him but we do not'.[11]

Mary recounted that Jesus had said to her: 'Blessed are you for not faltering at the sight of me: for where the mind is, there is the treasure'. Then 'Andrew responded, and said to the brethren, Say whatever you like about what has been said. I for one do not believe the Savior said that'. Peter, agreeing with Andrew, added, 'Would he really have spoken privately to a woman, and not freely to us?' At this,

> Mary wept and said to Peter ... Do you think that I thought this all up myself, or that I am not telling the truth about the Savior?
> Levi answered, and said unto Peter ... You have always been hot-tempered. Now I see you arguing with the woman as if you were enemies. But if the Savior found her worthy, who are you, indeed, to reject her? The Savior surely knows her well enough.

Levi', as we know,[12] was Matthew Annas, a priest and deputy of Alphaeus. His sensible opinion was the product of intellect and education. Peter and Andrew, on the other hand, were lesser educated villagers who, despite their length of time with Jesus and the more learned Apostles, still retained old establishment views of womanhood. Eventually, as we shall discover, Peter's sexist attitude was to achieve a position of prominence in the Romanized doctrine that was founded upon his teaching.

The early bishops of the Christian Church claimed their own Apostolic succession from Peter—the handing down of episcopal authority through the personal laying-on of hands. But those same bishops were described in the Gnostic Apocalypse of Peter as 'dry canals'.[13] It continues,

> They name themselves bishops and deacons as if they had received their authority directly from God ... Although they do not understand the mystery, they nonetheless boast that the secret of Truth is theirs alone.

As for the Resurrection, the matter remains a paradox. It is regarded as being of huge importance when it need not be; yet it has an express significance of which most people are quite unaware. The Gospel of Thomas quotes Jesus as saying, 'If spirit came into being because of the body, it is a wonder of wonders'.[14]

8

THE BLOODLINE CONTINUES

THE TIMES OF RESTITUTION

As we have seen, Mary Magdalene was three months pregnant at the time of the Crucifixion. She and Jesus had cemented their Second Marriage at the Bethany anointing in March 33 C.E. Apart from being able to derive this information directly from the Gospel sources, it is also a matter of straightforward calculation. A male heir to a dynastic succession was required ideally to have his first son at or close to his own fortieth birthday. (Four decades was the recognized period of royal generation.[1]) The birth of a dynastic son and heir should always have been planned to occur in (the equivalent of) September—the holiest month of the Jewish calendar—and it was for this reason that sexual relations were permitted only in the month of December.

First Marriages also took place in the holy month of September—the month that included the Day of Atonement. A dynastic marriage would, therefore, theoretically be scheduled for the September of the bridegroom's thirty-ninth birthday, with sexual activity commenced in the December immediately following. In practice, however, there was always the chance that the first child might be a daughter and provision for this contingency was made by bringing the First Marriage ceremony forward to the bridegroom's thirty-sixth September. The first chance of a child then fell in his thirty-seventh September. If there was no conception in the first December, the couple would try again a year later—and so on.

For a son to be born in or around the husband's fortieth year was fully acceptable within the generation standard.

Once a son was born, no further sexual contact between the parents was permitted for six years.[2] On the other hand, if the child was a daughter the ensuing period of celibacy was limited to three years until the 'times of restitution' (the return to the married state). As we have seen, the Second Marriage was solemnized in the March following conception, at which time the bride would be three months pregnant.

In accordance with these customs and rules, Jesus's First Marriage took place in September 30 C.E. (his thirty-sixth September), the very occasion on which Mary Magdalene first anointed his feet (Luke 7:37-38). There was, however, no conception that December, nor in the December of the next year. But, in December 32 C.E., Mary did conceive and duly anointed Jesus's head and feet at Bethany (Matthew 26:6-7, Mark 14:3 and John 12:1-3), formally sanctifying their Second Marriage in March 33 C.E.

Jesus had himself been born, against the rules, on March 1, 7 B.C.E. but, in order to regularize his status, he had been allocated the official birthday of September 15 in line with Messianic requirement. (It has long been customary for some monarchs to celebrate their actual birthdays and their separate official birthdays.) It was not until 314 C.E. that the Roman Emperor, Constantine the Great, arbitrarily changed the date of Jesus's official birthday to 25

December, on which date it is still celebrated, with many presuming it to be his real physical birthday. Constantine's reason for making this change was two-fold. Firstly, it separated the Christian celebration from any Jewish association, thereby suggesting that Jesus was himself a Christian and not a Jew. Secondly, the adjustment of Jesus's official birthday was designed to coincide with the customary pagan Sun Festival. However, in the contemporary setting of Jesus's own time, September 15, 33 C.E. (six months after the Crucifixion) was his thirty-ninth official birthday and in that month a daughter was born to

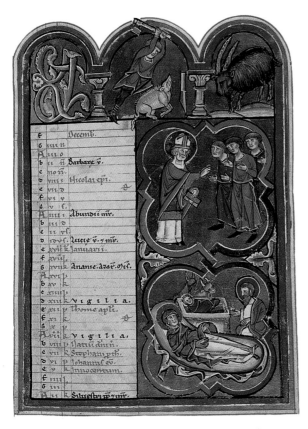

Christian calendar after the Roman strategic changing of Jesus's birthday to December 25

Mary Magdalene. She was named Tamar: 'Palm tree' (assimilated in Greek to the name *Damaris*), a traditional Davidic family name. Jesus was then required to enter a fully celibate state for three years until the 'times of restitution', as detailed in Acts 3:20-21.[3]

> And he shall send Jesus Christ, which before was preached unto you: Whom the heaven must receive until the times of restitution of all things, which God hath spoken by the mouth of all his holy prophets since the world began.

This month of September 33 C.E. coincided with Simon Zelotes being formally re-established as the Father of the Community, at which juncture Jesus was finally admitted to the priesthood—a ritual in which he 'ascended into Heaven'. Although recognized by many as the Davidic king, Jesus had long sought entry into the priesthood and particularly to the inner sanctum of the senior priests—the high monastery: the Kingdom of Heaven. Once Simon Zelotes had been reinstated, Jesus's wish was fulfilled: he was ordained and conveyed to Heaven by the Leader of the Pilgrims—his own brother James. In this fraternal context, James, by way of Old Testament imagery, was the designated 'Cloud'.[4] It was a cloud that had led the ancient Israelites into the Promised Land (Exodus 13:21-22) and the appearance of God to Moses on Mount Sinai had been accompanied not just by Thunder and Lightning, but also by a Cloud (Exodus 19:16). Thus (like Thunder, Lightning and Earthquake), Cloud was also retained as a symbolic designation within the Essene community.

Jesus's elevation to the priesthood is recorded in the New Testament by the event generally known as the Ascension. Not only did Jesus speak himself in parables, the Gospel writers did the same, applying allegories and parallels that were meaningful to these things, while they beheld, he was taken up, and a cloud received him out of their sight'. As Jesus departed into the priestly realm of Heaven, two angelic priests announced that he would eventually return in the same manner:

> Behold, two men stood by them, in white apparel, which also said, Ye men of Galilee, why stand ye gazing up into heaven? This same Jesus which is taken up ... shall so come in like manner as ye have seen him go ...
> (Acts 1:10-11)

And so Jesus left the everyday world for three years of which Mary Magdalene, the mother of his child, would have no physical contact with him. From her sixth month of pregnancy, Mary had the right to call herself *Mother*, but once her daughter was born and the three years of celibacy commenced, she would have been ranked as a *widow*. Dynastic children were brought up and educated at a monastic community center, in which their mothers (those designated *widows* or *crippled women*: wives in celibacy) also lived. It was because Jesus had himself been brought up in such enclosed conventual surroundings that so little is said about his childhood in the Gospels.

To Jesus a Son

Jesus's three-year period of monastic separation expired in September 36 C.E., following which physical relations with his wife were permitted once more in December.

One very clear property of the language used in the New Testament is that words, names and titles which have a cryptic meaning are used with that same meaning throughout—not only do they have the same meaning every time they are used,

A traditionally perceived image
of the Ascension
by William Hole, c.1890

'those with ears to hear'. Thus, passages of the Gospel texts which seem to be straightforward narrative (no matter how apparently supernatural their contexts) are also parables. As Jesus said to the disciples (Mark 4:11-12):

> Unto you it is given to know the mystery of the kingdom of God: but unto them that are without, all these things are done in parables: That seeing they may see, and not perceive; and hearing they may hear, and not understand ...

The Ascension, then, is another parable, as described in Acts 1:9: 'And when he had spoken but they are used every time that same meaning is required. Undoubtedly the most thorough studies to date in this field of research have been conducted by Dr. Barbara Thiering, based on information contained in the Dead Sea Scrolls commentaries on Old Testament books. These commentaries hold the secrets of the *pesharim* (the routes to vital clues) and they were produced by the learned Scribes at Qumrân.

In some cases, individual derivations of coded names or titles may be complex or obscure, but more often they are straightforward, though rarely obvious. Frequently, cryptic information in the Gospels is heralded by the statement that it is intended 'for those with ears to

The Sacred Allegory of Jesus and Mary Magdalene by Jan Provost, 1465-1529

hear'—this phrase is an inevitable precursor to a passage with a hidden meaning for those who know the code. The governing rules of the code are fixed and the symbolism remains constant— as in the case of Jesus himself.

By way of the inherent biblical *pesher* (singular of *pesharim* and meaning 'explanation' or 'solution'), Jesus is defined as the 'Word of God'— as established from the very outset in the Gospel of John:

> In the beginning was the Word, and the Word was with God ... And the Word was made flesh, and dwelt among us, and we beheld his glory ...
> (John 1:1,14)

There are no variables in the Gospel texts: whenever the phrase 'the Word of God' is used (with or without a capital 'W'), it means that Jesus either was present or is the subject of the narrative—as in Luke 5:1, when 'the word of God' stood by the lake.

The phrase was also used in Acts to identify Jesus's whereabouts after the Ascension. So when we read that 'the apostles which were at Jerusalem heard that Samaria had received the word of God' (Acts 8:14), we may immediately understand that Jesus was in Samaria.

It follows, therefore, that when we read 'the word of God increased' (Acts 6:7) we should apprehend at once that Jesus 'increased',[5] as symbolized through the *pesher* in the parable of the Sower and the Seed (Mark 4:8): 'And other [seed] fell on good ground, and did yield fruit that sprang up and increased'. In short, the Acts reference means that 'Jesus [yielded fruit and] increased'—that is to say, he had a son. Perhaps not surprisingly, this first son was also named Jesus and we shall return to him in due course.

As required by the Messianic rules, the birth took place in 37 C.E.—the year after Jesus returned to his marriage at the 'times of restitution'. Following the birth of a son, however, Jesus was now destined for no less than six more years of monastic celibacy.

In the Russian Church of St. Mary Magdalene, Jerusalem, there is a wonderful portrayal of Mary, which depicts her holding a red egg up to the viewer. This is the ultimate symbol of fertility and new birth. In a similar vein, *Sacred Allegory* by Jan Provost—a fifteenth-century esoteric painting—shows a sword-wielding Jesus together with his wife Mary, who is crowned and wears the black garb of a Nazarite priestess, while releasing the dove of the Holy Spirit.

THE GRAIL CHILD

During the early 40s C.E., Peter linked up with the newly converted Paul (previously an orthodox Hebrew called Saul of Tarsus) in Antioch, Syria, while James and his Nazarenes remained operative in Jerusalem. A further division in the ranks then became apparent when Simon (the Magus) Zelotes set up a separate base for his esoteric Gnostic sect in Cyprus.[6]

Peter had been Jesus's right-hand man and, as such, he should have become Mary Magdalene's guardian during the years of her separation (symbolic widowhood) but, although Peter had been married himself, he had a low opinion of women and was not prepared to be at the beck and call of a priestess. Paul's opinion of women was even less flattering and he strongly objected to their involvement in matters of religion. The two men, therefore, deliberately excluded Mary from any standing in their new movement and, to ensure her total alienation, they publicly declared her a heretic because she was a close friend of Simon Zelotes' consort, Helena-Salome.

In the course of this, Jesus and Mary once more resumed their married state in December 43 C.E., six years after the birth of their son. Jesus was not too concerned about Peter and Paul's attitude towards Mary, for he knew Peter well and he was aware of Paul's fanaticism. He was, in fact, perfectly happy for his wife to be associated with the Gnostic faction of Simon and Helena (or with the Nazarenes of his brother James), rather than with the new style of sexist ministry that was being promoted by Peter and Paul. After all, Mary (along with Martha) had been the devotional sister of Simon (Lazarus) in Bethany and they were very well acquainted. It was at this time that Mary once more conceived. By the spring of 44 C.E., Jesus had embarked on a mission to Galatia (in central Asia Minor) with the Chief Proselyte (Head of the Gentile converts), John Mark, perhaps better known as Bartholomew.

During this period, James and his Nazarenes became an increasing threat to Roman authority in Jerusalem. As a direct result, the Apostle James Boanerges was executed by Herod of Chalcis in 44 C.E. (Acts 12:1-2). Simon Zelotes took immediate retaliatory action and had Herod-Agrippa poisoned,[7] but was then obliged to flee. Thaddaeus, however, was not so fortunate; in trying to escape across the Jordan, he was seized by Chalcis and summarily executed. This placed the expectant Mary in a precarious situation, for Chalcis knew that she was a friend of Simon. She appealed for protection from Paul's one-time student, young Herod-Agrippa II (then aged seventeen), who duly arranged her passage to the Herodian estate in Gaul, where Herod-Antipas and his brother Archelaus had been sent into exile.

Later that year, Mary gave birth to her second son in Provence and there is a specific reference to this in the New Testament: 'The word of God grew and multiplied' (Acts 12:24).[8] This son was the all-important Grail Child and he was called Joseph.

HIDDEN RECORDS
AND THE DESPOSYNI

Having fulfilled his dynastic obligation to father two sons, Jesus was duly released from restrictions and able to lead a normal life once more. From 46 C.E., his elder son, the nine-year-old Jesus II, was schooled in Caesarea. Three years later, he underwent the ceremony of his Second Birth in Provence. In accordance with custom, he would have been symbolically born again from his mother's womb at the age of twelve—his designated 'First Year' as an initiate. In attendance was his uncle James (Joseph of Arimathea), who afterwards took his nephew to the West of England for a time.

In 53 C.E., Jesus junior was officially proclaimed Crown Prince at the synagogue in Corinth and duly received the Davidic Crown Prince's title of 'Justus' (the 'Righteous'—Acts 18:7).[9] He thereby formally succeeded his uncle, James the Just, as the kingly heir. Having reached the majority age of sixteen, Jesus Justus also became the Chief Nazarite, gaining entitlement to the black robe of that office—as worn by the priests of Isis, the universal Mother Goddess.[10]

His father, Jesus the Christ, went to Rome, via Crete and Malta, in 60 C.E.. Meanwhile, Paul returned to Jerusalem, having travelled extensively with Luke the physician. Once there, however, he was accused of conspiracy against Jonathan Annas, who had been murdered by Governor Felix. The Governor was sent for trial before Emperor Nero in Rome and Paul was obliged to follow. Then, after some time, Felix was acquitted, but Paul remained in custody because of his association with ex-pupil Herod-Agrippa II, whom Nero detested. During this period, Jesus Justus was also in the city (Colossians 4:11).

At about the same time, but far from the perils of Rome, Jesus Justus's younger brother, Joseph, had finished his education at a druidic college and was settled in Gaul with his mother. They were later joined by young Joseph's uncle James, who came permanently to the West, having been hounded out of Jerusalem in 62 C.E. His Nazarenes

Emperor Nero's punishment of the Christians
by Henryk Siemeradski, 1843-1902

had been subjected to brutal harassment by the Romans and the Sanhedrin Council had charged James with illegal teaching.[11] He was, consequently, sentenced to a public stoning and was excommunicated, to be declared spiritually 'dead' by the Jewish elders.[12] The once 'honorable counsellor' of the Sanhedrin and prospective Messiah of the Hebrews thus fell from the very pinnacle of civil and religious grace—an event which has often been symbolically portrayed as if he fell bodily from the Temple roof itself.

Having lost all spiritual credibility in the eyes of the law, James reassumed his hereditary style, Joseph of Arimathea, and made his way westward to join Mary Magdalene and her colleagues in Gaul. Back in Nero's Rome, Peter had arrived to assume responsibility for the Pauline sect, who were by then known as 'Christians'. Nero had developed a passionate hatred for the Christians and, to lessen their number, he instituted a fanatical regime of persecution. His favorite torture was to tie them to stakes in his palace gardens and to fire them as human torches at night.[13] This led to a major revolt by the Christians in 64 C.E., during the course of which Rome was engulfed by fire. The unbalanced Emperor was the suspected instigator, but he blamed the Christians and had both Peter and Paul put to death.

Before he died, Paul managed to relay a message to Timothy that Jesus was in a place of safety,[14] but he did not say where. It has been suggested by some that Jesus traced Thomas the Apostle's footsteps to India and he is reckoned to have died at Srinagar, Kashmir, where a tomb is attributed to him.[15]

Once James (Joseph of Arimathea) had settled permanently in the West, it was not long before Simon Zelotes led most of the Nazarenes out of Jerusalem in 65 C.E. He took them east of the Jordan and they spread into the region of old Mesopotamia (modern Iraq).

Nero's regime had caused considerable political nervousness and temperatures were raised to dangerous heights in the Holy Land. Early in 66 C.E., sporadic fighting broke out in Caesarea between the Zealots and Romans. The hostility quickly moved to Jerusalem, where the Zealots gained a number of strategic positions. They held the city for four years until a massive Roman army led by Flavius Titus arrived in 70 C.E., laying Jerusalem to waste. As Jesus had so rightly predicted many years before, the Temple fell and everything fell with it. Most of the inhabitants were slaughtered; the survivors were sold into slavery and the Holy City was an empty ruin for the next six decades.

In the wake of this destruction, the Jewish nation was in a state of turmoil. Not only did Jerusalem fall, but so too did Qumrân and, in time, the famous last bastion was the mountain fortress of Masada, southwest of the Dead Sea. There, fewer than a thousand Jews withstood repeated sieges by a mighty Roman army, but they were gradually deprived of all supplies and provisions. By 74 C.E., their cause was hopeless and the garrison commander, Eleazar Ben Jair, organized a program of mass suicide. Only two women and five children survived.[16]

Various waves of Nazarene refugees fled the Holy Land to perpetuate their tradition in the northern reaches of Mesopotamia, Syria and southern Turkey. The chronicler Julius Africanus, writing in around 200 C.E., while resident in the city of Edessa (now Urfa, in Turkey, as opposed to Edessa in Greece), recorded details of the exodus.[17] At the onset of the revolt, the Roman governors had caused all the public records in Jerusalem to be burned so as to prevent future access to the details of Jesus's family genealogy. During the Jewish Revolt, all records were fair game to the Roman troops, who were ordered to destroy private records as well—indeed, to destroy any relevant documentary evidence they could find. But,

'Noli me Tangere'. Jesus asks
Mary Magdalene not to touch him
by Correggio, 1489-1584

for all that, the destruction was not complete and certain papers remained successfully hidden.

Writing about this purposeful eradication of Messianic documentation, Africanus stated: 'A few careful people had private records of their own, having committed the names to memory or having recovered them from copies, and took pride in preserving the remembrance of their aristocratic origins'. He described these royal inheritors as the Desposyni ('Heirs of [or belonging to] the Lord [or the Master]'). Throughout the early centuries C.E., various Desposyni branches were hounded by Roman dictate—first by the Roman Empire and later by the Roman Church. Eusebius confirmed that, in Imperial times, the Desposyni leaders became the heads of their sects by way of a 'strict dynastic progression'. But, wherever possible, they were pursued to the death—hunted down like outlaws[18] and put to the Roman sword by Imperial command.

The full truth about this selective Inquisition was certainly concealed, but its mythology and tradition have survived. They have survived by way of Grail lore, the Tarot cards, Arthurian romance, the songs of the Troubadours, Unicorn tapestries, esoteric art and a continued veneration for the heritage of Mary Magdalene. So potent has been the tradition that, even today, the Holy Grail remains the ultimate relic of Quest. But all of this—no matter how enthralling or romantic—is deemed heretical by the orthodox ecclesiastical establishment. Why? Because the ultimate object of the enduring Quest still poses a daunting threat to a Church that dismissed the Messianic succession in favor of a self-styled clerical alternative.

MARY MAGDALENE

ROYAL BRIDE AND MOTHER

Mary Magdalene died in 63 C.E., aged sixty, at the place now called Saint Baume in southern France.[1] She is described in the New Testament as a woman 'out of whom went seven devils' (Luke 8:2) and later, in the same Gospel, she is said to be a 'sinner'. But in addition to this, she is portrayed in all the Gospels as a favorite and loyal companion of Jesus. However, Luke's descriptions of Mary are again a matter of cryptic coding.

Prior to marriage, Marys were under the authority of the Chief Scribe who, in Mary Magdalene's time, was Judas Sicariote. The Chief Scribe was also the Demon Priest Number 7,[2] and the 'seven demon priests' were established as a formal opposition group to those priests who were the 'seven lights of the Menorah'. It was their duty to supervise the community's female celibates. Upon her marriage, Mary Magdalene was naturally released from this arrangement. Hence, 'the seven demons went out of her' and she was permitted sexual activity on the regulated basis detailed earlier.

Mary Magdalene's father was the Chief Priest (subordinate to the High Priest) Syrus the Jairus. The Jairus priest officiated at the great marble synagogue at Capernaum and was ranked quite separately from the Zadok and the Abiathar. It had been a hereditary post from the time of King David, restricted to the descendants of Jair (Numbers 32:41).

The first mention of Mary in the New Testament is actually the story of how she was raised from death as Jairus's daughter in 17 C.E. Being raised (symbolically, from eternal darkness) related either to elevation of status within the Way or, as we have seen, to a release from spiritual death by excommunication. However, since women were not excommunicated, Mary's event was plainly an initiatory raising. First raisings for boys were at the age of twelve and for girls at

**Talmudic representation
of the Menorah**

fourteen. Given that Mary was raised in 17 C.E., this means that she was born in 3 C.E. and was therefore nine years younger than Jesus.

According to Gnostic tradition, Mary Magdalene was associated with Wisdom (Sophia), represented by the sun, moon and a halo of stars. The female gnosis of Sophia was deemed to be the *Holy Spirit*, thus represented on Earth by the Magdalene, who fled into exile bearing the child of Jesus. John, in Revelation 12:1-17, describes Mary and her son, and tells of her persecution, her flight into exile and of the continued Roman hounding of the 'remnant of her seed'.

In addition to Mary, other migrants to Gaul in 44 C.E. included Martha and her maid Marcella. There were also Philip the Apostle, Mary Jacob-Cleophas and Mary Salome-Helena. Their point of disembarkation in Provence was Ratis, which later became known as Les Saintes Maries de la Mer.[3] Despite Mary and Martha's prominence in the Gospel texts, there is no mention at all of them in Acts, nor in any of St. Paul's epistles after their westward departure in 44 C.E.

The Life of Mary Magdalene by Raban Maar (776-856), Archbishop of Mayence (Mainz) and Abbé of Fuld, incorporates many traditions about Mary dating back well beyond the fifth century. A copy of the Maar manuscript was unearthed at Oxford University in the early 1400s and the work had been cited in the *Chronica Majora* of Matthew Paris, in around 1190. It is also listed in the *Scriptorum Ecclesiasticorum Historia Literaria Basilae* at Oxford. Louis XI of France (1461-1483) was insistent on Mary's dynastic position in the royal lineage of France. *Saint Mary Magdalene* by the Dominican friar Père Lacordaire (published after the French Revolution) is a particularly informative work, as is *La Légende de Sainte Marie Madeleine* by Jacobus de Voragine, Archbishop of Genoa (born 1228). Both de Voragine and Maar state that Mary's mother Eucharia was related to

Mary Magdalene's 44 C.E. arrival in Provence. From the 15th-century Sforza Book of Hours

the royal house of Israel. (That was the Hasmonaean royal house, rather than the Davidic House of Judah.)

Another important work by Jacobus de Voragine is the famous *Legenda Aurea* (Golden Legend), one of the earliest books printed at Westminster, London, by William Caxton in 1483. Previously published in French and Latin, Caxton was persuaded by William, Earl of Arundel, to produce an English version from the European manuscripts. It is a collection of ecclesiastical chronicles detailing the lives of selected saintly figures. Highly venerated, the work was given public readings on a regular basis in medieval monasteries and churches.

One particular narrative from the *Legenda* is about St. Martha of Bethany and her sister, Mary Magdalene:

St. Martha, hostess to Lord Jesus Christ, as born into a royal family. Her father's name was Syro, and her mother's Eucharia; the father came from Syria. Together with her sister by inheritance through their mother, Martha came into possession of three properties: the castle Magdalene, and Bethany, and a part of Jerusalem.

After the Ascension of our Lord, when the disciples had departed, she, with her brother Lazarus and her sister Mary, also St. Maxim, embarked in a ship, on which—thanks to its preservation by our Lord—they all came safely to Marseilles. They thereafter proceeded to the region of Aix, where they converted the inhabitants to the faith.

The name 'Magdalene' derives from the Hebrew noun *migdal* (tower). In practical terms, the statement that the sisters possessed three castles is a little misleading, particularly since Marys (Miriams) were not allowed to own property. The joint heritage actually related to personal status—that is to say they inherited high community stations (castles/towers) of guardianship, as in Micah 4:8[4]: the Magdal-eder (watchtower of the flock).

The most active Magdalene cult was eventually based at Rennes-le-Château in the Languedoc region.[5] Elsewhere in France there were many shrines set up to Ste. Marie de Madeleine. These included her burial place at St. Maximus, where her sepulchre and alabaster tomb were guarded by Cassianite monks from the early 400s. Another important Magdalene seat was that of Gellone, where the Academy of Judaic Studies (the monastery of St. Guilhelm le Désert) flourished during the ninth century. The church at Rennes-le-Château was consecrated to Mary Magdalene in 1059 and, in 1096 (the year of the First Crusade), the great Basilica of St. Mary Magdalene was begun at Vézelay.

In drafting the Constitution for the Order of Knights Templars in 1128, the Cistercian abbot, St. Bernard de Clairvaux, specifically mentioned a requirement for 'the Obedience of Bethany, the castle of Mary and Martha'. It is evident, then, that the great *Notre Dame* cathedrals of Europe, which were wholly Cistercian-Templar instigated, were dedicated not to Jesus's mother Mary, but to 'Our Lady', Mary Magdalene.

St. Bernard de Clairvaux.
From Rev. Alban Butler's Lives of the Saints, 1926

SCARLET WOMAN—BLACK MADONNA

Early Christian texts describe Mary Magdalene as 'the woman who knew the all'. She was the one whom 'Christ loved more than all the disciples'; she was the apostle 'endowed with knowledge, vision and insight far exceeding Peter's and she was the beloved bride who anointed Jesus at the Sacred Marriage (the *Hieros Gamos*) at Bethany.

Disregarding all this, the Roman Church elected to discredit Mary Magdalene in an attempt to exalt her mother-in-law, Jesus's mother Mary. In order to accomplish this, they made use of ambiguous comments in the New Testament —comments that described the unmarried Magdalene as a 'sinner' (which actually meant that she was a celibate *almah* undergoing assessment in betrothal). The duplicitous bishops decided, however, that a sinful woman must be a whore and Mary was branded as such thereafter.

There is a fascinating parallel between Mary and her fellow migrant Helena-Salome. Because of his dislike for women (especially educated women), Peter had always regarded Helena-Salome as a witch. He paid no heed to the fact that she was close to Jesus's mother and had accompanied her at the Crucifixion. Helena was a High Priestess of the Order of Ephesus and, as such, was entitled to wear the red robe of the *hierodulai* ('sacred women'). The Roman Church, however, did not recognize such cardinal status in women and they too were classified as whores. Thus, the once venerated image of the *hierodulai* was transformed and (via medieval French into English) they became 'harlots', to be disparagingly referred to as 'scarlet women'.

Mary Magdalene was a Head Sister of the Nazarite Order (the equivalent of a senior bishop) and was entitled to wear black. In parallel with the early reverence for Mary Magdalene, a cult known

**The Black Madonna
of Vervieres**

as that of the Black Madonna emanated from Ferrières in 44 C.E.[6] Among the many Black Madonna representations that still exist, one of the finest statues is displayed at Verviers, Liège; she is totally black with a golden sceptre and crown, surmounted by Sophia's halo of stars. Her infant child also wears a golden crown of royalty.

In contrast to the Black Madonna image, it was also common for Mary Magdalene to be portrayed wearing a red cloak, often over a green dress (representing fertility).[7] An example is the famous *Saint Mary* fresco by Piero della Francesca, of about 1465, in the Gothic cathedral of Arezzo, near Florence. She is similarly clothed in Botticelli's *Mary at the Foot of the Cross*. The red is intended (like the scarlet of the *hierodulai*) to signify Mary's high clerical status. However, the concept of red-caped women of religious rank infuriated the Vatican hierarchy and, despite the Church's separate veneration of Jesus's mother, it was determined that she should not be dignified with the same privilege. In 1649, the bishops went so far as to issue a decree that all images of Jesus's mother should depict her wearing 'blue and white' only.[8] This had the effect that Jesus's mother Mary, although exalted by the Church was, nevertheless, denied any ecclesiastical recognition within the establishment.

Women were absolutely barred from ordination in the Catholic Church and the general relegation of women (other than Jesus's mother) from any venerable status pushed Mary Magdalene ever further into the background. By the same strategy, Jesus's own physical heirs were totally eclipsed and the bishops were enabled to reinforce their claim to holy authority by means of a self-devised male succession. This was not a Messianic descent from Jesus, as should have been the case, nor even a descent from the *ha-Rama-Theo* (Arimathea) prince, James the Just (brother of Jesus), but a contrived succession from Peter, the headstrong rustic Essene who despised women.

At the same time, the early Church was having to contend with a widespread veneration for the Universal Goddess—particularly in the Mediterranean environment—and this was actually to

Queen Isis, the Egyptian
nursing Madonna

heighten during the period of clerical squabbling over sexist issues. From prehistoric times, the Goddess had appeared in many guises and had been known by many names, including Cybele, Diana, Demeter and Juno. But however personified, she was always identified with Isis, who was said to be 'the Universal Mother, mistress of all the elements, primordial child of time, sovereign of all things and the single manifestation of all'.

To the ancient Egyptians, Isis was the sister-wife of Osiris, who was the founder of civilization and the judge of souls after death. Isis was specifically a maternal protectress and her cult spread far and wide. She was frequently portrayed holding her child, Horus, whose incarnations were said to be the pharaohs themselves. It is a well-established fact that the familiar image of the White Madonna is founded upon the depictions of Isis as the nursing mother. It was she too who inspired the mysterious Black Madonna, of whose image there were nearly 200 in France by the sixteenth century. Some 450 representations have now been discovered worldwide. Even the cherished patron goddess of France, *Notre Dame de Lumière* (Our Lady of Light), has her origins in the Universal Mother.

The image of the Black Madonna and her child has presented a constant dilemma for the Church—especially those statues at notable churches and shrines in continental Europe. In some cases they are black all over, but many have only black faces, hands and feet, although not negroid in character. A few have been overpainted in pale flesh tones to conform with the standard White Madonna representation, whilst many have simply been removed from the public gaze altogether. Some are modestly garbed, but others are displayed with various degrees of prestige and sovereignty, having ornately decorated clothing and crowns.

The Black Madonna has her tradition in Queen Isis and her roots in the pre-patriarchal Lilith. She thus represents the strength and equality of womanhood—a proud, forthright and commanding figure, as against the strictly subordinate image of the conventional White Madonna as seen in Church representations of Jesus's mother. It was said that both Isis and Lilith knew the secret name of God (a secret held also by Mary Magdalene, 'the woman who knew the All'). The Black Madonna is thus also representative of the Magdalene who, according to the Alexandrian doctrine, 'transmitted the true secret of Jesus'. In fact, the long-standing Magdalene cult was closely associated with Black Madonna locations. She is black because Wisdom (Sophia) is black, having existed in the darkness of Chaos before the Creation. To the Gnostics of Simon Zelotes, Wisdom was the Holy Spirit—the great and immortal Sophia who brought forth the first Father, Yaldaboath, from the depths. Sophia was held to be incarnate as the Holy Spirit in Queen Mary Magdalene and it was she who was said to bear the ultimate observance of the Faith.

MARY AND THE CHURCH

From the earliest days of the orthodox Christian movement, all venerators of the female principle were regarded as heretics. Long before the time of Emperor Constantine, Church Fathers such as Quintus Tertullian set the scene against female involvement, stating,

> It is not permitted for a woman to speak in church, nor is it permitted for her to baptize, nor to offer the Eucharist, nor to claim for herself a share in any masculine function—least of all in priestly office.

However, Tertullian was only following opinions expressed by his predecessors, notably Peter and Paul.

In the Gospel of Mary,[9] Peter challenges Mary Magdalene's relationship with Jesus, saying, 'Would he really have spoken privately to a woman, and not freely to us? Why should we change our minds and listen to her?' Again in the Coptic tractate called *Pistis Sophia* (Faith Wisdom),[10] Peter complains about Mary's preaching and asks Jesus to silence her, to stop her undermining his supremacy. Jesus instead rebukes Peter, whereupon Mary later confides, 'Peter makes me hesitate. I am afraid of him because he hates the female race'. Mary had good reason to be wary of Peter, for his attitude was made perfectly obvious on many occasions—as in the Gospel of Thomas.[11] Objecting to Mary's presence among the disciples, 'Simon Peter said unto them, Let Mary leave us, for women are not worthy of life'.

In the Gospel of Philip,[12] Mary Magdalene is regarded as 'the symbol of divine wisdom', but all such texts were excised by the bishops because they undermined the dominance of the male-only priesthood. Paul's New Testament teaching was expounded instead:

> Let the woman learn in silence with all subjection. But I suffer not a woman to teach, nor to usurp authority over the man, but to be in silence
> (1 Timothy 2:11-12).

Such authoritative pronouncements were especially useful because they actually masked the real issue. The point was that women had to be excluded at all costs. If they were not, the Magdalene's lingering presence would be seen to prevail. As the wife of Jesus she was not only the Messianic Queen but also the mother of the true heirs. There are, in the Gospels, no less than seven lists of the women who regularly accompanied Jesus and, in six of these, Mary Magdalene is the first named, even ahead of his own mother. For centuries after her death, Mary's legacy remained the greatest of all threats to a fearful Church that had bypassed Messianic descent in favor of a self-styled Apostolic succession.

In view of the Church's dread of Mary Magdalene, a special new document was produced, setting out what the bishop's reckoned to be her position within the scheme of things. Entitled *The Apostolic Order*, it was the transcript of a presumed discussion between the Apostles after the Last Supper and it claimed (which the Gospels do not) that both Mary and Martha were present,

Mary Magdalene reading
by Rogier van der Weyden, c.1435

90

thereby defeating part of its own objective. An extract from the supposed debate reads:

> John said: When the Master blessed the bread and the cup, and assigned them with the words, This is my Body and Blood, he did not offer them to the women who are with us.
>
> Martha said: He did not offer them to Mary because he saw her laugh.

On the basis of this purely imaginary story, the Church decreed that the first Apostles had decided that women were not to be allowed to become priests because they were not serious! The essence of this fabricated conversation was then adopted as formal Church doctrine and Mary Magdalene was thereafter pronounced a disbelieving recusant.

WOMEN AND THE GOSPEL SELECTION

The New Testament, as we know it, began to take shape in 367 C.E., when an initial selection of writings was collated by Bishop Athanasius of Alexandria, to be later ratified at the Council of Carthage in 397 C.E. There were, however, various criteria which governed the selection–the first being that the canonical Gospels must be written in the names of Jesus's own Apostles. But this ruling appears to have been disregarded from the outset. Although both Matthew and John were Apostles of Jesus, Mark and Luke were not; they are presented in the Acts as being later colleagues of St. Paul. On the other hand, Thomas and Philip were among the original twelve, but the Gospels in their names were excluded! Not only that, but

they were sentenced to be destroyed and, throughout the Mediterranean world, these and other books were buried and hidden in the fifth century. Subsequently, the New Testament was subjected to any number of edits and amendments, until the version with which we are now familiar was approved by the extended Council of Trento, in Northern Italy, as late as 1545-63.

Only in recent times have some of the early manuscripts been unearthed, with the greatest of all discoveries being that made in 1945 at Nag Hammadi. Although not rediscovered until recent times, the existence of these books had been no secret to historians. Indeed, certain of them, including the Gospel of Thomas, the Gospel of the Egyptians, the Gospel of Truth and others, are mentioned in the second-century writings of Clement of Alexandria, Irenaeus of Lyon and Origen of Alexandria.

What, then, was the criterion by which the Gospel selection was truly made? It was, in fact, a wholly sexist regulation which precluded anything that upheld the status of women in Church society. As mentioned, Peter and Paul's apparent dislike of women was used to set a strategically male-dominated scene, but even the quoted statements from these men were chosen very carefully, if not chosen out of context. In St. Paul's Epistle to the Romans, he made particular mention of his own female helpers; Phoebe, for example, whom he called a 'servant of the church' (16:1-2), along with Julia (16:15) and Priscilla, who laid down her neck for the cause (16:3-4). In fact, the New Testament is simply alive with women disciples, but the Roman Church bishops elected to ignore them all.

Indeed, the Church was so frightened of women that a rule of celibacy was instituted for its priests; a rule which became a law in 1138—a rule which persists even today. What really bothered the bishops, however, was not women as such, nor even sexual activity in general terms; it was the prospect of priestly intimacy with women which caused the problem. Why? Because women can become mothers and the very nature of motherhood is a perpetuation of bloodlines—a taboo subject which, at all costs, had to be separated from the necessary image of Jesus.

But, it was not as if the Bible suggested any such thing. In fact, quite the reverse was the case. St. Paul had actually said in his Second Epistle to Timothy (3:2-5) that a bishop should be the husband of one wife and that he should have children, for a man with his own household is better qualified to take care of the Church. Even though, in general terms, the bishops elected to uphold the teachings of Paul in particular, they chose to completely disregard this explicit directive so that Jesus's own marital status could be ignored.

LADY OF THE LAKE

In 633, a mysterious little boat sailed into the harbor of Boulogne-sur-mer in northern France. There was no one aboard, just a 3-foot (c. 1 meter) statuette of a Black Madonna and child, together with a copy of the Gospels in Syriac.[13] No one knew where the boat had come from, but it caused quite a stir and its enigmatic occupant—known as *Our Lady of the Holy Blood*—became the insignia of the Magdalene cathedral of *Notre Dame at Boulogne*.

The Black Madonna of Boulogne reinforced the connection between Mary and the sea (Latin: *mare*) in the popular mind and the 'Mary of the Sea' emblem (derived from the cathedral insignia) was used on pilgrims' badges before the time of Charlemagne. Indeed, a version of the device found its way into Scotland before armorial seals were common in Britain.[14] In eleventh-century Scotland, Edinburgh's Port of Leith incorporated its own official emblem—a depiction of Mary of the Sea and her Grail Child in a sailing boat protected by a cloud: a reference to James (Joseph of Arimathea) who was once the Cloud—the Leader of the Pilgrims.

For some reason, scholars of heraldry have largely seen fit to ignore the importance of such feminine devices, in just the same way that compilers of family trees and peerage registers have been guilty of dismissing female lineages. This was particularly so during the Georgian and Victorian eras in Britain, the volumes of which provide the basis for much of the unsatisfactory information available today. Maybe the current onset of the Age of Aquarius will see an end to male-dominated history but, for the time being, the majority of such works are published in the old style and format. Very little research is required, however, to discover that the ideal of *Noblesse Uterine* (matrilinear inheritance of nobility) was a concept thoroughly embraced throughout the Dark and early Middle Ages.

The libraries of Paris contain a number of manuscripts even older than Raban Maar's, which bear witness to Mary's mission in Provence. It is specifically mentioned in a hymn of the 600s (republished in the records of the *Acta Sanctorum*, issued by the Jesuit, Jean Bolland, in the seventeenth century).[15] Mary's companions, Mary-Salome (Helena) and Mary Jacob (the wife of Cleophas), are said to be buried in the crypt of *Les Saintes Maries* in the Camargue. Long before the ninth-century church was built, its predecessor was called *Sanctae Mariae de Ratis* and near the present main nave are the remains of a sculpture showing the Marys at sea.

Mary Magdalene's association with Gaul has been artistically depicted in two distinct ways:

May morning on the Magdalene Tower
by William Holman Hunt, 1890

representative and mystical. In some cases she is shown *en voyage* to Marseilles, as in the documented accounts. The most important example of this style of portrayal is perhaps that which has been exhibited at the ninth-century church of *Les Saintes Maries*: a painting by Henri de Guadermaris. It depicts the Marys' arrival in a boat off the coast of Provence and was shown at the Salon de Paris in 1886. Another famous picture on similar lines is *The Sea Voyage* by Lukas Moser, which forms part of the gold-and-silver-leafed altarpiece (*Der Magdalenenaltar*) at the Katholisches Pfarramt St. Maria Magdalena, Tiefenbronn, in southern Germany.

She is alternatively portrayed moving above the Earth to receive heavenly enlightenment (as apocryphal romance had her doing on a daily basis), or being carried westward as in the Revelation. A fine example of this style of representation is *Mary Magdalene Carried by the Angels*. This work of around 1606, by Giovanni Lanfranco, at the Galleria Nazionale di Capodimonte in Naples, shows the naked Magdalene together with three putti soaring above an empty European landscape.

Mary Magdalene's remains were preserved at the Abbey of St. Maximus, some 30 miles (c. 48 km) or so from Marseilles. Charles II of Sicily, Count of Provence, disinterred Mary's skull and humerus (upper arm bone) in 1279 in order to have them set in the gold and silver display casings in which they remain today.[16] Some of Mary's other bones and ashes were kept in an urn, but these were vandalized during the French Revolution.

Mary's cave of solitude is to be found nearby at La Sainte Baume. It was this cave which the Sire de Joinville visited in 1254 on returning from the Seventh Crusade with King Louis IX. Three centuries earlier, Wuillermus Gerardus, Marquis of Provence, made a pilgrimage to the cave, while the lofty grotto church at La Sainte Baume—with its various altars and fine sculpture of Mary Magdalene—has long been a noted place of pilgrimage.

**Mary Magdalene carried by the Angels
by Giovanni Lanfranco, 1582-1647**

Aix-en-Provence, where Mary Magdalene died in 63 C.E., was the old town of Acquae Sextiae.[17] It was the hot springs at Aix (Acqs) which gave it its name—*acqs* being a medieval derivative of the Latin word *aquae* (waters). In the Languedoc tradition, Mary is remembered as *la Dompna del Aquae*: the Mistress of the Waters. To the Gnostics (as indeed to the Celts), females who were afforded religious veneration were often associated with lakes, wells, fountains and springs. Indeed, gnosis (knowledge) and wisdom were attributed to the female Holy Spirit which 'moved on the face of the waters' (Genesis 1:2).

Earlier, we saw how the baptismal priests of the Gospel era were described as 'fishers' and, from the moment Jesus was admitted to the priesthood in the Order of Melchizedek (Hebrews 5), he too became a designated 'fisher'. The dynastic line of the House of Judah was thus uniquely established as a dynasty of Priest-Kings or, as Jesus's descendants became aptly known in Grail lore, Fisher Kings. The lines of descent from Jesus and Mary Magdalene, which emerged through the Fisher Kings, preserved the maternal Spirit of Aix to become the 'family of the waters'—the House del Acqs.

This family was prominent in Aquitaine—an area with a name that also has its roots in *acquae* ('waters') or *acqs*, as indeed does the town name of Dax, west of Toulouse, which stems from *d'Acqs*.[18] Here, Merovingian[19] branches that evolved from the Fisher Kings became Counts of Toulouse and Narbonne, also Princes of the Septimanian Midi (the territory between France and Spain).

Another family branch, related through the female line, was granted the Celtic Church heritage of Avallon, with Viviane del Acqs acknowledged as the hereditary High Queen in the early sixth century. Subsequently, in Brittany, a corresponding male branch of the Provençal House del Acqs became the Comtes (Counts) de Léon d'Acqs in descent from Viviane I's granddaughter Morgaine.

From the time that Chrétien de Troyes wrote his twelfth-century tale of *Ywain and the Lady of the Fountain*—in which the Lady corresponds to *la Dompna del Aquae*—the heritage of Acqs has persisted in Arthurian literature. The family legacy, which remained central to the Grail theme, was always directly related to the sacred waters and was always associated with Mary Magdalene. In 1484, Sir Thomas Malory's English *Le Morte d'Arthur* adjusted the distinction, by way of phonetic assimilation from *del Acqs to du Lac*, with the result that, in translation, Viviane II (Lady of the Fountain and mother of Lancelot del Acqs) became the Lady of the Lake.

IO

JOSEPH OF ARIMATHEA

THE GLASTONBURY CHAPEL

In the 1601 *Annales Ecclesiasticae*, the Vatican librarian, Cardinal Baronius, recorded that Joseph of Arimathea first came to Marseilles in 35 C.E. From there, he and his company crossed to Britain to preach the Gospel. This was confirmed much earlier by the chronicler Gildas III (516-570), whose *De Excidio Britanniae* stated that the precepts of Christianity were carried to Britain in the last days of Emperor Tiberius Caesar, who died in 37 C.E. Even before Gildas, such eminent churchmen as Eusebius, Bishop of Caesaria (260-340),[1] and St. Hilary of Poitiers (300-367) wrote of early apostolic visits to Britain. The years 35-37 C.E. are thus among the earliest recorded dates for Christian evangelism. They correspond to a period shortly after the Crucifixion—prior to the time when Peter and Paul were in Rome and earlier than the New Testament Gospels.

An important character in first-century Gaul was St. Philip.[2] He was described by Gildas and William of Malmesbury as being the inspiration behind Joseph's assignment in England. The *De Sancto Joseph ab Arimathea* states, 'Fifteen years after the Assumption [that is to say in 63 C.E.], he [Joseph] came to Philip the Apostle among the Gauls'. Freculphus, a ninth-century Bishop of Lisieux, wrote that St. Philip then sent the mission from Gaul to England, 'to bring thither the good news of the world of life and to preach the incarnation of Jesus Christ'.

Joseph of Arimathea in Britain
by William Blake, 1794

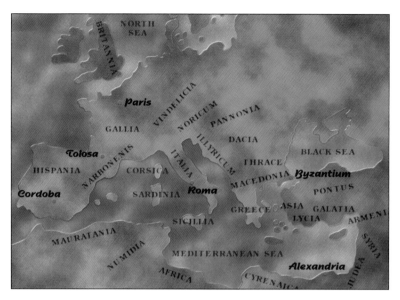

The Roman Empire

Upon their arrival in the West of England, Joseph and his twelve missionaries were viewed with some skepticism by the native Britons, but were greeted with some cordiality by King Arviragus of Siluria, brother of Caractacus the Pendragon. In consultation with other chiefs, Arviragus granted Joseph twelve hides of Glastonbury land. A hide is an area of land reckoned agriculturally to support one family for one year with one plough—equal in Somerset (the

**England's Domesday
Book of 1086**

Glastonbury shire) to 120 acres (c.48.5 hectares). Here they built their unique little church in a scale of the ancient Hebrew Tabernacle.[3] These grants remained holdings of free land for many centuries thereafter, as confirmed in the *Domesday Book* of 1086: 'The Church of Glastonbury has its own ville twelve hides of land which have never paid tax'. In Joseph's era, Christian chapels were hidden underground in the catacombs of Rome but, once the wattle chapel of St. Mary was built at Glastonbury, Britain could boast the first above-ground Christian church in the world.[4]

A monastery was subsequently added to the chapel and the Saxons rebuilt the complex in the eighth century. Following a disastrous fire in 1184, Henry II of England granted the community a Charter of Renovation in which Glastonbury was referred to as 'the mother and burying place of the saints, founded by the disciples of our Lord themselves'.[5] A stone Lady Chapel was constructed at that time. Later, the complex grew to become a vast Benedictine abbey, second in size and importance only to Westminster Abbey in London. Prestigious figures associated with Glastonbury included St. Patrick (the first Abbot in the fifth century) and St. Dunstan (Abbot from 940 to 946).

In addition to the accounts of Joseph of Arimathea at Glastonbury, others tell of his association with Gaul and the Mediterranean tin trade. John of Glastonbury (fourteenth-century compiler of *Glastoniensis Chronica*) and John Capgrave (Principal of the Augustinian Friars in England 1393-1464) both quoted from a book found by the Emperor Theodosius (375-395 C.E.) in the Jerusalem Pretorium. Capgrave's *De Sancto Joseph ab Arimathea* tells how Joseph was imprisoned by the Jewish elders after the Crucifixion. This is also described in the apocryphal *Acts of Pilate*. The historian, Bishop Gregory of Tours (544-595), similarly mentions the post-Crucifixion imprisonment of Joseph in his *History of the Franks* and, in the twelfth century, it was recounted yet again in *Joseph d'Arimathie* by the Burgundian Grail chronicler Sire Robert de Boron.

The *Magna Glastoniensis Tabula* and other manuscripts go on to say that Joseph subsequently escaped and was pardoned. Some years later he was in Gaul with his nephew, Joseph, who was baptized by Philip the Apostle. Young Joseph (Jesus and Mary's second son) is traditionally referred to as Josephes—the name that we shall continue to use in this book in order to distinguish him from his uncle, Joseph of Arimathea.

A good many valuable writings and relics were destroyed in the Glastonbury fire of 1184 and more were lost in the ravages of the Tudor dissolution of the monasteries. In the course of this latter destruction, Abbot Richard Whiting of Glastonbury was murdered (1539) by the henchmen of King Henry VIII. Fortunately, copies of some important manuscripts were salvaged—one of which (attributed to Gildas III) refers to Joseph of Arimathea as a '*noble decurio*'. The ninth-century Archbishop Raban Maar likewise described him as a '*noblis decurion*'. A Decurio was an overseer

The Grail Mass of Josephes
From the Cistercian Queste del Saint Graal, c.1351

of mining estates and the term originated in Spain, where Jewish metalworkers had been operative in the celebrated foundries of Toledo since the sixth century B.C.E..[6] It is not unlikely that Joseph's mining interest was the main reason for the generous land grant by King Arviragus.[7] Joseph was, after all, a well-known metal merchant and artificer in metals—a Master Craftsman, as was his father.

The *De Sancto Joseph* states that Joseph of Arimathea's wattle church of St. Mary was dedicated 'in the thirty-first year after our Lord's Passion' (that is, 64 C.E.). This conforms with 63 C.E. as its date of commencement, as given by William of Malmesbury. But, with regard to the fact that the dedication was to St. Mary (often presumed to be Jesus's mother), it has long been a point of debate that a church should have been consecrated to her some fifteen years after her Assumption and centuries before there was anything approaching a Virgin Mother cult. As confirmed in the twelfth- and thirteenth-century *Chronicles* of Matthew Paris, however, 63 C.E. was the very year in which the other Mary—Mary Magdalene—died at St. Baume.

Among the visits Joseph made to Britain, two were of great importance to the Church and were later cited by a number of clerics and religious correspondents. The first (as described by Cardinal Baronius) followed Joseph's initial seizure by the Sanhedrin after the Crucifixion. This visit in 35 C.E. ties in precisely with an account of St. James the Just in Europe—which is hardly surprising since Joseph of Arimathea and St. James were one and the same. The Rev. Lionel S. Lewis (Vicar of Glastonbury in the 1920s) also confirmed from his annals that St. James was at Glastonbury in 35 C.E. The second of Joseph's visits followed the 62 C.E. stoning and excommuni-

cation (spiritual death) of James the Just in Jerusalem.[8] Cressy, a Benedictine monk who lived shortly after the Reformation, wrote,

> In the one-and-fortieth year of Christ (that is, 35 C.E.), St. James, returning out of Spain, visited Gaul, Brittany and the towns of the Venetians, where he preached the Gospel, and so came back to Jerusalem to consult the Blessed Virgin and St. Peter about matters of great weight and importance.

The 'weighty matters' referred to by Cressy concerned the necessity for a decision on whether to receive uncircumcised Gentiles into the Nazarene Church. As Jerusalem's first bishop, Jesus's brother James presided at the Council meeting which handled the debate.

A number of old traditions relate to St. James in Sardinia and Spain, but they are often attributed to the wrong St. James. This is mainly because the Apostle James Boanerges (sometimes called St. James the Greater, as distinguished from James of Alphaeus—the Lesser) disappears from the New Testament for an unwarranted period.

Misunderstandings, caused by the apparent anomalies and duplicated entries concerning Joseph of Arimathea and St. James the Just, provoked some argument between the bishops at the Council of Basle in 1434. As a result, individual countries decided to follow their different traditions. It is St. Joseph who is most remembered in connection with Church history in Britain, whereas it is as St. James that he is revered in Spain. Even so, the English authorities compromised when linking him with the monarchy and the Royal Court in London became the Palace of St. James.

St. James's Palace, London

LORDSHIP OF THE GRAIL

The 'Joseph' distinction (Hebrew: *Yosef*, meaning 'he shall add') was conferred upon the eldest son of each generation in the Davidic succession. When a dynastic son of the House of Judah (by whatever personal name) succeeded to become the 'David', his eldest son (the Crown Prince) became the 'Joseph'. If there was no son at the time of a Davidic accession (or if the son was under sixteen years old), then the eldest brother of the David would temporarily hold the Joseph distinction. It would be relinquished to the senior line if and when a son was of age. Added to this was the *ha Rama-Theo* (Arimathea) style of the Divine Highness—equivalent to today's princely title of Royal Highness.

The bishops' debate followed an earlier dispute at the Council of Pisa in 1409 on the subject of the seniority, by age, of national Churches in Europe. The main contenders were England, France and Spain. The case was ruled in favor of England because the church at Glastonbury was founded by Joseph/James '*statim post passionem Christi*' (shortly after the Passion of Jesus). Henceforth, the monarch of France was entitled His Most Christian Majesty, while in Spain the appellation was His Most Catholic Majesty. The bitterly contested title of His Most Sacred Majesty was, however, reserved for the King of England.[9] Records of the debate—*Disputatio super Dignitatem Angliae et Galliae in Concilio Constantiano*—state that England won her case because the saint was not only granted land in the West Country by Arviragus, but was actually buried at Glastonbury. The possibility that the other Saint James (Boanerges, or James the Greater) might have visited Spain at some stage was not relevant to the debate.

St. Anne and the birth of Mary
by Albrecht Altdorfer, 1480-1538

The New Testament gives no real clue as to what Joseph of Arimathea had to do with Jesus's family; neither do the Gospels mention Joseph's age. Outside the scriptures, however, he is often presumed to have been Jesus's mother's uncle. Paintings and picture books, consequently, portray him as already rather elderly in the 30s C.E. That apart, a number of written accounts from a variety of sources record him as coming to Glastonbury thirty years later in 63 C.E.. Furthermore, Cressy's *Church History* (which incorporates the records of Glastonbury Monastery) asserts that Joseph of Arimathea died on July 27, 82 C.E.

If Jesus's mother, Mary, was born in about 26 B.C.E., as is generally reckoned, she would have been aged nineteen (or thereabouts) when Jesus was born. By the time of the Crucifixion she would have been in her middle fifties. If Joseph had been her uncle, he would have been, say, twenty years older than Mary—putting him somewhere in his middle seventies at that point in time. But then, thirty years afterwards (apparently at over 100 years of age) he is reputed to have begun a whole new life as an evangelist and decurio in the West! If that were not enough, the records then claim that he died twenty years later.

Clearly, none of this makes any sense and the hereditary aspect of the 'Joseph of Arimathea' distinction has to be applied. Hence, as established, the Joseph of the Crucifixion era was James the Just, born in 1 C.E. He died in 82 C.E., having been formally excommunicated in Jerusalem twenty years earlier.

It is also apparent that Jesus's mother's background and family are not accounted for in the Bible. This is not surprising since the Church interpretation of Mary's heritage is that she was a product of Immaculate Conception. The main sources concerning Mary are not the canonical Gospels but the apocryphal scriptures, *The Gospel of Mary*

and the *Protevangelion*. Many of the great artistic depictions of Mary's life and family are based on these, like Albrecht Dürer's famous *The Meeting of Anna and Joachim* (Mary's parents). The most comprehensive work on the subject is customarily accepted to be *La Leggenda di Sant' Anna Madre della Gloriosa Vergine Maria, e di San Gioacchino* (The Story of Saint Anna, Mother of the Blessed Virgin Mary, and of Saint Joachim). This work links her parents with the Royal House of Israel, but it does not mention Joseph of Arimathea as her uncle.

It was actually by way of a ninth-century Byzantine concept that the Church first promoted Joseph as Mary's uncle. There is no mention of him in that role beforehand. The concept arose at a time when the cautiously fearful Church councils were debating the approved content of the New Testament. So long as Joseph of Arimathea could be contained as a sideline character in the Davidic structure and, so long as he was not associated with the key Messianic line, his royal descendants could not embarrass the self-styled Apostolic structure of the Roman bishops.

By this strategy, the existence of Jesus and Mary's son, Josephes, was also conveniently disguised in the West. He was generally portrayed as Joseph of Arimathea's son, or sometimes as his nephew (which of course he was). In either role he was no threat to the orthodox scheme of things and, indeed, both definitions of his relationship (son and nephew) had genuine foundation, for he was the heir to the *ha Rama-Theo* distinction.

When Jesus became the 'David', his brother James became the 'Joseph'. This only changed when Jesus the younger was of an age to inherit the title. After the death of Jesus the Christ, his eldest son, Jesus the Justus, became the David. His younger son, Josephes (the new David's brother), then became the Joseph—the designated Crown Prince *ha Rama-Theo*. But until that time, while his brother Jesus Justus (called Gais or Gésu in Grail lore) was abroad in Rome and Jerusalem, Josephes' foster father and legal guardian was his uncle James, the prevailing Joseph of Arimathea.

Later, the firstborn son of Jesus Justus was Galains (called Alain in the Grail tradition).[10] In accordance with the custom of dynastic wedlock, Jesus Justus had first married in September 73 C.E.; his wife was a granddaughter of Nicodemus. The legacy of Davidic kingship (which was to become represented as Lordship of the Grail) was promised to Galains and was, in time, formally passed to him by his uncle and guardian, Josephes. But Galains became a committed celibate and died without issue. Hence, the Grail heritage reverted to Josephes' junior line—to be inherited by his son Josue,[11] from whom the Fisher Kings of Gaul descended.

As previously mentioned, Joseph of Arimathea had been to Britain with Mary's elder son, the twelve year-old Jesus Justus, in 49 C.E. This event is well remembered in West Country tradition and is evidenced in William Blake's famous song *Jerusalem*. The stories tell of how young Jesus walked upon the Exmoor coast and went to the Mendip village of Priddy. Because those royal feet did indeed 'walk upon England's mountains green' (albeit the son's feet rather than the father's), a stone in memory of his parents, Jesus and Mary Magdalene, was eventually set into the south wall of St. Mary's Chapel, Glastonbury. This stone, which remains on the site of the original first-century wattle chapel, is inscribed 'Jesus Maria' and, in due course, as one of the most venerated relics of the Abbey, it became a prayer station for pilgrims in the Middle Ages. The original

Nazarite bishop Josephes passes the Grail to his successor Alain.

13th-century French manuscript illustration

chapel was begun in 63 C.E. (immediately after Mary Magdalene's death) and the old annals[12] state that Jesus personally consecrated the chapel in honor of his mother. It was, therefore, to the Magdalene (not to Jesus the Christ's mother Mary) that the Glastonbury chapel was dedicated by her eldest son, Jesus Justus, in 64 C.E.

APOSTOLIC MISSIONS TO THE WEST

A most supportive colleague of Mary Magdalene in Provence was her friend Simon Zelotes who, no longer the active Father (the Abraham), assumed the style given to him by Jesus at his raising—that of Abraham's steward Eliezer, or Lazarus. Under this name he became the first Bishop of Marseilles and his statue is at St. Victor's church. A doorway from the nave of the church leads to a subterranean chapel (located on the site of Lazarus's residence) that was fiercely guarded by the monks in the early days. It was Lazarus—also known as the 'Great One' (Maximus)—who buried Mary Magdalene in her original alabaster sepulchre at St. Maximin in 63 C.E. Prior to this, he had been in Jerusalem and Antioch for a time and, after Mary's death, he went again to Jerusalem and Jordan before returning to join Joseph of Arimathea.

In Britain, Lazarus remained better known by his Apostolic name, Simon Zelotes. Nicephorus (758-829), Patriarch of Constantinople and Byzantine historian, wrote that

> St. Simon, surnamed Zelotes ... travelled through Egypt and Africa, then through Mauritania and all Libya, preaching the Gospel. And the same doctrine he taught to the peoples of the Occidental Sea and the islands called Britannia.

Nearly five centuries earlier, Bishop Dorotheus of Tyre wrote in his *Synopsis de Apostole* in 303 C.E. that 'Simon Zelotes preached Christ through all Mauritania, and Afric the less. At length he was crucified in Britannia, slain, and buried'. The 1601 *Annales Ecclesiasticae* of Cardinal Baronius confirm Simon's martyrdom in Britain. He was crucified by the Romans under Catus Decianus at Caistor, Lincolnshire. At the saint's own request, however, his mortal remains were later placed with those of the Magdalene in Provence.

Also associated with Joseph of Arimathea in Britain was Herod-Agrippa's uncle Aristobulus, who had been Mary Magdalene's particular ally when she was afforded protection by the Herodian establishment at Vienne, outside Lyon.[13]

An Archdruid in Dark Age Britain.
From R. Havel & Son, Engravers of London, 1815

The writings of the Roman churchman, Hippolytus (born about 160 C.E.), list Aristobulus as a Bishop of the Britons. Cressy maintains that he was a bishop in Britain ordained by St. Paul himself. The Greek Church *Martyrology* claims that Aristobulus was martyred in Britain 'after he had built churches and ordained deacons and priests for the island'. This is further confirmed by St. Ado (800-874), Archbishop of Vienne, in the *Adonis Martyrologia*. Earlier (303 C.E.), St. Dorotheus, Bishop of Tyre, wrote that Aristobulus was in Britain when St. Paul sent greetings to his household in Rome: 'Salute them which are of Aristobulus' household' (Romans 16:10). And the Jesuit *Regia Fides* additionally states, 'It is perfectly certain that before St. Paul reached Rome, Aristobulus was away in Britain'. He was, in fact, executed by the Romans at Verulamium (St. Albans)[14] in 59 C.E.

The Silurian Archdruid, Brân the Blessed, was married to Joseph of Arimathea's daughter Anna (Enygeus),[15] who is sometimes loosely referred to as 'a consabrina of the Blessed Mary' (that is Jesus the Christ's mother Mary). Because Joseph has sometimes been wrongly portrayed as Mary's uncle, the word 'consabrina' has often been taken to denote a cousin. In practice, however, the word was very obscure and denoted no more than a junior kinswoman. It was, therefore, the perfect word to use when a genealogical relationship was unspecific, or when it was deemed necessary for it to remain veiled.

In 51 C.E., Brân was taken hostage to Rome along with Caractacus the Pendragon. Resident in Rome, Gladys, the younger daughter of Caractacus, married the Roman senator Rufus Pudens[16] and thus became Claudia Rufina Britannica (as confirmed by the Roman poet,

Martial, in about 68 C.E.). Caractacus' other daughter was St. Eurgen of Llan Ilid (the wife of Salog, Lord of Salisbury). His famed son, Prince Linus, became the first appointed Bishop of Rome.[17] In his Second Epistle to Timothy 4:21 (New Testament), Paul writes: 'Eubulus greeteth thee, and Pudens and Linus, and Claudia, and all the brethren'. Eubulus (*eu-boulos*: 'well advised' or 'prudent') was a variation of Aristobulus (*aristo-boulos*: 'best advised' or 'noblest in counsel').

While in Britain, Joseph of Arimathea's enterprise was maintained by a close circle of twelve celibate anchorites (reclusive devotees). Whenever one died, he was replaced by another. In Grail lore these anchorites were referred to as 'the brethren of Alain (Galains)' who was one of their number. As such, they were symbolic sons of Brân the Patriarch (the 'Father' in the old order—as against the newly styled Bishop of Rome). This is why, in some literature, Alain is defined as the son of Brân (Bron). However, after Joseph's death in 82 C.E., the group disintegrated—mainly because Roman control had forever changed the character of England.

II

THE NEW CHRISTIANITY

GOOD KING LUCIUS

In the mid-second century, King Lucius, great-grandson of Arviragus, revived the spirit of the early disciples in Britain. In so doing, he was popularly held to have 'increased the light' of Joseph's first missionaries and, accordingly, became known as 'Lleiffer Mawr' (the Great

The Venerable Bede of Jarrow.
12th-century British manuscript illumination

Luminary). His daughter, Eurgen, forged the first link between the two key Davidic successions—that from Jesus and that from James (Joseph of Arimathea)—when she married Aminadab, the great-grandson of Jesus and Mary Magdalene in the line from Josephes, who had become the Nazarite Bishop of Saras (Gaza).

Lucius openly confirmed his Christianity at Winchester in 156 C.E. and his cause was heightened in 177 C.E. by a mass Roman persecution of Christians in Gaul. This was enforced especially in the old Herodian regions of Lyon and Vienne, where St. Irenaeus and 19,000 Christians were put to death thirty years later. During the persecution, a good many Gaulish Christians fled to Britain, especially to Glastonbury, where they sought the aid of Good King Lucius. He decided to approach Eleutherius, the Bishop of Rome, for advice (this was, of course, before the days of the formal Roman Church). Lucius wrote earnestly to Eleutherius, requesting instruction in Christian government.

The letter in reply, as contained in the *Sacrorum Conciliorum Collectio*, is still extant in Rome. Eleutherius suggested that a good king was always at liberty to reject the laws of Rome, but not the law of God. The following is an extract in translation:

> The Christian believers, like all the people of the kingdom, must be considered sons of the king. They are under your protection ... A king is known by his government, not by whether

104

Glastonbury in 1927

by A. Heaton Cooper, 1863-1929

he retains his power over the land. While you govern well, you will be a king. Unless you do this, the name of the king endures not, and you will lose the name of king.[1]

John Capgrave (1393-1464), the most learned of Augustinian friars, and Archbishop Ussher, in his *De Brittanicarum Ecclesiarum Primordiis*, both recounted that Lucius sent the missionaries Medway and Elfan to carry his request for advice to Rome. They eventually returned with the Bishop's emissaries Faganus and Duvanus (whom the Welsh annals name as Fagan and Dyfan) whose journey was confirmed by Gildas in the sixth century. The Venerable Bede of Jarrow (673-735) also wrote about the King's appeal, which is likewise mentioned in the *Anglo-Saxon Chronicle*.

Fagan and Dyfan reinstated the old order of anchorites at Glastonbury and have since been credited with the second foundation of Christianity in Britain. Following this, the fame of Lucius spread far and wide. He was already celebrated as the builder of the first Glastonbury

tower on St. Michael's Tor in 167 C.E. and now the church at Llandaff was dedicated to him as Lleurwgg the Great.[2]

Even more impressively, Lucius was responsible for founding the first Christian archbishopric in London. A Latin plaque above the vestry fireplace at St. Peter's, Cornhill, in the old City of London, reads:

In the year of our Lord 179, Lucius, the first Christian king of this island now called Britain, founded the first church in London, well known as the Church of St. Peter in Cornhill; and founded there the archiepiscopal seat, and made it the metropolitan church and the primary church of his kingdom. So it remained for the space of four hundred years until the coming of St. Augustine ... Then, indeed, the seat and pallium of the archbishopric was translated from the said church of St. Peter in Cornhill to Dorobernia, which is now called Canterbury.

The advice given by Bishop Eleutherius in response to Good King Lucius' plea is fascinating, for it is fully in keeping with the underlying principle of service that permeates the Messianic Grail Code. Kings of the Grail dynasties in Britain and France always operated on this basis: they were 'common fathers' to the people, never rulers of the lands. (The latter was a particularly feudal and Imperial concept that completely undermined the Code.) They understood, for example, the important difference in being 'Kings of the Franks' as against being Kings of France, or in being 'Kings of Scots' as against being Kings of Scotland. By virtue of this, the Grail monarchs were able to champion their nations rather than champion the clerics and politicians.

From the moment that a national monarchy becomes regulated by Acts of Parliament and Church decree, the titles of 'King' or 'Queen' are worthless. Under such circumstances there is no one left with authority enough to equal that of Church or Parliament and, therefore, no one to act solely on the people's behalf. Grail Kings were defined as Guardians of the Realm and, in this regard, Bishop Eleutherius' advice to Lucius was both profound and enlightened: 'All the people of the kingdom must be considered sons of the king. They are under your protection'.

RISE OF THE ROMAN CHURCH

In 66 C.E., the Hasmonaean scion, Flavius Josephus, had been appointed Commander in the defense of Galilee. He had previously trained for the Pharisee priesthood, but accepted military service when the Jews rose up against their Roman overlords. Josephus subsequently became the foremost historian of the era and his writings, *The Wars of the Jews* and *The Antiquities of the Jews*, provide a comprehensive insight into the long and complex history of the nation from the

Merovingian Gaul

time of the early patriarchs to the years of Roman oppression. In the context of his work it is interesting to note his one and only reference to Jesus.[3] It locates Jesus firmly within the historical fabric of the time, but without any reference to his divinity or to any scriptural motive:

Now it was at around this time that Jesus emerged–a wise man, if he may be called a man, for he was a worker of marvels. A teacher of such men as receive the truth with pleasure, he drew to him many of the Jews in addition to many of the Gentiles. He was the Christ, and when Pilate (at the suggestion of the principal men among us) had him condemned to be crucified, those that had loved him from the first did not forsake him, for he appeared to them alive again on the third day–just as the godly prophets had foretold about him, and ten thousand other wonderful things about him besides. And the sect of Christians, named after him, are still very much in existence even today.

Josephus' scholarly opus, comprising some 60,000 manuscript lines, was written during the 80s C.E. when he was in Rome, from where the Gospel of Mark had emerged a short while before. Although Peter and Paul were executed under Nero's regime, the Gospel writings of the era were not, on the face of it, anti-Roman. Indeed, the early Christians were more inclined to blame the Jews (rather than Pilate) for the persecution of Jesus and, because the Jewish uprising of 66-70 C.E. had failed, they firmly believed that God had switched allegiance from the Jews to themselves.

Notwithstanding this, the position of Christians within the expanding Roman Empire was hazardous; they were very much a minority group with no legal status. From Nero's crucifixion of Peter to the Edict of Milan in 313 C.E. (when Christianity was officially recognized), there were no fewer than thirty appointed Christian Bishops of Rome. The first Bishop, installed during Peter's lifetime by Paul in 58 C.E.,[4] was Britain's Prince Linus, the son of King Caractacus. (Linus is sometimes portrayed as if he had been a slave—but this was later Church propaganda and we shall return to it because it is of particular importance.)

By about 120 C.E., individual appointments had become the prerogative of group election and candidates had to be citizens of Rome. By the time of Bishop Hyginus (from 136 C.E.), there was little or no connection between the Pauline Christians and the Nazarene followers of Jesus's own Judaic doctrine. The latter had settled mainly in Mesopotamia, Syria, southern Turkey and Egypt—apart from the established movements in Britain and Gaul. In the meantime, the Christians of Rome had been constantly suppressed because their beliefs were thought to challenge the traditional divinity of the Caesars (Emperors). As time passed, the suppression became even more severe, until it once more reached the proportions of Nero's reign and became outright persecution.

The prevailing religion of Imperial Rome was polytheistic (observing many gods) and had emanated largely from the worship of natural deities such as those of the woods and waters. As Rome grew to statehood, the gods of her Etruscan and Sabine neighbors had been incorporated.

The Revels of Bacchus, god of wine.
Engraving by Bernard Picart, 1673-1733

EARLY EMPERORS AND BISHOPS OF ROME
44 BC - AD 337

Roman Emperors	Year	Bishops	Year
Augustus	44 BC - AD 14		
Tiberius	AD 14-37		
Gaius Caligula	37-41		
Claudius	41-54		
Nero	54-68		
Galba	68-69	Linus	58-78
Otho (joint)	69		
+ Vitellius	69		
Vespasian	69-79		
		Anacletus	78-89
Titus	79-81		
Domitian	81-96		
		Clement I	89-98
Nerva	96-98		
		Evaristus	99-106
Trajan	98-117	Alexander	107-115
		Sixtus I	116-125
Hadrian	117-138	Telesphorus	125-136
		Hyginus	136-140
Antoninus Pius	138-161	Pius I	140-154
		Anicetus	155-165
Marcus Aurelius	161-180	Soter	165-174
Commodus	180-192	Eleutherius	174-189
		Victor I	189-198
Pertinax (joint)	193		
+ Didius Julianus	193		
Lucius Severus	193-211	Zephyrinus	199-217
Caracalla	211-217		
Macrinus	217	Callixtus I	217-222
Heliogabalus	218-222		
Alexander Severus	222-235	Urban I	222-230
		Pontianus	230-235
Maximinus	235-238	Anterus	235-236
		Fabian	236-250

Gordian I (joint) + Gordian II	238		
Pupienus (joint) + Balbinus	238		
Gordian III	238-244		
Philip (the Arabian	244-249		
Decius	249-251		
Gallus	251-253	Cornelius	251-253
Aemilian	253		
Valerian (joint) + Gallienus	253-260 253-268	Lucius Stephen I Sixtus II Dionysius	253-254 254-257 257-258 259-268
Claudius	268-270	Felix I	269-274
Aurelian	270-275		
Tacitus	275		
Probus	276-282	Eutychianus	275-283
Carus	282-283		
Carinus (joint) + Numerianus	284 284	Gaius	283-296
Diocletian (joint) + Maximianus	284-305 286-305	Marcellinus	296-304
Constantius Chlorus	305-306		
Maxentius	306-312	Marcellus I	308-309
		Eusebius	309
		Miltiades	310-314
Constantine the Great (Britain and Gaul) (West)	306- 312-	Silvester I	314-335
(Overall)	324-337		

These included Jupiter (the sky god) and Mars (the god of war). Grecian cults were also embraced and, from 204 B.C.E., the orgies of Cybele (the Asiatic earth goddess) were evident, soon emulated by the hedonistic rituals of Dionysus/Bacchus (the god of wine). As the Roman Empire spread eastwards, so the esoteric cult of Isis, the Universal Mother, was introduced, along with the Persian veneration of Mithras (god of light, truth and justice). Eventually, the Syrian solar religion of *Sol Invictus* (the unconquered and unconquerable Sun) became the all-encompassing belief. Its vision of the sun as the ultimate giver of life enabled all other cults to be subsumed within it, with the Emperor as the earthly incarnation of the godhead.

By the middle of the second century, the original Nazarenes (the followers of Jesus and James's teachings) were unpopular not only with Rome, but were being severely harassed by the Pauline Christians—particularly by Irenaeus, Bishop of Lyon (born c.120 C.E.) He condemned them as heretics for claiming that Jesus was a man and not of divine origin as ruled by the new faith. In fact, he even declared that Jesus had himself been practising the wrong religion and that he was personally mistaken in his beliefs! Irenaeus wrote of the Nazarenes, whom he called *ebionites* (poor), that

> They, like Jesus himself, as well as the Essenes and Zadokites of two centuries before, expound upon the prophetic books of the Old Testament. They reject the Pauline epistles, and they reject the apostle Paul, calling him an apostate of the Law.

In retaliation, the Nazarenes of the Desposynic Church denounced Paul as a 'renegade' and a 'false apostle', claiming that his 'idolatrous writings' should be 'rejected altogether'.

In 135 C.E., Jerusalem was again crushed by Roman armies—this time under Emperor Hadrian—and the surviving Jews were scattered. Those who remained in Palestine were content (in their despair at such final military defeat) to concern themselves solely with rabbinical law and religion. Meanwhile, the Pauline sect (now quite divorced from its Judaic origins) was becoming ever more troublesome to the authorities.

Having reached the height of its glory in Hadrian's era (117-138 C.E.) Roman imperialism began to decline under Commodus. His ineffective rule (180-192 C.E.) prompted a good deal of disunity which led to many decades of civil war, pitting various generals against each other and against the central government. A conflict arose over who should wear the crown and opposing sections of the army began to elect their own sovereigns. Emperor Lucius Severus (193-211 C.E.) managed to restore some order by judicious use of the Praetorian Guard (the Emperor's personal bodyguard), but his discipline did not last for long. Throughout the third century, internal disputes left the borders of the Empire open to attack by Sassanians from Persia and Goths from the Black Sea regions.

In 235 C.E., the Emperor Maximinus decreed that all Christian bishops and priests should be seized, their personal wealth confiscated and their churches burned. The captives were sentenced to various forms of punishment and slavery, including penal servitude at the lead mines in Sardinia. On arrival, each captive would have one eye removed and the left foot and right knee damaged to restrict movement. The men were also castrated. If that were not enough, they were chained from their waists to their ankles so they could not stand upright and the fetters were permanently welded. Not surprisingly, the majority did not live for more than a few months. In those days, being a Christian was in itself dangerous, but to be a known leader was tantamount to signing a personal death warrant.

By the time of Emperor Decius (249 C.E.), the Christians had become so rebellious that they were proclaimed criminals and their mass persecution began on an official basis. This continued into the reign of Diocletian, who became Emperor in 284 C.E. He dispensed with any vestige of democratic procedure and instituted an absolute monarchy. Christians were required to offer sacrifices to the divine Emperor and they suffered the harshest punishments for disobedience. It was ruled that all Christian meetinghouses be demolished and disciples who convened alternative assemblies were put to death. All their property was confiscated by the magistrates, while all books, testaments and written doctrines of the faith were publicly burned. Christians of any prominent or worthy birthright were barred from public office and Christian slaves were denied any hope of freedom. The protection of Roman law was withdrawn and those who argued with the edicts were roasted alive over slow fires or eaten by animals in the public arena.

Diocletian attempted to counter the persistent aggressions of barbarian invaders by decentralizing control and establishing two separate divisions of the Empire. From 293 C.E., the West was managed from Gaul and the East was centered at Byzantium in (what is now) northwestern Turkey. But still the assaults continued, in particular new western invasions by the Germanic tribes of

Franks and Alamanni, who had previously been held across the Rhine. No longer were the Romans an invading power; they were now themselves the constant victims of insurgency from all sides.

One of the most ruthless of the persecutors under Diocletian was Galerius, governor of the eastern provinces. He ordered that anyone who did not worship the Emperor above all others would be painfully executed. Just before his death in 311 C.E., however, Galerius issued a surprising decree of relaxation, giving Christians the right to 'assemble in their conventicles without fear of molestation'. After some two and a half centuries of dread and suppression, the Christians entered a new age of conditional freedom.

From 312 C.E., Constantine became Emperor in the West—ruling jointly with Licinius in the East. By then, Christianity had increased its following considerably and was flourishing in England, Germany, France, Portugal, Greece, Turkey and all corners of the Roman domain. In fact, Christian evangelists were having more success in subduing the barbarians than were the legions of Rome— even in places as far afield as Persia and central Asia. It took little imagination for Constantine to realize that, while his Empire was falling apart at the seams, there could be some practical merit in his harnessing Christianity. He perceived in it a unifying force which could surely be used to his own strategic advantage.

Although Constantine had succeeded his father, he had a rival for the supreme Imperial rank in the person of his brother-in-law, Maxentius. In 312 C.E., their armies met at Milvian Bridge (a little outside Rome) and Constantine was victorious. This campaign was the prime moment of opportunity to establish his personal affiliation with Christianity and he announced that he had seen the vision of a cross in the sky, accompanied by the words 'In this sign conquer'. The Christian leaders were most impressed that a Roman Emperor had ridden to victory under their banner.

Constantine then summoned the ageing Bishop Miltiades. The Emperor's purpose was not to join the faith under the authority of the Bishop of Rome, but to take over the Christian Church in its entirety. Among his first instructions was that the nails from the Cross of Jesus be brought to him—one of which he would have affixed to his crown. His related pronouncement to the bewildered Miltiades was then destined to change the structure of Christianity for all time: 'In the future, We, as the Apostle of Christ, will help choose the Bishop of Rome'. Having declared himself an apostle, Constantine then proclaimed that the magnificent Lateran Palace was to be the Bishops' future residence.

When Miltiades died in 314 C.E., he was the first Bishop of Rome in a long succession to die in natural circumstances. Quite suddenly, Christianity had become respectable and was approved as an Imperial religion (in fact, as 'the' Imperial religion). Constantine subsequently became Caesar of all the Roman Empire in 324 C.E., thereafter to be known as Constantine the Great.

To replace Miltiades, Constantine (in breach of traditional practice) chose his own associate, Silvester, to be the first Imperial Bishop. He was crowned with great pomp and ceremony—a far cry from the shady backroom proceedings customary to previous Christian ritual. Gone were the days of fear and persecution, but the high price for this freedom was veneration of the Emperor—precisely what the Christian forebears had struggled so hard to avoid. The rank and file had no choice in the matter and the existing priests were quite simply instructed that their Church was now formally attached to the Empire. It was now the Church of Rome.

Silvester was too overwhelmed to perceive the trap into which he was leading the disciples of St. Peter. He saw only the route to salvation offered by Constantine. Although this monumental step gained Christians the right to move openly in society, their hierarchy was now to be encased in gold, ermine, jewels and all the trappings that the Christ himself had decried. Many followers of the faith were outraged, for their leaders had been seduced and corrupted by the very regime that had been the bane of their ancestors. They declared that the newfound status of acceptability was in no way a victory of conversion; it was an evil cloud of absolute defeat—a profanation of all the principles they had so long held sacred.

Up to that point, the Christian message had been gaining support in all quarters. Those spreading the Gospel knew that Constantine and his predecessors were sorely weakened in the face of the Church's evident gradual success. It was, after all, one of the reasons why Constantine's father had married Britain's Christian Princess Elaine (St. Helena). Silvester and his colleagues in Rome may have considered the new alliance to be a politically sound maneuver, but the emissaries in the field viewed it for precisely what it was: a strategic buyout by the enemy. They claimed that the spiritual message of St. Peter had been subverted by the idolatry of a self-seeking power striving to prevent its Imperial demise. In real terms, the very purpose of Christianity was nullified by the new regime. After nearly three centuries of strife and struggle, Jesus's own ideal had been forsaken altogether—handed over on a plate to be devoured by his adversaries.

Apart from various cultic beliefs, the Romans had worshipped the Emperors in their capacity as gods descended from others like Neptune and Jupiter. At the Council of Arles in 314 C.E.,[5] Constantine retained his own divine status by introducing the omnipotent God of the Christians as his personal sponsor. He then dealt with the anomalies of doctrine by replacing certain aspects of Christian ritual with the familiar pagan traditions of sun worship, together with other teachings of Syrian and Persian origin. In short, the new religion of the Roman Church was constructed as a hybrid to appease all influential factions. By this means, Constantine looked towards a common and unified world religion (Catholic meaning 'Universal') with himself at its head.

SAINT HELENA

Since the original 1996 publication of *Bloodline of the Holy Grail*, a number of readers have written to point out that the book's portrayal of St. Helena's British royal heritage differs from that generally taught by the Church. It certainly does and, in fact, hers is a good example of how personal histories have been manipulated to suit the strategic interests of the bishops. It is, therefore, worth looking at how the propagandist teaching came about in this regard.

Until the sixteenth-century Reformation, published information concerning the birthright of Empress Helena was always obtained from British records. In Britain, it was not until the eighteenth century that the historian, Edward Gibbon (1737-94), promoted the Roman fiction of Helena's birth when writing his *History of the Decline and Fall of the Roman Empire*, first published in 1776. This was followed by a vindication in 1779 after his spurious accounts of early Christian development were criticized. According to Gibbon (who had converted to Catholicism in 1753), Helena was born into an innkeeping family from the small town of Naissus in the Balkans. Later, he confirmed that this notion was a matter of conjecture but, notwithstanding this, his original claim has been slavishly followed by subsequent writers of histories and encyclopedias.

Pre-Gibbon records relate that Princess Elaine (Greco-Roman: Helen / Roman: Helena) was born and raised at Colchester and she became renowned for her expertise at political administration. Her husband, Constantius, was proclaimed

6th-century Byzantine ivory relief of an Archangel with the orb and staff of sovereignty

**11th-century Greek depiction of
Emperor Constantine and St. Helena**

Emperor at York (Caer Evroc). Prior to that, in 290 C.E., he had enlarged the York archbishopric at Helena's request and was subsequently buried at York. In recognition of Helena's pilgrimage to the Holy Land in 326 C.E. the church of Helen of the Cross was built at Colchester, where the city's coat of arms was established as her cross, with three silver crowns for its arms.

From the time of the Reformation, Rome undertook a structured program of disinformation about many aspects of Church history and this continued with increasing intensity. In practice, the revised Roman view about Helena is vague in the extreme, with the various accounts contradicting one another. Many put forward the Balkan theory, as repeated by Gibbon; some give Helena's birthplace as Nicomedia and others cite her as a Roman native.

Quite apart from the British records, the pre-Reformation information from Rome also upheld Helena's British heritage—as did other writings in Europe. These included the sixteenth-century *Epistola* of the German writer, Melancthon, who wrote: 'Helen was undoubtedly a British Princess'. The Jesuit records (even the Jesuit book *Pilgrim Walks in Rome*) state, when detailing Constantine's own birth in Britain: 'It is one of Catholic England's greatest glories to count St. Helena and Constantine among its children—St. Helena being the only daughter of King Coilus'.

The Roman document most commonly cited to uphold the anti-Britain message is a manuscript written in the late fourth century (after Helena's death) by Ammianus Marcellinus—from which the original information concerning Helena (c. 248-328 C.E.) has, very conveniently, gone missing. There is, however, a spuriously entered sixteenth-century margin note which gives the Church-approved details on which the Gibbonites and others base their opinion.

In all of this, the one person that the Church and its dutiful scholars have chosen to ignore is Rome's own Cardinal Baronius, the Vatican librarian who compiled the 1601 *Annales Ecclesiasticae*. In this work, he explicitly stated: 'The man must be mad who, in the face of universal antiquity, refuses to believe that Constantine and his mother were Britons, born in Britain'.

RELIGION AND THE BLOODLINE

DESPOSYNI AND THE EMPEROR

From the content of many books about early Christianity, it could easily be imagined that the Roman Church was the true Church of Jesus, whereas other Christ-related beliefs were heretical and ungodly. This is far from the truth; many branches of Christianity were actually far less pagan than the politically contrived Church of Rome. They despised the idols and opulent trappings of the Roman ideal and, for their pains, were accordingly outlawed by Imperial decree. In particular, the esoteric Gnostics were condemned as heathen for insisting that the 'spirit was good', but that 'matter was defiled'. This distinction certainly did not suit the highly materialistic attitudes of the new Church.

There were also those of the Nazarene tradition, who upheld the original cause of Jesus rather than the eccentric and embellished teachings of Paul that were so expediently misappropriated by Rome. These Judaic Christians of the traditional school controlled many of the principal churches of the Near East during the reign of Constantine. Moreover, they were led by none other than the bloodline descendants of Jesus's own family: the Desposyni ([Heirs] of the Lord).

In 318 C.E., a Desposyni delegation journeyed to Rome where, at the newly commissioned Lateran Palace, the men were given audience by Bishop Silvester. Through their chief spokesman Joses (a descendant of Jesus's brother Jude), the delegates argued that the Church should rightfully

be centered in Jerusalem, not in Rome. They claimed that the Bishop of Jerusalem should be a true hereditary Desposynos, while the bishops of other major centers—such as Alexandria, Antioch and Ephesus—should be related. Not surprisingly, their demands were in vain, for Silvester was hardly in a position to countermand the decrees of the Emperor. The teachings of Jesus had been superseded by a doctrine more amenable to Imperial requirement and, in no uncertain terms,

Truth Against the World (Y gwir erbyn y Byd)—the war cry of Queen Boudicca by Sir Peter Robson

The Madonna as the protector
of Constantinople.
10th-century Byzantine mosaic

Silvester informed the men that the power of salvation rested no longer in Jesus, but in Emperor Constantine!

Given that the Emperors had, for centuries, been revered as deities on Earth and that Constantine had officially claimed Apostolic descent, there was still one significant door left to close. After the visit of the Desposyni, he dealt with this very expediently at the Council of Nicaea in 325 C.E. The Pauline Christians had been expecting a Second Coming of their Messiah, sooner or later, and so Constantine had to demolish this expectation. The mission of Jesus to throw off Roman dominion had failed because of disunity among the sectarian Jews. Constantine took advantage of this failure by sowing the seed of an idea: perhaps Jesus was not the awaited Messiah as perceived. Furthermore, since it was the Emperor who had ensured the Christians' freedom within the Empire then surely their true Savior was not Jesus, but Constantine! After all, his mother, Helena, was of Arimatheac descent.

The Emperor knew, of course, that Jesus had been venerated by Paul as the Son of God, but there was no room for such a concept to persist. Jesus and God had to be merged into one entity so that the Son was identified with the Father. It thus transpired, at the Council of Nicaea, that God was formally defined as Three Persons in One: a deity comprising three coequal and coeternal parts—the Father, Son and Holy Spirit (or Holy Ghost). These aspects (persons) of the Trinity bore an uncanny resemblance to the three priestly designations, the *Father*, *Son* and *Spirit*, as used so long before by the Essenes at Qumrân.

There were, though, some bishops who opposed this new dogma. Many of the delegates were Christian theologians of the old school who averred that Jesus was the Son and, furthermore, that the Son had been created in the flesh by God, but he was not himself God. The leading spokesman for this faction was an aged Libyan priest of Alexandria named Arius. But when Arius rose to speak, Nicholas of Myra punched him in the face and that swiftly dealt with the opposition!

The Nicene Creed of the Trinity of God was established as the basis for the new, reformed, orthodox Christian belief. The followers of Arius (thereafter known as Arians) were banished. Some delegates, including Bishop Eusebius of Caesaria, were prepared to compromise, but this was not acceptable and they were compelled to relent fully in favor of the new Creed. And so it was that, with God designated as both the Father and the Son, Jesus was conveniently bypassed as a figure of any practical significance. The Emperor was now regarded as the Messianic godhead—not only from that moment, but as of right through an inheritance deemed reserved for him 'since the beginning of time'.

Within its revised structure, the Roman Church was presumed safe from the emergence of any alternative Christian champion. Indeed, once the historical Jesus had been strategically side-lined, the Christian religion was said to have been named after a man called Chrestus who, in 49 C.E., had been one of the early protagonists in Rome. There were now only two official objects of worship: the Holy Trinity of God and the Emperor himself—the newly designated Savior of the World. Anyone who disputed this was declared a heretic and Christians who attempted to retain loyalty to Jesus as the Messianic Christ were proclaimed by the Imperial Church to be heathens.

Meanwhile, it had been customary through the generations for the prevailing Bishop of Rome to nominate his own successor before he died, but

**A popular 19th-century portrayal
of the Holy Trinity.
(Unknown artist)**

this tradition was changed when Constantine proclaimed himself God's Apostle on Earth. It then became the Emperor's right to ratify appointments and the various candidates often came to blows, giving rise to a good deal of bloodshed in the streets. The theory of Apostolic Succession was retained, but the candidature was actually a farce because the Bishops of Rome were, thereafter, selected from the Emperors' own nominees.

In 330 C.E., Constantine declared Byzantium the capital of the Eastern (Byzantine) Empire, renaming it Constantinople. In the following year he convened a General Council in that city to ratify the decision of the earlier Council of Nicaea. On this occasion the doctrine of Arius (which had gained a significant following in the interim) was formally declared blasphemous. The Emperor's management of the Church was very much a part of his overall autocratic style; his rule was absolute and the Church was no more than a department of his Empire. Silvester might well have been the appointed Bishop of Rome, but his name barely featured in a sequence of events that was instigated by Constantine and forever changed the nature and purpose of Christianity.

Once this form of Roman Christianity had been established as the new Imperial religion, an even more totalitarian edict was to come at the behest of Emperor Theodosius the Great (379-395 C.E.). In 381 C.E., a second Ecumenical Council of Constantinople was convened with the purpose of ending the Arian dispute. Theodosius found it difficult to implement his sole divine right of Messianic appointment while the Arians still preached that the Son (Jesus) had been created by God and that the Holy Spirit passed from the Father to the Son. This concept had to be crushed and Jesus had to be permanently removed from the reckoning.

It was, therefore, decreed by the Church that the doctrine of the Trinity of God must be upheld by all: God was the Father, God was the Son and God was the Holy Spirit. There was to be no more argument!

DECLINE OF THE EMPIRE

Throughout this period, the Nazarene tradition was, however, upheld. From the days of the early Jewish revolts, the Nazarenes had retained their religion under the leadership of the Desposyni. They flourished in Mesopotamia, eastern Syria, southern Turkey and central Asia. Entirely divorced from the fabricated Christianity of the Roman Empire, their faith was closer to the original teachings of Jesus than any other and had an essentially Jewish base, rather than any idolatrous entanglement with sun worship or other mystery cults. In fact the Nazarenes were the purest of true Christians; their approach to the Trinity was a simple one: God was God and Jesus was a man—a hereditary human Messiah of the Davidic succession. They were absolutely emphatic about this and repudiated any notion that the Blessed Mary was a virgin.

St. Benedict welcomes the Gothic king Totila,
who sacked Rome in 546
by Giovanni, Il Sodoma, 1477-1549

At the same time, there were others who, although prepared to accept the doctrine of the Triune God, still retained a belief in the divinity of Jesus. Their view differed considerably from that of the Nazarenes, for they believed what Paul had said—that Jesus was the Son of God. This gave rise to yet another Creed, which emerged in about 390 C.E., to become known as the Apostles' Creed. It began, 'I believe in God the Father Almighty and in Jesus Christ, his only begotten Son, our Lord'. This frontline reintroduction of Jesus was hardly conducive to the Savior status of the Emperor but, within a few years, Rome was sacked by the Goths and the Western Empire fell into decline.

At that point, a new protagonist emerged in the dispute over the Trinity; he was Nestorius, Patriarch of Constantinople from 428 C.E.. In accord with the Nazarenes, Nestorius maintained that the argument over whether Jesus was God or the Son of God was totally irrelevant, for it was plain to all that Jesus was a man, born quite naturally of a father and mother. From this platform, Nestorius stood against his Catholic colleagues, who had brought Jesus back into the picture now that the Empire was failing. They referred to Mary as the *Theotokas* (Greek: 'bearer of God') or *Dei Genitrix* (Latin: 'conceiver of God'). As a result, the Nazarene-Nestorian precept that Mary was a woman like any other was condemned by the Council of Ephesus (431 C.E.) and she was venerated thereafter as a mediator (or intercessor) between God and the mortal world. As for Nestorius, he was declared a heretic and banished, but soon found himself among friends in Egypt and Turkey, establishing the Nestorian Church at Edessa in 489 C.E. It was here that Julius Africanus had previously recorded the Romans' purposeful destruction of the Desposynic papers of royal heritage, but had also confirmed the existence of continuing private accounts of lineage—describing the Davidic family sect as maintained by a 'strict dynastic succession'.

From the mid-fifth century, the Church of Rome continued in the West, while the Eastern Orthodox Church emerged from its centers at Constantinople, Alexandria, Antioch and Jerusalem. The unresolved debate over the Trinity had driven a wedge firmly between the factions and each claimed to represent the 'true faith'. The Church of Rome was reformed under the management of an appointed city administration: the Cardinals—a title derived from Latin *cardo* (pivot), thus 'key[man]', of whom there were twenty-eight appointees stationed at the Vatican.

While the Church of Rome was being restructured, the Western Empire collapsed—demolished by the Visigoths and Vandals. The last Emperor, Romulus Augustulus, was deposed by the German chieftain, Odoacer, who became King of Italy in 476 C.E. In the absence of an Emperor, the prevailing High Bishop, Leo I¹ gained the title of Pontifex Maximus (Chief pontiff or bridge-builder). In the East, however, the story was different and the Byzantine Empire was destined to flourish for another thousand years.

As the might of Rome crumbled, so too did Roman Christianity subside. The Emperors had themselves been identified with the Christian God, but the Emperors had failed. Their religious supremacy had been switched to the Chief Pontiff, but his was now a minority religion in a Christ-related environment of Gnostics, Arians, Nazarenes and the fast-growing Celtic Church.

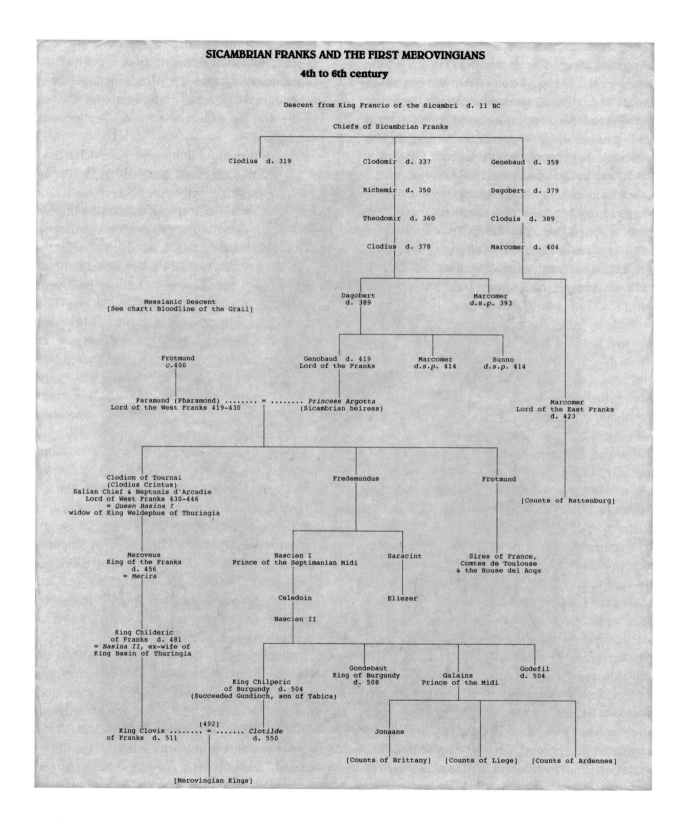

SICAMBRIAN FRANKS AND THE FIRST MEROVINGIANS

4th to 6th century

Descent from King Francio of the Sicambri d. 11 BC

Chiefs of Sicambrian Franks

Clodius d. 319

Clodomir d. 337

Genebaud d. 358

Richemir d. 350

Dagobert d. 379

Theodomir d. 360

Cloduis d. 389

Clodius d. 378

Marcomer d. 404

Dagobert d. 389

Marcomer d.s.p. 393

Messianic Descent
[See chart: Bloodline of the Grail]

Frotmund c.400

Genobaud d. 419
Lord of the Franks

Marcomer d.s.p. 414

Sunno d.s.p. 414

Faramund (Pharamond) .... = ... Princess Argotta
Lord of the West Franks 419-430   (Sicambrian heiress)

Marcomer
Lord of the East Franks
d. 423

Clodion of Tournai
(Clodius Crintus)
Salian Chief & Neptunis d'Arcadie
Lord of West Franks 430-446
= Queen Basina I
widow of King Weldephus of Thuringia

Fredemundus

Frotmund

[Counts of Rattenburg]

Meroveus
King of the Franks
d. 456
= Merira

Nascien I
Prince of the Septimanian Midi

Saracint

Sires of France,
Comtes de Toulouse
& the House del Acqs

Celedoin

Eliezer

Nascien II

King Childeric
of Franks d. 481
= Basina II, ex-wife of
King Basin of Thuringia

Gondebaut
King of Burgundy
d. 508

Galains
Prince of the Midi

Godefil
d. 504

King Chilperic
of Burgundy d. 504
(Succeeded Gundioch, son of Tabica)

(492)
King Clovis .... = ... Clotilde
of Franks d. 511   d. 550

Jonaans

[Counts of Brittany] [Counts of Liege] [Counts of Ardennes]

[Merovingian Kings]

THE MEROVINGIAN SORCERER KINGS

During the latter years of the declining Empire, the greatest of all threats to the Roman Church arose from a Desposynic royal strain in Gaul. They were the Merovingian dynasty—male line descendants of the Fisher Kings, with a Sicambrian female heritage. The Sicambrians took their name from Cambra, a tribal queen of about 380 B.C.E. They were originally from Scythia, north of the Black Sea, and were called the 'Newmage' (New Covenant).

The Bibliothèque Nationale, in Paris, contains a facsimile of the highly reputed *Fredegar's Chronicle*—an exhaustive seventh-century historical work of which the original took thirty-five years to compile. A special edition of Fredegar's manuscript was presented to the illustrious Nibelungen Court and was recognized by the State authorities as a comprehensive, official history. Fredegar (who died in 660) was a Burgundian scribe and his *Chronicle* covered the period from the earliest days of the Hebrew patriarchs to the era of the Merovingian kings. It cited numerous sources of information and cross-reference, including the writings of St. Jerome (translator of the Old Testament into Latin), Archbishop Isidore of Seville (author of the *Encyclopedia of Knowledge*) and Bishop Gregory of Tours (author of *The History of the Franks*).

Fredegar's *Prologue* asserts that his own researches were if anything even more painstaking than those of the writers he cited. Fredegar wrote,

I have judged it necessary to be more thorough in my determination to achieve accuracy ... and so I have included ... (as if source material for a future work) all the reigns of the kings and their chronology.

To achieve such accuracy, Fredegar, who was of high standing with Burgundian royalty, made use of his privileged access to a variety of Church records and State annals. He tells how the Sicambrian Franks—from whom France acquired its name—were themselves so called after their chief Francio, who died in 11 B.C.E.

In the fourth century, the Sicambrian Franks were in the Rhineland, to which they had moved from Pannonia (west of the Danube) in 388 C.E. under their chiefs, Genobaud, Marcomer and Sunno. Settling into the region of Germania, they established their seat at Cologne. Over the next century, their armies invaded Roman Gaul and overran the area that is now Belgium and northern France. It was at this stage that Genobaud's daughter, Argotta, married Fisher King Faramund (419-430 C.E.), who is often cited to have been the true founder of the French monarchy. Faramund was the grandson of Boaz-Anfortas (to whom we shall return) in the direct Messianic succession from Josue's son, Aminadab (Christine line), who married King Lucius' daughter, Eurgen (Arimatheac line).

Faramund, however, was not the only marital partner with a Messianic heritage. Argotta was herself descended from King Lucius' sister, Athildis, who married the Sicambrian chief Marcomer (eighth in descent from Francio) in about 130 C.E. Thus, the Merovingian succession which ensued from Faramund and Argotta was dually Desposynic.

Argotta's father, Genobaud, Lord of the Franks, was the last male of his line—and so Faramund and Argotta's son, Clodion, duly became the next Lord of the Franks in Gaul. In 488 C.E., Clodion's son, Meroveus, was proclaimed Guardian at Tournai and it was from him that the line became noted as the mystical dynasty of Merovingians, as they rose to prominence as Kings of the Franks. They reigned not by coronation or created

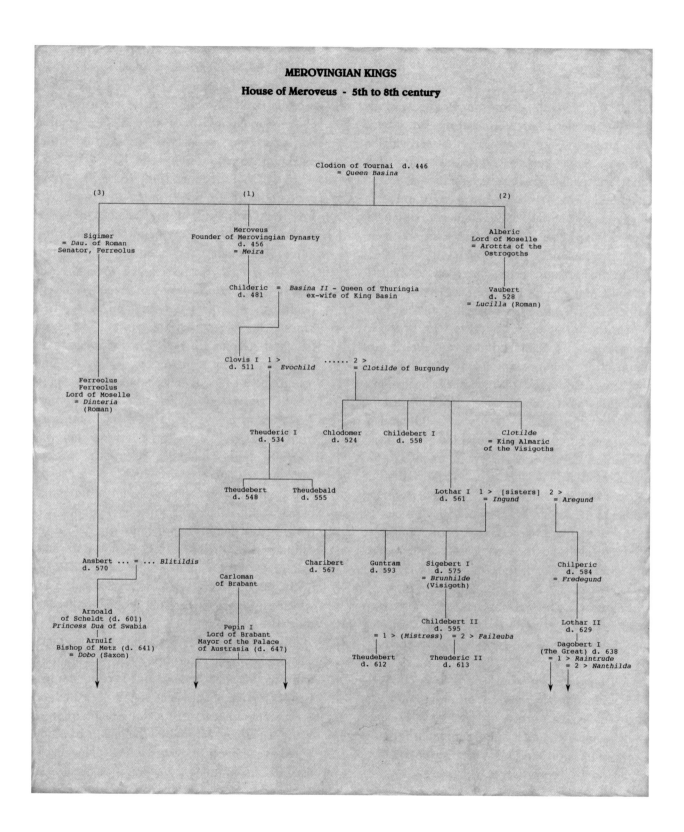

MEROVINGIAN KINGS

House of Meroveus - 5th to 8th century

Clodion of Tournai   d. 446
= *Queen Basina*

(3)

(1)

(2)

Sigimer
= *Dau.* of Roman
Senator, Ferreolus

Meroveus
Founder of Merovingian Dynasty
d. 456
= *Meira*

Alberic
Lord of Moselle
= *Arottta* of the
Ostrogoths

Childeric = *Basina II* - Queen of Thuringia
d. 481   ex-wife of King Basin

Vaubert
d. 528
= *Lucilla* (Roman)

Ferreolus
Ferreolus
Lord of Moselle
= *Dinteria*
(Roman)

Clovis I 1 >   ...... 2 >
d. 511   = *Evochild*   = *Clotilde* of Burgundy

Theuderic I
d. 534

Chlodomer
d. 524

Childebert I
d. 558

Clotilde
= King Almaric
of the Visigoths

Theudebert
d. 548

Theudebald
d. 555

Lothar I 1 > [sisters] 2 >
d. 561   = *Ingund*   = *Aregund*

Ansbert ... = ... *Blitildis*
d. 570

Charibert
d. 567

Guntram
d. 593

Sigebert I
d. 575
= *Brunhilde*
(Visigoth)

Chilperic
d. 584
= *Fredegund*

Carloman
of Brabant

Arnoald
of Scheldt (d. 601)
Princess Dua of Swabia

Arnulf
Bishop of Metz (d. 641)
= *Dobo* (Saxon)

Pepin I
Lord of Brabant
Mayor of the Palace
of Austrasia (d. 647)

Childebert II
d. 595

= 1 > *(Mistress)*   = 2 > *Faileuba*

Theudebert
d. 612

Theuderic II
d. 613

Lothar II
d. 629

Dagobert I
(The Great) d. 638
= 1 > *Raintrude*
= 2 > *Nanthilda*

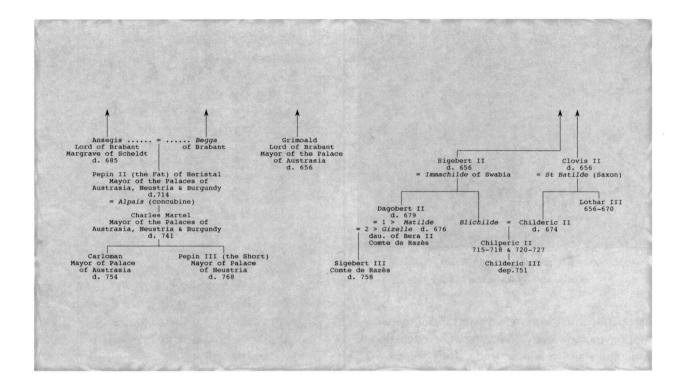

appointment, but by an accepted tradition that corresponded to the Messianic right of past generations.

Despite the carefully listed genealogies of his time, the heritage of Meroveus was strangely obscured in the monastic annals. Although the rightful son of Clodion he was, nonetheless, said by the historian Priscus to have been sired by an arcane sea creature, the *Bistea Neptunis*. There was evidently something very special about King Meroveus and his priestly successors, for they were accorded special veneration and were widely known for their esoteric knowledge and occult skills.[2] The sixth-century Gregory of Tours stated that the Frankish chiefs in the Sicambrian female line of their ancestry were not generally known for their ascetic culture, yet this learned dynasty (from what he called 'the foremost and most noble line of their race') emerged in the ancient Nazarite tradition to become known as the long-haired Sorcerer Kings.

Regardless of their ultimately Jewish heritage, the Merovingians were not practising Jews, but neither were other non-Roman Christians whose beliefs had sprung from Judaic origins. The Catholic bishop, Gregory of Tours, described them as 'followers of idolatrous practices', but the priestly Merovingians were not pagan in any sense of being unenlightened. In practice, their spiritual cult was not dissimilar to that of the Druids and they were greatly revered as esoteric teachers, judges, faith healers and clairvoyants. Although closely associated with the Burgundians, the Merovingians were not influenced by Arianism and their unique establishment was neither Gallo-Roman nor Teutonic. Indeed, it was said to be something entirely new and their culture seemed to appear from out of nowhere.

The Merovingian kings did not rule the land, nor were they politically active; governmental functions were performed by their Mayors of the Palace (Chief Ministers), while the kings were

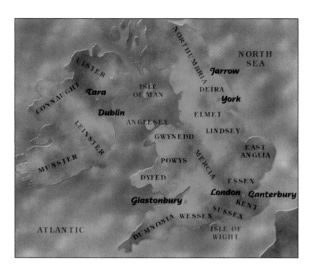

England, Ireland and Wales
(Celtic and Anglo-Saxon Lands)

more concerned with military and social matters. Among their primary interests were education, agriculture and maritime trade. They were avid students of proper kingly practice in the ancient tradition and their revered model was King Solomon,[3] the son of David. Their disciplines were largely based on Old Testament scripture but, notwithstanding this, the Roman Church proclaimed them irreligious.

When Meroveus's son Childeric died in 481 C.E., he was succeeded by his fifteen year-old son Clovis. During the next five years, he led his armies southward from the Ardennes, pushing out the Gallo-Romans so that, by 486 C.E., his realm included such centers as Reims and Troyes. The Romans managed to retain a kingdom at Soissons, but Clovis defeated their forces and the ruler, Syagrius, fled to the Visigoth court of King Alaric II. At this, Clovis threatened war against Alaric and the fugitive was handed over for execution. By his early twenties, with both the Romans and the Visigoths at his feet, Clovis was destined to become the most influential figure in the West.

At that time the Roman Church greatly feared the increasing popularity of Arianism in Gaul while Catholicism was dangerously close to being overrun in Western Europe, where the majority of active bishoprics were Arian. Clovis was neither Catholic nor Arian and it, therefore, occurred to the Roman hierarchy that the rise of Clovis could be used to their advantage. As it transpired, Clovis aided them quite inadvertently when he married the Burgundian Princess Clotilde.

Although the Burgundians were traditionally Arian in their beliefs, Clotilde was a Catholic and she made it her business to evangelize her version of the faith. For a time she had no success in promoting the doctrine to her husband, but her luck changed in 496 C.E. King Clovis and his army were then locked in battle against the invading Alamanni tribe near Cologne and, for once in his illustrious military career, the Merovingian was losing. In a moment of desperation he invoked the name of Jesus at much the same instant that the Alaman king was slain. On the loss of their leader, the Alamanni faltered and fell into retreat, whereupon Clotilde wasted no time in claiming that Jesus had caused the Merovingian victory. Clovis was not especially convinced of this, but his wife sent immediately for St. Remy, Bishop of Reims, and arranged for Clovis to be baptized.[4]

Word soon spread that the high potentate of the West had become a Catholic and this was of enormous value to Bishop Anastasius in Rome. A great wave of conversions followed and the Roman Church was saved from almost inevitable collapse. In fact, were it not for the baptism of King Clovis, the ultimate Christian religion of Western Europe might well now be Arian rather than Catholic. Nevertheless, the royal compliance was not a one-way bargain; in return for the king's agreement to be baptized, the Roman authorities pledged allegiance to him and his descendants.

Clovis, Merovingian King of the Franks,
invoking the name of Jesus
by William H. Rainey, 1852-1936

They promised that a new Holy Empire would be established under the Merovingians. Clovis had no reason to doubt the sincerity of the Roman alliance, but he unwittingly became the instrument of a bishops' conspiracy against the Messianic bloodline. With the blessing of the Church, Clovis was empowered to move his troops into Burgundy and Aquitaine. It was calculated that, by virtue of this, the Arians would be obliged to accept Catholicism, but the Romans also had a longer-term plan in mind—a plan to strategically maneuver the Merovingians out of the picture, leaving the Bishop of Rome supreme in Gaul.[5]

THE PENDRAGONS

ANFORTAS AND GALAHAD

The Sicambrian Franks, from whose female line the Merovingians emerged, were associated with Grecian Arcadia before migrating to the Rhineland. As we have seen, they called themselves the Newmage (People of the New Covenant), just as the Essenes of Qumrân had once been known.[1] This Arcadian legacy was responsible for the mysterious sea beast—the *Bistea Neptunis*—as symbolically defined in the Merovingian ancestry. The relevant sea lord was King Pallas, a god of old Arcadia, whose predecessor was the great Oceanus. In fact, the concept dated back as far as the ancient kings of Mesopotamia, who were said to be born of Tiâmat, the great mother of the primordial salt waters.

The immortal sea beast was said to be ever incarnate in a dynasty of ancient kings, whose symbol was a fish. This became an emblem of the Merovingian kings, along with the Lion of Judah and the *fleur-de-lys*, which was introduced in the late fifth century by King Clovis to denote the royal bloodline of France. Prior to this, the familiar Judaic trefoil had been emblematic of the covenant of circumcision. Both the rampant lion and the *fleur-de-lys* were later incorporated into the royal arms of Scotland.

In Arthurian lore, the Davidic sovereign lineage was represented by the Fisher Kings of the Grail Family and the patriarchal line was denoted by the name Anfortas, a symbolic style corrupted

The Legend of the Fleur-de-Lys.
15th-century French illumination for
the Bedford Book of Hours

from *In fortis* (Latin for 'In strength'). It was identified with the Hebrew name 'Boaz', the great-grandfather of David (similarly meaning 'In strength'), who is remembered in modern Freemasonry.

The name Boaz was given to the left-hand pillar of King Solomon's Temple (1 Kings 7:21 and 2 Chronicles 3:17). Its capitals, along with those of the right-hand pillar, Jachin, were decorated with brass pomegranates (1 Kings 7:41-42)—a symbol of male fertility, as identified in the *Song of Solomon* 4:13. It is not by chance that Botticelli's famous paintings, *The Madonna of the Pomegranate* and *The Madonna of the Magnificat*, both show the infant Jesus clutching a ripe, open pomegranate.[2] Indeed, from 1483 to 1510, Botticelli (more correctly, Sandro Filipepi) was the Nautonnier (Helmsman) of the Prieuré Notre Dame de Sion, an esoteric society with Grail connections. In the Grail tradition of Botticelli's time, the Arcadian sea lord, Pallas, was manifest in King Pelles: 'My name is Pelles, king of the foreign country and cousin nigh to Joseph of Arimathea'. It was his daughter, Elaine, who was the Grail Bearer of le Corbenic (*le Cors beneicon*: the Body blessed) and the mother of Galahad by Lancelot del Acqs.

Within the traditional Grail stories there is a consistency of names of Jewish, or apparently Jewish, extraction—names such as Josephes, Lot, Elinant, Galahad, Bron, Urien, Hebron, Pelles, Joseus, Jonas and Ban. In almost all of the legends, including Sir Thomas Malory's later fifteenth-century accounts, accentuated digressions constantly occur in relation to the Fisher Kings. In addition, there are many references to Joseph of Arimathea, King David and King Solomon. Even the priestly Judas Maccabaeus (who died in 161 B.C.E.) is

featured. Over the years, many have thought it strange that this well-born Hasmonaean hero of Judaea is treated with such high esteem in a seemingly Christian story:

> 'Sir Knight', said he to Messire Gawain, 'I pray you bide ... and conquer this shield, or otherwise I shall conquer you ... for it belonged to the best knight of his faith that was ever ... and the wisest.
> 'Who then was he?' said Messire Gawain.
> 'Judas Machabee was he ...'.
> 'You say true', saith Messire Gawain, 'and what is your name?'
> 'Sir, my name is Joseus, and I am of the lineage of Joseph of Abarimacie. King Pelles is my father, that is in the forest, and King Fisherman is my uncle'.[3]

It is known that some of the knights attributed to King Arthur were based upon real characters—particularly Lancelot, Bors and Lionel, who were connected to the del Acqs branch of the Grail Family. But what of the others? The indications are that many had factual origins, although not necessarily from the Arthurian era. When the majority of Grail romances were written in the Middle Ages, there was little love for the Jews in Europe. Dispersed from Palestine, many had settled in various parts of the West but, owning no land to cultivate, they turned to trade and banking. This was not welcomed by the Christians and so money-lending was prohibited by the Church of Rome. In the light of this, King Edward I had all Jews expelled from England in 1209, except for skilled physicians. In such an atmosphere, it is quite apparent that writers (whether in Britain or continental Europe) would not have found it natural or politically correct to use a string of

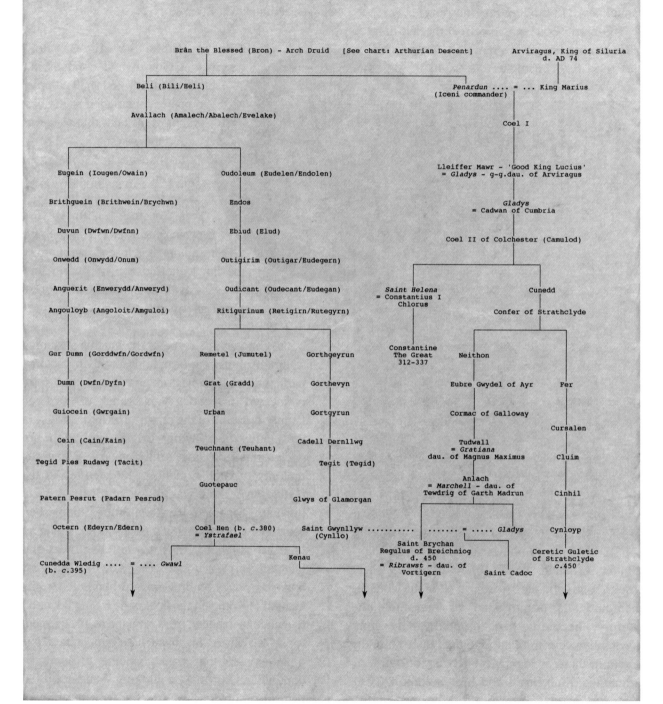

THE HOLY FAMILIES OF BRITAIN

Saints and the Sovereign Houses - 1st to 6th century

Brân the Blessed (Bron) - Arch Druid   [See chart: Arthurian Descent]   Arviragus, King of Siluria
d. AD 74

Beli (Bili/Heli)   Penardun .... = ... King Marius
(Iceni commander)

Avallach (Amalech/Abalech/Evelake)   Coel I

Eugein (Iougen/Owain)   Oudoleum (Eudelen/Endolen)   Lleiffer Mawr - 'Good King Lucius'
= Gladys - g-g.dau. of Arviragus

Brithguein (Brithwein/Brychwn)   Endos   Gladys
= Cadwan of Cumbria

Duvun (Dwfwn/Dwfnn)   Ebiud (Elud)   Coel II of Colchester (Camulod)

Onwedd (Onwydd/Onum)   Outigirim (Outigar/Eudegern)

Anguerit (Enwerydd/Anweryd)   Oudicant (Oudecant/Eudegan)   Saint Helena   Cunedd
= Constantius I
Chlorus

Angouloyb (Angoloit/Amguloi)   Ritigurinum (Retigirn/Rutegyrn)   Confer of Strathclyde

Gur Dumn (Gorddwfn/Gordwfn)   Remetel (Jumutel)   Gorthgeyrun   Constantine   Neithon
The Great
312-337

Dumn (Dwfn/Dyfn)   Grat (Gradd)   Gorthevyn   Eubre Gwydel of Ayr   Fer

Guiocein (Gwrgain)   Urban   Gortgyrun   Cormac of Galloway   Cursalen

Cein (Cain/Kain)   Cadell Dernllwg   Tudwall   Cluim
= Gratiana
dau. of Magnus Maximus

Tegid Pies Rudawg (Tacit)   Teuchnant (Teuhant)   Tegit (Tegid)   Anlach   Cinhil
= Marchell - dau. of
Tewdrig of Garth Madrun

Patern Pesrut (Padarn Pesrud)   Guotepauc   Glwys of Glamorgan   Cynloyp

Octern (Edeyrn/Edern)   Coel Hen (b. c.380)   Saint Gwynllyw .... = ... Gladys   Ceretic Guletic
= Ystrafael   (Cynllo)   of Strathclyde
c.450

Saint Brychan
Regulus of Breichniog
d. 450
= Ribrawst - dau. of
Vortigern

Cunedda Wledig .... = ... Gwawl   Kenau   Saint Cadoc
(b. c.395)

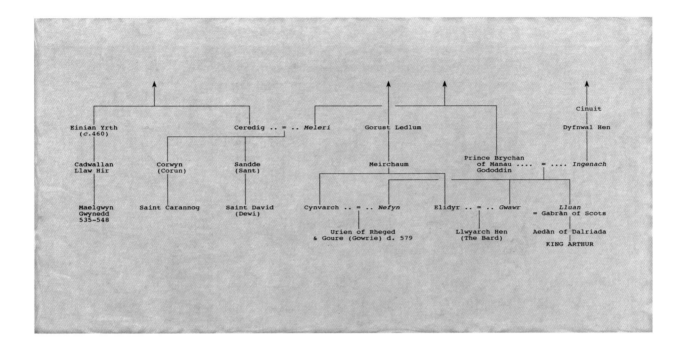

Jewish-sounding names for local heroes, knights and kings. Yet the names persist, from those of the early protagonists such as Josephes, to that of the later Galahad.

In the early Grail stories, Galahad was identified by the Hebrew name Gilead. The original Gilead was a son of Michael, the great-great-grandson of Nahor, brother of Abraham (1 Chronicles 5:14). Gilead means 'a heap of testimony'; the mountain called Gilead was the 'Mount of Witness' (Genesis 31:21-25) and Galeed was Jacob's cairn, the 'Heap of the Witness' (Genesis 31:46-48). In the footsteps of Bernard de Clairvaux, the Lincolnshire Abbot, Gilbert of Holland, equated the Arthurian Galahad directly with the family of Jesus in the Cistercian *Sermons on the Canticles*. Christian writers would not have exalted men of Jewish heritage to high positions in a chivalric environment unless their names were already known and well established. Evidently, therefore, the characters were based upon some historical foundation, even though their individual time frames were brought into common alignment for the romances.

CAMELOT

From around 700 B.C.E., Celtic tribes (*keltoi* meaning 'strangers') from Central Europe settled in Britain and, through the Iron Age, their culture developed to an advanced stage until they controlled all of lowland Britain. Over successive centuries, they were joined by further waves of European Celts. The last settlers were the Belgic tribes, who moved into the Southeast. The previous inhabitants spread northwards and westwards, establishing such places as Glastonbury in Somerset and Maiden Castle in Dorset. When the Romans arrived in the later B.C.E. year, the Celts were driven more generally westwards, despite their ongoing resistance under such formidable leaders as Caractacus and Boudicca (Victoria).

DESCENT TO THE HOUSES OF WALES AND BRITTANY

Arimatheac descent - 1st to 10th century

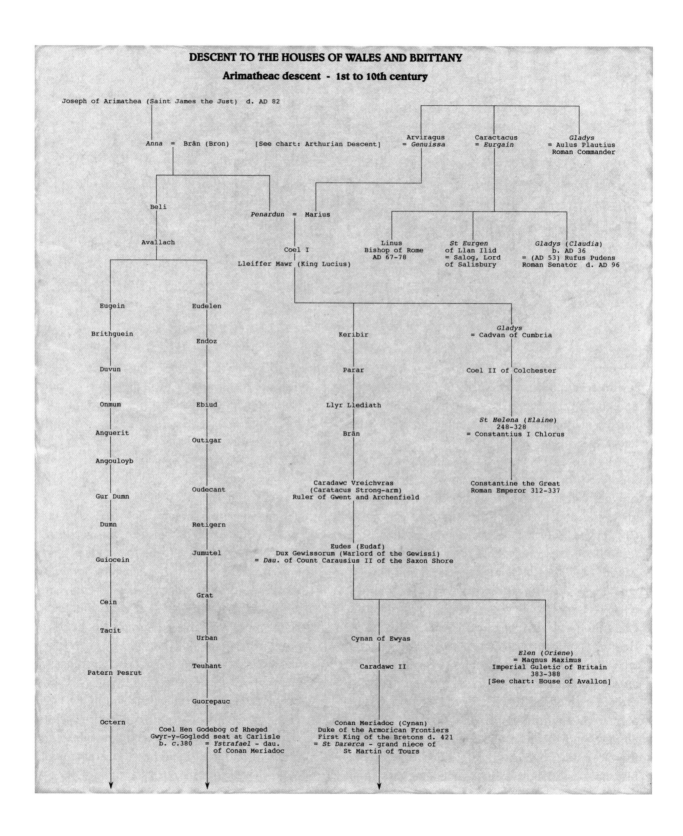

Joseph of Arimathea (Saint James the Just) d. AD 82

Anna = Brân (Bron)   [See chart: Arthurian Descent]   Arviragus = *Genuissa*   Caractacus = *Eurgain*   *Gladys* = Aulus Plautius Roman Commander

Beli

Penardun = Marius

Avallach

Coel I
Lleiffer Mawr (King Lucius)

Linus
Bishop of Rome
AD 67-78

St Eurgen
of Llan Ilid
= Salog, Lord
of Salisbury

Gladys (Claudia)
b. AD 36
= (AD 53) Rufus Pudens
Roman Senator d. AD 96

Eugein   Eudelen

Brithguein   Keribir   *Gladys*
= Cadvan of Cumbria
          Endoz

Duvun   Parar   Coel II of Colchester

Onmum   Ebiud   Llyr Llediath

Anguerit   Brân   *St Helena (Elaine)*
248-328
= Constantius I Chlorus
          Outigar

Angouloyb

Gur Dumn   Oudecant   Caradawc Vreichvras
(Caratacus Strong-arm)
Ruler of Gwent and Archenfield

Constantine the Great
Roman Emperor 312-337

Dumn   Retigern

Guiocein   Jumutel   Eudes (Eudaf)
Dux Gewissorum (Warlord of the Gewissi)
= *Dau.* of Count Carausius II of the Saxon Shore

Cein   Grat

Tacit

Urban   Cynan of Ewyas

Elen (Oriene)
= Magnus Maximus
Imperial Guletic of Britain
383-388
[See chart: House of Avallon]

Teuhant   Caradawc II

Patern Pesrut

Guorepauc

Octern   Coel Hen Godebog of Rheged
Gwyr-y-Gogledd seat at Carlisle
b. c.380 = *Ystrafael* - dau.
of Conan Meriadoc

Conan Meriadoc (Cynan)
Duke of the Armorican Frontiers
First King of the Bretons d. 421
= *St Darerca* - grand niece of
St Martin of Tours

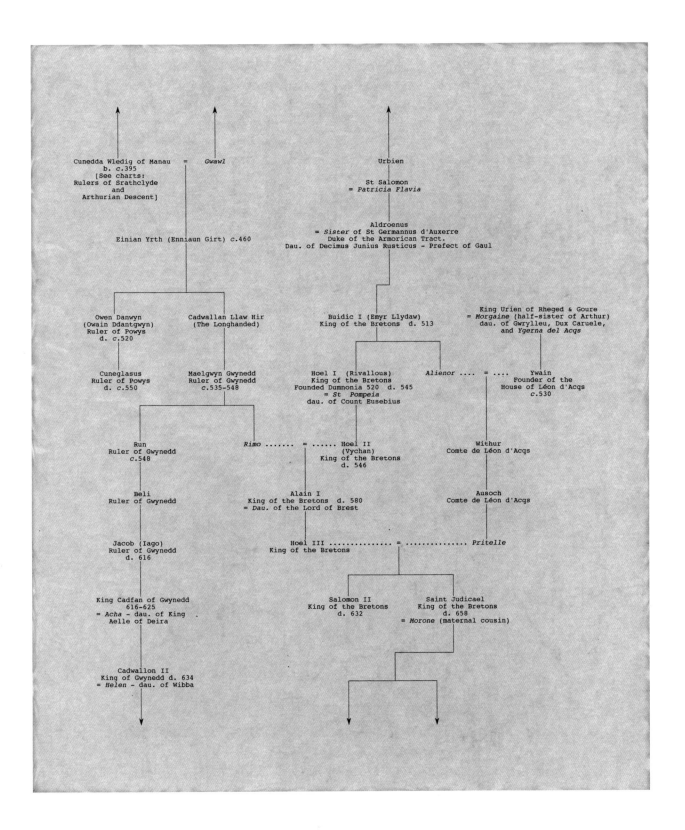

Cunedda Wledig of Manau = Gwawl
b. c.395
[See charts:
Rulers of Srathclyde
and
Arthurian Descent]

Urbien

St Salomon
= Patricia Flavia

Einian Yrth (Enniaun Girt) c.460

Aldroenus
= Sister of St Germannus d'Auxerre
Duke of the Armorican Tract.
Dau. of Decimus Junius Rusticus - Prefect of Gaul

Owen Danwyn
(Owain Ddantgwyn)
Ruler of Powys
d. c.520

Cadwallan Llaw Hir
(The Longhanded)

Buidic I (Emyr Llydaw)
King of the Bretons d. 513

King Urien of Rheged & Goure
= Morgaine (half-sister of Arthur)
dau. of Gwrylleu, Dux Caruele,
and Ygerna del Acqs

Cuneglasus
Ruler of Powys
d. c.550

Maelgwyn Gwynedd
Ruler of Gwynedd
c.535-548

Hoel I (Rivallous)
King of the Bretons
Founded Dumnonia 520 d. 545
= St Pompeia
dau. of Count Eusebius

Alienor .... = ... Ywain
Founder of the
House of Léon d'Acqs
c.530

Run
Ruler of Gwynedd
c.548

Rimo .... = ... Hoel II
(Vychan)
King of the Bretons
d. 546

Withur
Comte de Léon d'Acqs

Beli
Ruler of Gwynedd

Alain I
King of the Bretons d. 580
= Dau. of the Lord of Brest

Ausoch
Comte de Léon d'Acqs

Jacob (Iago)
Ruler of Gwynedd
d. 616

Hoel III .... = ... Pritelle
King of the Bretons

King Cadfan of Gwynedd
616-625
= Acha - dau. of King
Aelle of Deira

Salomon II
King of the Bretons
d. 632

Saint Judicael
King of the Bretons
d. 658
= Morone (maternal cousin)

Cadwallon II
King of Gwynedd d. 634
= Helen - dau. of Wibba

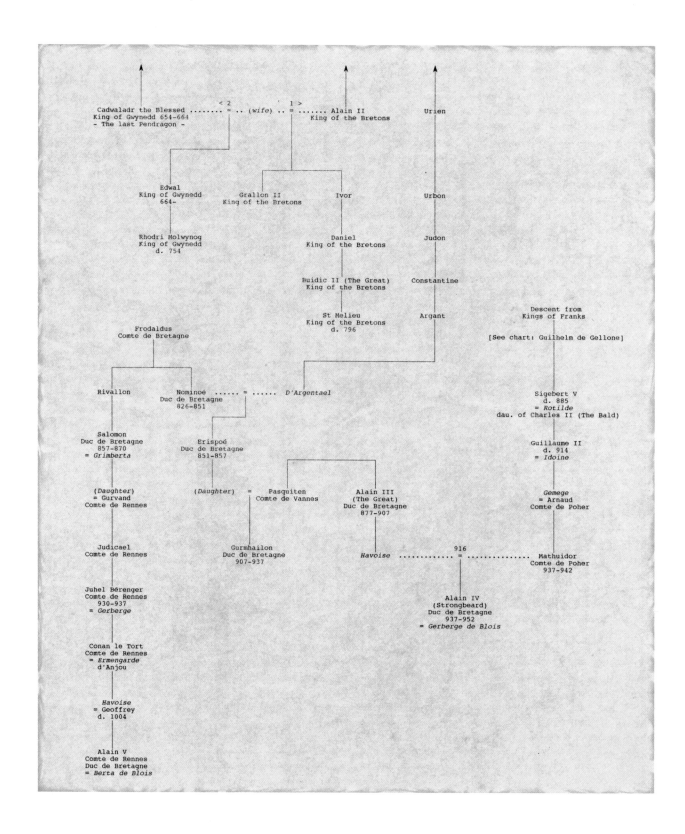

The Romans had considerable success in their conquest of Britain, but they could never defeat the Picts of Caledonia in the far north and, because of this, Emperor Hadrian (117-138 C.E.) had built a great wall across the country to separate the cultures. A majority of Celts south of the wall adapted to the Roman way of life, but their fiery northern cousins kept on fighting, as did the Scots Gaels of Northern Ireland.

In Wales, the early rulers of Powys and Gwynedd descended from Avallach in the line of Beli Mawr (sometimes called Billi or Heli). Beli the Great (Mawr)—a first-century BC.E. overlord of the Britons—is a good example of a character whose time frame is often confused because of the fables that have grown around him. His grandson was the Archdruid Brân the Blessed (son-in-law of Joseph of Arimathea). By virtue of their historical association, Beli and Brân are often muddled with the earlier brothers Belinus and Brennus (the sons

of Porrex), who contended for power in northern Britain in around 390 B.C.E. and were regarded as gods in the old Celtic tradition.

More potential confusion arises in that Brân the Blessed is often cited as the father of Caractacus. They were indeed contemporaries in the first century C.E., but Caractacus' father was Cymbeline of Camulod. The persistent anomaly has fostered no end of complications in books dealing with lineage in the Dark Ages, but the cause is easily explained. Brân's father, in descent from Beli Mawr, was King Llyr (Lear). Some generations later, however, in a succession from King Lucius, the names were repeated during the third and fourth centuries, when the Welsh chief, Llyr Llediath, was the father of another Brân, father of Caradawc (a variant of the name Caractacus).

In descent from Beli Mawr, the mighty Cymbeline was the Pendragon of mainland Britain during Jesus's lifetime. The Pendragon, or

**The Emperor supervises the building
of Hadrian's Wall.
Illustrated London News, April 1, 1911**

Queen Boudicca of the Iceni
by Archibald Stevenson Forrest, 1869-1963

tribal revolt against Roman domination from 60 C.E.—yelling her famous war cry 'Y gwir erbyn y Byd' (The Truth against the World). It was immediately after this that Joseph of Arimathea came from Gaul to set up his Glastonbury church in the face of Roman imperialism.

The concept of the Dragon in kingly terms emerged from ancient Dragon Lords of Mesopotamia, but more directly from the holy crocodile (the *Messeh*) of the Egyptians. The Pharaohs were anointed with crocodile fat and, thereby, attained the fortitude of the Messeh, from which stems the Hebrew term, 'Messiah' (Anointed One). The image of the intrepid Messeh evolved to become the Dragon, which in turn became emblematic of mighty kingship, as detailed in *Genesis of the Grail Kings*.

Following the Romans' withdrawal from Britain in 410 C.E., regional leadership reverted to tribal chieftains. One of these was Vortigern of Powys in Wales, whose wife was the daughter of the previous Roman governor, Magnus Maximus. Having assumed full control of Powys by 418 C.E., Vortigern was elected Pendragon of the Isle in 425 C.E. and made good use of the dragon emblem, which subsequently became the Red Dragon of Wales.

By that time, various kingly branches had emerged in the Arimatheac lines from Joseph's daughter, Anna, and her husband, Brân the Blessed. Among the most prominent of these local kings was Cunedda, the northern ruler of Manau, by the Firth of Forth. In a parallel family branch was the wise Coel Hen who led the 'Men of the North' (the *Gwyr-y-Gogledd*). Fondly remembered in nursery rhyme as 'Old King Cole', he governed the regions of Rheged from his Cumbrian seat at Carlisle (the northern *Camu-lot* fortress). Another noted leader was Ceretic, a descendant of King Lucius.[5] From his base at Dumbarton, he governed the regions of Clydesdale. Together with

Head Dragon of the Island (*Pen Draco Insularis*), was the King of Kings and Guardian of the Celtic Isle. The title was not dynastic; Pendragons were appointed from Celtic royal stock by a Druid council of elders. Cymbeline governed the Belgic tribes of the Catuvellauni and Trinovantes from his seat at Colchester—the most impressive Iron Age fort in the land. Colchester was then called 'Camulod' (or Romanized, 'Camulodunum')—from the Celtic *camu lot* meaning 'curved light'. This fortified settlement became the later model for the similarly named and seemingly transient Court of Camelot in Arthurian romance.[4] North of Cymbeline's domain, in Norfolk, the people known as the Iceni were ruled by King Prasutagus, whose wife was the famous Boudicca (or Boadicea). She led the great, but unsuccessful,

Vortigern, these three kings were the most powerful overlords in fifth-century Britain. Theirs were the families who also bore the most famous Celtic saints and were accordingly known as the Holy Families of Britain.

In the middle 400s C.E., Cunedda and his sons led their armies into North Wales to expel unwanted Irish settlers at the request of Vortigern. In so doing, Cunedda founded the Royal House of Gwynedd in the Welsh coastal region west of Powys. The Picts of Caledonia in the far north then took advantage of Cunedda's absence and began a series of Border raids across Hadrian's Wall. An army of Germanic Jute mercenaries, led by Hengest and Horsa, was swiftly imported to repel the invaders but, having succeeded, they turned their attentions to the far south and seized

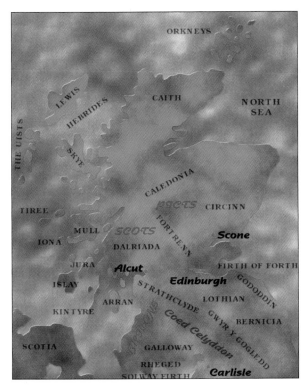

Early Scotland

(Caledonia, Dalriada and Gwyr-y-Gogledd)

the kingdom of Kent for themselves. Other Germanic Saxon and Angle tribes subsequently invaded from Europe. The Saxons took the south, developing the kingdoms of Wessex, Essex, Middlesex and Sussex, whilst the Angles occupied the rest of the land from the Severn estuary to Hadrian's Wall, comprising Northumbria, Mercia and East Anglia. The whole became known as England (Angle-land) and the new occupants called the Celtic western peninsula Wales (*weallas* meaning 'foreigners').

Because Ireland was separated by sea from the tempestuous British mainland, it became a perfect haven for monks and scholars. Eire-land is said by some to mean 'land of peace', but the ancient name derived more directly from Eire-amhon (father of King Irial of Tara) who married Tamar, the daughter of King Zedekiah of Judah, in about 586 B.C.E. (Eire was also the name of the Tuatha Dé Danann wife of King Ceathur, who reigned in much the same era.) A unique and indigenous culture thus developed in the form of Celtic Christianity. It emerged primarily from Egypt, Syria and Mesopotamia, with precepts that were distinctly Nazarene. The liturgy was largely Alexandrian and, because Jesus's teachings (rather than his person) formed the basis of the faith, the Mosaic content of the Old Testament was duly retained. The old Jewish marriage laws were observed, together with the celebrations of the Sabbath and Passover, while the divinity of Jesus and the Roman dogma of the Trinity played no part in the doctrine. The Celtic Church had no diocesan bishops, but was under the direction of abbots (monastic elders) and the whole was organized upon a clan structure, with its activities focused on scholarship and learning.

Cunedda remained in North Wales and, after Vortigern's death in 464 C.E., he succeeded as Pendragon, also becoming the supreme military commander of the Britons. The holder of this latter post was called the Guletic. When Cunedda died, Vortigern's son-in-law, Brychan of Brecknock, became Pendragon and Ceretic of Strathclyde became the military Guletic. Meanwhile, Vortigern's grandson Aurelius—a man of considerable military experience—returned from Brittany to lend his weight against the Saxon incursion. In his capacity as a druidic priest, Aurelius was the designated Prince of the Sanctuary of the Ambrius—a holy chamber, symbolically modelled upon the ancient Hebrew Tabernacle (Exodus 25:8—'And let them make me a sanctuary; that I may dwell

among them'). The Guardians of the Ambrius were individually styled 'Ambrosius' and wore scarlet mantles. From his fort in Snowdonia, Aurelius the Ambrosius maintained the military defense of the West and succeeded as the Guletic when Brychan died.

SAINT COLUMBA AND MERLIN

In the early 500s, Brychan's son (also Brychan) moved to the Firth of Forth as Prince of Manau. There he founded another region of Brecknock in Forfarshire, which the Welsh people referred to as 'Breichniog of the North'. His father's seat had been at Brecon in Wales—and so the northern fortress was likewise called Brechin. Brychan II's daughter married Prince Gabràn[6] of Scots Dalriada (the Western Highlands), as a result of which Gabràn became Lord of the Forth, inheriting a castle at Aberfoyle.

At that time, the Irish Gaels were in dispute with the Brychan house and, under King Cairill of Antrim, launched an assault against Scots Manau in 514. The invasion was successful and the Forth area was brought under Irish rule. Brychan duly called for assistance from his son-in-law, Prince Gabràn, and from the Guletic commander, Aurelius. Rather than attempt to remove the Irish from Manau, the leaders decided to launch a direct sea offensive against Antrim. In 516, Gabràn's Scots fleet sailed from the Sound of Jura with the Guletic troops of Aurelius. Their objective was the castle of King Cairill, the formidable hill-fort at Dun Bædàn (Badon Hill). The Guletic forces were victorious, and Dun Bædàn was overthrown.[7] In 560, the chronicler Gildas III (516-570) wrote about this battle in his *De Excidio Conquestu Britanniae* (The Fall and Conquest of Britain) and the great battle featured in both the Scots and Irish chronicles.[8] Some years after the Battle of

St. Mark in the Irish Book of Kells

Dun Bædàn, Gabràn became King of Scots in 537, with his West Highland court at Dunadd, near Loch Crinan.

At that time, the Pendragon was Cunedda's great-grandson, the Welsh king, Maelgwyn of Gwynedd. He was succeeded in this appointment by King Gabràn's son, Aedàn of Dalriada, who became King of Scots in 574 and was the first British king to be installed by priestly ordination, when anointed by St. Columba.

Born of Irish royal stock in 521, Columba was eligible to be a king in Ireland—but abandoned his legacy to become a monk, attending the ecclesiastical school at Moville, County Down. He founded monasteries in Derry and around, but his greatest work was destined to be in the Western Highlands and islands of Scots Dalriada, having been banished from Ireland in 563. Columba had mustered an army against the unjust King of Sligo, following which he was imprisoned at Tara and then exiled at the age of forty-two. With twelve disciples, he sailed to Iona and established the famous Columban monastery. Later, further north in Caledonia, Columba's royal heritage was well received by King Bruide of the Picts and he attained prominence as a political statesman at the druidic court. With a fleet of ships at his disposal, Columba visited the Isle of Man and Iceland, setting up schools and churches wherever he went—not only in Caledonia and the islands but also in English Northumbria (Saxonia).

At that time, the Scottish Lowlands (below the Forth) consisted of thirteen separate kingdoms. They bordered on the Northumbrian realm to the south and on the Pictish domain to the north. Although geographically outside Wales, the regions of Galloway, Lothian, Tweeddale and Ayrshire were all governed by Welsh princes. One of these dynastic

**Iona Abbey today on the site
of St. Columba's mission**

**Carlisle Castle in Cumbria—
a center of operations,
called Caruele, in Arthurian times**

regions above Hadrian's Wall was that of the Gwyr-y-Gogledd (Men of the North), whose chief was King Gwenddolau.

Shortly before Aedàn's kingly ordination by Columba, King Rhydderch of Strathclyde had killed King Gwenddolau in battle near Carlisle. The battlefield sat between the River Esk and Liddel Water, above Hadrian's Wall. (It was here, at the Moat of Liddel, that the Arthurian tale of *Fergus and the Black Knight* was set.)

Gwenddolau's chief adviser (the Merlin of Britain) was Emrys of Powys, the son of Aurelius. On Gwenddolau's death, however, the Merlin fled to Hart Fell Spa in the Caledonian Forest and then sought refuge at King Aedàn's court at Dunnad.

The title, 'Merlin' (applied to the Seer to the King), was long established in the Druid tradition. Prior to Emrys, the appointed Merlin was Taliesin the Bard, husband of Viviane I del Acqs. At his death in 540, the title passed to Emrys of Powys, who was the famous Merlin of Arthurian tradition. Emrys was an elder cousin of King Aedàn and was, therefore, in a position to request that the new king take action against Gwenddolau's killer. Aedàn, therefore, complied and duly demolished Rhydderch's Court of Alcut at Dumbarton.

In those days the most important urban center in the north of Britain was Carlisle. It had been a prominent Roman garrison town and, by 369 C.E., was one of the five provincial capitals. In his *Life of St. Cuthbert*, Bede refers to a Christian community in Carlisle long before the Anglo-Saxons penetrated the area. A little south of Carlisle, near Kirkby Stephen in Cumbria, stands the ruin of Pendragon Castle. Carlisle was also called Cardeol or Caruele in Arthurian times and it was here that Grail writers such as Chrétien de Troyes located King Arthur's second royal court. *The High History of the Holy Grail* refers specifically to Arthur's court at Carlisle, which also features in the French *Suit de Merlin* and in the British tales, *Sir Gawain and the Carl of Carlisle* and *The Avowing of King Arthur.*

14

KING ARTHUR

THE HISTORICAL WARLORD

Jt is often claimed that the first quoted reference to Arthur comes from the ninth-century Welsh monk, Nennius, whose *Historia Brittonum* cites Arthur at numerous identifiable battles. But, Arthur was recorded long before Nennius in the seventh-century *Life of St. Columba*. He is also mentioned in the Celtic poem *Gododdin*, written in about 600.

When King Aedàn of Dalriada was installed by St. Columba in 574, his eldest son and heir (born in 559) was Arthur. In the *Life of St. Columba*, Abbot Adamnan of Iona (627-704) related how the Saint had prophesied that Arthur would die before he could succeed his father. Adamnan further confirmed that the prophecy was accurate, for Arthur was killed in battle a few years after Columba's own death in 597.

The name 'Arthur' is generally reckoned to derive from the Latin *Artorius*, but this is quite incorrect. In fact, the reverse is the case. The Arthurian name was purely Celtic, emerging from the Irish 'Artur'. The third-century sons of King Art were Cormac and Artur. Irish names were not influenced by the Romans and the root of 'Arthur' can be found as far back as the fifth century B.C.E., when Artur mes Delmann was King of the Lagain.

In 858, Nennius listed various battles at which Arthur was victorious. The locations included the Caledonian Wood north of Carlisle (Cat Coit Celidon) and Mount Agned—the fort of Bremenium in the Cheviots, from which Anglo-Saxons

Queen Guinevere Maying
by John Collier, 1850-1934

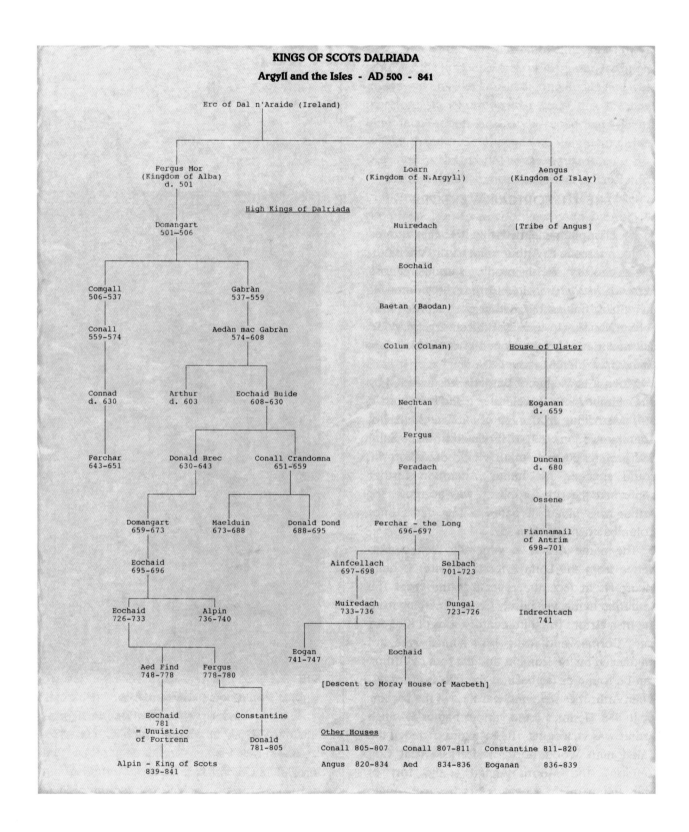

KINGS OF SCOTS DALRIADA

Argyll and the Isles - AD 500 - 841

Erc of Dal n'Araide (Ireland)

Fergus Mor
(Kingdom of Alba)
d. 501

Loarn
(Kingdom of N.Argyll)

Aengus
(Kingdom of Islay)

High Kings of Dalriada

Domangart
501-506

Muiredach

[Tribe of Angus]

Eochaid

Comgall
506-537

Gabràn
537-559

Baetan (Baodan)

Conall
559-574

Aedàn mac Gabràn
574-608

Colum (Colman)

House of Ulster

Connad
d. 630

Arthur
d. 603

Eochaid Buide
608-630

Nechtan

Eoganan
d. 659

Fergus

Ferchar
643-651

Donald Brec
630-643

Conall Crandomna
651-659

Feradach

Duncan
d. 680

Ossene

Domangart
659-673

Maelduin
673-688

Donald Dond
688-695

Ferchar - the Long
696-697

Fiannamail
of Antrim
698-701

Eochaid
695-696

Ainfcellach
697-698

Selbach
701-723

Eochaid
726-733

Alpin
736-740

Muiredach
733-736

Dungal
723-726

Indrechtach
741

Aed Find
748-778

Fergus
778-780

Eogan
741-747

Eochaid

[Descent to Moray House of Macbeth]

Eochaid
781
= Unuisticc
of Fortrenn

Constantine

Donald
781-805

Other Houses

Alpin - King of Scots
839-841

Conall 805-807   Conall 807-811   Constantine 811-820

Angus 820-834   Aed   834-836   Eoganan   836-839

were repelled. Also featured was Arthur's battle by the River Glein (Glen) in Northumbria, where the fortified enclosure was the center of operations from the middle 500s. Other named Arthurian battlegrounds were the City of the Legion (Carlisle) and the district of Linnuis—the old region of the Novantae tribe, north of Dumbarton, where Ben Arthur stands above Arrochar at the head of Loch Long.

To place Arthur in his correct context, it is necessary to understand that such apparent names as 'Pendragon' and 'Merlin' were actually titles. They applied to more than one individual over the course of time. Arthur's father, King Aedàn mac Gabràn of Scots, became Pendragon by virtue of the fact that he was Prince Brychan's grandson. In this line, Aedàn's mother, Lluan of Brecknock, was descended from Joseph of Arimathea. There never was an Uther Pendragon, even though he was grafted into English charts of the era in sixteenth-century Tudor times. The name 'Uther Pendragon' was invented in the twelfth century by the romancer, Geoffrey of Monmouth (later Bishop of St. Asaph) and the Gaelic word 'uther' was simply an adjective meaning 'terrible'. Historically, there was only ever one Arthur born to a Pendragon: he was Arthur mac Aedàn of Dalriada.

On his sixteenth birthday in 575, Arthur became sovereign Guletic (commander) of the British forces and the Celtic Church accepted his mother, Ygerna del Acqs, as the true High Queen of the Celtic kingdoms. Her own mother (in the hereditary lineage of Jesus and Mary Magdalene) was Viviane I, dynastic Queen of Burgundian Avallon. The priests, therefore, anointed Arthur as High King of the Britons following his father's ordination as King of Scots. At the time of her conception of Arthur by Aedàn, Ygerna (Igraine) was still married to Gwyr-Llew, Dux of Carlisle. The *Scots Chronicle* records the event as follows:

Becaus at ye heire of Brytan was maryit wy tane Scottis man quen ye Kinrik wakit, and Arthure was XV yere ald, ye Brytannis maid him king be ye devilrie of Merlynge, and yis Arthure was gottyn onn ane oyir mannis wiffe, ye Dux of Caruele.

In the *Historia Regum Britanniae* (History of the Kings of Britain) by Geoffrey of Monmouth (c. 1147), Gwyr-Llew, the Dux of Caruele (Warlord of Carlisle), was literally spirited away to the southern West Country to become Gorlois, Duke of Cornwall.[1] This adjustment of the facts was deemed necessary because Geoffrey's Norman patron was Robert, Earl of Gloucester. The *Historia* was funded by Norman money, with an express requirement to cement King Arthur into the English tradition, even though he did not feature in the *Anglo-Saxon Chronicle*.

Although presented as a factual history, Geoffrey's work was known to be inaccurate in many respects. The historian William of Malmesbury called it 'dubious stuff' and William of Newburgh went even further, stating, 'Everything that the man took pains to write concerning Arthur and his predecessors was invented'.

Many were particularly baffled by Geoffrey's Duke Gorlois of Cornwall because there were no Dukes in sixth-century England. The early title of 'Dux' was quite different from that of the later ducal nobility; it was a strictly military distinction and held no feudal tenure of land ownership. Another anomaly was the assertion by Geoffrey that the sixth-century Arthur had been born at Tintagel Castle—but there was no castle at Tintagel until the first Earl of Cornwall built one in the early twelfth century. Previously there had been only a ruined Celtic monastery on the site.

Another misappropriation of the Pendragon's son was manifest in Wales and the tradition persists today. There actually was an Arthur in sixth-century Wales—in fact, he was the only other royal Arthur of the era, but he was not the son of a Pendragon and he was not the Arthur of Grail lore. This other Arthur was installed as Prince of Dyfed by St. Dubricius in 506, even though he and his forebears were enemies of the native Welsh. He was descended from disinherited Déisi royalty, expelled from Ireland in the late fourth century. When the Roman troops left South Wales in 383 C.E., the Déisi leaders came from Leinster to settle in Dyfed (Demetia). Arthur, Prince of Dyfed, features as a notorious tyrant in *The Lives of the Saints* (in the tales of Carannog and others) and he is generally portrayed as a troublesome regional interloper.

In Arthurian romance, the confusion between the Scots and Welsh Arthurs arose mainly because of the Merlin connection. As we have seen, Merlin Emrys was the son of Aurelius. But Aurelius' wife

**The ruin of Tintagel Castle
in Cornwall**

was Arthur of Dyfed's sister, Niniane. Aurelius had married her in an effort to curtail the Déisi invasions of Powys, but his strategy was short-lived. This, of course, meant that Merlin Emrys was Arthur of Dyfed's nephew while, at the same time, he was a cousin to the Pendragon Aedàn mac Gabràn and was the appointed guardian of Aedàn's son, Arthur of Dalriada.

According to the tenth-century *Annales Cambriae* (Annals of Wales), Arthur perished at the Battle of Camlann. But to which Arthur do the annals refer? The answer is that, being composed so long after the event, they actually refer to a composite Arthur—a character forged from both the Dyfed and Dalriadan princes, along with some other memorable characters.

The fifteenth-century *Red Book of Hergest* (a collection of Welsh folktales) states that the Battle of Camlann was fought in 537. If this location relates to Maes Camlan, south of Dinas Mawddwy, then it is quite possible that Arthur of Dyfed fought there. He was renowned for leading incursions into both Gwynedd and Powys. What is certain, however, is that Arthur of Dalriada fought a later battle at Camelon, west of Falkirk. *The Chronicles of the Picts and Scots* refer to this northern conflict as the 'Battle of Camelyn'. He also fought at Camlanna (or Camboglanna) by Hadrian's Wall— the battle which led to his demise.

As for Geoffrey of Monmouth, he decided to ignore all the geographical locations, siting his fanciful battle by the River Camel in Cornwall. Geoffrey also associated the Irish battle of Badon Hill (Dun Bædàn) with a battle at Bath, because the latter place had once been known as Badanceaster.

In the *Life of Saint Columba*, Abbot Adamnan related that, in the late 500s, King Aedàn of Scots had consulted St. Columba about his due successor in Dalriada, asking, 'Which of [my] three sons is to reign: Arthur, or Eochaid Find, or Domingart?' Columba replied,

ARTHURIAN DESCENT

Houses of Siluria, Camulod, Dalriada and Gwynedd

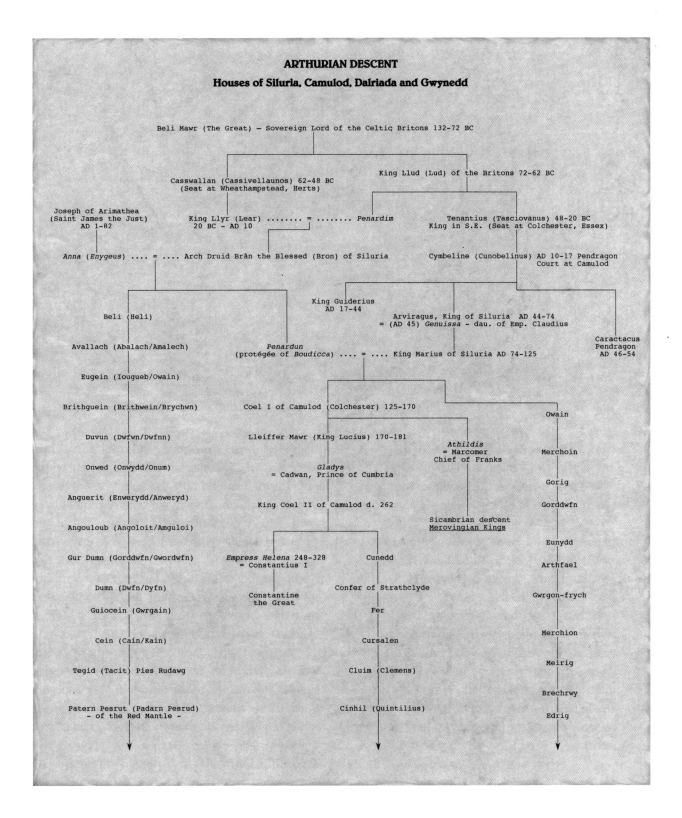

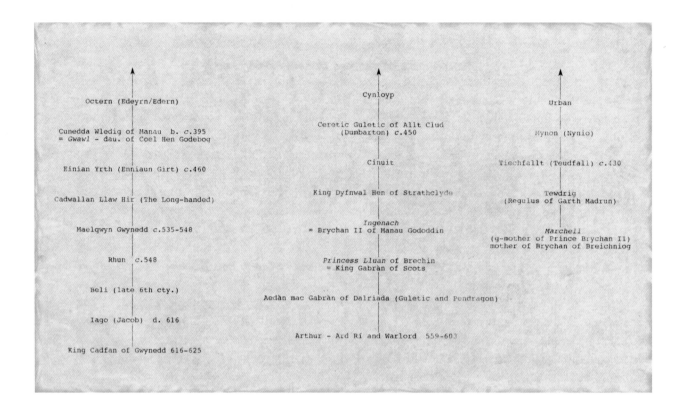

```
Octern (Edeyrn/Edern)                      Cynloyp                              Urban

Cunedda Wledig of Manau  b. c.395     Ceretic Guletic of Allt Clud          Mynon (Nynio)
= Gwawl - dau. of Coel Hen Godeboq      (Dumbarton) c.450

Einian Yrth (Enniaun Girt) c.460           Cinuit              Tiechfallt (Teudfall) c.430

Cadwallan Llaw Hir (The Long-handed)  King Dyfnwal Hen of Strathclyde              Tewdrig
                                                                          (Regulus of Garth Madrun)
Maelgwyn Gwynedd c.535-548                Ingenach                       Marchell
                                      = Brychan II of Manau Gododdin      (g-mother of Prince Brychan II)
                                                                          mother of Brychan of Breichniog
Rhun  c.548                            Princess Lluan of Brechin
                                       = King Gabràn of Scots

Beli (late 6th cty.)

                                   Aedàn mac Gabràn of Dalriada (Guletic and Pendragon)
Iago (Jacob)  d. 616

                                      Arthur - Ard Rí and Warlord  559-603
King Cadfan of Gwynedd 616-625
```

None of these three will be ruler, for they will fall in battle, slain by enemies; but now if thou hast any other younger sons, let them come to me.

A fourth son, Eochaid Buide, was summoned and the saint blessed him, saying to Aedàn, 'This is thy survivor'. Adamnan's account continues:

And thus it was that afterwards, in their season, all things were completely fulfilled; for Arthur and Eochaid Find were slain after no long interval of time in the Battle of the Miathi. Domingart was killed in Saxonia; and Eochaid Buide succeeded to the kingdom after his father.

The Miathi (as mentioned by Adamnan) were a tribe of Britons who settled in two separate groups,

north of the Antonine and Hadrian Walls respectively. The Antonine Wall extended between the Firth of Forth and the Clyde estuary. Hadrian's Wall traversed the lower land between the Solway Firth and Tynemouth. In 559, the Angles had occupied Deira (Yorkshire) and had driven the Miathi northwards. By 574, the Angles had also pushed up into Northumbrian Bernicia. Some of the Miathi decided to stay by the lower Wall and make the best of it, while others moved further north to settle beyond the upper Wall.

The main stronghold of the northern Miathi was at Dunmyat, on the border of (modern) Clackmannanshire, in the district of Manau on the Forth. Here, they had cast their lot with the Irish settlers, which made them none too popular with the Scots and Welsh. Despite King Cairill's 516 defeat in Antrim, the Irish remained boisterously obstructive in Manau. The Guletic forces,

ARTHUR AND THE HOUSE OF AVALLON DEL ACQS

Merlin, Vortigern and Aurelius - 4th to 6th century

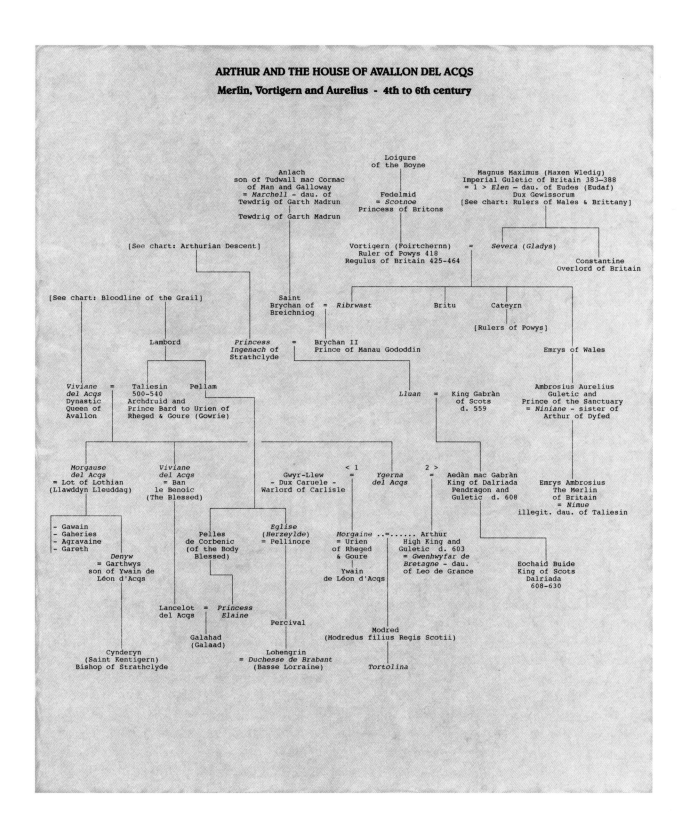

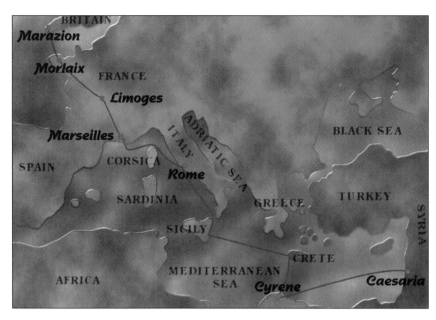

Route of the 1st-century Metal Traders

consequently, made another incursion into Ulster in 575. This second assault at Dun Bædàn is the one mentioned by Nennius, who rightly described Arthur's presence, whereas the Gildas account relates to the earlier 516 battle and, correctly, gives Ambrosius Aurelius as the commander. Nennius gives Arthur rather more credit than his due, however, for on this second occasion the Scots were defeated and Arthur's father, King Aedàn, was obliged to submit to Prince Bædàn mac Cairill at Ros-na-Rig on Belfast Lough.[2]

Following King Bædàn mac Cairill's death in 581, Aedàn of Scots finally managed to expel the Irish from Manau and the Forth. Later, in 596, Arthur's cavalry drove the Irish out of Scots Brecknock. King Aedàn was present at the battles, but Arthur's younger brothers Brân and Domingart were killed at Brechin on the Plain of Circinn.

In confronting the Irish at Manau, the Guletic troops also had to face the Miathi Britons. They were successful in driving many of them back to their southern territory, but those who remained when the Guletic troops departed had to contend with the Picts, who promptly moved into their domain. By the end of the century, the Picts and Miathi were united against the Scots, whom they met at the Battle of Camelyn, north of the Antonine Wall. Once again the Scots were victorious and the Picts were driven northwards. Afterwards, a nearby ironworks foundry construction was dubbed *Furnus Arthuri* (Arthur's Fire) to mark the event. It was a long-standing attraction and was not demolished until the eighteenth-century Industrial Revolution.

Three years after Camelyn, the Scots faced the southern Miathi and the Northumbrian Angles. This confrontation was a protracted affair fought on two battlegrounds—the second conflict resulting from a short-term Scots retreat from the first. The forces initially met at Camlanna, an old Roman hill-fort by Hadrian's Wall. Unlike the previous encounter, however, the 'Battle of Camlanna' was a complete fiasco for the Scots.

LORDS OF STRATHCLYDE AND THE GWYR-Y-GOGLEDD
Supplement to Arthur and Avallon chart

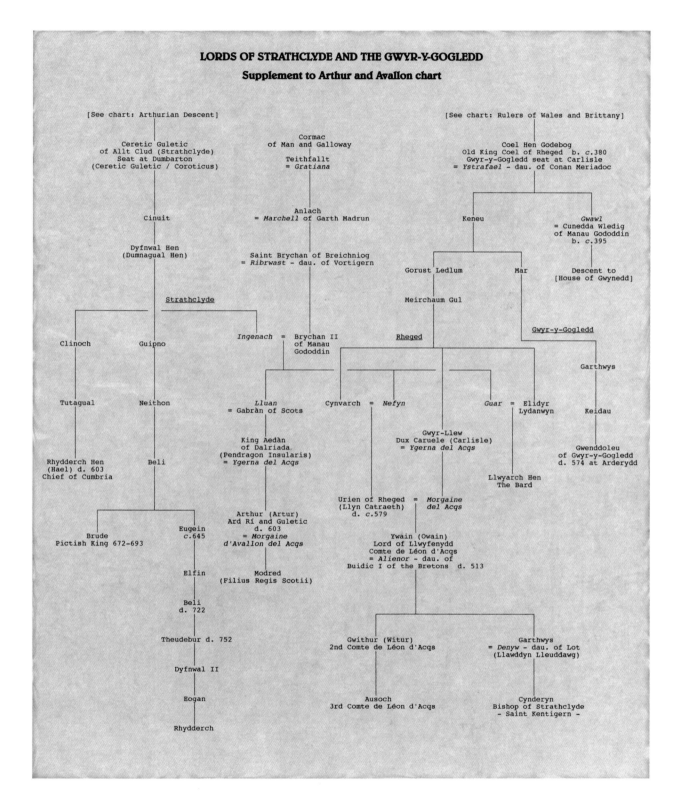

Falling for a diversionary tactic by the Miathi, the Scots allowed the Angles to move behind them in a concerted northwesterly push towards Galloway and Strathclyde. The unlucky definition of a *Cath Camlanna* has been applied to many a lost battle thereafter.

Only a few months earlier, the Angle king, Aethelfrith of Bernicia, had defeated King Rhydderch at Carlisle, thereby acquiring new territory along the reaches of the Solway. The Dalriadan forces under Aedàn and Arthur were therefore under some pressure to intercept and halt the Angles' northward advance. They were said to have assembled immense forces, drawn from the ranks of the Welsh princes and they even gained support from Maeluma mac Bædàn of Antrim, the son of their erstwhile enemy. By that time, the Irish were themselves daunted by the prospect of an Anglo-Saxon invasion.

MODRED AND MORGAINE

It is important to note that King Aedàn was a Celtic Church Christian of the Sacred Kindred of St. Columba. Indeed, the Dalriadans were generally associated with the Sacred Kindred, which was distinctly grounded in the Nazarene tradition, but incorporated some customary druidic and pagan ritual.

Arthur, however, became obsessed with Roman Christianity, to the extent that he began to regard his Guletic cavalry as a holy army. This disposition led to considerable disturbance within the Celtic Church for Arthur was, after all, destined to be the next King of Scots. The elders were particularly worried that he might try to implement a Romanized kingdom in Dalriada and it was on this account that Arthur made an enemy of his own son Modred, Archpriest of the Sacred Kindred. Modred was an associate of the Saxon

King Cerdic of Elmet (the West Riding of Yorkshire) and Cerdic was allied to Aethelfrith of Bernicia. It was not difficult, therefore, to persuade Modred to oppose his father on the battlefield and to ally himself with the Angles in his bid to save the Scots kingdom from losing its ancient druidic heritage.

And so it was that, when the Scots faced the Angles and Miathi at Camlanna in 603, Aedàn and Arthur found themselves not only against King Aethelfrith, but also against their own Prince Modred. The initial affray at Camlanna was short-lived and the Celtic troops were obliged to chase after the Angles, who had swept past them. They caught up again at Dawston-on-Solway (then called Degsastan in Liddesdale) and the *Chronicles*

Morgan le Fay (Morgaine), the half-sister of King Arthur.
Engraved from a painting by
George Frederick Watts, 1817-1904

of Holyrood and *of Melrose* refer to the battle site as 'Dexa Stone'. Archpriest Modred's appearance with the invaders severely downcast the Celtic spirits and it was here that Arthur (aged forty-four) fell alongside Maeluma mac Bædàn.

The battle, which began at Camlanna and ended at Dawston, was one of the fiercest in Celtic history. The *Tigernach Annals* call it 'the day when half the men of Scotland fell'. Although Aethelfrith was victorious, heavy losses were sustained by all. His brothers Theobald and Eanfrith were slain, along with all their men, and King Aedàn fled the field having lost two sons, Arthur and Eochaid Find, along with his grandson, Archpriest Modred.

Aethelfrith never reached Strathclyde, but his success at Dawston enabled the Northumbrian territory to be extended northwards to the Firth of Forth, incorporating the Lothians. Ten years later, in 613, Aethelfrith besieged Chester and brought Cumbria fully under Angle control. This drove a permanent geographical wedge between the Welsh and the Strathclyde Britons. The Mercian Angles then pushed westwards, forcing the Welsh behind what was eventually to be the line of Offa's Dyke, while the Wessex Saxons encroached beyond Exeter, annexing the south-west peninsula.

In time, the once conjoined Celtic lands of Wales, Strathclyde and Dumnonia (Devon and Cornwall) were totally isolated from each other and the Kindred of St. Columba blamed it all on Arthur. He had failed in his duties as Guletic and

New Year procession of the Druids
by R. Hope, 1908

The death of King Arthur in Avalon.

19th-century engraving by Bellenger

High King. His father, King Aedàn of Dalriada, died within five years of the Camlanna disaster, which was said to have opened the door to the final conquest of Britain by the Anglo-Saxons. The days of Celtic lordship were done and, after more than six centuries of tradition, Cadwaladr of Wales (twenty-sixth in line from Joseph of Arimathea) was the last Pendragon.

In the wake of Arthur's defeats at Camlanna and Dawston (jointly called *di Bellum Miathorum*: the Battle of the Miathi), the old kingdoms of the North existed no more. The Scots, who were physically separated from their former allies in Wales, perceived that their only route towards saving the land of Alba (Scotland) was to become allied with the Picts of Caledonia. This was achieved in 844, when Aedàn's famed descendant, King Kenneth MacAlpin, united the Picts and Scots as one nation.[3] The records of Kenneth's installation support

his truly important position in the family line by referring to him as a descendant of the Queens of Avallon.

Had Modred survived he would undoubtedly have become Pendragon, for he was a great favorite of the Druids and the Celtic Church. Arthur's mother, Ygerna, was the elder sister of Morgause, who married Lot of Lothian, the ruler of Orkney. Lot and Morgause were the parents of the Orkney brothers Gawain, Gaheries and Gareth. Morgause was also, like Ygerna, a younger sister of Viviane II, the consort of King Ban le Benoic,[4] a Desposynic descendant of Faramund and the Fisher Kings. Viviane and Ban were the parents of Lancelot del Acqs.

On the death of her first husband, the Dux of Carlisle, Ygerna married Aedàn of Dalriada, thereby legitimating Arthur before his titles were granted. By way of this union, the lineages of Jesus and

James (Joseph of Arimathea) were combined in Arthur for the first time in about 350 years, which is why, despite his shortcomings, he became so important to the Grail tradition.

Arthur's maternal grandmother, Viviane I, was the dynastic Queen of Avallon, a kinswoman of the Merovingian kings. His aunt, Viviane II, was the official Keeper of Celtic Mysticism and this heritage fell, in due course, to Ygerna's daughter, Morgaine. Arthur was married to Gwenhwyfar of Brittany, but she bore him no children. On the other hand, he did father Modred by Morgaine. Old Registers, such as the *Promptuary of Cromarty*, suggest that Arthur also had a daughter called Tortolina, but she was actually his granddaughter (the daughter of Modred). Morgaine (alternatively known as Morganna or Morgan le Faye) was married to King Urien of Rheged and Gowrie (Goure)[5] who, in Arthurian romance, is called Urien of Gore. Their son was Ywain, founder of the Breton House de Léon d'Acqs, who held the rank of Comte (Count). In her own right, Morgaine was a Holy Sister of Avallon and a Celtic High Priestess.

Writers have sometimes considered Arthur's sexual relationship with his half-sister Morgaine to be incestuous, but this was not the way it was regarded in Celtic Britain. At that time, the anciently perceived dual nature of God prevailed, as did the equally ancient principle of the sacred sister-bride. In this regard, the prayer of the Celts began, 'Our Father-Mother in the heavens' and, in conjunction with this, specifically defined rites were performed to denote the mortal incarnation of the dual 'male-female' entity. As the earthly manifestation of the goddess Cerridwin, Morgaine represented the female aspect, while Arthur was her true male counterpart in the established tradition of the pharaohs.

At the festival of Beltane (the Spring equinox), Arthur was apprehended as a god in human form and was obliged to participate in a ritual of sacred intercourse between the twin aspects of the incarnate Father-Mother. In view of Arthur and Morgaine's presumed divinity during this rite, any male offspring from the union would be deemed the Celtic Christ and would be duly anointed as such. By virtue of this, although Arthur was destined to become the prominent subject of romantic history, it was his son Modred who held the highest spiritual position; he was the designated Christ of Britain, the ordained Archpriest of the Sacred Kindred and an anointed Fisher King.

In his maturity, Arthur upheld the Roman tradition, but it was Archpriest Modred who strove to amalgamate the old Celtic teachings with those of the Christian Church, treating both Druids and Christian priests on an equal basis. It was this essential difference between father and son that drove them against each other. Arthur became significantly Romanized, whereas Modred upheld religious toleration in the true nature of Grail kingship. Despite the extraordinary success of Arthur's early career, his eventual Catholic leaning caused him to betray his Celtic Oath of Allegiance. As High King of the Britons he was supposed to be the Defender of Faith but, instead, he imposed specific ritual upon the people. When he and Modred perished in 603, Arthur's death was not mourned by the Celtic Church, but he will never be forgotten. His kingdom fell because he forsook the codes of loyalty and service. His ultimate neglect facilitated the completion of the Saxon conquest and his knights will roam the wasteland until the Grail is returned. Contrary to all myth and legend, it was the dying Archpriest Modred (not Arthur) who was carried from the field by his mother Morgaine's Holy Sisters.

THE HOLY SISTERS

In Geoffrey of Monmouth's *Historia*, Morgan le Faye's nine Holy Sisters are cited as guardians of the Isle of Avalon. As far back as the first century, the geographer Pomponius Mela had similarly written of nine mysterious priestesses living under vows of chastity on the Isle of Sein, off the Brittany coast near Carnac. Mela told of their powers to heal the sick and foretell the future, in much the way that Morgaine del Acqs was a Celtic High Priestess with prophetic and medicinal powers. The Roman Church, however, would not tolerate such attributes in a woman and, because of this, the Cistercian monks were obliged to transform Morgan le Faye's image in the Arthurian *Vulgate Cycle*.

The Cistercians were closely identified with the Knights Templars of Jerusalem and Grail lore was born directly from the Templar environment. The Counts of Alsace, Champagne and Léon (with whom writers like Chrétien de Troyes were associated) all had affiliations with the Order, but the Catholic Church still held sway in the public domain. Consequently, women were afforded no rights to fulfill any ecclesiastical or sacred function and, to this end, from the middle 1200s, Morgaine (dynastic heiress and Celtic holy sister of Avallon) was portrayed as Morganna the malevolent sorceress. In the English poem *Gawain and the Green Knight* (written in around 1380), it is the jealous Morganna who transforms Sir Bercilak into the Green Giant in order to frighten Guinevere.

In a manner similar to the matriarchal practice of the Picts, Morgaine's honorary Avallonian dynasty was perpetuated in the female line. The difference was that the Queens' daughters held supreme position rather than their sons—thus the honor was eternally female in concept. Originating from the same lineage of Jesus, the Celtic nominal Queens of Avallon emerged alongside the Merovingian kings, while other important offshoots were the lines of the Septimanian and Burgundian royal successions.

Morgaine's son Ywain (Eógain) founded the noble house of Léon d'Acqs in Brittany and the later arms of Léon bore the black Davidic Lion on a gold shield (in heraldic terms: 'Or, a lion rampant, sable'). The province was itself so named because *Léon* was Septimanian-Spanish for 'lion'. The English spelling appeared in the twelfth century as a variant of the Anglo-French *liun*. Until the fourteenth century, the Scots Lord Lyon, King of Arms, was still called the *Léon Héraud*.

**The temptation of Sir Percival
by Arthur Hacker, 1894**

In some books, it is suggested that Ywain's son, Comte Withur de Léon d'Acqs (often corrupted to d'Ah), is identical with Uther Pendragon because of the similarity of first name. But actually Withur was a Basque name, derived from the Irish *Witur*, whose Cornish equivalent was *Gwythyr*. The Comité (County) of Léon was established in about 530 at the time of the Breton King Hoel I. He was of Welsh Arimatheac descent and his sister Alienor was Ywain's wife.

At that time, there were two levels of authority in Brittany. In the course of a protracted immigration from Britain, Breton Dumnonia had been founded in 520, but it was not a kingdom as such. There emerged a line of kings such as Hoel, but they were not Kings of Brittany, they were Kings of the immigrant Bretons. Throughout this period, the region remained a Merovingian province and the local kings were subordinate to Frankish authority by appointed Counts: the *Comites non regis*. The supreme Frankish Lord of Brittany 540-544 was Chonomore, a native of the Frankish State with Merovingian authority to oversee the development of Brittany by the settlers. Chonomore's forebears were Mayors of the Palace of Neustria and he was the hereditary Comte de Pohor. In time, the descendants of Ywain's aunt Viviane II became overall Counts of Brittany.

Brittany features prominently in Arthurian romance. At Paimpont, about 30 miles (c.48 kilometers) from Rennes, is the enchanted Forest of Broceliande, from which stretches the Valley of No Return, where Morganna confined her lovers. Also to be found are the magic Spring of Barenton and Merlin's Garden of Joy, although most of the stories of Broceliande were actually transposed from far earlier accounts of the historical Merlin Emrys in the Caledonian Forest of Scotland.

THE ISLE OF AVALON

As indicated in Geoffrey of Monmouth's romance, Avalon was traditionally associated with the magical Otherworld. It was here that the legendary Arthur was tended by the maidens in his eternal abode. Morgan le Faye promised to heal Arthur's wounds if he would remain on the Isle and nothing was ever said of his death. The implication was, therefore, that Arthur might one day return.

When Geoffrey wrote his story, he was clearly unaware of the furor it would cause. Not only was the account inaccurate in many respects, but he had suggested a possible Second Coming of the King. This, along with the sacred powers he attributed to women, was quite unacceptable to the Roman Church and the later writer, Sir Thomas Malory, took a route of compromise. He simply had Bedevere place the wounded Arthur in a barge full of women who would transport him to Avalon. Then Bedevere walked through the forest and came upon a chapel in which Arthur's body had been interred.

Although Geoffrey's Avalon was based on the Otherworld of Celtic tradition (A-val or Avilion), his interpretation was more related to classical writings about the Fortunate Islands, where the fruit was self-tending and the people immortal. In mythological terms, such places were always 'beyond the western sea'. At no point did any of the early writers identify a location for the mystic Isle; it did not have to be anywhere in particular—certainly not within the mortal domain, for its enchantment was that of an eternal paradise.

All of this changed in 1191, however, when the Isle of Avalon was suddenly identified with Glastonbury in Somerset. The definition of this inland location as an island was justified on the basis that Glastonbury stood amid watery marshland and the nearby lake—villages of Godney and Meare dated from about 200 B.C.E. Nevertheless, because of the geographical anomaly, the name 'Vale of Avalon' became a popular alternative. Prior to this date there had been no recognized connection between Arthur and Glastonbury, except for a passing mention by Cardoc of Llancarfan.[6] He wrote, in 1140, that the Abbot of Glastonbury had been instrumental in Gwynefer's release from King Melwas of Somerset, but he did not suggest that Glastonbury was Avalon—neither did anyone else.

**The Lady Chapel of St. Mary
at Glastonbury Abbey**

What happened in 1191 was that the monks of Glastonbury made use of Arthurian tradition in a manner that would truly impress today's marketing specialists. Some writers have since labelled their actions an outright fraud, while others have tried to make the case that the monks were themselves deluded by circumstance. Whatever the truth of the matter, they not only saved their Abbey from extinction, but gave birth to a whole new Glastonbury tradition. The Abbey had been badly damaged by fire in 1184 and Henry II began to fund the reconstruction. When he died in 1189, his son Richard I came to the throne, but he was more concerned with applying Treasury resources to the Holy Land Crusade. As a result, the Glastonbury funding was terminated, leaving the Abbot and his monks penniless. So what did they do but dig a hole between a couple of Saxon monuments south of the Lady Chapel where, to the amazement of all, they found the supposed remains of King Arthur and Queen Guinevere!

Some 16 feet (c. 4.8 meters) below ground, in a hollowed oak canoe, they unearthed the bones of a tall man, along with some smaller bones and a tress of golden hair. Such a find was of little consequence in its own right, but the monks were in luck, for not far above the log coffin there was said to have been a leaden cross embedded in stone. Upon the cross was inscribed *Hic Iacet Sepultus Inclytus Rex Arthurius In Insula Avallonia Cum Uxore Sua Secunda Wenneveria* ('Here lies interred the renowned King Arthur in the Isle of Avalon with his second wife Guinevere'). Not only had they found Arthur's grave but they had also conveniently found written proof that Glastonbury was the Isle of Avalon!

16th-century Flemish illustration of the Canterbury pilgrims

However, the Roman Church officials were far from happy that Guinevere was described as the king's 'second' wife and it was asserted that the inscription was obviously incorrect.[7] This posed something of an immediate problem but, soon afterwards the legend reappeared, miraculously changed in spelling and format. This time it dispensed with Guinevere altogether, so that it was far more in keeping with requirement: *Hic Iacet Sepultus Inclitus Rex Arturius In Insula Avalonia* ('Here lies interred the renowned King Arthur in the Isle of Avalon').

Quite why the monks should have dug in that particular spot is unclear—and even if they did find the bones as stated, there was nothing to associate them with King Arthur. The identification came only from the inscription on the leaden cross, yet the Latin was plainly of the Middle Ages, differing from Arthurian Latin to the extent that today's English differs from that of Tudor times.

Whatever the facts, the monks' purpose was well served and, following a successful publicity campaign, pilgrims flocked in their thousands to Glastonbury. The Abbey was substantially enriched with their donations and the complex was rebuilt as planned. As for the alleged bones of Arthur and Guinevere, they were deposited in two painted chests and placed in a black marble tomb before the high altar.

The entombed remains proved to be such a popular attraction that the monks determined to benefit further from their newfound tourist trap. It was apparent that if Arthur's bones created such a stir, then the relics of a saint or two would have a significant impact. So they took to their spades once more and, very soon, other discoveries were announced: the bones of St. Patrick and St. Gildas, along with the remains of Archbishop Dunstan, which most people knew had lain at Canterbury Cathedral for 200 years!

By the time of Henry VIII's dissolution of the monasteries, Glastonbury Abbey was boasting dozens of relics, including a thread from Mary's gown, a sliver from Aaron's rod and a stone that Jesus had refused to turn into bread. At the dissolution, though, the Abbey's days of monastic activity were done and the said relics disappeared without trace. Since that time, no one has seen the supposed bones of Arthur and Guinevere; all that remains is a notice marking the site of the tomb. To many people, nonetheless, Glastonbury will always be associated with Avalon. Some prefer Geoffrey's idea of Tintagel, while others stake their claims on Bardsey or Holy Island. Yet, apart from the reality of Avallon in Burgundy, it is plain that the Celtic Otherworld was a mythical realm, with a tradition dating back beyond record.

If the mystic Isle existed within the mortal plane, then it was akin to that eternal paradise which the pre-Goidelic Fir-Bolg tribe called Arunmore. From Connacht in Ireland, the Fir-Bolg installed their King Oengus mac Umóir, on the timeless island haven in the ancient days B.C.E.. It was to this place that the warriors fled after their defeat by the Tuatha Dé Danann at the legendary battle of Magh Tuireadh.[8] The Enchanted Isle was said to lie in the sea between Antrim and Lethet (the stretch of land between the Clyde and the Forth). Arunmore was the Isle of Arran, the traditional home of Manannan, the sea god. Arran was also called Emain Ablach (the place of apples)[9] and this association was perpetuated in the *Life of Merlin*, which referred specifically to the *Insula Pomoru*—the Isle of Apples.

**On the
Isle of Arran**

15

INTRIGUE AGAINST THE BLOODLINE

THE EVOLVING CHURCH

Having been separated from the Byzantine Church, the Church of Rome developed the theme of the Apostles' Creed sometime after the year 600. Passages were incorporated that are still familiar today: God became 'the maker of heaven and earth' and, in a thoroughly non-biblical portrayal, Jesus (having suffered under Pontius Pilate) 'descended into hell', before rising on the third day. The Creed also, at this time, introduced the concept of the Holy Catholic Church and the Communion of Saints.

During the sixth and seventh centuries, the supposedly heretical Nestorian belief spread into Persia, Iraq and southern India—even as far east as China, where missionaries arrived at the Imperial Court of the T'ang Emperor T'ai-tsung in 635. He was so inspired by the new doctrine that he had the Nestorian Creed translated into Chinese and sanctioned the building of a commemorative church and monastery. Nearly a century and a half later, in 781, a monument in honor of Nestorius was erected at Sian-fu.

In the meantime, the Arians—who also denied Jesus's divinity—had gained a very strong foothold

The descent of Christ in Hell —
in accordance with the Apostles' Creed
by Jacopo Bellini, 1400-70

in European society. Christian history generally uses the term 'barbarian' to describe Arians such as the Goths, Visigoths (West Goths), Ostrogoths (East Goths), Vandals (Wends), Lombards and Burgundians, but the description refers to no more than cultural differences; it does not mean these peoples were heathen ruffians. The open hostility of the said barbarians towards Rome and Byzantium was no more barbaric than the Romans' own savage empire-building. Although once wholly pagan (as indeed were the Romans themselves), these tribes had, in large measure, become followers of Arius during the fourth century. From Spain and southern France, through to the Ukraine, most of Germanic Europe was Arian Christian in the 600s.

Another doctrine which had, to some extent, become associated with the Nestorians and Arians was a remnant of the fourth-century cult of Priscillian of Avila. His alternative Christian movement had begun in northwestern Spain and had made significant inroads into Aquitaine. Fundamental to the Priscillian belief—which came out of Egypt, Syria and Mesopotamia—was the mortality of the Blessed Mary, as against her semi-divine image in the Roman Church. Priscillian had been executed in 386 C.E., at Trier (north of Metz), although his body was later transferred for burial in Spain.[1]

In view of these widespread alternatives to orthodox Christianity, it is quite apparent that the Catholic Church was far from paramount in the West. Catholicism was surrounded and infused with various other forms of the faith. However, they were generally based on Judaic traditions, rather than on the Pauline concept which had been adopted and revised by Rome. With the exception of some spiritually based factions within in the Gnostic movement, they retained beliefs

akin to the Desposyni tradition, promoting the Nazarene doctrine of Jesus's own humanity and preaching his message rather than venerating his person.

While the Roman Church was busily concerned with dogma and ecclesiastical structure, the Celtic Church was showing an interest in the hearts and minds of the people. By 597, Celtic Christianity was so widespread that Bishop Gregory of Rome sent the Benedictine monk, Augustine, to England specifically to establish the Roman Church more firmly in that country. His arrival was deliberately timed to follow the death that year of the prominent Father of the Sacred Kindred, the gentle St. Columba. Augustine began his work in southeastern England, in Kent to be precise, where the local King Aethelbert's wife was already a confirmed Catholic. In 601, Augustine was proclaimed the first Archbishop of Canterbury and, two years later, he attempted to become Primate of the Celtic Church as well. However, such an endeavor could only fail against an establishment that remained far more Nazarene than Roman. Indeed, Augustine's plan was not for a unification of Churches, but for the strategic subjugation of a traditional Church which Rome had declared more or less heretical.

It was not until 664, at the Synod of Whitby in North Yorkshire, that Rome achieved the first doctrinal victory over the Celtic Church. The main debate concerned the date of Easter, for the Chief Pontiff of the day had decided that Easter should no longer be formally associated with the Jewish Passover. Against all prevailing custom and against all Celtic tradition, the Catholic bishops succeeded in getting their own way—so displacing for all time the historic Jewish and Celtic ties. Traditionally, however, Britain's Easter festival was not a Passover celebration in the Jewish style, neither was it anything to do with Jesus. Easter (in both name and season) actually represented Eostre, the goddess of Spring, whose feast day was observed long before any association with Christianity.

Following the Synod, the Catholic Church increased its strength in Britain, but the Celtic Church could not be suppressed without an open declaration of war against Ireland. However, the days of Roman imperialism were over and no army that the Roman Church could muster would ever defeat the fierce troops of the Irish kings. The Celtic Church, consequently, remained very active

Artists often defied the ruling that the Madonna should be depicted in blue and white only by introducing a little cardinal red and such Grail symbolism as bunches of grapes. From The Flight into Egypt by Gerard David, 1510

in Britain and the Sacred Kindred of St. Columba eventually became the ecclesiastical seat of the Kings of Scots.

Through all this, the Bishop of Rome's biggest problem was his inability to gain supremacy over the royal houses of Celtic Britain. Rome had seen a measure of potential success with the conversion of King Arthur, but Arthur had been killed and the Druid style Nazarene heritage remained firm through the successors of his half-brother Eochaid Buide. Shortly after Eochaid's accession, Bishop Boniface IV adopted the new Roman style of 'Pope' (Papa) in 610, as an alternative to being called a 'bridge-builder' (pontiff). This was a blatant and positive attempt to compete with the long-standing Celtic distinction of 'Father', inherited from the Essene tradition. But when the new papal supremacy was tested on Dianothus, Abbot of Bangor, he responded that neither he nor his colleagues recognized any such authority. They were prepared, he said, to acknowledge the Church of God, 'but as for other obedience, we know of none that he whom you term the Pope (or Bishop of Bishops) can demand'. A local letter written to the Abbot of Iona in 634 referred unequivocally to St. Patrick (the prevailing Father) as 'Our Pope'.

Over the centuries, various attempts were made to deny the priestly and patriarchal heritage of the Celtic Church (which was more than authoritative enough to cause concern in the Vatican).[2] Roman Catholic holy orders were supposed to rely on Apostolic Succession, but no such succession could be proved, for the Apostle Peter (on whom the succession supposedly hinged) had never held any formal office. The first appointed Bishop of Rome was Britain's Prince Linus (son of Caractacus the Pendragon) and, as recorded in the *Apostolic Constitutions*, Linus began the true succession, having been installed by St. Paul during Peter's lifetime in 58 C.E.

Later, in 180 C.E., Irenaeus, Bishop of Lyon, wrote, 'The Apostles having founded and built up the Church at Rome, committed the ministry of its supervision to Linus'. In attempts to veil the royal heritage of Linus, he has often been portrayed as if he were a lowly slave, but this has not removed the thorn from the Church's side and, because of it, the papal doctrine has to be considered 'infallible' when emanating from the throne. If not, then the whole concept of a structured progression of High Bishops in Apostolic succession from Peter collapses, since Peter was never a Bishop of Rome, neither of anywhere else.

SCHISM IN CHRISTIANITY

Rome's final split with the Eastern Church occurred in 867, when the latter announced that it upheld the true Apostolic Succession. The First Vatican Council disagreed and so Photius, Patriarch of Constantinople, actually excommunicated Pope Nicholas I of Rome!

This led to a whole new round of argument about the definition of the Trinity. The Catholics of western Christendom decided to ratify what was called the 'Filioque Article', which had been introduced at the Council of Toledo in 598. It declared that the Holy Spirit proceeded 'from the Father and *from* the Son' (Latin: *filioque*). The Eastern Church claimed otherwise, stating that the Spirit proceeded 'from the Father *through* the Son' (Greek: *dia tou huiou*). It was a somewhat intangible and quite extraordinary point of theological dispute, but it was apparently good enough to split formal Christianity down the middle. In reality, of course, it was simply a trivial excuse to perpetuate the debate over whether the Church should be politically managed from Rome, or from Constantinople. The final result was the formation of two quite distinct Churches from the same original.[3]

As time progressed, the Eastern Church changed relatively little. From its primacy at Constantinople, it continued to adhere strictly to scriptural teachings and its focus of worship became the Eucharist ('thanksgiving') ritual with bread and wine.

Catholicism, on the other hand, underwent numerous changes: new doctrines were added and old concepts were amended or further substantiated. From the twelfth century, seven Sacraments were deemed to embody the grace of God in a person's physical life (though not all were necessary for individual salvation). They were classified as: baptism, holy communion, confirmation, confession and penance, ordination to holy orders, the solemnization of matrimony and the anointing of the seriously ill and dying ('extreme unction' or the 'last rites'). It was further decreed that the bread and wine of the Communion were actually transformed, upon consecration, into the physical body and blood of Jesus (the doctrine of Transubstantiation).

Inasmuch as Constantine's Roman Church had commenced as a hybrid, so too was the structure to remain composite. New methods and ideologies were introduced to maintain efficient control of congregations from a distance in an expanding Catholic society. In this way, Roman Catholicism evolved in a strictly regulated fashion and some doctrines that seem today to be traditional are actually quite recently implemented features. It was not until Victorian times that certain aspects of the Catholic creed (hitherto only implied) were determined as explicit items of faith. The doctrine of the Immaculate Conception, for instance, was not formally expressed until 1854, when Pope Pius IX decreed that Mary, the mother of Jesus, was herself conceived free from Original Sin. Mary's Assumption into Heaven was not defined until the 1950s by Pope Pius XII, whilst Pope Paul VI did not proclaim her Mother of the Church until 1964.

Such decrees were themselves rendered possible by the ultimate assertion of authority— that of 'papal infallibility'. The dogma to this effect was proclaimed at the First Vatican Council in 1870 and stated, in a way that brooked no opposition, that 'the Pope is incapable of error when defining matters of Church teaching and morality from his throne'!

CONTROL OF RELIGIOUS ART

The Roman Catholic Church was not only concerned with retaining control over historical records and romantic literature. Indeed, the bishops set their sights against anything that appeared contrary to their dogmatic notions and, to this effect, an orthodox correctness was implemented and regulated throughout the creative sphere. That the Madonna should be depicted only in blue and white has already been mentioned, but there were other rules which governed sacred art in general. Some artists, such as Botticelli and Poussin, successfully introduced symbolic elements into their works—elements that the uninitiated would not comprehend but, in general terms, the art of much of Europe was constrained by strict Vatican guidelines.

From the earliest days of the Roman Church, the male relatives of Jesus had posed a problem, but this was successfully countered when they were pushed into the background of Church tradition while Mary, the mother of Jesus, was brought to the fore. The unfortunate Joseph, father of Jesus and James (the true link in the royal succession) was deliberately sidelined, while the cult of the Virgin Mother grew out of all proportion. By way of this considered strategy, public knowledge of the continuing bloodline of Judah was conveniently suppressed.

Rules were laid down by the Church as to who might be portrayed in art and how.[4] Anne (Anna), the mother of Mary, was seldom introduced into paintings with her daughter because

The Virgin and Child with St. Anne
(showing the mother positioned
behind her daughter)
by Leonardo da Vinci, 1452-1519

her presence would detract from Mary's divine status. If Anne's visible attendance was essential, she was placed in a subordinate position. Francesco da San Gallo's *Saint Anne and the Madonna* provides a good example of how the mother is seated behind her daughter. Cesi's *The Vision of Saint Anne* shows Anne kneeling before a vision of Mary. Leonardo da Vinci's *The Virgin and Child with Saint Anne* is cleverly contrived to position the adult Mary on her mother's knee, thereby keeping the Madonna to the fore. Similarly, Anne stands behind her daughter in Pietro Perugino's *The Family of the Virgin*.

Mary's husband, Joseph, and her father, Joachim, were generally confined to inferior or background positions within pictorial artwork. Both characters created problems because their paternal functions were contrary to the purported Immaculate Conception and Virgin Birth. As early as the fresco paintings of Taddeo Gaddi (died

Adoration of the Shepherds
(depicting an elderly, disinterested Joseph)
by Domenico Ghirlandaio, 1485

1366), it was preferred to reduce Joachim's status by showing him at his least dignified. He was often, therefore, portrayed being ejected from the Temple by the High Priest Issachar, having presumed to offer a feast-day lamb although he was not yet a father. In Michelangelo's *The Holy Family*, Mary is raised upon a central throne, while her husband Joseph leans over a background balustrade, seemingly contemplating some unrelated matter.

The Church would gladly have denied that the Blessed Mary ever married, but artists could not escape the directness of the Gospels. Nevertheless, there was no room for any suggestion of physical attachment between Joseph and Mary. Joseph was, for that reason, generally depicted as being considerably older than his wife—balding and taking little interest in his family, as in Ghirlandajo's *The Adoration of the Shepherds* (c.1485). The famous *Doni Tondo* by Michelangelo (1504) similarly features a very bald and white-bearded Joseph, as does Caravaggio's *The Rest on the Flight into Egypt*. Indeed, Joseph was not infrequently shown as positively infirm, leaning uncomfortably on a crutch, while Mary remained always beautiful and serene, as in Paolo Veronese's *The Holy Family*.

Joseph's necessary presence was a cause of some difficulty for artists depicting the Nativity. But the difficulty was overcome in such paintings as Alessandro Moretto's sixteenth-century *The Nativity* by showing him as elderly with a supportive staff. Sometimes Joseph even appears to be in his dotage, or asleep, as in Lorenzo di Credi's portrayal. One way or another, this kingly descendant of the House of David was, time after time, reduced to being a superfluous onlooker (as in Hans Memling's *The Adoration of the Magi*) and he was seldom permitted to be a part of any relevant action. Moreover, in such pictures as Van Dyck's *Repose in Egypt*, Joseph

**Rest on the Flight to Egypt (with Joseph white
and balding, while Mary remains young and serene)
by Caravaggio, 1571-1610**

seems hardly capable of any action—being more ready to collapse at Mary's feet and to join her father, Joachim, on the official road to oblivion.

FROM MEROVINGIAN TO CAROLINGIAN

By the mid-seventh century, Rome was in a position to begin dismantling the Merovingian succession in Gaul—a plan which, as we saw earlier, was contrived at the baptism of King Clovis. In 665, the Mayor of the Austrasian Palace (akin to a Prime Minister) was firmly under papal control. When King Sigebert II died, his son Dagobert was only five years old—at which point Mayor Grimoald took action. To begin, he kidnapped Dagobert and had him conveyed to Ireland, to live in exile among the Scots Gaels. Then, not expecting to see the young heir again, Grimoald told Queen Immachilde that her son had died.

Prince Dagobert was educated at Slane Monastery, near Dublin, and he married the Celtic Princess Matilde when he was fifteen. Subsequently, he went to York under the patronage of St. Wilfred. But then Matilde died and Dagobert decided to return to France, much to the

Charles Martel against
the Moors at Poitiers
by William H. Rainey, 1852-1936

overshadowed the supremacy of the Pope. Dagobert's jealous enemies included his own powerful Mayor, Pepin the Fat of Heristal. Two days before Christmas 679, Dagobert was hunting near Stenay in the Ardennes when he was confronted by one of Pepin's men and lanced to death—impaled to a tree. The Church of Rome was quick to approve the assassination and immediately passed the Merovingian administration in Austrasia to the ambitious Mayor.

Pepin the Fat was, in due course, succeeded by his illegitimate son, the well-known Charles Martel (the 'Hammer') who gained recognition by turning back the Moorish invasion near Poitiers in 732. He then sustained the Roman endeavor by gaining control of other Merovingian territories. When Martel died in 741, the only Merovingian of any notable authority was Dagobert II's nephew, Childeric III. Martel's son, Pepin the Short, was the Mayor of Neustria. Up to that point (except for the Grimoald affair), the Merovingian monarchy had been strictly dynastic; hereditary succession was an automatic and sacred right—a matter in which the Church had no say whatsoever. But that tradition was destined to be overturned when Rome grasped the opportunity to 'create' kings by papal authority. In 751, Pepin the Short, in league with Pope Zachary, secured Church approval for his own coronation as King of the Franks in place of Childeric. The Church's long-awaited ideal had come to fruition and, from that time onwards, kings were endorsed and crowned only by self-styled Roman prerogative.

So Pepin became king with the full blessing of the Pope and Childeric was deposed. The pledge of allegiance made by the Roman Church in 496 C.E. to King Clovis and his descendants was broken. After two and a half centuries, the Church was suitably geared to usurp the ancient legacy of the Merovingian bloodline and to take control of the Frankish realm by appointing its own kings.

amazement of his mother. In the meantime, Grimoald had placed his own son on the Austrasian throne, but Wilfred of York and others spread word of the mayoral treachery and the House of Grimoald was duly discredited. Having secondly married Gizelle de Razès, a niece of the Visigoth king, Dagobert was reinstated in 674 (after an absence of nearly twenty years) and the Roman intrigue was thwarted—but not for long.[5]

Dagobert II's reign was short but effective; his major success was in centralizing the Merovingian sovereignty, but the Catholic movement set itself firmly to negate his Messianic heritage because it

Childeric was publicly humiliated by the bishops. His hair (kept long in the Nazarite tradition) was cut brutally short and he was incarcerated in a monastery, where he died four years later. Thus began a new dynasty of French kings, the Carolingians—so named after Pepin's father, Charles (Carolus) Martel.[6]

KING OF THE JEWS

After their defeat by Charles Martel in the 730s, the Islamic Moors retreated to the city of Narbonne in the south of France, which became their base for further military resistance. This posed a difficult and prolonged problem for Pepin the Short, who duly sought assistance from the Jews of Narbonne. He finally gained their support—but at a price. The Jews agreed to deal with the problem if Pepin guaranteed the setting up of a Jewish kingdom within the territory of Burgundy—a kingdom that would have at its head a recognized descendant of the Royal House of David.[7]

Pepin agreed and the Jews defeated the Moors from within the city. The Jewish kingdom of Septimania (the Midi) was then established in 768, from Nimes to the Spanish frontier, with Narbonne as its capital. The previous governor of the region was the Merovingian, Theuderic IV (Thierry), who had been ousted from power in Neustria and Burgundy by Charles Martel in 737. Theuderic (known to the Moors as Makir Theodoric) was married to Pepin the Short's sister Alda. It was their son, Count Guilhelm de Toulouse, who then acceded to the new throne as the King of Septimania in 768. Guilhelm was not only of Merovingian lineage, but was a recognized Potentate of Judah, holding the distinction of 'Isaac' in the patriarchy.

Pepin's son, Charles, was the ruler who became known as Charlemagne the Great. As King of the Franks from 771 and Emperor of the West from 800, Charlemagne was pleased to confirm Guilhelm's entitlement to dynastic sovereignty in Septimania. The appointment was also upheld by the Caliph of Baghdad and, reluctantly, by Pope Stephen in Rome. All acknowledged King Guilhelm of the House of Judah to be a true bloodline successor of King David. Guilhelm was particularly influential at the Carolingian Court and he had an illustrious military career. In spite of his prominent position, Guilhelm was greatly influenced by St. Benedict's monastic asceticism and founded his own monastery at Gellone. In 791 he instituted his famous Judaic Academy of St. Guilhelm and was later featured by the Holy Grail chronicler Wolfram von Eschenbach.

King Pepin the Short—

first of the Carolingians

by H. de Viel Castel (19th century)

THE CAROLINGIANS

House of Charlemagne - 8th to 10th century

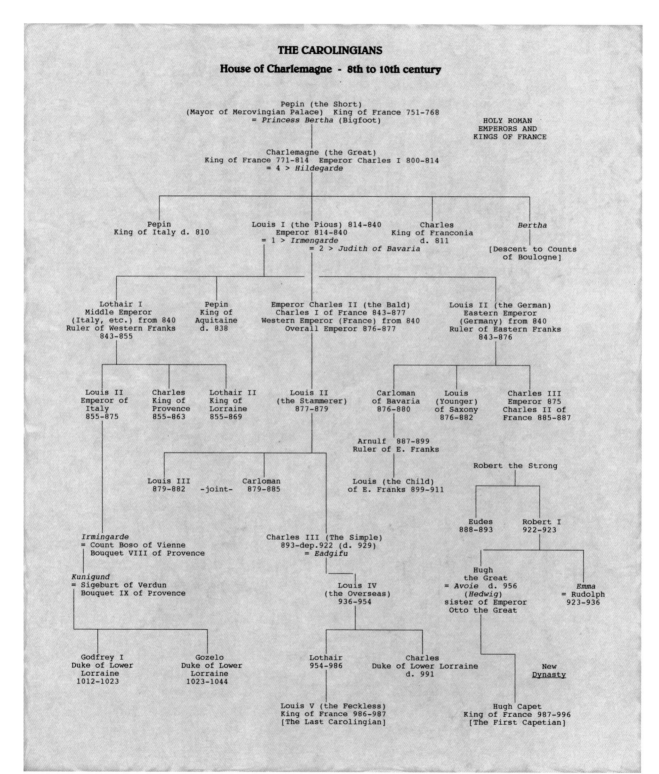

Pepin (the Short)
(Mayor of Merovingian Palace)   King of France 751-768
= *Princess Bertha* (Bigfoot)

HOLY ROMAN
EMPERORS AND
KINGS OF FRANCE

Charlemagne (the Great)
King of France 771-814   Emperor Charles I 800-814
= 4 > *Hildegarde*

Pepin
King of Italy d. 810

Louis I (the Pious) 814-840
Emperor 814-840
= 1 > *Irmengarde*
= 2 > *Judith of Bavaria*

Charles
King of Franconia
d. 811

Bertha

[Descent to Counts
of Boulogne]

Lothair I
Middle Emperor
(Italy, etc.) from 840
Ruler of Western Franks
843-855

Pepin
King of
Aquitaine
d. 838

Emperor Charles II (the Bald)
Charles I of France 843-877
Western Emperor (France) from 840
Overall Emperor 876-877

Louis II (the German)
Eastern Emperor
(Germany) from 840
Ruler of Eastern Franks
843-876

Louis II
Emperor of
Italy
855-875

Charles
King of
Provence
855-863

Lothair II
King of
Lorraine
855-869

Louis II
(the Stammerer)
877-879

Carloman
of Bavaria
876-880

Louis
(Younger)
of Saxony
876-882

Charles III
Emperor 875
Charles II of
France 885-887

Arnulf 887-899
Ruler of E. Franks

Louis III
879-882   -joint-

Carloman
879-885

Louis (the Child)
of E. Franks 899-911

Robert the Strong

Eudes
888-893

Robert I
922-923

Irmingarde
= Count Boso of Vienne
Bouquet VIII of Provence

Charles III (The Simple)
893-dep.922 (d. 929)
= *Eadgifu*

Hugh
the Great
= *Avoie* d. 956
(*Hedwig*)
sister of Emperor
Otto the Great

Emma
= Rudolph
923-936

Kunigund
= Sigeburt of Verdun
Bouquet IX of Provence

Louis IV
(the Overseas)
936-954

Godfrey I
Duke of Lower
Lorraine
1012-1023

Gozelo
Duke of Lower
Lorraine
1023-1044

Lothair
954-986

Charles
Duke of Lower Lorraine
d. 991

New
Dynasty

Louis V (the Feckless)
King of France 986-987
[The Last Carolingian]

Hugh Capet
King of France 987-996
[The First Capetian]

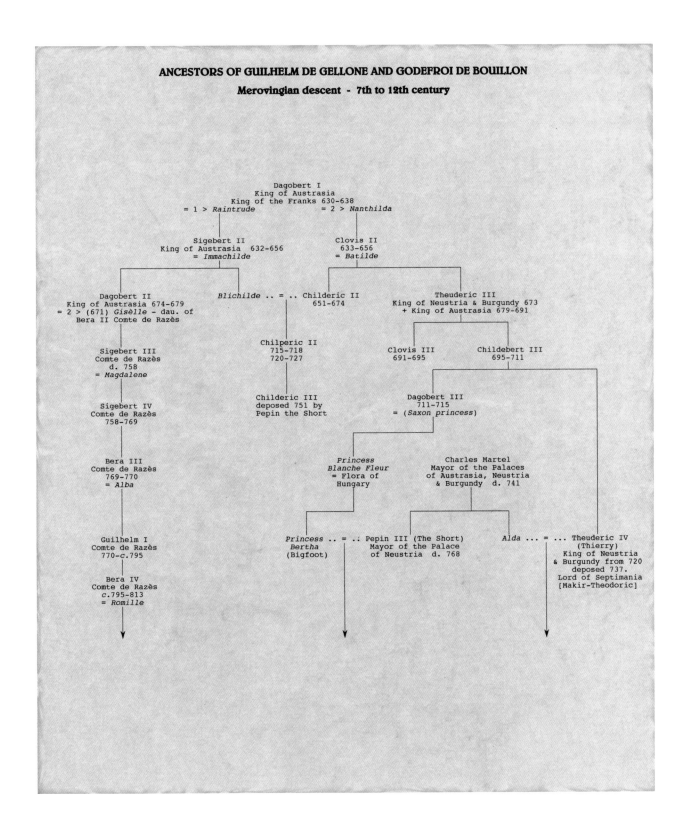

ANCESTORS OF GUILHELM DE GELLONE AND GODEFROI DE BOUILLON

Merovingian descent - 7th to 12th century

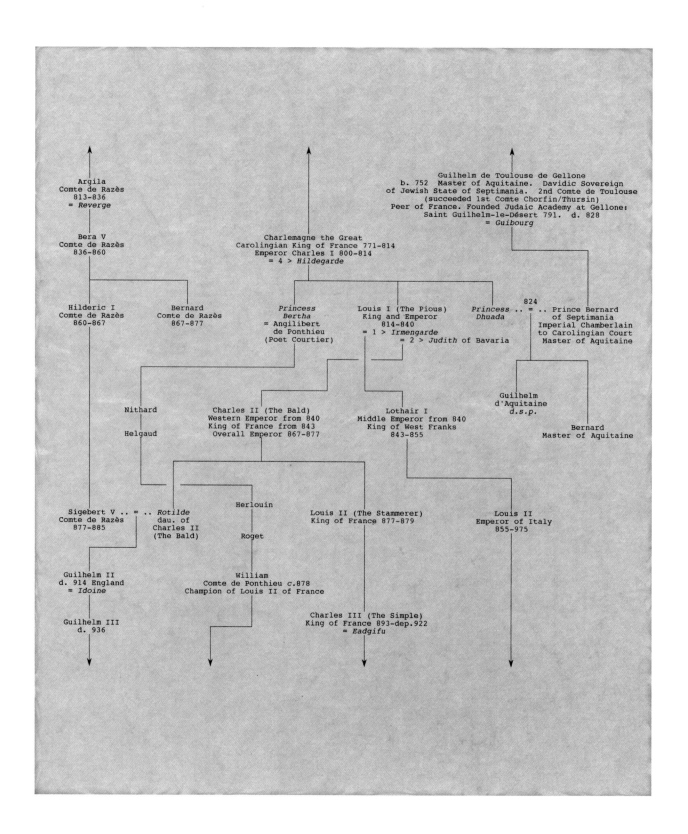

Argila
Comte de Razès
813-836
= *Reverge*

Bera V
Comte de Razès
836-860

Hilderic I
Comte de Razès
860-867

Bernard
Comte de Razès
867-877

Guilhelm de Toulouse de Gellone
b. 752 Master of Aquitaine. Davidic Sovereign
of Jewish State of Septimania. 2nd Comte de Toulouse
(succeeded 1st Comte Chorfin/Thursin)
Peer of France. Founded Judaic Academy at Gellone:
Saint Guilhelm-le-Désert 791. d. 828
= *Guibourg*

Charlemagne the Great
Carolingian King of France 771-814
Emperor Charles I 800-814
= 4 > *Hildegarde*

*Princess
Bertha*
= Angilibert
de Ponthieu
(Poet Courtier)

Louis I (The Pious)
King and Emperor
814-840
= 1 > *Irmengarde*
    = 2 > *Judith* of Bavaria

*Princess ..
Dhuada*

824
= .. Prince Bernard
of Septimania
Imperial Chamberlain
to Carolingian Court
Master of Aquitaine

Nithard

Helgaud

Charles II (The Bald)
Western Emperor from 840
King of France from 843
Overall Emperor 867-877

Lothair I
Middle Emperor from 840
King of West Franks
843-855

Guilhelm
d'Aquitaine
d.s.p.

Bernard
Master of Aquitaine

Herlouin

Roget

Sigebert V .. = .. *Rotilde*
Comte de Razès   dau. of
877-885   Charles II
           (The Bald)

Louis II (The Stammerer)
King of France 877-879

Louis II
Emperor of Italy
855-975

Guilhelm II
d. 914 England
= *Idoine*

William
Comte de Ponthieu *c.*878
Champion of Louis II of France

Guilhelm III
d. 936

Charles III (The Simple)
King of France 893-dep.922
= *Eadgifu*

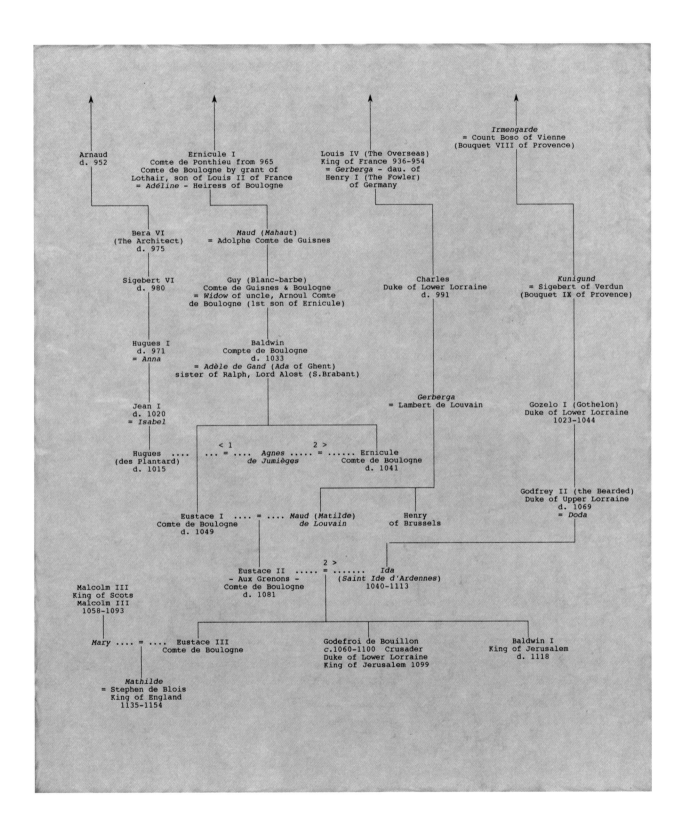

The gold and enamel tomb of
Emperor Charlemagne (died 814)

More than 300 years later, the Davidic succession was still extant in the Spanish Midi, although the notional kingdom had ceased to function as a separate State within a State. In 1144 the English monk, Theobald of Cambridge, stated (when initiating a charge of ritual murder against the Jews of Norwich):

> The chief men and rabbis of the Jews who dwell in Spain assemble together at Narbonne, where the Royal Seed resides, and where they are held in the highest esteem.

In 1166, the chronicler, Benjamin of Tudela, reported that there were still significant estates held by the prevailing Davidic heirs:

> Narbonne is an ancient city of the Torah8 ... Therein are sages, magnates and princes, at the head of whom is Kalonymos, son of the great Prince Todros of blessed memory, a descendant of the House of David, as stated in his family tree. He holds hereditaments and other landed properties from the rulers of the country, and no one may dispossess him.

By his wife Guibourg, Guilhelm's eldest son and heir was Prince Bernard of Septimania; his other sons were Heribert, Bera and Theodoric. Bernard became Imperial Chamberlain and was second in authority to the Carolingian Emperor. He was the leading Frankish statesman from 829 and married Charlemagne's daughter Dhuada at the Imperial Palace of Aix-la-Chapelle in June 824. They had two sons: William (born November 826) and Bernard (born March 841). William became a prominent military leader and Bernard II held the reins of Aquitaine, to rival King Louis II in power and influence within the region.

TEMPLE OF THE GRAIL

LEGACY OF THE GRAIL

Of all Arthurian themes, the most romantic is that of the Holy Grail yet, because of the Grail's enduring tradition, there is a lingering uncertainty about its place in time. Its champions have been portrayed in the first century, in the Arthurian period and in the Middle Ages. In essence, the Grail is timeless.

The Grail has been symbolized by many things: a chalice, a platter, a stone, a casket, an aura, a jewel and a vine. It is sought by some and seen by others. It is sometimes tangible, with appointed guardians and maidenly bearers, but is often ethereal, appearing in a variety of guises including that of Jesus himself. Its powers include those of rejuvenation, knowledge and provision. Just as Jesus was a healer, teacher and provider, so too is the Grail. In name it has been the *Graal*, the

Saint Graal, the *Seynt Grayle*, the *Sangréal*, the *Sankgreal*, the *Sangrail*, the *Sank Ryal* and the *Holy Grail* but, however defined, its spirit remains at the very center of achievement.

Despite a background that is both romantic and sacred, Grail lore remains an unproclaimed heresy, having been associated with pagan tradition, blasphemy and unholy mysteries. Moreover, the Roman Church has openly condemned the Grail because of its strong female associations—particularly with the ethos of *Courtly Love* (Amour Courtois) in the Middle Ages. The romantic notions of Chivalry and the songs of the Troubadours were despised by Rome because they placed womanhood on a pedestal of veneration, contrary to Catholic doctrine. To a far greater extent, though, the Church's reluctance to accept the Sangréal tradition derives from the Grail Family's specifically defined Messianic lineage.

Vision of the Grail
by William Morris, 1890

In its most popular role, the Holy Grail is identified as the cup used by Jesus at the Last Supper. After the Crucifixion, it was supposedly filled with Jesus's blood by Joseph of Arimathea. This concept first arose in the twelfth century, but its perpetuation was largely due to Alfred, Lord Tennyson's *Holy Grail*, published in 1859.

It was Sir Thomas Malory who first used the words 'Holy Grayle' in his fifteenth-century adaptation of the French *le Saint Graal*. Malory referred to 'the holy vessel', but also wrote of the *Sankgreal* as being 'the blessed blood of Christ', with both definitions appearing in the same story. Apart from such mentions, Malory gave no description of the Grail—only that it appeared at Camelot 'covered in white samite' (fine silk). It was seen by Lancelot in a vision and eventually achieved by Galahad. In Malory's account, the Grail champions are Bors, Perceval, Lancelot and his son Galahad. Who was described as 'a young knight of kings' lineage and of the kindred of Joseph of Arimathea, being the grandson of King Pelles'.

Medieval tradition related that Joseph of Arimathea brought the Holy Grail to Britain, while even earlier European lore told how Mary Magdalene originally brought the Sangréal into Provence. It is a significant fact that, prior to the fifteenth century, the majority of Grail romances came out of continental Europe.

The earliest written account of *le Seynt Graal* comes from the year 717, when a British hermit called Waleran saw a vision of Jesus and the Grail. Waleran's manuscript was referred to by Heliand, a French monk of the Abbey of Fromund, in around 1200; also by John of Glastonbury in the *Cronica sive Antiquitates Glastoniensis Ecclesie* and later by Vincent of Beauvais in his 1604 *Speculum Historiale*. Each of these texts relates how Jesus placed a book in Waleran's hands. It began:

**Sir Galahad—The Quest
by Arthur Hughes, 1870**

Here is the Book of thy Descent.
Here begins the Book of the Sangréal.

In the public domain, the literary Grail did not appear until the 1180s, at which stage it was described simply as a 'graal'; it was neither explained as a holy relic, nor associated with the blood of Jesus. In his le Conte del Graal—roman de Perceval, Chrétien de Troyes states:

A damsel came in with the squires, holding between her two hands a graal ... And as she entered ... there was such a brilliant light that the candles lost their brightness. After her came a damsel holding a dish of silver. The graal which preceded her was of refined gold, and it was set with precious stones of many kinds ... The youth [Perceval] watched them pass, but he did not dare to ask concerning the graal and whom one served with it.

On this first occasion, at the castle of the wounded Fisher King, the graal is not described as a cup, neither is it associated with blood. But later in the story Chrétien explains:

> Do not think that he [the Fisher King] takes from it a pike or a lamprey, or a salmon; the holy man sustains and refreshes his life with a single mass wafer. So sacred a thing is the graal, and he himself is so spiritual, that he needs no more for his sustenance than the Mass wafer which comes with the graal.

If Chrétien's graal was big enough to accommodate a large fish, it was clearly not a cup in this context, but a sizable tureen. Its mystery, however, lies in the fact that it served just a single Mass wafer. Elsewhere in Chrétien's work, there is mention of a hundred boars heads served on graals while, in around 1215, the Abbot of Froidmont, centring upon this explanation, described a graal as a deep dish used by the rich.

Up to that point, there was no link between the Fisher King's graal and the traditional Sangréal. But, in the 1190s, the Burgundian writer, Sire Robert de Boron, changed this with his poem *Joseph d'Arimathie—roman de l'Estoire dou Saint Graal*. He redefined Chrétien's Fisher King (previously contemporary with King Arthur) as Bron (a kinsman by marriage of Joseph of Arimathea) and reclassified the relic as *le Saint Graal*: a 'chalice of holy blood'.

According to de Boron, Joseph obtained the Passover cup from Pilate and collected Jesus's blood when removing him from the cross. He was imprisoned by the Jews, but managed to pass the cup to his brother-in-law Hebron, who travelled to the Vales of Avaron. There he became Bron the Rich Fisher. Bron and his wife Enygeus (Joseph's sister) had twelve sons, eleven of whom married, while the twelfth, Alain, remained celibate. Meanwhile, Joseph joined the family abroad and constructed a table to honor the Graal. At this table there was a particular seat called the Siege Perilous. It represented the seat of Judas Iscariot and was reserved especially for Alain. In later stories it was to be the virgin knight Galahad for whom the *Siege Perilous* was reserved at the Round Table of Camelot.

At about the same time as de Boron's *Joseph d'Arimathie*, another related work appeared by a writer known as Wauchier. It was very much a continuation of Chrétien's account but, in this tale, the Graal acquired a different aspect, performing a physical role:

**The Grail Maiden of Castle Corbenic
by Arthur Rackham, 1867-1939**

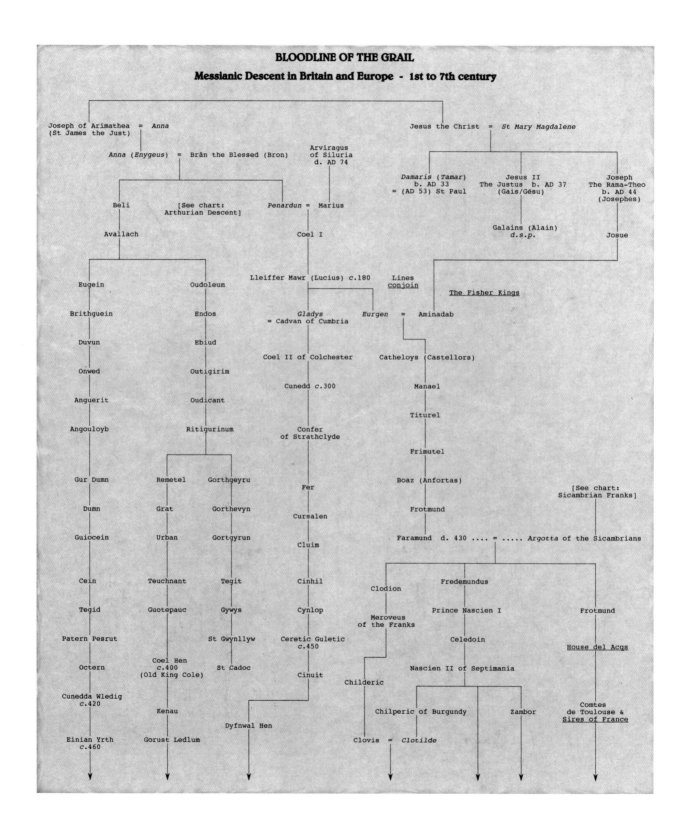

BLOODLINE OF THE GRAIL

Messianic Descent in Britain and Europe - 1st to 7th century

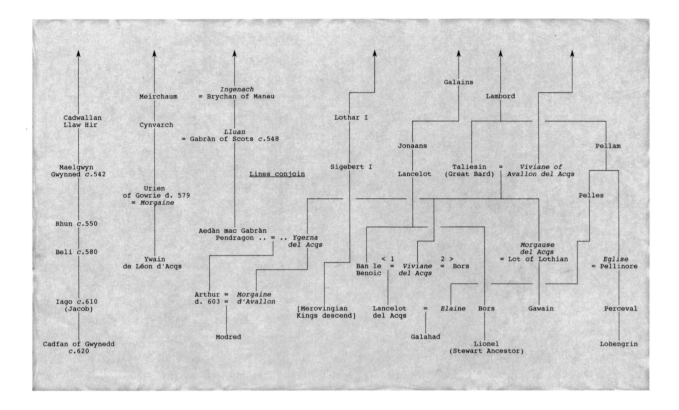

Then Gawain saw entering by the door the rich Graal, which served the knights and swiftly placed bread before each one. It also performed the butler's office—the service of wine, and filled large cups of fine gold, and decked the tables with them. As soon as it had done this, without delay it placed at every table a service of food in a large silver dish. Sir Gawain watched all this, and marvelled much how the Graal served them. He wondered sorely that he beheld no other servant, and hardly dared to eat.

In some respects, Wauchier's version brought the Chrétien and de Boron stories together. King Arthur's knights were featured, but the author also recounted the tradition of Joseph of Arimathea. He explained that Joseph's lineal descendant was Guellans Guenelaus, the deceased father of Perceval and that, in keeping with previous texts, Perceval's mother was a widow.

The story known as the *Perlesvaus*, or the *High History of the Holy Grail*, is a Franco-Belgian work dating from about 1200. It is very specific about the importance of Grail lineage, asserting that the Sangréal is the repository of royal heritage, thereby reiterating the important dynastic principle of Waleran's eighth-century manuscript. In the *Perlesvaus*, the Grail is not defined as a material object, but as a mystic aura that contains various images of Messianic significance. In this work, the *Corpus Christi* of Chrétien's Mass wafer emerges as the continuing presence of the Christ. In respect to the cup symbolism, the *Perlesvaus* states:

> Sir Gawain gazes at the Grail, and it seems to him that there is a chalice within it, although at the same time there is not one.

Medieval France

Gawain, Lancelot and Perceval are all featured in the *Perlesvaus* and the paramount question is 'Whom does the Grail serve?' Only by asking this question can Perceval heal the groin wound of the Fisher King and return the barren Wasteland to fertility. In the *Perlesvaus*, the Fisher King (Priest-King) is called Messios, denoting his Messianic standing. Other accounts refer to the Fisher King Anfortas (effectively the same name as Boaz, thus 'in strength'—thereby identifying the Davidic lineage). Alternatively, the Fisher King is sometimes called Pelles (from Pallas, the ancient *Bistea Neptunis* of the Merovingian ancestry).[1]

Not the least important feature of the *Perlesvaus* is its evident reference to the Knights Templars. On the Island of the Ageless, Perceval comes to a glass hall, to be met by two Masters. One acknowledges his familiarity with Perceval's royal descent. Then, clapping their hands, the Masters summon thirty-three other men who are 'clad in white garments' each bearing 'a red cross in the midst of his breast'. Perceval also carries the red cross of the Templars upon his shield. The tale is basically Arthurian, but it is set in a later period, at a time when the Holy Land is in the hands of the Saracens.

Also from the early 1200s comes a most important Grail romance called *Parzival*, by the Bavarian knight Wolfram von Eschenbach. Once again a Templar association is evident, for the Knights of the Templeise are portrayed as guardians of the Temple of the Grail, located on the Mount of Salvation (Munsalvaesche). Here, the Fisher King officiates at the Grail Mass and is specifically depicted as a Priest-King in the style of Jesus, the Merovingians and the Kings of Scots. Munsalvaesche has long been associated with the mountain fortress of Montségur in the Languedoc region of southern France.

Wolfram stated that Chrétien's Grail story was wrong, giving his own source as being Kyôt le Provenzale, a Templar attaché who wrote of an early Grail manuscript from Arabia. It was by the learned Flegetanis,

> A scholar of nature, descended from Solomon, and born of a family which had long been Israelite until baptism became our shield against the fire of hell.

As with the *Perlesvaus*, Wolfram's *Parzival* lays great stress on the importance of Grail lineage. Wolfram also introduced Perceval's son Lohengrin, the Knight of the Swan. In the Lorraine tradition, Lohengrin was the husband of the Duchess of Brabant (Lower Lorraine). *Parzival* explains that Perceval's father was Gahmuret (as against Guellans in the Wauchier account) and that the Fisher King of Perceval's day was Anfortas, son of Frimutel, son of Titurel. The Fisher King's sister, Herzeylde, was Perceval's mother: the 'widow lady' of tradition. Expounding at length on the various mystical attributes of the Grail, the text names its bearer as the Queen of the Grail Family, Repanse de Schoye, declaring:

**Galahad, Bors and Percival are
fed with the Sanct Grael
by Dante Gabriel Rossetti, 1828-82**

She was clad in the silk of Arabia, and she bore, resting on a green silk cloth, the perfection of earthly paradise, both roots and branches. It was a thing men call the Grail, which surpassed every earthly ideal.

Despite the reference to roots and branches, the Grail is said to be a 'stone of youth and rejuvenation'. It is called *Lapsit Exillis* (sometimes *Lapis Elixis*)—a variant of Lapis Elixir, the alchemical Philosophers' Stone. Wolfram explains:

By the power of that stone the Phoenix burns to ashes, but the ashes speedily restore him to life again. Thus doth the Phoenix moult and change its plumage, after which he is bright and shining as before.

At the Fisher King's sacrament of the Eucharist, the Grail Stone records the names of those called to its service—but it is not possible for everyone to read those names:

Around the end of the stone, an inscription in letters tells the name and lineage of those, be they maids or boys, who are called to make the journey to the Grail. No one needs to erase the inscription, for as soon as it has been read it vanishes.

In very similar terms (the relevance of which is fully explained in *Genesis of the Grail Kings*), the New Testament (Revelation 2:17) states:

> To him that overcometh will I give to eat of the hidden manna [divine food, as in the Eucharist], and will give him a white stone, and in that stone a new name written, which no man knoweth saving he that receiveth it.

Wolfram (who also wrote of Guilhelm de Gellone, King of Septimania) said that the original Flegetanis manuscript was held by the House of Anjou, a noble house that was closely allied with the Templars. He also claimed that Perceval was himself of Angevin blood. In *Parzival*, King Arthur's Court is set in Brittany, while in another work Wolfram located the Grail Castle in the Pyrenees. He also made specific mention of the Countess of Edinburgh (Tenabroc) as being among the Grail Queen's retinue.

The Cistercian *Vulgate Cycle* of around 1220 contains the *Estoire del Graal*, the *Queste del Saint Graal* and the *Livres de Lancelot*, as well as other tales of Arthur and Merlin. In these, the descriptions of the Grail are largely influenced by Chrétien and de Boron, while the earlier 'Graal' spelling is reinstated. In the *Estoire*, the story of Joseph of Arimathea is extended to include his time in Britain, while his heir, Bishop Josephes of Saraz, is identified as the head of the Grail fraternity. Bron (de Boron's Rich Fisher) reappears as the *Estoire's* Fisher King. The Graal, meanwhile, has become the miraculous escuele (dish) of the Paschal Lamb. In both the *Estoire* and the *Queste*, Grail Castle is symbolically called 'le Corbenic' (the Body blessed).[2] The *Queste* identifies Galahad as being 'descended from the high lineage of King David' but, more importantly, it specifically notes his descent in the succession from King Solomon.

The *Livres de Lancelot* (which feature Gawain in the first instance) go on to expand the story of Galahad, detailing him as the son of Lancelot by the daughter of Pelles. She is the Grail princess Elaine le Corbenic and Pelles is the son of the wounded Fisher King, whereas in Malory's later account Pelles is himself the King.

King Arthur certainly received mentions in the early Grail literature, but it was not until the thirteenth-century *Vulgate Cycle* that he was fully established in this regard. However, after the Holy Land fell in 1291, the Grail legends slipped from the public arena. It was not until the fifteenth century that Sir Thomas Malory revived the theme with his tale of *The Sankgreal: The Blessed Blood of Our Lord Jesus Christ*.

**Sir Galahad is introduced
to the Round Table
by Walter Crane, 1845-1915**

THE VESSEL AND THE VINE

In its representation as a stone or jewel the Holy Grail is the repository of spiritual wisdom and cosmological knowledge, signifying 'fulfilment'. As a dish (*escuele*) or platter it carries the Mass wafer of the Eucharist or the Paschal Lamb and symbolizes the ideal of 'service'. Its most popular representation as a chalice containing the blood of Jesus is, however, a purely female image. To the Church, sacred vessels had pagan associations and Grail imagery was thus moved into the convenient wings of mythology.

In the pagan tradition, the Grail was likened to the mystical cauldrons of Celtic folklore: the horns of plenty, which held the secrets of provision and rebirth. The father of the Irish god-kings, Dagda of the Tuatha Dé Danaan, had a cauldron that would only cook for heroes. Likewise, the horn of Caradoc would not boil meat for cowards. The pot of the goddess Ceridwen contained a potion of great knowledge and the Welsh gods, Matholwch and Brân, possessed similar vessels.[3] The similarity of the name Brân to that of Bron the Rich Fisher has often been cited, with the suggestion that perhaps one derived from the other.

The vessel of mystery to the ancient Greeks was the 'Krater'. (In mundane contexts, a crater was a stone bowl for mixing wine.)[4] In philosophical terms, the Krater contained the elements of life and Plato referred to a Krater which contained the light of the sun. Alchemists similarly had their own vessel from which was born Mercurius, the *filius philosophorum* (son of the philosophers), a divine child who symbolized the wisdom of the *vas-uterus*, while the Hermetic vessel itself was called the 'womb of knowledge'. It is this uterine aspect of the enigmatic vessel that is so important in Grail science.

The medieval *Litany of Loretto* went so far as to describe Jesus's mother Mary as the vas *spirituale* (spiritual vessel). In esoteric lore, the womb was identified as the 'vessel of life' and was represented by a cup or chalice. The Holy Grail became likened to a vessel because it was said to carry the perpetual blood of Jesus and, just as the kraters and cauldrons contained their various secrets, so too was the blood of Jesus (the Sangréal) held to be contained within a cup.

In *Parzival*, it is said of the Grail Queen that 'she bore ... the perfection of earthly paradise, both roots and branches'. According to the New Testament Gospel of John 15:5, Jesus said, 'I am the vine, ye are the branches'. Psalm 80:8 reads, 'Thou hast brought a vine out of Egypt: thou hast cast out the heathen, and planted it'.

The lineage of the Merovingian kings was called the Vine and the Bible classifies the descendants of Israel as a Vine; the line of Judah being described at some length as the Lord's cherished plant (Isaiah 5:7). Indeed, some medieval portrayals of Jesus show him in a wine press, accompanied by the statement 'I am the true vine' (John 15:1). Some Grail emblems and watermarks depict a chalice containing clusters of grapes—the fruit and seeds of the vine.[5] From the grape comes wine—and the wine of the Eucharist is the eternal symbol of the Messianic bloodline.

In the original Grail legends there were constant references to the Grail Family, the Grail dynasty and the custodians (or guardians) of the

Grail. Quite apart from legend, the Knights Templars of Jerusalem were the Guardians of the Sangréal. The associated Prieuré Notre Dame de Sion became allied to the Merovingian bloodline in particular and it was the Merovingian descendant Godefroi de Bouillon, Duke of Lower Lorraine, who was installed as Defender of the Holy Sepulchre and King of Jerusalem in 1099.

The importance of the Grail exists in its definition as the 'Sangréal'. From this came San Greal = San Graal = Saint Grayle = Holy Grail. More correctly, it was the Sang Réal—the Blood Royal, carried by the uterine Chalice of Mary Magdalene. It was she who inspired the 'Dompna' (Great Lady) of the Troubadours—who were so callously treated by the Inquisition—and they called her the 'Grail of the World'.

As detailed in medieval literature, the Grail was identified with a family and a dynasty. It was the Desposynic Vine of Judah, perpetuated in the West through the blood of Jesus. This lineage included the Fisher Kings and Lancelot del Acqs. It descended to the Merovingian Kings of France and the Stewart Kings of Scots, incorporating such reputed figures as Guilhelm de Gellone and Godefroi de Bouillon.

In descent from Jesus's brother James (Joseph of Arimathea), the Grail Family founded the House of Camulod (Colchester) and the Princely House of Wales. Notable in these lines were King Lucius, Coel Hen, Empress Helena, Ceredig Gwledig and King Arthur. The divine legacy of the Sangréal was perpetuated in the sovereign and most noble houses of Britain and Europe and it is still extant today.

Having established that the Vine represents the Messianic bloodline, it follows that the Vineyard is the place where that vine will flourish. About two centuries after the Council of Constance in 1417, Archbishop Ussher of Armagh (the seventeenth-century compiler of Bible chronology) commented on the Council records. From these he quoted 'Immediately after the passion of Christ, Joseph of Arimathea ... proceeded to cultivate the Lord's Vineyard, that is to say, England'.[6]

It is apparent from the annals of saintly genealogy and bardic pedigree that the Messianic line of the Sangréal came into Britain from first-century Gaul. In the Lord's Vineyard the line flourished to become the Princely House of Wales and from this early root stemmed the Gwyr-y-Gogledd chiefs of the northern regions.

In parallel, another branch of the Vine conjoined with the great kings of Camulod and Siluria. It was by no chance that Prince Linus, son of Caractacus, became the first Bishop of Rome. Neither was it a fluke of circumstance that Helena (Princess Elaine of Camulod), daughter of Britain's Coel II, married Emperor Constantius.[7] By way of this alliance Rome was attached to the Judaean royal succession which it had tried so hard to suppress by other means. St. Helena's son was Constantine the Great and, having a Celtic Christian mother[8] of a Desposynic line, he was not slow to proclaim himself the true Messiah, even though his father's predecessors had been savage persecutors of the Christian movement.

17

GUARDIANS OF THE GRAIL

THE CRUSADER KNIGHTS

From the onset of the eighth-century Carolingian dynasty in France, the Church implemented a new territorial dominion, fronted by its puppet-kings, across western and central Europe. This became the Holy Roman Empire, which persisted until its termination in 1806. During this period, Imperial history was compiled by Vatican scribes, or by those who operated by Vatican authority. The inevitable result was that accounts of the murdered Merovingian King Dagobert were suppressed to the point of his nonexistence in the chronicles. Not for another thousand years did the true facts of his life become generally known and, only then in the seventeenth century, did it become apparent that Dagobert had a son called Sigebert, whose descendants included the famous crusader, Godefroi de Bouillon, Defender of the Holy Sepulchre.

By the time of the Norman conquest of Britain in 1066, the Merovingians of Gaul had been formally ignored for some 300 years. During their reign, however, they had established a number of governmental customs which prevailed thereafter. One of the Merovingian innovations was a system of regional supervision by chief officers called 'Comtes' (Counts). As deputies of the Kings, the Counts acted as chancellors, judges and military leaders. They were not unlike the Celtic Earls of Britain, although the nature of both titular groups became changed to incorporate land tenure during feudal times.

In the eleventh century, the Counts of Flanders and Boulogne emerged at the very forefront of Flemish society. Given Godefroi de Bouillon's Davidic inheritance through the Merovingians, it was fitting that he (a brother of Count Eustace III of Boulogne) should become the designated King of Jerusalem after the First Crusade. This military venture was sparked in 1095 by the Muslim seizure of Jerusalem, subsequent to which Pope Urban II

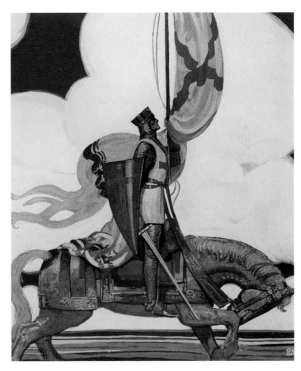

**The 11th-century Crusader ideal
to recover the Holy Land.
From H. G. Wells' The Outline of History**

A crusader keeps vigil at the
Holy Sepulchre in Jerusalem
by Adolf Closs, 1900

raised a formidable army, led by the best knights in Europe.

At that point, Godefroi de Bouillon was Duke of Lower Lorraine. He had succeeded to the title through his famous mother, St. Ida, from whom he gained the castle and lands of Bouillon— estates which he mortgaged to the Bishop of Liège in order to fund his Holy Land campaign. By the time the First Crusade was under way, Godefroi had become its overall commander and, on its eventual success in 1099, he was proclaimed King of Jerusalem.

Of the eight Crusades, which persisted until 1291 in Egypt, Syria and Palestine, only Godefroi's First Crusade was to any avail, but even that was marred by the excesses of irresponsible troops who used their victory as an excuse for wholesale slaughter of Muslims in the streets of Jerusalem. Not only was Jerusalem important to the Jews and Christians, but it had become the third Holy City of Islam, after Mecca and Medina. As such, the city sits at the heart of continuing disputes today.

During this crusading era, various knightly Orders emerged, including the Ordre de Sion (Order of Sion),[1] founded by Godefroi de Bouillon in 1099. Others were the Knights Protectors of the Sacred Sepulchre and the Knights Templars. Godefroi de Bouillon died in 1100, soon after his Jerusalem triumph, to be succeeded as King by his younger brother, Baldwin of Boulogne. After eighteen years, Baldwin was followed, in 1118, by his cousin, Baldwin II du Bourg. According to the orthodox accounts, the Knights Templars were founded in that year as the Poor Knights of Christ and of the Temple of Solomon. They were said to have been established by a group of nine Frenchmen, who took vows of poverty, chastity and obedience, and swore to protect the Holy Land.

The Frankish historian, Guillaume de Tyre, wrote at the height of the Crusades (in around

Knights preparing to embark for the Crusade.
From the Statutes of the Order
of the Holy Ghost at Naples

1180) that the function of the Templars was to safeguard the highways for pilgrims. But, given the enormity of such an obligation, it is inconceivable that nine poor men succeeded without enlisting new recruits until they returned to Europe in 1128. In truth, there was a good deal more to the Order than is conveyed in Guillaume's account. The Knights were in existence for some years before they were said to have been founded by Hugues de Payens, a cousin and vassal of the Comte de Champagne. Their function was certainly not highway patrol and the King's chronicler, Fulk de Chartres, did not portray them in that light at all. They were the King's frontline diplomats in a Muslim environment and, in this capacity, they endeavored to make due amends for the actions of unruly Crusaders against the Sultan's defenseless subjects. The Bishop of Chartres wrote about the Templars as early as 1114, calling them the

Milice du Christi (Soldiers of Christ). At that time, the Knights were already installed at Baldwin's palace, which was located within a mosque on the site of King Solomon's Temple.

When Baldwin moved to the domed citadel on the Tower of David, the Temple quarters were left entirely to the Order of Templars.

The task of ministering to the pilgrims was actually performed by the Hospitallers of St. John of Jerusalem. The separate Knights Templars were a very select and special unit. They had sworn a particular oath of obedience—not to the King or to their leader, but to the Cistercian Abbot, St. Bernard de Clairvaux (died 1153),[2] who was also related to the Count of Champagne. Indeed, it was on land donated by the Count that Bernard built the Cistercian monastery of Clairvaux in 1115. It was St. Bernard who rescued Scotland's failing Celtic Church and rebuilt the Columban monastery on Iona.[3] It was St. Bernard who (from

1128) first translated the sacred geometry of King Solomon's masons, and it was St. Bernard who preached the Second Crusade at Vézelay to King Louis VII and a congregation of 100,000. At Vézelay stood the great Basilica of St. Mary Magdalene and St. Bernard's Oath of the Knights Templars required the 'Obedience of Bethany—the castle of Mary and Martha'.[4]

Deep beneath the Jerusalem Temple site was the great stable of King Solomon, which had remained sealed and untouched since Bible times. The enormous underground shelter was described by a Crusader as 'a stable of such marvellous capacity and extent that it could hold more than 2000 horses'.[5] To open up this capacious repository was the original secret mission of the Knights Templars, for it was known by

St. Bernard to contain the wealth of Old Testament Jerusalem, including the Ark of the Covenant which, in turn, held the greatest of all treasures: the Tables of Testimony.[6]

By 1127, the Templars' search was over. They had retrieved not only the Ark and its contents, but an untold wealth of gold bullion and hidden treasure, all of which had been safely stowed below ground long prior to the Roman demolition and plunder of 70 C.E. It was not until 1956 that confirmatory evidence of the Jerusalem hoard came to light at Manchester University. The deciphering of the Qumrân *Copper Scroll* was completed that year and it revealed that an 'indeterminable treasure', along with a vast stockpile of bullion and valuables, had been buried beneath the Temple.

King Solomon and the treasures of the Temple
by Frans Francken the Younger, 1581-1642

In the light of the Templars' overwhelming success, Hugues de Payens received a summons from St. Bernard to attend a forthcoming Council at Troyes. It was to be chaired by the papal ambassador, the Cardinal Legate of France. Hugues and a company of knights duly left the Holy Land with their auspicious find and St. Bernard announced that the Jerusalem mission had been fulfilled. He wrote,

> The work has been accomplished with our help, and the Knights have been sent on a journey through France and Burgundy, under the protection of the Count of Champagne, where all precautions can be taken against all interference by public or ecclesiastical authority.[7]

The Champagne Court at Troyes was well prepared for the cryptic translation work to follow and, in readiness, the Court had long sponsored an influential school of Kabbalistic studies. The Council of Troyes was held in 1128, at which time St. Bernard became the official Patron and Protector of the Knights Templars. In that year, international status as a Sovereign Order was conferred upon the Templars and their Jerusalem headquarters became the governing office of the capital city. The Church established the Knights as a religious Order and Hugues de Payens was installed as Grand Master.

After the Council of Troyes, the Templars' rise to international prominence was remarkably swift. They became engaged in high-level politics and diplomacy throughout the western world and were advisers to monarchs and parliaments alike. Just eleven years later, in 1139, Pope Innocent II (another Cistercian) granted the Knights international independence from obligation to any authority save himself. Irrespective of kings, cardinals or governments, the Order's only superior was the Pope. Even prior to this, however, they were granted vast territories and substantial property across the map from Britain to Palestine. The *Anglo-Saxon Chronicle* states that when Hugues de Payens visited England's Henry I, 'the King received him with much honor, and gave him rich presents'. The Spanish King, Alfonso of Aragon, passed a third of his kingdom to the Order and the whole of Christendom was at their feet.

NOTRE DAME

When news spread of the Templars' incredible find, the Knights became revered by all and, notwithstanding their Jerusalem wealth, large donations were received from all quarters. No price was too high to secure affiliation and, within a decade of their return, the Templars were probably the most influential body the world has ever known. Nevertheless, despite the prodigious holdings of

Rielvaux Abbey, North Yorkshire.
A ruin of the Cistercian Order,
founded 1131 in the Rye Valley

**Flying buttresses at
Chartres Cathedral**

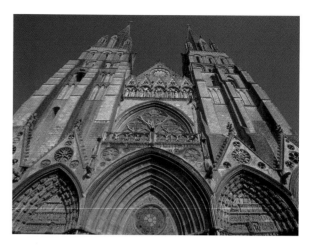

**The soaring face of
Notre Dame de Bayeux**

of the Templars' knowledge of the universal equation. City skylines began to change as the great *Notre Dame* cathedrals, with their majestic Gothic arches, rose from the earth. The architecture was phenomenal—impossible, some said. The pointed ogives reached incredible heights, spanning hitherto insurmountable space, with flying buttresses and thinly ribbed vaulting. Everything pulled upwards and, despite the thousands of tons of richly decorated stone, the overall impression was one of magical weightlessness.

By referencing the Tables of Testimony, the cosmic law and its sacred geometry were applied by the Templar masons to construct the finest holy monuments ever to grace the Christian world. At the northern door of *Notre Dame* de Chartres (the Gate of the Initiates), a relief carving on a small column depicts the Ark of the Covenant undergoing transportation. The inscription reads *Hic amititur Archa cederis*: 'Here, things take their course—you are to work through the Ark'.[8]

The cathedrals were all built at much the same time, even though some took more than a century to complete in their various stages.[9] *Notre Dame* in

the Order, the individual Knights were bound to a vow of poverty. Whatever his station in life, every Templar was obliged to sign over title to his possessions—yet still the sons of nobility flocked to join the Order. Being so well funded, the Templars established the first international banking network, becoming financiers for the Levant and for practically every throne in Europe.

Just as the Order grew to high estate, so too did the Cistercians' fortune rise in parallel and, within twenty-five years of the Council of Troyes, they could boast more than three hundred abbeys. But that was not the end of it, for the people of France then witnessed the most astounding result

Paris was begun in 1163, Chartres in 1194, Reims in 1211 and Amiens in 1221. Others of the same era were at Bayeux, Abbeville, Rouen, Laon, Evreux and Etampes. In accordance with the Hermetic principle 'As above, so below', the combined ground-plan of the *Notre Dame* cathedrals replicates the Virgo constellation.[10] Of all these, the *Notre Dame* at Chartres is said to stand on the most sacred ground.

Notable among the authorities on the history of Chartres is Louis Charpentier, whose research and writings have done much to increase the understanding of Gothic architecture in general. He tells that at Chartres the telluric earth currents are at their highest and the site was recognized for its divine atmosphere even in druidic times. So venerated is the location of Chartres that it is the only cathedral not to have a single king, bishop, cardinal, canon, or anyone interred in the soil of its mound. It was a pagan site, dedicated to the traditional Mother Goddess— a site to which pilgrims travelled long before the time of Jesus. The original altar was built above the Grotte des Druides, which housed a sacred dolmen[11] and was identified with the Womb of the Earth.

One of the greatest mysteries of Gothic architecture is the stained glass used in the cathedral windows. This first appeared in the early twelfth century, but disappeared just as suddenly a hundred years later. Nothing like it had ever been seen before, and nothing like it has been seen since. Not only is the luminosity of Gothic glass greater than any other, but its light-enhancement qualities are far more effective. Unlike the stained glass of other architectural schools, its interior effect is the same whether the light outside is bright or dim. Even in twilight, this glass retains its brilliance way beyond that of any other.

Gothic glass also has the unique power to transform harmful ultraviolet rays into beneficial light, but the secret of its manufacture was never revealed, although it was known to have been a product of Hermetic alchemy. Those employed to perfect the glass were Persian philosophical mathematicians such as Omar Khayyam, whose adepts claimed their method incorporated the *Spiritus Mundi*—the cosmic breath of the universe. Only very recently, as detailed in *Genesis of the Grail Kings*,[12] has the secret manufacturing process become known—a process which has stunning implications way beyond the glass itself.

Grail image of Jesus in a wine-press —

'I am the true vine' (John 15:1)

by John R. Spencer-Stanhope, 1864

Throughout the Gothic cathedrals works of architectural art abound, depicting biblical history and the Gospel stories, in which much attention is given to the life of Jesus. Some of the work currently visible was added after the 1300s, but during the true Gothic era there was not one portrayal of the Crucifixion. On the basis of pre-Gospel writings discovered in Jerusalem, the Templars denied the Crucifixion sequence as described in the New Testament and, for that reason, never depicted the scene. The twelfth-century window in the West front of Chartres includes a medallion of the Crucifixion, but this was transferred from elsewhere at a later date—probably from St. Denis,

St. Anne immaculately conceiving

her daughter Mary

by Jean Bellagambe, 1467-1535

just north of Paris. There are similarly inherited windows at other *Notre Dame* cathedrals.

In addition to the Jerusalem bullion, the Templars also found a wealth of ancient manuscripts in Hebrew and Syriac, providing first-hand accounts that had not been edited by any ecclesiastical authority. In the light of these, it was widely accepted that the Knights possessed an insight which eclipsed orthodox Christianity—an insight which permitted them the certainty that the Church had misinterpreted both the Virgin Birth and the Resurrection.

In times to follow, however, the once revered knowledge of the Templars caused their persecution by the savage Dominican friars of the Inquisition. It was at that point in the history of Christianity that the last vestige of free thinking disappeared. Neither special knowledge nor access to truths counted for anything against the hard new party line of Rome. So too did all traces of the female aspect disappear, with only the Blessed Mary left to represent all womankind. In practice, her semi-divine Virgin-Madonna status was so far removed from any reality that she represented no one. But despite this, a ray of hope has prevailed, for another female light shines from the cathedrals of *Notre Dame*, wherein the veneration of Mary Magdalene remains central to the theme. The beautiful Magdalene window at Chartres has an inscription which reads 'Donated by the Water-carriers'—the Aquarians. Mary was the bearer of the Holy Grail and she will undoubtedly become more prominent as the great new inspiration of the Aquarian Age—the age of renewed intellect, wisdom and the Universal Law of the Ark.

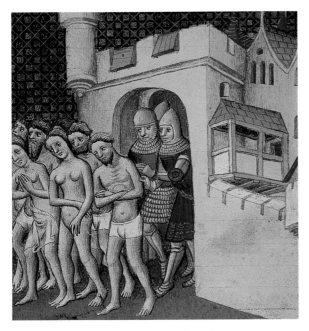

**Inquisitional herding of
French heretics at Carassonne**

SLAUGHTER IN LANGUEDOC

West northwest of Marseilles, on the Golfe du Lion, stretches the old province of Languedoc where, in 1208, the people were admonished by Pope Innocent III for unchristian behavior. In the following year, a papal army of 30,000 soldiers descended upon the region under the command of Simon de Montfort. They were deceitfully adorned with the red cross of the Holy Land Crusaders, but their purpose was very different. They had, in fact, been sent to exterminate the ascetic 'Cathari' sect (the Pure Ones) who, according to the Pope and King Philippe II of France, were heretics. The slaughter went on for thirty-five years, claiming tens of thousands of lives and culminating in the hideous massacre at the seminary of Montségur, where more than 200 hostages were set up on stakes and burned alive in 1244.[13]

In religious terms, the doctrine of the Cathars was essentially Gnostic; they were notably spiritual people, who believed that the spirit was pure but that physical matter was defiled. Although their convictions were unorthodox in comparison with the avaricious pursuits of Rome, the Pope's dread of the Cathars was actually caused by something far more threatening. They were said to be the guardians of a great and sacred treasure associated with a fantastic and ancient knowledge. The Languedoc region was substantially that which had formed the eighth-century Jewish kingdom of Septimania and was steeped in the traditions of Lazarus (Simon Zelotes), whilst the inhabitants regarded Mary Magdalene as the Grail Mother of Christendom.[14]

Like the Templars, the Cathars were expressly tolerant of the Jewish and Muslim cultures. They also upheld the equality of the sexes[15] but, for all that, they were condemned and violently suppressed by the Catholic Inquisition (formally instituted in 1233) and were charged with all manners of blasphemy and sexual deviance. Contrary to the charges, the witnesses brought to give evidence spoke only of the Cathars' Church of Love and of their unyielding devotion to the ministry of Jesus. They believed in God and the Holy Spirit, recited the Lord's Prayer and ran an exemplary society with its own welfare system of charity schools and hospitals. They even had the Bible translated into their own tongue—the *langue d'oc* (hence the regional name).

In practical terms, the Cathars were simply non-conformists, preaching without licence and having no requirement for appointed priests or the richly adorned churches of their Catholic neighbors. St. Bernard had said that 'No sermons are more Christian than theirs and their morals are pure'—yet still the papal armies came, in the outward guise of a holy mission, to eradicate their community from the landscape.

The edict of annihilation referred not only to the mystical Cathars themselves, but to all who supported them—which included most of the people of Languedoc. At that time, although geographically a part of France, the region was actually an independent State. Politically, it was more associated with the northern Spanish frontier, having the Count of Toulouse as its overlord. Classical languages were taught, along with literature, philosophy and mathematics. The area was generally quite wealthy and commercially stable, but all this was to change in 1209 when the papal troops arrived in the foothills of the Pyrenees. In allusion to the Languedoc center at Albi, the savage campaign was called the Albigensian Crusade[16]—at least that is what we are generally told. However, the name has a far more important implication. 'Albi' was, in fact, a variant of the old European word *ylbi* (a female elf) and the Cathars referred to the Messianic Sangréal as the *Albi gens*: the 'Elven bloodline'.

Of all the religious cults that flourished in medieval times, Catharism was the least menacing and the fact that the Cathars were associated with a particular ancient knowledge was no new revelation; Guilhelm de Toulouse de Gellone, King of Septimania, had established his Judaic Academy more than four centuries earlier. However, this fact (along with the notion that the Cathars held an unsurpassed treasure more historically meaningful than the root of Christianity) led Rome to only one conclusion: the Ark, the Tables of Testimony and the Jerusalem manuscripts must be hidden in Languedoc. This, it was felt, was enough to blow the lid off the fundamental concept of the orthodox Roman Church. There was only one solution for a desperate and fanatical regime—and so the word went out: 'Kill them all!'

PERSECUTION OF THE KNIGHTS TEMPLARS

The mock Crusade ended in 1244, but it was to be another sixty-two years before Pope Clement V and King Philippe IV were in a position to harass the Knights Templars in their bid for the arcane treasure. By 1306 the Jerusalem Order was so powerful that Philippe IV of France viewed them with trepidation; he owed a great deal of money to the Knights and was practically bankrupt. He also feared their political and esoteric might, which he knew to be far greater than his own. With papal support, King Philippe persecuted the Templars in France and endeavored to eliminate the Order in other countries. Knights were arrested in England, but north of the Border in Scotland the papal Bulls were ineffective. This was because King Robert the Bruce and the whole Scottish nation had been excommunicated for taking up arms against Philippe's son-in-law, King Edward II of England.[17]

Until 1306, the Knights had always operated without papal interference, but Philippe managed to change this. Following a Vatican edict forbidding him to tax the clergy, the French king arranged for the capture and murder of Pope Boniface VIII. His successor, Benedict XI, also met his end in very mysterious circumstances, to be replaced in 1305 by Philippe's own candidate, Bertrand de Goth, Archbishop of Bordeaux, who duly became Pope Clement V. With a new Pope under his control, Philippe drew up his list of accusations against the Knights Templars. The easiest charge to lay was that of heresy, for it was well known that the Knights did not hold to the established view of the Crucifixion and they would not bear the upright Latin cross. It was also known that the

Templars' diplomatic and business affairs involved them with Jews, Gnostics and Muslims.

On Friday, October 13, 1307, Philippe's henchmen struck and Templars were seized throughout France. Captured Knights were imprisoned, interrogated, tortured and burned. Paid witnesses were called to give evidence against the Order and some truly bizarre statements were obtained. The Templars were accused of a number of assorted practices deemed unsavory, including necromancy, homosexuality, abortion, blasphemy and the black arts. Once they had given their evidence, under whatever circumstances of bribery or duress, the witnesses disappeared without trace. But, despite all this, the King did not achieve his primary objective, for the treasure remained beyond his grasp. His minions had scoured the length and breadth of Champagne and Languedoc but, all the while, a majority of hoard which had not been strategically secreted prior to the event, was hidden away in the Treasury vaults of Paris.

At that time, the Grand Master of the Order was Jacques de Molay. Knowing that Pope Clement V was a pawn of King Philippe, Molay arranged for the Paris hoard to be removed in a fleet of eighteen galleys from La Rochelle. Most of these ships sailed to Scotland[18] (and some to Portugal), but Philippe was quite unaware of this and negotiated with various monarchs to have the Templars generally pursued outside France. Subsequently, Philippe forced Pope Clement to outlaw the Order in 1312 and two years later Jacques de Molay was burned at the stake.

**In Inquisitional imagery,
the Templars were accused of
trampling upon the Crucifix!**

KINGDOM OF THE SCOTS

BANQUO AND LADY MACBETH

From the time of the usurped Merovingians, the most significant reigning dynasty in the Desposynic succession was Scotland's Royal House of Stewart, whose heritage was part Scots and part Breton. In respect to their Scottish ancestry, one of the most important characters was Banquo, the eleventh-century Thane of Lochaber.

From the time when Kenneth MacAlpin united the Picts and Scots in 844, the individual Kings of Scots inherited their crowns by way of Tanist descent in accordance with Pictish custom. Although the Scots maintained their kingship by succession through the male line, the Pictish tradition had been matrilinear. An arrangement was therefore devised by which Pictish princesses married Scots kings, thus maintaining the *status quo*, but the descent was not set in one family line. Kings were selected in advance from sons, nephews and cousins in parallel lines of descent from a common source. In this particular case, the common source was King Kenneth. The great advantage of this selective arrangement was that minors never achieved the crown, as happened to Scotland's detriment in later times after the system was discarded.

Following nearly 200 years of alternating Tanist succession in the Scots descent, a furious dispute arose when the tradition was discarded by King Malcolm II. Instead of correctly affording the kingship to his younger cousin, Boede of Duff (Dubh), he decided that his own immediate offspring should inherit the crown. The problem was that Malcolm had no son, but he did have three daughters, of whom Bethoc, the eldest, was married to Crinan, Archpriest of the Sacred Kindred of St. Columba.[1] Like Columba himself, Crinan was descended from the Tir Conaill royalty of Ireland. Malcolm's second daughter, Donada, was married to Findlaech MacRory, Mormaer of Moray, while Olith (the youngest) was married to Sigurd II, Norse Prince and Jarl (Earl) of the Orkneys. An additional complication was caused because King Malcolm's sister Dunclina was married to Kenneth of Lochaber who, through the structure of Tanistry, had a secondary claim to the crown as a cousin of Boede in descent from Kenneth MacAlpin.

The sons of these various marriages were each and all in the running for kingship when Malcolm II died in 1034 and, among these sons, the heir with the closest right to succession was Dunclina's son Banquo Thane of Lochaber. Yet, in accordance

EARLY KINGS OF SCOTS

Carolingian Contemporaries - 8th to 10th century

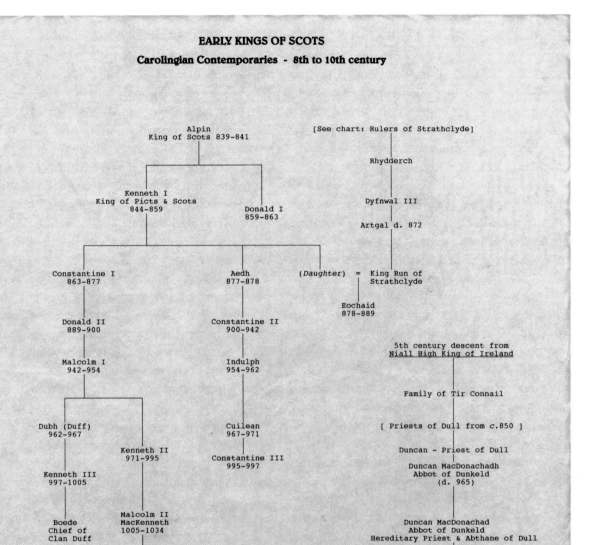

Alpin
King of Scots 839-841

[See chart: Rulers of Strathclyde]

Rhydderch

Kenneth I
King of Picts & Scots
844-859

Donald I
859-863

Dyfnwal III

Artgal d. 872

Constantine I
863-877

Aedh
877-878

(Daughter) = King Run of
Strathclyde

Eochaid
878-889

Donald II
889-900

Constantine II
900-942

5th century descent from
Niall High King of Ireland

Malcolm I
942-954

Indulph
954-962

Family of Tir Connail

[Priests of Dull from c.850]

Dubh (Duff)
962-967

Cuilean
967-971

Duncan - Priest of Dull

Kenneth II
971-995

Duncan MacDonachadh
Abbot of Dunkeld
(d. 965)

Kenneth III
997-1005

Constantine III
995-997

Boede
Chief of
Clan Duff

Malcolm II
MacKenneth
1005-1034

Duncan MacDonachad
Abbot of Dunkeld
Hereditary Priest & Abthane of Dull

Olith = Sigurd II
Jarl of Orkneys

Donada = Finlaech
Mormaer of Moray
d. 1057

Bethoc = Crinan
Abbot of Dunkeld
Thane of the Isles
d. 1045

Thorfinn II
Jarl of Orkneys
d. 1057

- [joint kings] - Macbeth
1040-1057
(Slain by Malcolm, son of Duncan)

Duncan I
1034-1040
(Slain by Macbeth)

with Malcolm's wishes, the son of his eldest daughter Bethoc succeeded as King Duncan I. Being also the son and hereditary heir of Archpriest Crinan (who was slain by Vikings in 1045), Duncan became Scotland's first Priest-King in the style of the earlier Merovingians of Gaul. This concept of the monarch as both the sovereign representative and the religious patriarch remained at the core of Scots culture thereafter.

Prior to Malcolm's death, a revolt against the planned succession had been instigated by Gruoch, senior daughter of the logical Tanist, Boede of Duff, who had no living son. Consequently, King Malcolm slew Boede, thereby leaving Gruoch with a significant sovereign claim by the rule of Tanistry. She, thereupon, mustered fierce opposition against the King, who responded by killing her husband, Gillacomgen of Moray. Gruoch (who was pregnant at the time) fled to the protection of her cousin-in-law Macbeth, the son of Donada and Findlaech. Then, shortly afterwards in 1032, she married her protector and was henceforth Lady Macbeth.

When Malcolm II died in 1034, Gruoch persuaded Macbeth to challenge his cousin Duncan's succession. She was not alone in her resentment of Duncan and a series of riots ensued, led by various Clan chiefs. Not even the influential Banquo of Lochaber, a captain in Duncan's army, could contain the riots. A military council was therefore convened at which Macbeth gained control of the King's troops, managing to subdue the revolt. He thus became more popular than the King himself, further elevating the ambitions of Lady Macbeth, who knew the crown was within her husband's grasp. But what of King Duncan? The truth of his demise in 1040 is still uncertain. History relates that he was killed in an affray at Bothnagowan (Pitgaveny, near Elgin), whereas romantic literature tells that he was murdered in Macbeth's castle. Whatever the case, Macbeth duly became King south and west of the Tay, while his cousin Thorfinn of Caithness (the son of Olith and Sigurd) ruled the rest of Scotland.

For seventeen years Macbeth ran an orderly realm, while his wife hosted a popular court. At the beginning, however, Thane Banquo endeavored to regain the crown for Duncan's son, Malcolm Canmore, Prince of Cumbria. In the course of the dispute, Macbeth slew two of Banquo's sons and arranged for Banquo and his eldest son, Fleance, to be ambushed. Banquo was killed in the fight, but Fleance escaped to the castle of Prince Gruffyd ap Llewelyn of Gwynedd (Northwest Wales). There he became the first husband of Gruffyd's daughter Nesta, with whom he remained for some time. Then, following his eventual death, Nesta married Osbern Fitz Richard de Léon.

Throughout Macbeth's reign, Malcolm persisted with his claim, gaining the support of Thorfinn and, in 1057, their combined armies forced Macbeth's retreat at Lumphanan. Conceding absolute defeat, Lady Gruoch Macbeth committed suicide and, soon afterwards, Macbeth was slain. Thorfinn was also killed in the battle and his widow, Ingibjorg, was obliged to marry Malcolm Canmore. Despite his victory, Malcolm did not accede to the crown immediately, for the Macbeth party was still in control and placed Lady Gruoch's son Lulach (by her first husband Gillacomgen) on the throne. A few months later, however, Lulach was slain at Strathbogie and, in 1058, Malcolm III Canmore was proclaimed King of Scots.[2]

The accounts of Macbeth, Lady Macbeth and Banquo have been treated very sparingly by historians, but their legendary status lives on in William Shakespeare's popular play based on the *Chronicles of Englande, Scotlande, and Irelande* by Raphael Holinshed (died 1580). Shakespeare's *Macbeth* was written nearly six centuries after the historical event. Therefore, when constructing the prophecies of the three weird sisters, the playwright already knew precisely what had followed in history. On consulting their auguries early in the play, the witches inform Macbeth that he will be King. They also tell Banquo that, although he will never reign, he will beget a line of future kings—as indeed he did.

THE HIGH STEWARDS

The name Stewart derives from the 'Steward' distinction, as used in the Middle Ages in Scotland. The early Stewarts became Kings of Scots in 1371 and the royal branch later adopted the French corrupted name 'Stuart' (as did some other branches also). From their earliest days it was known that the Stewarts were descended from Banquo of Lochaber and their descent through this noble Thane (ultimately from King Alpin, the father of Kenneth I) was listed in all relevant genealogies. It was also a fact, however, that the Stewarts emerged from the eleventh-century Seneschals (Stewards) of Dol in Brittany.[3] In sovereign terms, their conjoined legacies were of enormous significance, for their Scots lineage was of the Arimathea succession, while their Breton inheritance was that of Jesus himself, through the Fisher Kings.

The pre-Scotland forebear of the Breton line was Alan, Seneschal of Dol and Dinan, a contemporary of Banquo and Macbeth in the second quarter of the eleventh century. Alan's sons were Alan and Flaald (hereditary Stewards of Dol) and Rhiwallon (Lord of Dol). The senior son, Alan (Alanus Siniscallus), was a commander in the First Crusade and appears in the *Cartulary of St. Florent* as a benefactor of the Abbey. His brother Flaald (Fledaldus) was the Baron of St. Florent and married Aveline, the daughter of Arnulf, Seigneur de Hesdin of Flanders. The third brother, Lord Rhiwallon, became Abbot of St. Florent de Saumur in 1082.

Certain peerage registers cite Aveline as the wife of Flaald's son, Alan, but such entries are incorrect.[4] Alan Fitz Flaald was born with the 'de

Hesdin' title inherited from his mother Aveline (Ava). She is described in the *Cartulary of St. George, Hesdin* as being of an age to consent to her father's gifting of English estates to the Priory in 1094. When Seigneur Arnulf (the brother of Count Enguerrand de Hesdin) joined the Crusade in 1090, Aveline became his deputy and heiress in England. She was styled 'Domina de Norton' (Lady of Norton) and her son was Alan Fitz Flaald de Hesdin, Baron of Oswestry in the reign of King Henry I. Alan married Adeliza, the daughter of Sheriff Warine of Shropshire,[5] thereby inheriting that same office. He also founded Sporle Priory in Norfolk as a cell of St. Saumur.

Alan the Steward's sons were William and Jordan Fitz Alan. William succeeded to the Oswestry and Shropshire titles after the death of his cousin Alan and, from him, the Fitzalan Earls of Arundel descended. Jordan inherited the hereditary Stewardship of Dol and also the lands of Tuxford, Burton and Warsop in England. Alan also had a daughter, Emma, who married Walter, Thane of Lochaber—the son of Fleance (son of

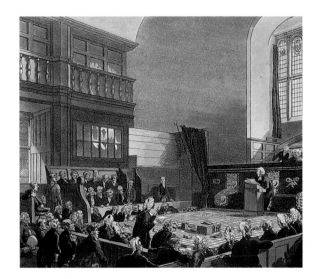

The Court of the Exchequer in London.
From W. H. Pyne's
The Microcosm of London, 1808-11

195

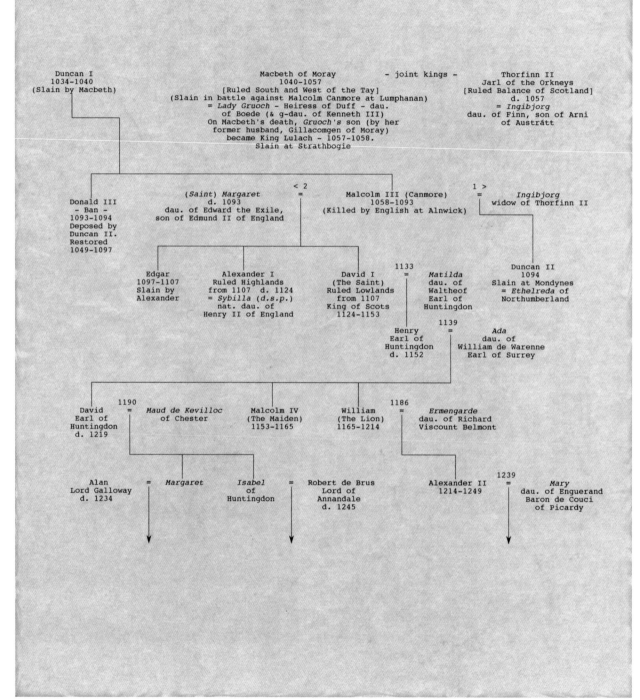

FROM MACBETH TO THE STEWARTS

Scotland: 1040-1371

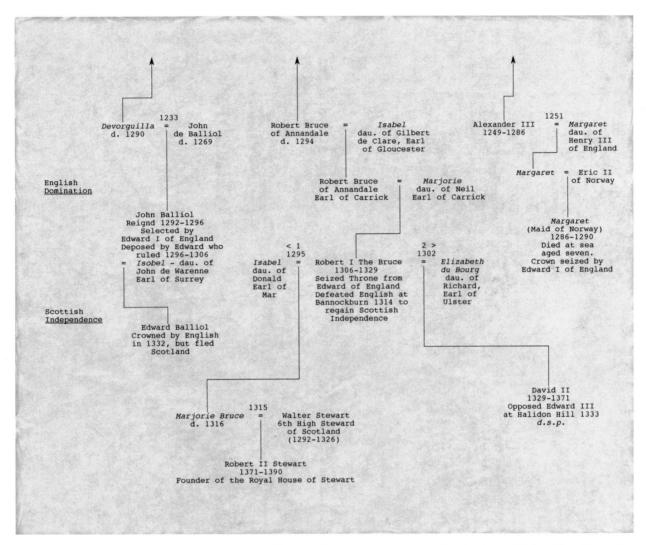

English
Domination

Scottish
Independence

	1233			
Devorguilla	=	John		
d. 1290		de Balliol		
		d. 1269		

Robert Bruce = Isabel
of Annandale dau. of Gilbert
d. 1294 de Clare, Earl
of Gloucester

	1251	
Alexander III	=	Margaret
1249-1286		dau. of
		Henry III
		of England

Margaret = Eric II
of Norway

John Balliol
Reignd 1292-1296
Selected by
Edward I of England
Deposed by Edward who
ruled 1296-1306
= Isobel - dau. of
John de Warenne
Earl of Surrey

Robert Bruce = Marjorie
of Annandale dau. of Neil
Earl of Carrick Earl of Carrick

Margaret
(Maid of Norway)
1286-1290
Died at sea
aged seven.
Crown seized by
Edward I of England

< 1
1295
Isabel =
dau. of
Donald
Earl of
Mar

Robert I The Bruce
1306-1329
Seized Throne from
Edward of England
Defeated English at
Bannockburn 1314 to
regain Scottish
Independence

2 >
1302
= Elizabeth
du Bourg
dau. of
Richard,
Earl of
Ulster

Edward Balliol
Crowned by English
in 1332, but fled
Scotland

David II
1329-1371
Opposed Edward III
at Halidon Hill 1333
d.s.p.

	1315	
Marjorie Bruce	=	Walter Stewart
d. 1316		6th High Steward
		of Scotland
		(1292-1326)

Robert II Stewart
1371-1390
Founder of the Royal House of Stewart

Banquo) and Princess Nesta of Gwynedd. Their son, Alan of Lochaber, married his cousin, Adelina of Oswestry (the daughter of Alan Fitz Flaad) and they were the parents of Walter Fitz Alan (died 1177), who became the first High Steward of Scotland.

Some published charts of Stewart genealogy mistakenly identify Walter the High Steward with his grandfather Walter, Thane of Lochaber. The mistake arose because an alternative form of the name Alan was Flan and this became confused with Fleance, the name of the son of Banquo.[6]

It was actually the latter Walter Fitz Alan who was appointed to the Scots Grand Stewardship of King David I (1124-1153). Walter arrived in Scotland in about 1138 and was granted lands in Renfrewshire and East Lothian by King David I. On becoming the High Steward of Scotland, Walter gained the highest of conferred positions and was also made Chancellor of Treasury Revenues. This latter office gave rise to the *Fesse Chequey* in the armorial bearings of the Stewarts: the 'chequey' represents the chequered (or checked) table that was used for monetary calculation and from this derived the term 'Exchequer', as applied to the State Treasury Department.

During the reign of David's grandson, Malcolm IV, Walter founded the Cluniac Paisley Priory and was appointed Commander of the King's Army. In 1164 the Renfrew coast was invaded by 160 Norse warships of the mighty Somerled, Thane of the Isles. The ships contained more than 6000 warriors bent on conquest but, once ashore, they were defeated by a much smaller force under the command of Walter's Household Knights. In the Library of Corpus Christi College, Cambridge, there is a manuscript by the monk William of Glasgow, which gives an eyewitness account of the 1164 Battle of Renfrew. He states that Somerled was killed early in the fight, following which the invaders were routed with heavy slaughter. The battle is also described in the *Chronicles of Man, of Holyrood* and *of Melrose*.

Of all the Scots kings, young Malcolm IV (known as the 'Maiden') was the weakest, as he proved by giving away the long-prized territories of Cumbria to Henry II of England. He then went to Toulouse at the age of fourteen and spent most of his remaining ten years abroad. It was just as well for Scotland that Walter the Steward was there to manage political, military and financial affairs in the King's stead. Malcolm IV was succeeded by his brother William in 1165; he was a much stronger character, nicknamed the 'Lion'. A while after his accession, William sought to regain Northumberland and Cumberland from Henry II at Alnwick in 1174. By that time, King Henry of England was married to Eleanor of Aquitaine (the former wife of Louis VII of France), but their sons (with Eleanor's approval) sided with William of Scots

in the Cumbrian dispute, standing against their father on the battlefield. In the event, William was defeated and captured, following which he was obliged to sign the Treaty of Falaise, recognizing the English King as Lord Paramount of Scotland. William was thereafter held in custody and, once more, Walter the High Steward took the reins.

Walter Fitz Alan died in 1177 and was succeeded by his son Alan as the Second High Steward. In 1189, Alan joined the Third Crusade with Henry II's son and successor, Richard I *Coeur*

King Richard I of England and the Third Crusade by Henry Justice Ford, 1860-1941

de Lion (the Lionheart). Before leaving for the Holy Land with Alan, King Richard declared the Treaty of Falaise null and void, reaffirming Scotland's right to independence. Alan the Steward died in 1204 and his son Walter became Third High Steward to William's son and heir, Alexander II. This Walter was the first to use the name 'Stewart' and it was he who raised Paisley Priory to the status of an Abbey in 1219. By 1230 he was Justiciar North of the Forth as well as Chancellor.

The succeeding King Alexander III became one of Scotland's most impressive monarchs although, in the early days, his reign was subject to the partial regency of the Fourth High Steward, Walter's son Alexander. At that time the Norse invaders were proving troublesome once more and, in 1263, the fleet of the Norwegian King Haakon arrived at Clydeside. They were defeated at the Battle of Largs by Scots forces under the command of Alexander Stewart, who was rewarded with the Lordship of Galloway.

King Alexander III married Margaret, the daughter of Henry III Plantagenet of England and, in order to keep the peace with the King of Norway, their daughter, Princess Margaret of Scotland, was married to the future King Eric II. Unfortunately, she died in childbirth soon afterwards—two years before the death of her father, who left no surviving sons. This meant that the sole heiress to the Kingdom of Scots was Alexander's granddaughter, the 'Maid of Norway', who was then only three years old. And so the Fifth High Steward, Sir James (Alexander Stewart's son), became Regent in Scotland.

The Scots were then concerned that their nation might come under rule from Norway. The Bishop of Glasgow approached the Maid's uncle, King Edward I of England, for advice in the matter but, in view of Plantagenet aspirations towards control of Scotland, Edward's response was predictable. He suggested that Margaret, Maid of Norway, should be married to his own son Edward Caernarvon and that she should be brought up at the English Plantagenet court. From that moment, Edward I considered his suggestion to be a positive betrothal, but the Scots did not think of it as a binding agreement. Four years later, however, it was decided to bring the young heiress to Scotland in any event.

In September 1290, Margaret, the seven-year-old Queen of Scots, set sail for her sovereign land—only to die suddenly and mysteriously when her ship reached Orkney. In the aftermath of this tragedy Sir James Stewart endeavored to keep the peace, but the emergent Wars of Succession and Independence were destined to plague Scotland for many years.

ROBERT THE BRUCE

The three main contenders for Margaret's inheritance were John Comyn (in descent from King Donald Ban), John Balliol (in descent from Prince David, Earl of Huntingdon) and Robert Bruce, Lord of Annandale (in another descent from Prince David). Bruce was the initial favorite, but Edward I of England proclaimed himself Lord Paramount of Scotland in view of the supposed betrothal of his son. He gained permission from a few Scots nobles to adjudicate and, by political maneuver, took control of the nation's key fortresses. Then, with a specially appointed committee, whom he called 'the wisest in England', Edward made his selection. The Plantagenet council was insistent that the new King of Scots must be prepared to rule under the

**Robert the Bruce defies
King Edward III of England.
From Jean Froissart's Chronicles, c.1350**

King of England. Robert Bruce was the Scots' own choice, but he refused to submit to Edward, stating,

> If I can get the aforesaid kingdom by means of my right and a faithful assize, well and good. But if not, I shall never, in gaining that kingdom for myself, reduce it to thraldom'.

John Balliol, on the other hand, agreed to the requirement and thereupon became the appointed King, swearing the necessary oath:

> I, John, King of Scotland, shall be true and faithful to you, Lord Edward, by the grace of God, King of England, the noble and superior Lord of the Kingdom of Scotland, the which I hold and claim to hold of thee.

Balliol gained the throne in 1292, at which time the High Steward was still Sir James Stewart. Sir James was himself a supporter of Robert Bruce and a stern opponent of King Edward and Balliol. Edward compelled Balliol to provide money and troops for the English army—a move that stirred many to form a martial resistance movement under the Paisley-born knight Sir William Wallace. With the support of James Stewart, Wallace achieved some initial success, whereupon Edward deposed Balliol in 1296 and began to rule Scotland himself. Wallace won a good victory at Stirling in 1297, after which he was proclaimed Warden of Scotland but, in the following year, he was defeated by Edward's longbowmen at Falkirk. In 1305 he was captured and executed by the English, who impaled his head on London Bridge and sent the rest of his body in pieces to cities in Scotland and the North.

From that time, a new leader took up the Scots cause. He was Robert the Bruce, the succeeding heir of Robert Bruce the contender. Irrespective of the presumed Plantagenet interest, the Scots crowned Robert I Bruce in 1306. Then, when Edward II invaded Scotland in 1314, Bruce defeated him at Bannockburn and declared his nation's independence.

THE ROYAL HOUSE OF STEWART

Sir James Stewart died within three years of Bruce's coronation and was succeeded by his son Walter Stewart, the Sixth High Steward. Walter had commanded the left wing of the Scots army at Bannockburn and been knighted by Bruce on the battlefield. Then, in the following year, Walter married King Robert's daughter

Marjorie. Some months later Robert went to Ireland, leaving Walter Stewart as his Regent in Scotland, but Marjorie then died in a riding accident, still within a year of her marriage. At the time of her death she was pregnant, but her unborn son Robert was saved by caesarian operation and, in time, became the Seventh High Steward. By the age of nineteen, Robert was the Regent for Bruce's son, King David II, holding the office until David was of age in 1341.

Soon afterwards, Edward III Plantagenet began the Hundred Years' War with France. David decided to take up the French cause, but was defeated and captured by the English at Nevill's Cross in 1346. He was held in custody for eleven years, during which time Robert the High Steward took charge in Scotland. King David was eventually freed in 1357, but not before he had come to an arrangement with Edward III. Addressing the Scottish Parliament, David announced that, should he die without issue, the crown of Scotland would pass to the King of England, but the response echoed loud and clear: 'So long as one of us can bear arms, we will never permit an Englishman to reign over us'. From that moment, David was disregarded by the Scots and, when he died without an heir in 1371, the people decided to make their own choice for his successor.

There was only one man who could possibly succeed—the man who had been running Scotland for years and whose ancestors had been deputy kings for six generations. He was Robert Stewart, the Seventh High Steward.

On March 26, 1371, the Royal House of Stewart was founded by King Robert II. For the first time since the sixth-century Arthur mac Aedàn of Dalriada, the key Grail successions of Britain and Europe had conjoined in Scots royalty and the Stewarts' ancient legacy of kingship was fulfilled.

King Robert I Bruce of Scots at Bannockburn in 1314.
From Cassell's History of England

19

THE AGE OF CHIVALRY

ARTHURIAN ROMANCE

The romantic legends of King Arthur, which became popular from the Middle Ages, had little to do with the historical Arthur —a Celtic Ard Rí (High King) and warlord, whose Guletic warriors gained a fearsome reputation in the sixth century. Nonetheless, Grail lore had brought Arthur into the public domain and, when England's Noble Order of the Garter was founded by Edward III in 1348, Arthur's cavalrymen were updated to become gallant armored champions of the day. The great 18-foot (c. 5.5 meters) oak Round Table of the Plantagenet era now hangs in Castle Hall, Winchester. It has been carbon-dated to about the reign of Henry III (1216-1272), but its symbolic Arthurian paintwork was a later addition, probably designed in the Tudor reign of King Henry VIII.

We have already considered the historical Arthur in a previous chapter,[1] but it is appropriate now to look at the legendary Arthur who so inspired the Age of Chivalry—the Arthur whose story was born when Geoffrey of Monmouth produced his colorful *Historia Regum Britanniae* in about 1147. Commissioned by the Norman Earl of Gloucester, Geoffrey transposed Arthur mac Aedàn of Dalriada into a West Country environment. He also transformed Gwyr-Llew, Dux of Caruele, into Gorlois, Duke of Cornwall, while inventing Uther Pendragon and introducing various other themes to suit the feudal requirement.

**The Round Table at the
Great Hall, Winchester**

Amid all this, one of Geoffrey's most romantic introductions was Arthur's magic sword, Caliburn, which had been forged on the Isle of Avalon.

In 1155, the Jersey poet Robert Wace composed the *Roman de Brut* (Story of Brutus). This was a poetical version of Geoffrey's *Historia*, based upon a tradition that civilization in Britain was founded in around 1130 B.C.E. by Prince Brutus of Troy.[2] A copy of Wace's poem, which included the very first reference to the Knights of the Round Table, was presented to Eleanor of Aquitaine. In this notable work, Geoffrey's Queen Guanhumara[3] appeared more correctly as Gwynefer (from the Celtic *Gwen-hwyfar*: 'fair spirit') and Arthur's Caliburn was renamed Excalibur.[4]

In about 1190, the Worcestershire priest Layamon compiled an English version of Wace's poem but, prior to this, a more exciting romance emerged from France. Its author was Chrétien (Christian) de Troyes, whose mentor was Marie, Countess of Champagne. Chrétien transformed Arthur's already adventurous tradition into thoroughly inspired legend and gave Gwynefer the more poetic name of Guinevere. His five related tales appeared in about 1175 and it was in his tale of Lancelot, entitled *Le Chevalier de la Charrette*, that Camelot first appeared as the royal court. Chrétien moved in aristocratic circles and such stories of his as *Yvain—le Chevalier au Lion* were based on a number of noble characters from sixth to eleventh-century Léon. The distinctive heraldic arms of the Comtes de Léon d'Acqs incorporated a black lion on a golden shield and they were accordingly known as Knights of the Lion.

It was at this stage that continental European writers began amalgamating Arthurian literature with the lore of the Holy Grail. At the request of Count Philippe d'Alsace, Chrétien commenced his famous tale of Perceval in *Le Conte del Graal* (the Story of the Grail). But Chrétien died during the course of this and the work was concluded by other writers.

Next on the Arthurian scene was the Burgundian poet Robert de Boron. His verses of the 1190s included *Joseph d'Arimathie—Roman l'Estoire dou Saint Graal*. However, unlike Chrétien's story of the *Sangréal*, de Boron's was not contemporary with King Arthur. In essence it was more concerned with the time frame of Joseph of Arimathea.

From about the same era came an anonymous manuscript entitled *Perlesvaus*. This work had Templar origins and declared that Joseph of Arimathea was Perceval's great uncle. Then, in about 1200, emerged the tale of *Parzival*, a detailed and expanded story of the Grail Family by the Bavarian knight Wolfram von Eschenbach.

King Arthur was brought more fully into the picture by a series of five stories from the period 1215-1235, which became known as the *Vulgate Cycle*. Written by Cistercian monks, these works featured Lancelot's son Galahad, whose mother was the Fisher King's daughter, Elaine le Corbenic. Arthur's greatest knight, Perceval, also remained a central character. The *Vulgate Cycle* retained Wace's Excalibur as Arthur's sword and established the theme of his obtaining it from the Lady of the Lake. At this stage, the story of Arthur's drawing a sword from a stone had nothing whatever to do with Excalibur. This stemmed from a quite separate incident in Robert de Boron's *Merlin* and it was not until the nineteenth century that Excalibur and the stone were brought together.

Arthur withdraws Excalibur
from the stone
by Walter Crane, 1845-1915

Throughout this period of Franco-European lore, King Arthur had little prominence in Britain except for brief appearances in such works as the thirteenth-century *Black Book of Carmarthen*. Geoffrey of Monmouth had claimed that the Welsh town of Carmarthen was named after Merlin (as *Caer Myrddin*: 'Seat of Merlin') but, in fact, the name had nothing whatever to do with Merlin; it derived from the Roman name for the settlement, *Castra Maridunum*.

The English poem *Arthour and Merlin* appeared in the latter 1200s and, from Wales in around 1300, came the *Book of Taliesin*, which featured Arthur in the supernatural Otherworld. He also made appearances in the *White Book of Rhydderch* (c. 1325) and the *Red Book of Hergest* (c. 1400). The Welsh *Triads* included some Arthurian references, as did the *Four Branches of the Mabinogi* which, in the nineteenth century, were translated into English by Lady Charlotte Guest under the revised title of *The Mabinogion*.

Not until the fifteenth century—around 800 years after the time of the historical Arthur—did all the legends consolidate into the general format that we know today. This occurred in the collected writings of Sir Thomas Malory of Warwickshire. They were printed in 1485 under the title *Le Morte d'Arthur* (The Death of Arthur). Being one of the first books published in print by William Caxton, Malory's Arthurian cycle was acknowledged as the standard work on the subject, although it has to be said that it was not an original account of anything. The work was commissioned by Margaret Beaufort of Somerset, the mother of the man who, by force of arms in that very year, became King Henry VII, the first of the reigning House of Tudor.

It was also during that same period that Uther Pendragon and Arthur began to appear in newly assembled genealogies and there was an express reason for this. When Henry VII (son of Edmund Tudor of Richmond) usurped the Plantagenet throne of Richard III, his only claim to succession was through his mother, a great-great-granddaughter of Edward III. In order to present his own Tudor heritage in a favorable light, Henry commissioned new genealogies to show an impressive descent from the princely House of Wales. However, in preparing these charts, the genealogists sought to add a spark of intrigue and, for good measure, the names of Uther and Arthur were introduced into a related Cornish line.

Malory's famous tales were a compilation of the most popular traditions from various sources. All the familiar names were brought into play and,

**The rescue of Guinevere by Sir Lancelot
by N. C. Wyeth, 1882-1945**

to appease Henry Tudor, Camelot was located at Winchester in Hampshire. In addition, the old tales were greatly enhanced and many new story lines were conceived. Not the least of these was the love affair between Lancelot and Guinevere. Chivalric principles were central to Malory's portrayal, even though he was himself a criminal of some renown, having been imprisoned for theft, rape, cattle rustling, debt, extortion and the attempted murder of the Duke of Buckingham. At various stages between 1451 and 1470, he was held under lock and key in the cells of Coleshill, Colchester Castle, Ludgate, Newgate and the Tower of London.

Malory settled Arthur firmly into the Middle Ages and his characters forsook their Celtic garb for suits of shining armor. He entitled his inspired work *The Whole Book of King Arthur and His Noble Knights of the Round Table*. In all, there were eight interlaced stories: *The Tale of King Arthur, The Noble Tale of King Arthur and Emperor Lucius, The Noble Tale of Sir Lancelot du Lake, The Tale of Sir Gareth, The Book of Sir Tristram de Lyonesse, The Tale of the Sangréal, The Book of Sir Lancelot and Queen Guinevere* and *The Most Piteous Tale of the Morte Arthur*.

From the days of Thomas Malory, the Arthurian legends became an integral part of British heritage. They achieved a great revival with the birth of nineteenth-century Romanticism—a largely nationalistic movement which appealed to the Victorians' nostalgia for a lost Golden Age. During this era, the Poet Laureate, Alfred, Lord Tennyson, wrote his famous *Idylls of the King* and Arthurian themes were very apparent in the striking paintings of the Pre-Raphaelite Brotherhood.

The Damsel of Sanct Grael
by Dante Gabriel Rossetti, 1828-82

MERRIE ENGLAND

The turbulent medieval times have often been referred to as the age which saw the flowering of 'Merrie England'—a tag that persists despite the severe plagues and hardships of the era. In truth, the description had little to do with the fact that England was 'merry'. The description derives rather more precisely from Mary Jacob (St. Mary the Gypsy), who had come to Western Europe with Mary Magdalene in 44 C.E. Alongside the veneration of the Magdalene, the cult of Mary the Gypsy was widespread in England during the Middle Ages. The name Mary is an English form (based on a Greek variant) of the Egyptian name *Mery*, meaning 'beloved' (Hebrew: *Miriam*). As we have seen, the name had long been associated with the sea (Latin: *mare*) and with water in general—as a result of which, Mary the Gypsy was identified with the goddess Aphrodite, who was said to have been born from the sea foam.

Mary Jacob (the wife of Cleophas, according to John 19:25) was a first-century priestess and is sometimes referred to as Mary the Egyptian. Her Oath of Wedlock was called the 'Merrie' (again from 'beloved')—whence probably derives the English verb 'to marry'. Outside Catholic doctrine, the Holy Spirit was considered to be female and was always associated with water. Often depicted with a fish tail, St. Mary was a traditional merri-maid (mermaid) and was given the attributive name Marina. She is portrayed alongside Mary Magdalene (*la Dompna del Aquae*) in a window at the Church of St.Marie in Paris. As Maid Marian, her cult is incorporated in the Robin Hood legends, while Mary Magdalene's incarnation appears in the Celtic tradition as Morrigan, the Great Queen of Fate. The individual identification of the

The Birth of Venus
by Sandro Botticelli, c.1485

two Marys is often confusing because both are associated with Provence and the sea.

In the early days of Christianity, Emperor Constantine banned the veneration of Mary the Gypsy, but her cult continued and was introduced into England from Spain. Mary Jacob-Cleophas had landed at Ratis (Saintes Maries de la Mer) together with Mary Magdalene and Mary Helena-Salome, as detailed in *The Acts of Magdalene* and the ancient MS *History of England* in the Vatican Archive. Her most significant emblem was the scallop shell, depicted so effectively along with her Aphrodite status in Botticelli's famous painting, *The Birth of Venus*. Even today, the Compostela pilgrims carry the shells of the aphrodisiac fish to the supposed St. James's tomb at Santiago. Mary the Gypsy—sacred harlot and love cultess—was ritually portrayed by the Anglo-Saxons as the May Queen and her dancers, 'Mary's Men', still perform their rites under the corrupted name of 'Morris Men' in English rural festivities. Another reference to Mary's Men is found in the rebellious 'Merrie Men' of the Greenwood legends.

SCOTLAND AND THE GRAIL

Many of the Scottish families so often accredited with Norman descent are actually of Flemish origin.[5] Their ancestors were actively encouraged to emigrate to Scotland during the twelfth and thirteenth-century reigns of David I, Malcolm IV and William the Lion. A policy of purposeful settlement was implemented because the Flemings were very experienced in trade, agriculture and urban development, with their strategic arrival in Scotland being quite unlike the unwanted Norman invasion of England. Such families as Balliol, Bruce, Comyn, Douglas, Fleming, Graham, Hay, Lindsay and many others

all have their heraldic origins in Flanders. In recent years some excellent in-depth research has been conducted in this field by the heraldic historian Beryl Platts.

There were few Normans of note in medieval Scotland, but one Norman family who did achieve great prominence from the eleventh century was that of St. Clair. Henri de St. Clair was a Crusader with Godefroi de Bouillon. More than two centuries later, his descendant (also Henri de St. Clair) was a commander of the Knights Templars at the Battle of Bannockburn. The St. Clairs (who eventually became the Sinclair Earls of Caithness) were of Viking heritage through both the Dukes of Normandy and the Jarls of Orkney. Following the Inquisition of the Templars and their settlement in Scotland, the St. Clairs became Scots Ambassadors to both England and France. Henry de St. Clair (son of Henri the Crusader) was a Privy Councillor and his sister, Richilde, married into the de Chaumont family, who were kin to Hugues de Payens, the original Grand Master of the Templars.

The Templar legacy of the St. Clairs is particularly apparent just south of Edinburgh, near to the original Templar center at Ballantradoch. Here, in the village of Roslin, stands the fifteenth-century Rosslyn Chapel which, at first glance, resembles a miniature Gothic cathedral with its pointed-arch windows and climbing buttresses topped with elaborate pinnacles. Closer inspection reveals, however, that it is actually a strange combination of Nordic, Celtic and Gothic styles.

The St. Clairs received the Barony of Roslin from Malcolm III Canmore in 1057 and, in the following century, they built their castle in the vicinity. Deep beneath this fortress, it is said that the sealed vaults still contain some of the Templar treasure brought from France during the Catholic Inquisition. When the Templar Fleet left the coast of Brittany in 1307, the majority of ships and their valuable cargo went to Scotland by way of Ireland and the Western Isles.[6] Some went to Portugal, however, where the Templars became reincorporated as the Knights of Christ. The famous Portuguese navigator Vasco da Gama, who pioneered the Cape route to India in 1497, was a Knight of Christ, while the earlier Prince Henry the Navigator (1394-1460) was the Order's Grand Master.

In addition to the French evacuees, Scotland also received the Templars who escaped from England, where their headquarters from 1185 had been at Temple, south of Fleet Street in London. Since their fourteenth-century proscription, the site has been occupied by two Inns of Court: the Inner Temple and Middle Temple. Nearby stands the twelfth-century round church of the Templars, while Temple Bar, the Westminster gateway to the City, stood between Fleet Street and The Strand.

From the time that Roslin came into St. Clair possession, prominent family members were buried there, with the exception of Rosabelle, the wife of Baron Henri the Crusader. She was drowned off the coast to leave a haunting memory, as recalled by Sir Walter Scott during the nineteenth century. In his *The Lay of the Last Minstrel*, he wrote,

And each Sinclair was buried there,
With candle, book and knell;
But the sea-caves rung,
And the wild winds sung
The dirge of lovely Rosabelle.

Throughout their early years, the St. Clair Barons of Roslin were of the highest ranking Scots nobility and they were numbered among the closest confederates of the kings. In the thirteenth century, Sir William de St. Clair was Sheriff of Edinburgh, Lothian, Linlithgow and Dumfries, while also appointed Justiciar for Galloway. King

Alexander III additionally selected him as foster father to the Crown Prince of Scotland.

Following the death of Robert the Bruce in 1329, a later Sir William de St. Clair set out with Bruce's heart in a silver casket.[7] Along with Sir James Douglas and two other knights, he was to bury the casket in Jerusalem but, on reaching Andalusia in southern Spain, the party was confronted by the Moorish cavalry. Seeing no way out, the four men charged the invincible foe and were duly slain. The Moors were so impressed with the knights' courage that they returned the casket to Scotland, where Bruce's heart was later buried at Melrose Abbey.

It was a descendant William Sinclair, Earl of Caithness, Grand Admiral and Chancellor of Scotland, who founded Rosslyn Chapel in 1446. The family of St. Clair (having adapted their name to Sinclair in the late 1300s) were by then the eminent guardians of the Kings—the Sangréal (Blood Royal)—in Scotland. Five years earlier, King James II Stewart had also appointed William to the post of Hereditary Patron and Protector of Scottish Masons. These were not speculative freemasons but operative, working stonemasons, proficient in the application of mathematics and architectural geometry. William was thus able to call upon the finest craftsmen and builders in the country. Once the Rosslyn foundations were laid, building work commenced in 1450 and the Chapel was completed in 1486 by William's son Oliver. It was meant to be part of a larger collegiate church, but the rest was never built, although the foundations are still discernible.

In spite of its age, the Chapel is in remarkable condition (though currently undergoing repair) and is still in regular use. The building is 35 feet x 69 feet (c. 10.7 meters x 21 meters), with a roof height of 44 feet (c. 13.4 meters). Many hundreds of stone carvings adorn the walls and ceilings. They tell stories from the Bible and depict numerous

Masonic symbols and examples of Templar iconography. There are swords, compasses, trowels, squares and mauls in abundance, along with various images of King Solomon's Temple. Rosslyn Chapel provides such an unusually stimulating visual and spiritual experience as to commend itself to visitors. The historian and biographer Andrew Sinclair has written at length about the history of Rosslyn and the Sinclairs, imparting a detailed account of the Sinclair fleet's transatlantic voyage in 1398, long before the supposed discovery of America by Christopher Columbus. Indeed, there are various original American corncob carvings at Rosslyn, which confirm the fact.

Apart from the Judaic and esoteric carvings, the Christian message is also evident, with an assortment of related depictions in stone. Also, there are constant traces of Islam and the whole is strangely bound within a pagan framework of winding serpents, dragons and woodland trees. Everywhere, the wild face of the Green Man peers from the stone foliage of the pillars and arches, symbolizing the constant earth forces and the lifecycle. And all of this is enveloped in a vast array of fruits, herbs, leaves, spices, flowers, vines and the emblematic plants of the garden paradise. Inch for inch, Rosslyn is probably the most extravagantly decorated church in the country, although not one crafted image can be construed as being art for art's sake. Every carving has a purpose and each purpose relates to the next while, despite the seeming ambiguity of the scene, an almost magical harmony reigns throughout.

The name St. Clair derives from the Latin, *Sanctus Clarus*, meaning 'Holy Light' and, above all else, Rosslyn is the ultimate Chapel of the Holy Grail, with the mystical quest paramount in its imagery. The Knights Templars were the Guardians of the Grail Family and the family shield of St. Clair bore an engrailed (scalloped) black cross upon silver to denote its bearer as a Knight of the Grail. At Rosslyn and elsewhere in Scotland, wall carvings and tombs of the Grail Knights bear the emblem of a tall-stemmed Chalice with the bowl face-forward. In its bowl, the Rosy Cross (with its *fleur-de-lys* design) signifies that the *vas-uterus* contains the Blood Royal.

JOAN OF ARC

During the 1400s, when Rosslyn Chapel was being built, the Grand Helmsman of the Prieuré Notre Dame de Sion was René d'Anjou. He was the Count of Bar, Provence, Piedmont and Guise; also Duke of Calabria, Anjou and Lorraine. Additionally, he was a titular King of Jerusalem, being a scion of Godefroi de Bouillon's House of Lorraine. In his capacity as Helmsman, René was succeeded by his daughter Yolande, whose own successors in this regard included Botticelli and Leonardo da Vinci. René's other daughter, Margaret, married King Henry VI of England.

Joan of Arc kisses the Sword of Liberation by Dante Gabriel Rossetti, 1863

It is from René d'Anjou that the familiar Cross of Lorraine derives. The cross, with its two horizontal bars, became the lasting symbol of Free France and was the emblem of the French Resistance during World War II. Among René's most prized possessions was a magnificent Egyptian cup of red crystal, which he obtained in Marseilles. It was said to have been used at the wedding of Jesus and Mary Magdalene, bearing the later inscription (translated):

> He who drinks well will see God.
> He who quaffs at a single draught
> will see God and the Magdalene.[8]

René d'Anjou's literary work, entitled *Battles and the Order of Knighthood and the Government of Princes*, exists today in the translation of the Rosslyn-Hay Manuscript in the library of Lord William Sinclair. It is the earliest extant work of Scottish prose and its leather-bound oak cover bears the names 'Jhesus, Maria, Johannes' (Jesus, Mary, John). Similarly, a mason's inscription at Melrose Abbey reads, 'Jhesus, Mari, Sweet Sanct John'.[9]

St. John (Jesus's 'beloved disciple') was greatly venerated by the Grail Knights and Templars. He was the inspiration for the Hospitallers of Saint John of Jerusalem and Britain's later St. John Ambulance Association. It is significant that the New Testament Gospel of John makes no mention of the Virgin Birth, only of Jesus's Davidic descent. More importantly, it gives the New Testament's only account of the historically significant wedding at Cana (John 2:1-11). Interestingly, the Rosslyn manuscript symbolizes St. John by way of a Gnostic serpent and a Grail emblem.

Among René d'Anjou's colleagues was the famous Maid of Orléans, Jeanne d'Arc (Joan of Arc). Born in 1412, Joan was the daughter of a Domrémy farmer in the Duchy of Bar. In the following year Henry V (probably the most power-crazed of all English monarchs) became King of England. He was described by his own nobles as a cold, heartless warmonger, even though historical propaganda has since conferred upon him the mantle of a patriotic hero. At the time of his accession, the Plantagenet war against France had subsided, but Henry decided to revive Edward III's claim to the kingdom of France. This he did on the basis that Edward's mother of a whole century before was the daughter of King Philippe IV.

Henry V, with 2000 men-at-arms and 6000 archers, swept through Normandy and Rouen, defeating the French at Agincourt in 1415. He was subsequently proclaimed Regent of France at the Treaty of Troyes. With the aid of the faithless French Queen Isabau, Henry then married the French King's daughter, Katherine de Valois, and set a course towards overthrowing her brother,

The 1415 Battle of Agincourt.
From a 15th-century French manuscript

the Dauphin, who was married to René d'Anjou's sister Mary. It transpired, however, that Henry V died two years later, as did King Charles VI of France. In England the heir to the throne was Henry's infant son, whose uncles—the Dukes of Bedford and Gloucester—became Overlords of France. The French people were somewhat concerned about their future prospects, but all was not lost for along came the inspired Joan of Arc. In 1429 she appeared at the fortress of Vaucouleurs, near Domrémy, announcing that she had been commanded by the saints to besiege the English at Orléans.

At the age of seventeen, Joan departed for the Royal Court at Chinon, along with the Dauphin's brother-in-law, René d'Anjou. Once at Chinon on the Loire, she proclaimed her divine mission to save France from the invaders. At first the Court resisted Joan's military ambitions, but she gained the support of Yolande d'Aragon, who was the Dauphin's mother-in-law and the mother of René d'Anjou. Joan was then entrusted with the command of more than 7000 men, including the prestigious Scots Royal Guard of the *Gendarmes Ecossais* and the most prominent captains of the day. With René d'Anjou at her side, Joan's troops destroyed the blockade at Orléans and overthrew the English garrison. Within a few weeks the Loire Valley was again in French hands and, on July 17, 1429, Charles the Dauphin was crowned at Reims Cathedral by Archbishop Regnault of Chartres.

Less than a year after her success, the Maid of Orléans was captured while besieging Paris and the Duke of Bedford arranged for her trial by Pierre Cauchon, Bishop of Beauvais, who condemned her to life imprisonment on bread and water. When Joan refused to submit to rape by her captors, the Bishop pronounced her an ungrateful sorceress and, without further trial, she was burned alive in the Old Market Square at Rouen on May 30, 1431.

**Joan of Arc in prison
by Howard Pyle, 1904**

When the Dauphin was crowned at Reims, the brave shepherdess of Lorraine had stood alongside the new King with her now famous banner, which bore the names 'Jhesus-Maria': the same as on the sacred stone at the Glastonbury Chapel ('Jesus-Maria');[10] as repeated (along with St. John) in the Rosslyn-Hay manuscript ('Jhesus-Maria') and as etched at Melrose Abbey ('Jhesus-Mari')—the names which at all times relate to the marriage of Jesus and Mary Magdalene, and to the perpetual Bloodline of the Holy Grail.

HERESY AND INQUISITION

THE HAMMER OF WITCHES

Following the persecution of the Knights Templars and their allies, the Holy Office of the Catholic Inquisition continued its work mainly in France and Italy. The Pope's appointed Inquisitors were essentially Dominican Black Friars and Franciscan Grey Friars. Their power was considerable and they gained a terrible reputation for their cruelty. Torture had been granted papal sanction in 1252 and the trials were all held in secret. Victims who confessed to heresy were imprisoned and burned, whilst those who made no such confession were given exactly the same punishment for their disobedience.

By the fifteenth century, the Inquisition had lost some of its momentum, but new impetus was gained in Spain from 1480, when the wrath of the Spanish Inquisition was largely directed against Jews and Muslims. The Grand Inquisitor was the

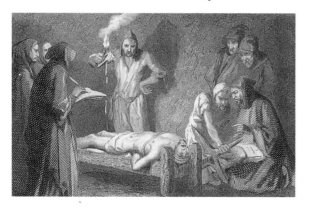

Torture of the Inquisition
by Tony Johannot, 1803-52

brutal Dominican, Tomâs de Torquemada, senior confessor to Ferdinand II and Queen Isabella. A few years after its implementation, however, the Spanish Inquisition set its sights towards another apostate cult. The resultant oppression was to last for more than two centuries—not only in Spain, but throughout Christian Europe. The unsuspecting prey were described as 'the most diabolical heretics who ever conspired to overthrow the Roman Church'.

In 1484, two Dominicans, Heinrich Kramer and James Sprenger, published a book called the *Malleus Maleficarum* (the 'Hammer of Witches'). This evil but imaginative work gave full details of what was perceived to be the hideous new threat posed by practitioners of satanic magic. The book was so persuasive that, two years later, Pope Innocent VIII issued a Bull to authorize the suppression of this blasphemous sect.[1] Up to that point, the cult known as witchcraft had not really constituted a threat to anyone, resting mainly in the continuation of pagan ritual and fertility rites by the peasant classes. In real terms, it was little more than the vestige of a primeval belief in the divine power of natural forces, focused above all on Pan, the mischievous Arcadian god of the shepherds. Pan was traditionally portrayed with the legs, ears and horns of a goat, but the creative Dominicans had other ideas about the pipe-playing Horned One. They blackened his image so that he was seen to correspond to the Devil himself and the friars invoked a passage from the ordinances of Exodus 22:18-19, which stated,

The English word 'witch' derives from an ancient variant of 'willow'—the tree of the Triple Moon Goddess (maiden, woman and hag). Willow worshippers were said to possess supernatural powers of divination (as graphically portrayed by the three weird sisters—the triple hecate of William Shakespeare's *Macbeth*)—and this enabled the Church to include all manner of magicians and fortune-telling gypsies within its loose classification of 'witchcraft'. Indeed, the revised definition was so all-embracing that just about anybody who did not conform precisely to the orthodox dogma was under suspicion as a practitioner of the black arts.

Although some generally anti-establishment characters were caught in the ever widening net as a method of circumventing courtroom trial, the organized witch hunts were, for the most part, directed against the defenseless rural classes. The unfortunate victims were either strangled, drowned, or burned alive, having been accused of venerating the Devil at nocturnal orgies and of consorting with evil spirits. Meanwhile, those of the privileged class who possessed true esoteric skills and Hermetic knowledge were obliged to conduct their business in the secrecy of their lodges and underground clubs.

Saint Dominic, founder of the Black Friars
by Claudio Coello, 1630-93

THE PROTESTANT REVOLT

During the early years of this persecution, the Dominican monk, Johann Tetzel, implemented a lucrative scheme to replenish the Vatican coffers. The scheme concerned the forgiveness of sins, which had hitherto been expiated by means of penances such as fasting, repetition of the rosary and other acts of repentance. Tetzel's concept replaced these traditional penalties with Indulgences—formal declarations of

Thou shalt not suffer a witch to live. Whosoever lieth with a beast shall surely be put to death.

Then, by means of a blatant misapplication of the Bible text, they condemned the Pan cultists firstly as witches and, secondly, as people who performed hideous revels with a familiar animal. Since the Inquisitors were all men, it was determined that witchcraft must be a form of depravity linked to the insatiable wantonness of women!

The sale of Indulgences supervised by the Pope
by Hans Holbein, 1497-1543

guaranteed absolution, which were available for cash. Approved by papal decree, the sale of Indulgences soon became a source of considerable revenue for the Church.

For centuries, the orthodox clergy and its associated monastic Orders had suffered a series of outrageous measures imposed by an avaricious hierarchy that was becoming ever more corrupt. Through it all, they had upheld successive Vatican dictates with as much loyalty as they could muster, but the trading of Christian salvation for money was more than some could tolerate. The practice was, therefore, openly challenged. In October 1517, an Augustinian monk and professor of theology at the University of Wittenberg, Germany, nailed his written protest to the door of his local church—an act of formal objection that was destined to split the Western Church permanently in two. On receiving a papal reprimand, he publicly set fire to it and was excommunicated for his pains. His name was Martin Luther and his fellow protesters became known as Protestants.

Luther's attempt to reform a particular Church practice actually gave rise to a much larger scale Reformation movement and the establishment of an alternative Christian society outside Vatican control. In England, the most significant consequence of the ensuing Reformation was the

formal rejection of the Pope's authority and his replacement as Head of the English Church by the Tudor King Henry VIII. This was, in due course, followed by the establishment of the independent Church of England under Queen Elizabeth I, who was excommunicated by Rome in 1570. Scotland's formal secession from a somewhat limited vestige of papal control occurred in 1560 under the influence of the Protestant reformer John Knox.

It was by no chance that Martin Luther's protest gained support in some very influential circles, for Rome had many enemies in high places. Not the least of these enemies were the Knights Templars and the underground Hermetic societies, whose esoteric crafts had been condemned by the Catholic Inquisition. The truth was not so much that Luther gained the support of others, but that he was the willing instrument of an already active movement which endeavored to dismantle the rigid international domination of the Pope.

The Protestant split with Rome facilitated an environment of democratic freethinking, which culminated in the achievements of Britain's Royal Society and fuelled the cultural and intellectual ideals of the Renaissance. Indeed, the High Renaissance movement of 1500-1520 set the perfect scene for Luther's stand against the politically motivated bishops. This was the age of the individual and of human dignity; it was the age when Leonardo da Vinci, Raphael and Michelangelo developed the harmony of classical art to its highest form; it was the age in which the excitement of pagan-orientated scholarship re-emerged in a burst of color to cross new frontiers of science, architecture and design. Above all else, the Reformation countered all aspirations to recreate the supreme lordship of Imperial Rome.

Ever since the Catholic Church had ousted the Merovingian kings in the eighth century, there had been a calculated move to reflect earlier glories through the contrived Holy Roman Empire. But the Reformation undermined all of this as the nations of Europe polarized and divided. Germany, for instance, separated into a predominantly Protestant north and a Roman Catholic south. As a result, the Spanish Inquisition against Jews and Muslims was extended to include Protestants as well. Initially, they were hounded mainly in the Low Countries, but then, in 1542, an official Roman Inquisition against all Protestants was established by Pope Paul III. Not surprisingly, the Protestants took up arms.

The powerful Catholic Habsburgs, who governed Spain and the Empire, took the brunt of the Protestant retaliation. They suffered a devastating blow when King Philip II's Spanish Armada was scattered to the winds in 1588. They were additionally plagued by the lengthy Protestant Revolt in the Netherlands from 1568, and by the Thirty Years' War in Germany from 1618—a conflict that began when the Bohemian Protestants rebelled against Habsburg rule from Austria. They offered their crown instead to the German Prince Friedrich V, Elector Palatine of the Rhine. He was the nephew of the French Huguenot leader, Henri de la Tour d'Auvergne, Duc de Bouillon. On his acceptance of the Bohemian

honor, however, the wrath of the Pope and the Holy Roman Emperor descended and the lengthy war was begun. During the strife, Bohemia's cause was joined by Sweden, along with Protestant France and Germany. In time, the Imperial territories were severely depleted, to the extent that the Emperor retained purely nominal control in the Germanic states.

In 1562, the French Protestants (Huguenots) rose against their own Catholic monarchy and the ensuing civil struggles (which lasted until 1598) became known as the 'Wars of Religion'. The House of Valois was then in power, but the contemporary Regent of France was the Florentine Catherine de Medici. She was the

**The betrothal of Mary and Joseph
by Raphael, 1483-1520**

Defeat of the Spanish Armada.
16th-century English School at the National Maritime Museum

niece of Pope Clement VII and was largely responsible for the notorious St. Bartholomew's Day Massacre of August24, 1572. On that ill-fated day more than 3000 Huguenots were slaughtered in Paris, while another 12,000 were killed elsewhere in France. This clearly delighted Pope Gregory XIII, who sent a personal note of congratulation to the French court!

From the early days of the Frankish kings, the papal administrators had managed to displace any powerful institution that threatened the evolving Holy Roman Empire. But, quite suddenly, it had been confronted by an unforeseen opponent—a revised and generally more acceptable image of itself—a parallel, independent Christian Church. Moreover, this opposition movement was upheld by the same victims of persecution and proclaimed heresy that the Vatican had thought suppressed. In the newly enlightened Age of

Reason, the Protestants emerged under the unified banner of the Red (Rosy) Cross—an emblem incorporated in Martin Luther's own personal seal.

The 'Rosicrucians' (as they were styled) preached liberty, fraternity and equality. They were the constant challengers of tyrannical oppression and, in time, were destined to be instrumental in both the American and French Revolutions. Following the Reformation, the Rosicrucian Order was largely responsible for the establishment of a new spiritually aware environment. People discovered that the Apostolic history of the Roman bishops was an outright fraud and that the Church had deliberately sabotaged the story of Jesus. It also became apparent that the Rosicrucians (like the Cathars and Templars before them) had access to an ancient knowledge which held more substance than anything promulgated by Rome.

Against the weight of this onslaught, Rome's only defense was to continue with its well-tried declarations of heresy. Threats of violence were issued against anyone who opposed the Catholic doctrine. In fact, a new charge had to be found— a charge that was not so lightweight as that of heresy, which had sufficed in the past. The opposers of Catholicism, in whatever form, were therefore specifically defined as 'devil worshippers' and the Hammer of Witches Inquisition was implemented against an imagined satanic conspiracy fronted by sorcerers. The problem was that nobody really knew who these presumed sorcerers were—and so a series of ludicrously tragic trials and tests was devised to root them out. In the midst of all of this, the harsh Puritan sect became politically allied to the Roman strategy, implementing their own witch hunts in England and America. Over a period of some 250 years, more than a million innocent men, women and children were murdered by the delegated authority of the Witch-finders.

ORDER OF THE ROSY CROSS

In 1614 and 1615, two tracts known as the 'Rosicrucian Manifestos' emerged from Germany. They were the *Fama Fraternitatis* and the *Confessio Fraternitatis*. These were followed in 1616 by an associated romance called *The Chemical Wedding*, written by the Lutheran pastor Johann Valentin Andreae. The earlier Manifestos were by related authors, if not also by Andreae, who was a senior official of the Prieuré Notre Dame de Sion. The publications announced a new age of enlightenment and Hermetic liberation in which certain universal secrets would be unlocked and made known. In view of the advent of the Stuarts' scientific Royal Society a few decades later in Britain, the prophecies were correct enough but, at the time, they were veiled in allegory. The writings centerd on the travels and learning of a mysterious character named Christian Rosenkreutz, a Brother of the Rosy Cross. His name was plainly designed to have Rosicrucian significance and he was depicted wearing the apparel of the Templars.

The action of *The Chemical Wedding* takes place in the magical Castle of the Bride and Bridegroom—a palace filled with lion effigies, where the courtiers are students of Plato. In a setting worthy of any Grail romance, the Virgin Lamplighter arranges for all present to be weighed on the scales, while a clock tells the motions of the heavens and the Golden Fleece is presented to the guests. Music from strings and trumpets is played throughout and all is cloaked in an atmosphere of chivalry, with knights in Holy Orders presiding. Beneath the castle stands a mysterious sepulchre bearing strange inscriptions, while outside in the harbor lie twelve ships of the Golden Stone flying their individual flags of the Zodiac. Amid this curious reception, a fantasy play is conducted to tell the compelling story of an unnamed princess who, cast ashore in a wooden chest, marries a prince of similarly obscure background and thereby causes a usurped royal heritage to be restored.

When combined with the two earlier publications, *The Chemical Wedding's* Grail significance was blatantly obvious. The Church, therefore, wasted no time in bringing the full weight of its condemnation against the Manifestos. The setting was mythical, but to illustrate the scene the Rosicrucians only ever used one actual castle in their depictions: the Castle of Heidelberg, the abode of the Palatine Lion—the home of Prince

Friedrich of the Rhine and his wife, Princess Elizabeth Stuart, the daughter of King James VI of Scots (James I of England).

Notwithstanding the Rosicrucian awakening of the Reformation, the Brotherhood of the Order of the Rosy Cross had a very ancient history, dating back to the Egyptian Mystery School of Pharaoh Tuthmosis III (c.1468-1436 B.C.E.). The old teachings were furthered by Pythagoras and Plato, to later find their way into Judaea through the ascetic Egyptian Therapeutate, which presided at Qumrân in the days before Jesus. Allied to the Therapeutate were the Samaritan Magi of West Manasseh, at whose head was the Gnostic leader Simon (Magus) Zelotes, a lifelong confederate of Mary Magdalene. The Samaritan Magi, whose representatives were apparent at the Nativity, were founded in 44 B.C.E. by Menahem, a Diaspora Essene and the grandfather of Mary Magdalene. Menahem's descent was from the priestly Hasmonaeans—the family of Judas Maccabaeus, who is so revered in the Arthurian Grail story of Gawain.

The 'beloved disciple', John Mark (sponsor of the Gospel of John and also known as Bartholomew), was a specialist in curative healing and remedial medicine, attached to the Egyptian Therapeutate (cognate in name with the English adjective 'therapeutic'). It was because of this that John became the revered saint of the Knights Hospitallers of Jerusalem. John Mark was the disciple to whom Jesus entrusted the care of his mother at the Crucifixion: 'And from that hour the disciple took her unto his own' (John 19:27). Some Bibles—including the King James Authorized Version—erroneously add an extra word (generally in *italics*): '... unto his own *home*'. But the word *home* was not applicable to the original Gospel text. John was, in fact, appointed as Mary's 'paranymphos' (personal attendant) and those defined as 'his own', unto whom he took Mary, were the nurses of the Therapeutate.

The symbol of the Therapeutate healers was a serpent—the same as is shown (along with the Rosy Cross Grail emblem) to denote St. John in the Rosslyn-Hay Manuscript of King René d'Anjou. The Gnostic Serpent of Wisdom is used as part of the caduceus[2] insignia of many international medical associations today. It was because of John's particular closeness to Jesus's family that he recognized the true significance of the sacred wedding feast at Cana. The kingly dynasty of Jesus was of great merit, but so too was the Hasmonaean and royal heritage of Mary Magdalene. She was the original *Notre Dame des Croix*, the bearer of the Messianic vase, the Lady of the Light—and it is in her Chalice that the Rosy Cross of the Sangréal is always found.

Among the notable Rosicrucian Grand Masters was the Italian poet and philosopher Dante Alighieri, author of *The Divine Comedy* in around 1307.[3] One of Dante's most avid students was Christopher Columbus who, in addition to his patronage by the Spanish court, was sponsored by Leonardo da Vinci, a member of René d'Anjou's Order of the Crescent (a revival of an earlier crusading Order established by Louis IX). Another prominent Grand Master was Dr. John Dee, the astrologer, mathematician, Secret Service operative and personal adviser to Queen Elizabeth I. Also, the lawyer and philosophical writer Sir Francis Bacon, Viscount St. Albans, was Grand Master in the early 1600s. Under King James VI (I) Stuart, Bacon became Britain's Attorney General and Lord Chancellor. Because of the continuing Inquisition, he was greatly troubled by the prospect of large-scale Catholic settlement in America, as a result of which he became particularly involved with Britain's own transatlantic colonization, including the famous *Mayflower* voyage of 1620. Among Bacon's Rosicrucian colleagues was the noted Oxford physician and theological philosopher Robert Fludd, who assisted with the English translation of the King James Authorized Version of the Bible.

In Britain's seventeenth-century Stuart era, the Rosicrucians were inextricably linked with the scientific Royal Society and such academics as Robert Boyle and Sir Christopher Wren were prominent within the Order of the Rosy Cross. The aims and ambitions of the Order, along with the eminent scholars Sir Isaac Newton, Robert Hooke, Edmund Halley and Samuel Pepys, were straightforward: to advance the study and application of ancient science, numerology and cosmic law. Rosicrucians also undertook to encourage the ideals of the Egyptian Therapeutate by promoting international medical aid for the poor. It is not in the least coincidental that the most influential agency in the field of emergency relief throughout the world (as established by the Geneva Convention of 1864) is identified by its familiar Red Cross.

THE FORGOTTEN MONARCHY OF SCOTLAND

At this stage in the 1996 first edition of *Bloodline of the Holy Grail* we continued the story of Scotland's Royal House of Stewart, citing it as Britain's most significant reigning dynasty in the Desposynic succession. In the course of this study, an overview of Scotland's national heritage was given, highlighting such notable characters as Mary, Queen of Scots, King James VII and Bonnie Prince Charlie, from whom the present heir to the Royal House descends. We saw how it was that, from medieval times, Scotland was under constant threat from the Monarchs and Parliaments of England, who sought to gain control north of the Border—an enterprise which culminated in the 1707 Treaty of Union, which has been challenged by many Scots because it contravenes the Written Constitution of Scotland: the 1320 *Declaration of Arbroath*.

Now, from July 1, 1999, Scotland has moved into an exciting new era, with the benefit of her own Parliament, devolved from Westminster. This is a far cry from the separate Scottish Parliament which prevailed until 293 years ago, but it is a significant step on the road towards governmental autonomy and, perhaps, a fully regained independence in time.

A key feature of our previous overview of Scotland was the fact that, from the time of the 1688 deposition of the Royal House of Stewart (Stuart) by the Anglican Church and the Whig Parliament, the family line of de jure princes has continued down to date, with the present Head of the House being HRH Prince Michael Stewart of Albany, President of the European Council of Princes.

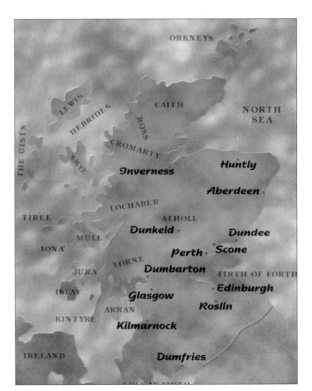

Kingdom of the Scots

It was announced in earlier editions of *Bloodline of the Holy Grail* that the Scottish content of those editions would be superseded by Prince Michael's own compelling book, *The Forgotten Monarchy of Scotland*, which would cover the related subject matter in far greater detail. In view of the fact that this publication is currently available, there is little point in duplicating aspects of the content, for it is not now within the scope of *Bloodline of the Holy Grail* to do justice to one of the most enthralling and astonishing family histories ever written. Not only does Prince Michael's work delve into an amazing web of political conspiracy and intrigue, but it provides the best of all published accounts concerning the Knights Templars and the rise of western Freemasonry. This work is thoroughly recommended reading.

PRECEPT OF THE HOLY GRAIL

These days it is generally understood that establishment history is largely based on recorded propaganda. It was originally compiled to suit the political needs of the era when written rather than necessarily being an accurate record of events. In short, it is generally a slanted version of the truth. For example, the English historical version of the 1415 Battle of Agincourt understandably differs from that of the French viewpoint. Similarly, the Christian perception of the Crusades is not necessarily shared by the Muslims. There are at least two sides to most stories.

Beneath the streets of Rome, the catacombs of early times hold the remains of more than six million Christians. Laid in a single row the passages would extend for 550 miles (880 kilometers). Ironically, the later fanaticism of the Inquisitions accounted for more than a million additional lives because the victims were supposedly 'not'

Christian! Through the centuries, millions of Jews have been persecuted and killed as a result of anti-Semitism initiated by members of the Christian Church. This was managed mostly under cover of the accusation of deicide (with the Jews being blamed for the execution of Jesus). It ran completely out of control during the holocaust of the early 1940s, but anti-Semitism still lingers. Tens of millions of Soviet Russian lives were lost during Stalin's brutal dictatorship, an autocratic totalitarianism that despised religion in any form. Vast numbers such as these are beyond the bounds of practical imagination, but their memory cannot be confined to savage regimes of the past. Worldwide religious feuds continue just as in the days of old and the 'ethnic cleansing' of the Inquisition is still very apparent today.

In theory, Communism was introduced to fulfill a socialist ambition, but the dream soon died as the giant machine rose to power by military oppression. Capitalism, on the other hand, is equally ruthless because it venerates balance-sheets above the welfare of people; as a result, millions are condemned to starvation in the poorer regions, while vast food mountains stockpile elsewhere. Even in the United States, where the Constitution promotes the ideal of liberty and equality, we see an ever widening gap between the privileged and subordinate groups. Rich communities are now barricading themselves within walled environments, while the welfare systems of the West are crumbling into bankruptcy.

History has proved many times over that absolute rule by monarchs or dictators is a road to social disparity. Yet the democratic alternative of elected government has often proved similarly inequitable. Even elected Parliaments can become egotistic and dictatorial in a world where those entrusted to serve may regard themselves, instead, as the masters.

Bloodline of the Holy Grail
by Sir Peter Robson

Additionally, in countries such as Britain, with its multi-party political structure, the people are regularly faced with the rule of ministers empowered by a minority vote. In such circumstances, who is there to champion the rights of individuals? Trade unions, some might say—but, quite apart from being politically biased in themselves, such organizations are still subject to governmental control. Although they might have a weight of membership, they have no final authority to equal that of Parliament. As far as the judicial system is concerned, its purpose is to uphold legal justice, not moral justice. The people of Britain may cite the Queen as their national guardian, but Britain has a Parliamentary Monarchy and, by virtue of the 1689 Bill of Rights, the Throne is held only by

consent of the Westminster Government. Hence, the monarchs are quite powerless to champion individual rights and liberties with any effect.

A popular alternative to absolute monarchy or dictatorship has been found in outright Republicanism. The Republic of the United States was created primarily to free the emergent nation from the despotism of the House of Hanover. Yet its citizens still tend to be fascinated by the concept of monarchy. No matter how Republican the spirit, the need for a central symbol remains. Neither a flag nor a president can fulfill this unifying role, for by virtue of the Party system presidents are always politically motivated. Republicanism was devised on the principle of fraternal status, yet an ideally classless society can never exist in an environment that promotes displays of eminence and superiority by degrees of wealth and possession.

During the recent and current centuries, many radical events have taken place: the American Revolution, the French Revolution, the Russian Revolution, two major World Wars and a host of changes as countries have swapped one style of government for another. Meanwhile, civil and international disputes continue just as they did in the Middle Ages. They are motivated by trade, politics, religion and whatever other banners are flown to justify the constant struggle for territorial and economic control. The Holy Roman Empire has disappeared, the German Reichs have failed and the British Empire has collapsed. The Russian Empire fell to Communism, which has itself been disgraced and crumbled to ruin, while Capitalism teeters on the very brink of acceptability. With the Cold War now officially ended, America faces a new threat to her economic superpower status from the Pacific countries. In the meantime, the nations of Europe band together in what was once a seemingly well conceived economic community, but which is already suffering from the same pressures of individual custom and national sovereignty that beset the Holy Roman Empire.

Whether nations are governed by military regimes or elected parliaments, by autocrats or democrats, and whether formally described as monarchist, socialist or republican, the net product is always the same: the few control the fate of the many. In situations of dictatorship this is a natural experience, but it should not be the case in a democratic environment. True democracy is 'government by the people for the people', in either direct or representative form, ignoring class distinctions and tolerating minority views. The American Constitution sets out an ideal for this form of democracy but, in line with other nations, there is always a large sector of the community that is not represented by the party in power. Because presidents and prime ministers are politically tied and, because political parties take their respective turns at individual helms, the inevitable result is a lack of continuity for the nations concerned. This is not necessarily a bad thing, but there is no reliable ongoing institution to champion the civil rights and liberties of people in such conditions of ever-changing leadership. Consequently, we are faced, at all times, with 'government *of* the people'.

Is there an answer to the anomaly—an answer that could bring not just a ray of hope but a shining light for the future? There certainly is, but its energy relies on those in governmental service appreciating their roles as representatives of society rather than presuming to stand at the head of society. It is, therefore, necessary for those on self-made pedestals to kick them aside in the interests of harmony and unity. Jesus was not in the least humbled when he washed his Apostles' feet at the Last Supper; he was raised to the realm of a true Grail King—the realm of equality and princely service. This is the eternal Precept of the Sangréal and it is expressed in Grail lore with the utmost clarity: Only by asking 'Whom does the Grail serve?' will the wound of the Fisher King be healed and the Wasteland returned to fertility.

NOTES AND REFERENCES

CHAPTER 1: ORIGINS OF THE BLOODLINE

1. As also mentioned in Hugh Schonfield, *The Passover Plot*, Element Books, Shaftesbury, 1985, ch. 5, p. 245.

2. Eusebius of Caesarea, *Ecclesiastical History* (trans. C. F. Crusé), George Bell, London, 1874, III, 11.

3. Malachi Martin, *The Decline and Fall of the Roman Church*, Secker and Warburg, London, 1982, p. 43.

4. Massue, Melville Henry, 9th Marquis of Ruvigny and Raineval, *The Jacobite Peerage, Baronetage, Knightage and Grants of Honour*, 1904, Introduction.

5. The date of 4004 was calculated by Archbishop James Ussher of Armagh in his *Annales Veteris Testamenti* of 1650. Adam's creation has been separately dated at 5503 B.C.E. by means of Alexandrian texts and at 5411 B.C.E based on the Greek Septuagint. The standard Jewish reckoning for the Creation (on which the Judaic calendar relies for its emergent year) is 3760 B.C.E.

    Ussher's date provides a satisfactory mean and is often used in today's chronologies. The *Universal History's* error was in confusing Adam's date (see note 7) with the Earth's creation.

    The Septuagint was produced by 72 translators of Old Testament texts in around 270 B.C.E.

6. Darwin was not the first in the field of evolutionary research. The French naturalist Comte George de Buffon, Keeper of the Jardin du Roi, published the *Epochs of Nature* in 1778; the Scottish physician James Hutton (sometimes known as the 'founder of geology') published his *Theory of the Earth* in 1785; the French anatomist Baron Georges Cuvier (the 'father of palaeontology') published his *Tableau elementaire de l'histoire naturelle des animaux* in 1798, followed by his great work *Le regne animal*; the French naturalist le Chevalier Jean Baptiste de Monet Lamark, Professor of Zoology at the University of Paris, published his *Philosophie zoologique* in 1809, and followed it with the Histoire naturelle des animaux sans vertebres; and the Scotsman Sir Charles Lyell published his *Principles of Geology* in the early 1830s.

7. For Adam to have appeared somewhere around Ussher's mean year of 4004 B.C.E (see note 5) would put him notionally in the tribal Bronze Age of his locality. From around 6000 B.C.E there were villages and organized farming communities. By 5000 B.C.E there was municipal structure, complete with civic councils run by the Halafans of Tel Halaf. In Jordan, Jericho was an established urban residential center from about 6000 BC and, in China, the Yangtze Basin (the basin of the Chang Jiang) was developed in the same era. By 4000 B.C.E (the said time of Adam), the plough, wheel and sailing ship were all in widespread use.

8. Prior to *The Descent of Man*, Darwin's On *the Origin of the Species by Means of Natural Selection* was published in 1859.

9. The Hebrew language at the time the books of the Pentateuch (the first five books of the Old Testament) were written did not distinguish between past tenses as we do in English. There was only one past tense and it referred to events that 'happened', 'have happened' and 'had happened' with equal relevance. Linguistically, there was no difference between what took place a thousand years ago and what occurred yesterday.

Moreover, the Hebrew words for 'day' and 'year' were used with total flexibility, which made translation into languages with more concrete ideas of time very difficult. See Mary Ellen Chase, *Life and Language in the Old Testament*, Collins, London, 1956, ch. 3, pp. 32-9.

10. A derivation of the name Israel is from *ysra* ('ruler'), plus the element *El* (Lofty one or, later, God)—found in various forenames such as Elizabeth and Michael—thus 'El is ruler' or 'El rules'. See Ahmed Osman, *The House of the Messiah*, Harper Collins, London, 1992, ch. 17, p. 96. (Also see note 11 below.)

11. Jacob was renamed Israel (Genesis 32:28, 35:10) after his wrestling with God. Some say, therefore, that Israel means 'God wrestles', but there is no apparent foundation for this. The descendants of Jacob-Israel were called Israelites.

12. *Oxford Concordance to the Bible*, ref. Ramesses (2).

13. Ahmed Osman, *The House of the Messiah*, ch 1, p. 11.

14. *Ibid.*, ch. 12, p. 67.

15. The Tabernacle of the Congregation (also translated as the Tent of the Meeting) was a wooden-framed rectangular tent or booth covered with cloth and skins. It was used as a portable place of worship during the wanderings in the Wilderness. (See the *Oxford Concordance to the Bible*).

CHAPTER 2: IN THE BEGINNING

1. The subject is fully covered by Dr. Raphael Patai, a noted authority on historical Judaic culture, in *The Hebrew Goddess*, Wayne State University Press, Detroit, 1967.

2. Some of the Old Testament, however, derived directly from the Book of the Law that was discovered in the Temple of Jerusalem (2 Kings 22:8-13) some 35 years before the Babylonian Exile during the reign of King Josiah of Judah (640-609 B.C.E). The existing Hebrew text of the Old Testament corresponds to that produced by the Massoretic scholars in around 900 C.E., although it is based on earlier manuscripts, some from the 1st century B.C.E.

3. Eridu (modern Abu Shahrein) was the most sacred city of ancient Mesopotamia—a jewel within a green and fertile land that, to the inhabitants of Canaan, would have seemed a veritable paradise. In acknowledgment of its lush surroundings the city was dedicated to the water god Enki (or Ea), and has been identified with the Garden of Eden.

4. According to Sir Charles Leonard Woolley (one-time Director of the British Museum and of the University of Pennsylvania's archaeological expedition to Mesopotamia) in *Ur of the Chaldees* (1, 21-32), the Flood, as narrated in Genesis, took place in around 4000 B.C.E.

5. The Tower of Babel, a huge ziggurat, was constructed on the Babylonian Plain of Shinar. Such richly decorated, multi-levelled ziggurats (Babylonian for 'high place' or 'tower') were features of Sumerian cities. They were surmounted by small temples to the primary deities of the regions. The Great Ziggurat was sited at the city of Uruk (from which modern Iraq derives its name) and its temple was consecrated to the goddess Ishtar.

6. To the Jews, the Underworld was known as *Sheol*. It was an equivalent to the Graeco-Roman kingdom of Hades, the infernal region in which souls dwelt in mournful darkness, separated from their earthly bodies.

7. The first five Books of Moses correspond to the first five books of the Old Testament (also called the Pentateuch): Genesis, Exodus, Leviticus, Numbers and Deuteronomy.

8. The Books of the Prophets are technically those written by or about the Jewish prophets, as opposed to books that are narrative histories—although the general definition does include some historical books such as Judges, Samuel and Kings. The balance of the Old Testament is called the Hagiographa (Holy writings).

9. Other Jewish holy writings are the Mishnah and the Talmud. The Mishnah (Repetition) is an early codification of Jewish law, based upon ancient compilations and edited in Palestine by the Ethnarch (Governor) Judah I in the early 3rd century C.E. It consists of traditional law (Halakah) on a wide range of subjects, derived partly from old custom and partly from Biblical law (Tannaim) as interpreted by the rabbis (teachers).

   The Talmud is basically a commentary on the Mishnah, compiled originally in Hebrew and Aramaic. It derives from two independently important streams of Jewish tradition: the Babylonian and the Palestinian.

10. Rev. John Fleetwood, *The Life of Our Lord and Savior Jesus Christ*, William MacKenzie, Glasgow, *c.*1900, ch. 1, p. 3: the entry by Dr. G. Redford.

11. Twelve other works dating from and related to the last part of the Old Testament era constitute the Apocrypha (Hidden things). Although included in the Greek Septuagint, they were not, however, contained in the Hebrew canon. They originated in the Hellenist Judaism of Alexandria, but are not accepted by orthodox Jews. The books are, nevertheless, included in St. Jerome's Latin Vulgate (c. 385 C.E.) as an extension to the Old Testament, and are recognized by the Roman Catholic Church. But, they are omitted by almost all Protestant Bibles, having been sidelined by the prime reformer Martin Luther (1483-1546) and largely ignored by translators. The twelve books are: Esdras, Tobit, Judith, the Rest of Esther, the Wisdom of Solomon, Ecclesiasticus [of Jeremiah], Baruch with the Epistle of Jeremy, the Song of the Three Holy Children, the History of Susanna, Bel and the Dragon, the Prayer of Manasses, and Maccabees.

12. J. T. Milik, *Ten Years of Discovery in the Wilderness of Judaea* (trans. J. Strugnell), SCM Press, London, 1959, ch. 1, pp. 11-19.

13. In the New Testament, 2 Corinthians 4:3-7 similarly states: 'If our Gospel be hid, it is hid to them that are lost ... But we have this treasure in earthen vessels'.

14. James Robinson and the Coptic Gnostic Project, *The Nag Hammadi Library*, E. J. Brill, Leiden, 1977.

15. *Bedouin* is used in English as a singular adjective, whereas it is technically a plural noun. In Arabic, *bedu* is 'desert' and the *bedu'een* are the 'people of the desert'.

16. Josephus, *Antiquities of the Jews* (trans. W. Whiston), Thomas Nelson, London, 1862, XV, ch. 5, p. 2.

17. J. T. Milik, *Ten Years of Discovery in the Wilderness of Judaea*, ch. 3, pp. 51-3.

18. John Allegro, *The Dead Sea Scrolls*, Penguin, Harmondsworth, 1964, ch. 5, p. 94.

19. *Ibid.*, ch. 5, p. 93.

20. Barbara Thiering, *Jesus the Man*, Doubleday/Transworld, London, 1992, ch. 4, pp. 20-1.

21. Eschatology: the study (or branch of theology) that has to do with the end of the world—the Last Things (death or judgment).

22. John Allegro, *The Dead Sea Scrolls*, ch. 6, p. 104.

23. *Pesharim*: 'Interpretations', thus 'Commentary' or 'Exegesis'. The singular is *pesher*.

24. Barbara Thiering, *Jesus the Man, passim*.

25. *Ibid.*, Appendix III, p. 339.

26. Josephus, *The Jewish Wars*, II, ch. 8, p. 6.

27. Barbara Thiering, *Jesus the Man*, ch. 12, p. 65; Appendix III, p. 344.

28. During the earlier era of polytheistic religions, Zoroaster (or Zarathustra) modified the concept and devised the world's first genuinely dualist creed. He became the archpriest and prophet of Ahura Mazda (Ormuzd), god of life and light, who was opposed by Ahriman (Angra Mainyu), the evil lord of death and darkness. These ancient deities were destined to wage a continual war, Light against Darkness, until Light won in the Final Judgment. At that time, Ahura Mazda would resurrect the dead to create a Paradise on Earth.

   Over the centuries thereafter, and as the tradition altered with the differing cultural influences, much of the legend remained fixed. At the time of the Essenes of Qumrân (as the years B.C.E drew to a close), the story of the dualist war was still current, although generally as an allegory related to the hoped-for overthrow of Roman imperialism.

   Later, Roman Christianity retained the basic idea, result that many Christians still believe there is a Final Judgment to come.

CHAPTER 3: JESUS, SON OF MAN

1. Rev. John Fleetwood, *The Life of Our Lord and Savior Jesus Christ*, ch. 1, pp. 21-2. For the various interpretations of the prophecy, see *Dr. Smith's Bible Dictionary*.

2. A. N. Wilson, *Jesus*, Sinclair Stevenson, London, 1992, ch. 4, p. 79.

3. Nancy Qualls-Corbett, *The Sacred Prostitute*, Inner City Books, Toronto, 1988, ch. 2, p. 58.

4. The concept that Mary was 'ever-virgin' was established at the Council of Trullo in 692 C.E.

5. A. N. Wilson, *Jesus*, ch. 4, p. 83.

6. An old monastic complex stood on the outskirts of Qumrân. Among its buildings was the house where Essene children conceived out of wedlock were born. The community referred to this house as 'Bethlehem of Judaea' (as opposed to the quite separate Bethlehem settlement, south of Jerusalem). Matthew 2:5 states that Jesus was born 'in Bethlehem of Judaea'. (See Barbara Thiering, *Jesus the Man*, ch. 9, pp. 50-2.)

   The Gospel narratives were geared to comply with the prophecy of Micah 5:2, which dates from about 710 B.C.E: 'But thou, Bethlehem Ephratah, though thou be little ... yet out of thee shall he come forth unto me that is to be ruler in Israel'.

7. *Dr. Smith's Bible Dictionary* says that the Hebrew word translated as 'inn' in English more literally signifies a 'lodging-place'. Inns, in the modern sense, were unknown in the ancient Near East, where it was common to invite travellers into one's home, and was regarded as a pious duty to do so.

8. A. N. Wilson, *Jesus*, ch. 4, p. 80.

9. Ahmed Osman, *The House of the Messiah*, ch. 5, p. 31. *Robinson's Bible Researches*, on the other hand, gives the Arabic name as *enNusara*. (See Rev. John Fleetwood, *The Life of our Lord and Savior Jesus Christ*, ch. 1, p. 10.)

10. The Old Testament does not refer to Nazareth. Neither does the Hebrew Talmud, and nor does Josephus mention the town in his 1st-century *The Antiquities of the Jews* or in *The Jewish Wars*. Nazareth first appeared around 70 C.E. and became a place of pilgrimage only from the 6th century (Ahmed Osman, *The House of the Messiah*, ch. 5, pp. 30-2).

11. Rev. John Fleetwood, *The Life of Our Lord and Savior Jesus Christ*, 1, 4, confirms the information in *Dr. Smith's Bible Dictionary* that the name Gabriel in this context represents a title corresponding to angelic office.

12. Josephus, *The Jewish Wars*, II, ch. 8, p. 7.

13. Barbara Thiering, *Jesus the Man*, Appendix III, pp. 335-8. The name Gabriel means 'Man of God'. Appendix III, p. 340. The name Michael means 'Who [is] like God'.

14. Luke 1:5—Elizabeth was a daughter of the priestly house of Aaron.

15. Luke 2:25.

16. Rev. John Fleetwood, *The Life of our Lord and Savior Jesus Christ*, ch. 1, pp. 10-11; an extract by Dr. Paxton outlines the customary rules of Jewish matrimony as distinct from the more restrictive dynastic regulations.

17. Barbara Thiering, *Jesus the Man*, p. 8; Appendix I, p. 177.

18. Josephus, *The Jewish Wars*, 11, ch. 8, p. 13.

19. Barbara Thiering, *Jesus the Man*, ch. 7, p. 42: Appendix I, p. 209.

It was not until 314 C.E. that Emperor Constantine the Great arbitrarily changed the date of Jesus's birthday to December 25 so as to coincide with the pagan sun festival.

It will be noticed that the dates of some New Testament events as given in this book do not conform to the traditional dates. The year of Jesus's birth, for example, is often considered to have been 5 B.C.E., but herein is 7 B.C.E. The date of the Crucifixion is similarly often shown as 30 C.E. whereas it is given here as 33 C.E. The first published sequence of Biblical dates appeared in 526 C.E., being calculations of the monk Dionysius Exiguus. By his reckoning Jesus was born in the Roman year 754 A.U.C. (*Anno Urbis Conditae*: 'Years after the founding of the city [of Rome]')—equivalent to 1 C.E. But Herod the Great died four years before this, in 750 AUC (= 4 B.C.E.). Because it was known that Herod was still alive at the time of Jesus's birth, the monk's chart was, therfore, adjusted to set the Nativity a year before Herod's death—in the year 749 AUC (= 5 B.C.E.). This became the accepted date, and the rest of the Gospel time-frame was recalculated accordingly.

20. In relating Jesus's lineage, Matthew and Luke do not agree on the genealogy from King David. Matthew gives the kingly line from Solomon, whereas Luke details a descent from another of David's sons, Nathan. This segment of the list in Matthew contains 22 ancestors, against 20 in Luke. However, both lists eventually coincide at Zerubbabel, whom they agree was the direct and immediate heir of Shealtiel. But even this is subject to debate for, whereas the Old Testament books of Ezra (3:2) and Haggai (1:1) confirm that Zerubbabel was born into Shealtiel's family, there could have been a generation between the two—a possible son of Shealtiel named Pedaiah, who would then have been Zerubbabel's father. The account in 1 Chronicles 3:19 is confusing in this regard.

The main difference between Matthew and Luke concerns the ancestors from the time of David to the era of the Israelites' return from Babylonian captivity. For this term, the equivalent list in 1 Chronicles is in general accord with Matthew's genealogy. Then, having converged on Zerubbabel, the lists in Matthew and Luke diverge again. Matthew traces Jesus's descent through a son named Abiud, while Luke takes a course through a son called Rhesa (a titular name meaning 'chieftain').

Jesus's paternal grandfather is called Jacob according to Matthew 1:16 but, in Luke 3:23, he is said to be Heli. Both versions are correct, however, for Joseph's father, Heli, held the distinction of 'Jacob' in his patriarchal capacity. (See Barbara Thiering, *Jesus the Man*, ch. 5, p. 29.)

The genealogical list in Matthew, from David to Jacob-Heli (spanning about 1000 years) contains 25 generations at 40 years each. Luke, on the other hand, gives 40 generations at 25 years each. Hence, Luke places Jesus in the 20th generation from Zerubbabel, whereas Matthew places him in the 11th. Through this latter period of around 530 years, the Matthew list supports a 53-year generation standard, while Luke is more comprehensible with its 28-year standard.

21. The original Zadok was the High Priest who anointed David's son King Solomon in around 1015 B.C.E (1 Kings 1:38-40), as celebrated by Handel in the anthem sung at British coronations since the 18th century.

CHAPTER 4: THE EARLY MISSION

1. Barbara Thiering, *Jesus the Man*, Appendix II, p. 299.

2. *Ibid.*, Appendix I, pp. 325-30.

3. Rev. John Fleetwood, *The Life of Our Lord and Savior Jesus Christ*, ch. 1, pp. 11-12; extract from *Dr. Smith's Bible Dictionary*.

4. The Samaritans believed that Simon (Zelotes) Magus represented the 'Power of God' (Acts 8:9-10).

5. Steve Richards, *Levitation*, Thorsons, Wellingborough, 1980, ch. 5, pp. 66-7.

6. Barbara Thiering, *Jesus the Man*, ch. 15, p. 80.

7. Judas the Galilean died in 6 C.E.

8. The Syrian Semitic verb *skariot* was an equivalent of the contemporary Hebrew *sikkarti*: 'to deliver up'. It has been suggested that Judas Iscariot was therefore 'Judas the Deliverer', referring to his betrayal of Jesus. (See Ahmed Osman, *The House of the Messiah*, ch. 15, p. 81.)

9. *Jacob* is synonymous with *Jacobus*, of which there was a Latin variant *Jacomus*, from which (via the Norman French) English now has the variant nominal form of *James*. The connection between the forms has never been forgotten and is the reason why, from the 17th century, adherents of the Stuart King James VII of Scotland (James II of England) were known as Jacobites (i.e., Jacob-ites).

10. Matthew was regarded with considerable hostility by the Pharisees. Their strict, orthodox Jewish outlook caused them to be petty in the extreme about the observance of laws that predated the Books of Moses (the Pentateuch or Torah), to the extent that they believed Israel could not be redeemed until all Jews were purified. To them, such essential purification was incompatible with monetary affairs or political intrigues, and someone who was involved in both—like a publican, and especially one who collected taxes—could only be regarded as a sinner.

11. The Proselytes were Gentile converts to the Jewish faith.

12. Shem was a son of Noah and an ancestor of Abraham; he represents the ancient lineage of the S[h]emitic peoples.

13. The name Bartholomew derives from *Bar-Ptolemy* (Aramaic: 'servant of Ptolemy') and thus has its own Egyptian connotations.

14. Thomas was born Philip, the son of Herod the Great and Mariamne II. In due course he became the first husband of Herod's granddaughter Herodias, with whom he had a daughter, Salome (who requested the head of John the Baptist from Herod-Antipas of Galilee). Well known for her 'dance of the seven veils', Salome is not mentioned by name in the New Testament, but features in Flavius Josephus' *The Antiquities of the Jews*, XVIII, ch. 5, sect 4.

15. Genesis 16:7-12.

16. Numbers 22:21-35.

17. Judges 13:3-19.

18. Judges 6:11-22.

19. 1 Enoch 4:9 and the Qumrân *War Scroll* 9:15-17. See also A. Dupont-Sommer, *The Essene Writings From Qumrân* (trans. G. Vermes), Basil Blackwell, Oxford, 1961, V, p. 183 (re. the angelic shields).

20. Josephus, *The Jewish Wars*, II, ch. 7, p. 7.

21. Tabulated details of the angelic and priestly structures are given in Barbara Thiering, Jesus the Man, Appendix III.

22. The spiritual energy of springs and streams was numerically represented in the Solar Force as 1080. (See John Michell, *Dimensions of Paradise*, Thames and Hudson, London, 1988, ch. 1, p. 18.)

CHAPTER 5: THE MESSIAH

1. The Qumrân *Manual of Discipline* (the *Scroll of the Rule*), ch. 6, pp. 4-5; annex 18-20.

2. There was a good deal of speculation over whether John the Baptist or Jesus was the awaited Messiah. John was, after all, the prevailing Zadok and anointed as such, thereby holding Messianic status (*Messiah*: 'Anointed One'). But when asked directly about the Savior Messiah, John 'confessed, and denied not; but confessed, I am not the Christ' (John 1:20).
The Qumrân Scrolls indicate that the community lived in expectation of two important Messiahs. One was to be of the priestly caste, whom they called the Teacher of Righteousness; the other would be a Prince of the line of David—a warrior who would restore the kingdom of his people.

   John the Baptist made it quite clear that he was not the Kingly Messiah (John 3:28): 'I said, I am not the Christ, but that I am sent before him '. For the Qumrân notion of the two Messiahs, see also John Allegro, *The Dead Sea Scrolls*, ch. 13, pp. 167-72.

3. The Hebrew calendar was lunar in origin, and its 12-month year totals 354 days although, to make up for the deficiency of 11 days in relation to the solar calendar year, it adds a complete calendar month in 7 years of a 19-year cycle. The Hellenists in Palestine adopted the Romans' Julian (365-day) calendar in 44 B.C.E.—a system that suited the Samaritan Magi, who made astronomical calculations according to the solar calendar, which added 10 days per year to the lunar calendar. The difference in calendars over a number of centuries might account for a displacement of seven years in a forecast relating to a time sufficiently far ahead.

4. Josephus, *The Antiquities of the Jews*, XVIII, ch. 3, p. 2.

5. Barbara Thiering, *Jesus the Man*, ch. 20, pp. 97-100.

6. Spikenard was a fragrant, sweet-smelling ointment compounded from the nard plant, which grew only in the Himalayan mountains at heights of around 15,000 feet (c. 4570 meters) and was very expensive.

7. In the Gospels of Matthew and Mark, Jesus's entry into Jerusalem occurs before the anointing at Bethany. A political motivation lies behind this textual switch of events in their accounts. In John, the anointing is correctly related in conjunction with the raising of Lazarus and, for Jesus to be accredited as the Messiah, it was imperative that he be anointed.

8. Spikenard was also used as an unguent in funerary rites. It was customary for a grieving widow to place a broken vial of the ointment in her late husband's tomb. (See Margaret Starbird, *The Woman With the Alabaster Jar, Bear*, Santa Fe, New Mexico, 1993, ch. 2, pp. 40-1.)

9. Margaret Starbird, *The Woman With the Alabaster Jar*, ch. 11, pp. 35-6.

10. Of the academic works on the subject of sacred marriage, Samuel Kramer's *The Sacred Marriage Rite* (especially ch. 3, p. 63) is worthy of particular study. From the female stand-point, however, nowhere is the story of the Lost Bride more compassionately conveyed than in the writings of Margaret Starbird.

11. Ahmed Osman, *The House of the Messiah*, ch. 28, p. 152.

12. Barbara Thiering, *Jesus the Man*, Appendix III, pp. 366-71.

13. The Sanhedrin was the Jewish assembly that held supreme authority in all religious and civil matters. It consisted of priests, scribes and elders, who formed the Supreme Court of Judicature (*Oxford Concordance to the Bible*).

14. Salome's baptismal name was Helena. As the spiritual adviser to Salome, daughter of Herodias, she too was called Salome in accordance with custom. Helena-Salome was the spiritual mother of the Apostles, James and John Boanerges.

15. Barbara Thiering, *Jesus the Man*, Appendix III, pp. 366-71.

16. Morton Smith, *The Secret Gospel*.

17. *Ibid.*, ch. 7, p.51.

18. In the 4th century C.E., when the New Testament was first collated, the Gospel manuscripts of Mark ended at the present Chapter 16 verse 8, before the narration of the Resurrection events. These shorter manuscripts are part of the *Codex Vaticanus* and the *Codex Sinaiticus*. (See Baigent, Leigh and Lincoln, *The Holy Blood and the Holy Grail*, ch. 12, pp. 282-3; notes, p. 432.)

19. Baigent *et al.*, ch. 12, p. 296.

CHAPTER 6: BETRAYAL

1. John the Baptist had initially supported a prediction known as the Prophecy of Enoch. This gave a date for the restoration of the Zadokite and Davidic hereditary lines as being 'the end of the eighth World Week'—that is 3920 years after the supposed Creation. This had been calculated to occur in the year now defined as 21 B.C.E., but nothing had happened. Calendar revision allowed for an extension to 29 C.E., but judicious recalculation further extended the deadline date to 31 C.E. (See Barbara Thiering, *Jesus the Man*, ch. 13, pp. 67-8). John's whole reputation, with all its wild mystique, hung on this prediction. Following John's execution, the prophecy was recalculated yet again to fall on the vernal equinox of 33 C.E.

2. Josephus, *The Antiquities of the Jews*, XVIII, ch. 1, sect. 3.

3. John Allegro, *The Dead Sea Scrolls*, ch. 7, p. 131; ch. 12, p. 164; ch. 13, p. 168.

4. The Scroll of *The Rule*, Annex II, 17-22.

5. Barbara Thiering, *Jesus the Man*, ch. 21, p. 102.

6. Baigent, Leigh and Lincoln, *The Holy Blood and the Holy Grail*, ch. 12, p. 309.

7. Barbara Thiering, *Jesus the Man*, ch. 22, p. 105.

8. Baigent, Leigh and Lincoln, *The Holy Blood and the Holy Grail*, ch. 12, p. 309; notes, p. 433.

9. *The Apostolic Constitutions*, VI, sect. 9. See Clement (Cults and Religions) in Bibliography.

10. Gnostic tradition has it that Simon the Cyrene was crucified 'in the place of Jesus'. This does not mean instead of Jesus, but in what should have been Jesus's location. Understanding Jesus to represent the kingly Davidic heritage, with Simon to represent the priestly line (and therefore Judas to represent the line of the prophets), the positioning of the three crosses should have been made to observe the formal hierarchical ranks. According to this scheme, the position of the King should have been to the west (on the left); the position of the Priest should

have been in the center; and the position of the Prophet should have been to the east (on the right). But the Gospels state that Jesus's cross was in the middle. If, though, the Cyrene was crucified in this place instead of Simon (as the Priest), Jesus (as the King) would have been correctly positioned to the west.

CHAPTER 7: CRUCIFIXION

1. Barbara Thiering, *Jesus the Man*, ch. 24, p. 113.

2. *Ibid.*, Appendix II, p. 312.

3. *Ibid.*, Appendix III, p. 353.

4. *Ibid.*, ch. 26, p. 122.

5. The translation to 'pound' in this case represents the Greek *litra* (a variant of the Roman *libra*), a measure of weight equal to one nineteenth of a *talantaios* (talent). In modern terms this approximates to 330 grams or 12 ounces *avoirdupois*. 100 New Testament 'pounds' is thus roughly equal in modern terms to 33 kilograms or 75 pounds (more than 5 stones) *avoirdupois*—a considerable quantity for Nicodemus to manage alone.

6. Christianity did survive, although for many the Crucifixion was seen as the blow which should have put an end to it. Senator Cornelius Tacitus (born c. 55 C.E.), referring to the Crucifixion, wrote ruefully: 'In spite of this temporary setback, the deadly superstition [Christianity] had broken out afresh, not only in Judaea where the mischief had started, but even in Rome' (Tacitus, *The Annals of Imperial Rome*, XIV, ref. 64 C.E.).

7. See Chapter 5, *The King and His Donkey*.

8. Baigent, Leigh and Lincoln. *The Messianic Legacy*, ch. 6, p. 68.

9. Gladys Taylor, *Our Neglected Heritage*, Covenant Books, London, 1974, Vol. 1, p. 42.

10. The Gnostics were so called because they were accredited with gnosis (Greek: 'knowledge'—especially esoteric insight). The Gnostic movement originated in Samaria, where Simon Zelotes (Simon the Magus) was head of the Samaritan Magi (men of wisdom) of West Manasseh. Later, it was further developed in Syria, again with Simon as its principal proponent, before spreading into the pre-Roman Christian environment.

11. *Nag Hammadi Codex* BG 8502, 1.

12. See Chapter 4, *Who Were the Apostles?* (under Thaddaeus, James and Matthew).

13. *Nag Hammadi Codex* VII, 3.

14. *Nag Hammadi Codex* II, 2.

CHAPTER 8: THE BLOODLINE CONTINUES

1. Barbara Thiering, *Jesus the Man*, Appendix I, p. 177 and p. 196.

2. *Ibid.*, Appendix III, p. 177.

3. The fact that Jesus is mentioned in connection with the 'times of restitution' (Acts 3:21) indicates that he had become a parent and was, therefore, obliged to lead a celibate existence for a predetermined time. There is no suggestion that this child was a son, which means that the child was a daughter. Note that Damaris is mentioned in Acts 17:34.

4. Barbara Thiering, *Jesus the Man*, Appendix I, p. 297 and p. 299; Appendix III, pp. 363-4.

5. *Ibid.*, ch. 29, p. 133.

6. Simon is honored as the first missionary priest in Cyprus. The main church in Larnaca is dedicated to him under his other New Testament name, Lazarus. He is said to have been the first Bishop of Larnaca.

7. Barbara Thiering, *Jesus the Man*, ch. 31, pp. 143-4.

8. *Ibid.*, ch. 31, p. 141.

9. *Ibid.*, Appendix I, p. 268.

10. The color black, as used for ecclesiastical garb, has associations far older than Christianity.

    The tall black statue of Isis at the Church of St. Germain, Paris, was identified as the Virgin of Paris until the 16th century. The original abbey on the site was built for Childebert I on top of a Temple of Isis. It housed Childebert's relics from the Treasures of Solomon and was a burial place for the Merovingian kings. (See Ean C. M. Begg, *The Cult of the Black Virgin*, Arkana, London, 1985, ch. 2, p. 66.) The Benedictine monks of St. Germain-des-Prés wore black cassocks in the Nazarite tradition.

    A statue of St. Genevieve was erected in the Benedictine chapel. She was perceived as a successor to Isis in France, and was a close friend of King Clovis.

11. It was in 62 C.E. that Ananus the younger, a Sadducee brother of Jonathan Annas, became High Priest. As such, he was predisposed towards furthering the Sanhedrin's opposition to James and his Nazarene ideals.

12. The stoning took place in 62 C.E., according to Josephus' 1st-century *Antiquities of the Jews*, XX, ch. 9, p. 1.

13. Tacitus, *The Annals of Imperial Rome*, XV, 43: ref. 64 C.E.

14. 2 Timothy 2:9: 'The word of God is not bound'.

15. Andreas Faber-Kaiser, *Jesus Died in Kashmir*, Abacus/Sphere, London, 1978.

16. The only time that Jewish forces ever again dented Roman military pride was when, in 132 C.E., they revolted once more under the leadership of Simon Ben Kochba, Prince of Israel. Simon assembled a large army of native volunteers, together with professional mercenary soldiers from abroad. His battle plan included many strategic operations, some of which made use of tunnels and underground chambers beneath Jerusalem. Within one year, Jerusalem was recaptured from the Romans. Jewish administration was established and maintained for two years. But outside the city the struggle continued and the final strategy depended on military assistance from Persia. However, just when the Persian forces were meant to set out for the Holy Land, Persia was invaded. Its troops had to stay and defend their own territory—with the result that Simon and his gallant band were not able to counter the advance of the twelve Roman legions, who had regrouped in Syria at the command of Emperor Hadrian. Simon's men were eventually overwhelmed at Battin, west of Jerusalem, in 135 C.E.

17. Julius Africanus made his reputation by translating into Latin a series of works written by the 1st-century disciple Abdias, the Nazarene Bishop of Babylon. The *Books of Abdias* amounted to ten volumes of firsthand Apostolic history. However, like so many other important eyewitness accounts of the era, they were rejected outright for inclusion in the eventual New Testament.

18. Malachi Martin, *The Decline and Fall of the Roman Church*, p. 44.

CHAPTER 9: MARY MAGDALENE

1. John W Taylor, The Coming of the Saints, Covenant Books, London, 1969, ch. 7, p. 138.

2. Barbara Thiering, *Jesus the Man*, ch. 17, p. 88; also ch. 15, pp. 80-1.

    As Chief of the Scribes, Judas Sicariote also held the post of the Tempter. It was thus with Judas that Jesus debated when he was 'led up of the Spirit into the wilderness to be tempted of the devil' (Matthew 4:1). Judas was at that time seeking to become the Father in the place of John the Baptist. The basis of

Judas's negotiation with Jesus was that if he would aid him to priestly eminence, he would assist him, in return, to become king: 'All this power I will give thee, and the glory of them: for that is delivered unto me; and to whomsoever I will give it. If thou therefore wilt worship me, all shall be thine' (Luke 4:6-7).

3. Ean Begg, *The Cult of the Black Virgin*, ch. 4, p. 98.

4. Margaret Starbird, *The Woman With the Alabaster Jar*, ch. 3, p. 50.

5. Henry Lincoln, *The Holy Place*, Jonathan Cape, London, 1991, ch. 7, p. 70.

6. Ean Begg, *The Cult of the Black Virgin*, Introduction, p. 20.

7. Margaret Starbird, *The Woman With the Alabaster Jar*, ch. 6, p. 123.

8. *Ibid.*, ch. 6, p. 123.

9 . *Nag Hammadi* Codex BG 8502-1.

10. Elaine Pagels, *The Gnostic Gospels*, Weidenfeld and Nicolson, London, 1980, ch. 3, p 65.

11. *Nag Hammadi Codex* II, 2.

12. *Ibid.*, II, 3.

13. Ean Begg, *The Cult of the Black Virgin*, ch. 2, p. 68.

14. Beryl Platts, *Origins of Heraldry*, Proctor Press, London, 1980, ch. 1, p. 33.

15. John W Taylor, *The Coming of the Saints*, ch. 6, p. 103.

16. Rev. Père Lacordaire, *St. Mary Magdalene*, Thomas Richardson, Derby, 1880, pp. 106-8.

17. *Dictionnaire Étymologique des noms de lieux en France.*

18. *Ibid.*

19. The Merovingians were the dynasty of Frankish kings in the 5th to 8th centuries, who founded and established what became the monarchy of France.

CHAPTER 10: JOSEPH OF ARIMATHEA

1. In *De Demonstratione Evangelii*, Eusebius wrote: 'The Apostles passed over the ocean to the islands known as Britain'. (See Rev. Lionel Smithett Lewis, *Joseph of Arimathea at Glastonbury*, A. R. Mobray, London, 1927, p. 54.)

2. Archbishop Isidore of Seville (600-636) wrote: 'Philip of the city of Bethsaida, whence also came Peter, preached Christ to the Gauls, and brought barbarous nations and their neighbors ... into the light of knowledge ... Afterwards he was stoned and crucified, and died in Hierapolis, a city of Phrygia'. This information was confirmed by Freculphus, 9th-century Bishop of Lisieux.

3. The Tabernacle of the Hebrews is described in Exodus 26 and 36.

4. Rev. Lionel Smithett Lewis, *Joseph of Arimathea at Glastonbury*, pp. 15-16.

5. Writing in about 600 C.E., St. Augustine described: 'There is on the western confines of Britain a certain royal island called in ancient speech Glastonia ... In it, the earliest Angle neophytes of the Catholic doctrine—God guiding them—found a church not made by any man, they say, but prepared by God Himself for the salvation of mankind, which church the Heavenly Builder Himself declared (by many miracles and mysteries of healing) he had consecrated to Himself and to Holy Mary, Mother of God '. (See William of Malmesbury, *The Antiquities of Glastonbury*, Talbot/JMF Books, Llanerch, 1980, p. 1.)

6. The route used by the Jewish tin traders was described by Diodorus Siculus in the days of Emperor Augustus (63 B.C.E.-14 C.E.): 'The tin ore is transported from Britain into Gaul, the merchants carrying it on horseback through the heart of

Celtica to Marseilles and the city called Narbo[nne]'. It was then taken by ship across the Mediterranean to any of several destinations. See John W Taylor, *The Coming of the Saints*, ch. 8, p. 143.

7. Tin is essential to the production of bronze, and the most important tin mines were in southwestern England—an area also rich in copper and lead, for which there was a great market in the expanding Roman Empire. The British Museum contains two splendid examples of lead from the Mendip mines near Glastonbury, dated 49 C.E. and 60 C.E. respectively. In Latin, one bears the name of 'Britannicus, son of the Emperor Claudius', and the other is inscribed, 'British lead: property of the Emperor Nero'.

8. It is important to note that stoning was not generally a method of execution. It was more often a way of hounding a denounced victim out of one area of the city, or out of the city altogether.

9. Rev. Lionel Smithett Lewis, *Joseph of Arimathea at Glastonbury*, p. 15. Following the union of Scotland with England and Wales, the king's title was adjusted to the less pious 'His Britannic Majesty'.

10. Professor Roger Sherman Loomis, in *The Grail: From Celtic Myth to Christian Symbolism*, University of Wales Press, Cardiff, 1963, makes the point that proper names in manuscript transmission sometimes lose their initial letter—although mutation of the initial letters of names is a feature of the Celtic languages. By this process, Morgaine is sometimes found as Orguein and, with specific relevance to the present case, Galains (Galaain) became Alain (Alaain).

11. The *Grand Saint Grail* confirms that on the death of Alain the Lordship of the Grail passed to Josue—although defining him as Alain's brother rather than his cousin.

12. Including, for example, *De Sancto Joseph ab Arimathea* and William of Malmesbury's *De Antiquitate*.

13. Herod-Antipas, the Tetrarch of Galilee, was banished by Rome to Lyon in Gaul following his beheading of John the Baptist. It was also at Lyon, from June 28, 208 C.E., that 19,000 Christians were put to death at the personal direction of Emperor Lucius Severus.

14. Verulam or Verulamium was renamed St. Albans after a 4th-century martyr: the Roman soldier Alban, who was beheaded by his military superiors in 303 C.E. (the Diocletian era) for sheltering a Christian priest. He is often referred to as 'the first Christian martyr in England' which, of course, he was not. Modern St. Albans is a busy market city in Hertfordshire, with a spectacular abbey.

15. *Genealogies of the Welsh Princes*, Harleian MS 3859, confirms that Anna was the daughter of Joseph of Arimathea.

16. Gladys Taylor, *Our Neglected Heritage*, I, p. 33.

17. Peter was never formally appointed Bishop of Rome. Linus—appointed by Paul in 58 C.E. (during Peter's lifetime: *Apostolic Constitutions*)—was therefore the first pope. (See Gladys Taylor, *Our Neglected Heritage*, I, pp. 40-5.)

CHAPTER 11: THE NEW CHRISTIANITY

1. A transcript of Eleutherius' reply to King Lucius in 177 C.E. is given in John W. Taylor, *The Coming of the Saints*, Appendix K.

2. Lucius died on December 3, 201 and was buried at St. Mary le Lode in Gloucester. His remains were later reinterred at St. Peter's, Cornhill, London.

References in Roman martyrology to the burial of Lucius at Chur in Switzerland are inaccurate on two counts. They actually relate to King Lucius of Bavaria (not to Lucius the Luminary of Britain); also the Bavarian Lucius died at Curia in Germany, not at Chur in Switzerland.

3. The reference to Jesus in the *Antiquities of the Jews* (XVIII, ch. 3, p. 3) is regarded by some as a later Christian interpolation. Origen, writing before 245 C.E., does not mention the passage, although Eusebius in his *Demonstration of the Gospel* written in around 320 C.E., does. It may therefore be held to have been interpolated after Origen but before Eusebius. (See Ahmed Osman *The House of the Messiah*, ch. 3, pp. 19-20). But the basis of such a claim is tenuous, to say the least. The passage is not really Christian in sentiment: it defines neither Jesus's status as the Messiah, nor his relationship to God. It states only that he was 'the Christ', a 'wise man', a 'worker of marvels' and a 'teacher'—in much the way that the Jews of the era would have perceived him. (See A. N. Wilson, *Jesus*, ch. 4, p. 89.)

4. George F. Jowett, *The Drama of the Lost Disciples*, Covenant Books, London, 1961, ch. 12, pp. 125-6.

5. Three British bishops attended the Council of Arles in 314: those of London, York, and Lincoln.

CHAPTER 12: RELIGION AND THE BLOODLINE

1. In 452 C.E., Bishop Leo I of Rome and an unarmed body of monks confronted the fearsome Attila the Hun and his army by the River Po in northern Italy. At that time, Attila's empire stretched from the Rhine right across into Central Asia. His well-equipped hordes were ready with chariots, ladders, catapults and every martial device to sweep on towards Rome. The conversation lasted no more than a few minutes, but the outcome was that Attila ordered his men to vacate their encampments and retreat northwards. What actually transpired between the men was never revealed, but afterwards Leo the Great was destined to wield supreme power.

Some time earlier, in 434 C.E., an envoy sent by the Byzantine Emperor Theodosius II had met the dreaded Hun in similar circumstances by the Morava River (south of modern Belgrade). He had given Attila the contemporary equivalent of millions of dollars as a ransom for peace in the East. Bishop Leo's arrangement was probably much the same. (See Malachi Martin, *The Decline and Fall of the Roman Church*. Also, for further reading on the subject, see Norman J. Bull, *The Rise of the Church*, Heinemann , London, 1967.)

2. The word 'occult' is today often associated with sinister magic—but it actually means no more than 'hidden' or 'obscure'. Initiates of the occult during the Middle Ages revered the planet Venus as representative of Mary Magdalene, who was regarded as a medium of secret revelation. Over its regular 8-year cycle, Venus traces a precise pentangle (a five-pointed star) in the night sky. This same figure is formed by the five mountain peaks around the Magdalene center at Rennes-le-Chateau in Languedoc. See Henry Lincoln, *The Holy Place*, ch. 7, pp. 65-70.

3. The esoteric tradition of Solomon spanned the centuries to the era of Gnostic Christianity, which preceded the Merovingian age. The Gnostics, whose texts referred to the *Book of Solomon*, were the inheritors of the early Jewish sects of Babylonia. Their form of Christianity was thus closely allied to the metaphysical doctrines of Plato and Pythagoras; their creeds were largely founded on astrology and on cosmic awareness. In addition they claimed a particular insight (*gnosis*: 'knowledge') into Jesus's teaching that was unknown to the Church of Rome.

4. What traditional history makes of this baptism is that the pagan Clovis became a Christian. What actually transpired was that the already Christian Clovis became a Roman Catholic.

5. The whole subject of the relationship between Clovis and the Vatican is well covered in Baigent, Leigh and Lincoln, *The Holy Blood and the Holy Grail*, ch. 9, p. 209 and elsewhere.

CHAPTER 13: THE PENDRAGONS

1. John Allegro, *The Dead Sea Scrolls*, ch. 7, p. 110.

2. Some art historians maintain that the pomegranates in these paintings denote the Resurrection through classical associations with the story of Persephone. She was the ancient Greek goddess (a daughter of Zeus and Demeter) who was carried off to the Underworld by Hades (Pluto). A condition of her eventual rescue was that she could spend only part of each year thereafter on the Earth's surface, and her annual return is marked by the regeneration of natural life that characterizes the spring.

This story is an allegory of the growth and decay cycle of vegetation and has nothing whatever to do with bodily resurrection from the dead. Such a connotation was conferred on Botticelli's paintings by a fearful establishment wishing to conceal the facts. Botticelli was a Grail student, a leading esotericist and a designer of Tarot cards. His pomegranate seeds represent fertility in accordance with the pomegranates of the *Song of Solomon* and the pillar capitals of Solomon's Temple, which was built around a thousand years before Jesus was crucified.

3. From The High History of the Holy Grail, compiled in around 1220 from an earlier manuscript by the clerk Josephus.

4. Henry VIII's antiquary, John Leland, in 1542 identified the Iron Age hill-fort at South Cadbury in Somerset as Camelot, mainly on the grounds that a couple of villages nearby included the river-name Camel. Excavations at Cadbury during the 1960s unearthed the remains of a Dark Age feasting hall but, appealing as it was to the tourist industry, there was nothing to associate the camp with Arthur. Indeed, more than 40 constructions of similar age and type have been found in the southwest of England alone, and there are many more elsewhere in the country. See Michael Wood, *In Search of the Dark Ages*, BBC Books, London, 1981, ch. 2, p. 50.

5. Lucius was the grandson of Brân's daughter Penardun of Siluria. She is sometimes held to have been the daughter of Beli Mawr, or sometimes his sister. She was, however, the sister of the later Beli, son of Brân. Penardun was a protégée of Queen Boudicca.

6. Gabràn was a grandson of Fergus mac Erc, who was born of Gaelic Scots royalty in descent from the High King Conaire Mor of Ireland. Fergus left Ireland in the latter 5th century in order to colonize the Western Highlands, taking with him his brothers Loarn and Angus. Loarn's family occupied the region of northern Argyll, thereafter known as Loarna (or Lorne), based at Dunollie, Oban.

7. Individual annals cite different names for this conflict and/or its location. Names for the location include Mount Badon, Mons Badonicus, Dun Bædàn and Cath Badwn (in which mount and mons imply a hill; *dun* implies either a hill or a hill-fort, and *cath* represents a stronghold). Names for the battle include *Bellum Badonis* and *Obsessio Badonica* (the first suggesting a war and the second a siege).

8. The battle is cited in the Bodleian Manuscripts, the *Book of Leinster*, the *Book of Ballymote* and the *Chronicles of the Scots*—and all give the date as 516. The Scots commander is generally named as Aedàn mac Gabràn of Dalriada, but Aedàn had not yet been born. The leader was actually his father, Gabràn, who became King of Dalriada in 537. Aedàn and his eldest son, Arthur, fought at the second battle of Dun Bædàn, which took place in 575. Despite the definitive date of 516

quoted in the chronicles, there has been a great deal of speculation about this (first) battle, much of which has arisen
because researchers have been directed to the wrong historian Gildas. All too often it is Gildas II who is mistakenly identified as the author of *De Excidio*. But he lived 425-512, and was
thus already dead when Gildas III was born in 516—the very
year of the battle, as he made a point of saying.

Other selected works on the subject of Britain in the
Dark Ages are Myles Dillon and Nora K. Chadwick, *The Celtic
Realms*; Hector Munro Chadwick *et al., Studies in Early British
History*; Hector Munro Chadwick, *Early Scotland*; W. F. Skene,
Celtic Scotland; R. Cunliffe Shaw, *Post-Roman Carlisle and the
Kingdoms of the North-West*; Eoin MacNeill, *Celtic Ireland*, and
Peter Hunter Blair, *The Origins of Northumbria*.

Chapter 14: King Arthur

1. In the time of Arthur, the southwest peninsula of the British
   mainland was called Dumnonia (from which the name Devon
   derives). The name *Cornwall* did not emerge until the 9th
   century.

2. *Tract on the Tributes Paid to Bædàn, King of Ulster* in the
   Chronicles of the Picts and Scots.

3. This was at a time before the unified nation of England. It was
   not until 927 that Alfred the Great's grandson, Aethelstan, was
   recognized as overall king by the majority of Anglo-Saxon
   territorial groupings.

4. The distinction of *'le Benoic'* derives from Latin *ille benedictum*:
   'the Blessed'.

5. Urien is most famous for effecting a coalition of Strathclyde
   rulers against the Northumbrian Angles of Bernicia.

6. Geoffrey Ashe, *Avalonian Quest*, ch. 3, sect. 2, p. 48.

7. The tradition that Arthur had two wives is yet another manifestation of the confusion caused by the convergence in mythology of the two princely Arthurs (Arthur of Dalriada and Arthur
   of Dyfed) described as if they were one in the *Annales
   Cambriae*.

8. Thomas F. O'Rahilly, *Early Irish History and Mythology*, Dublin
   Institute for Advanced Studies, 1946, ch. 6, p. 145.

9. William J. Watson, *The History of the Celtic Place Names of
   Scotland*, William Blackwood, Edinburgh, 1926, ch. 3, p. 97.

Chapter 15: Intrigue against the Bloodline

1. Some useful information on Priscillian is to be found in
   Baigent, Leigh and Lincoln, *The Messianic Legacy*, ch. 8,
   pp. 99-101.

2. For further information about the Celtic Church, See Nora K.
   Chadwick, *The Age of Saints in the Celtic Church*, Oxford
   University Press, 1961; Dom Louis Gougaud, *Christianity in
   Celtic Lands*, and E. G. Bowen, *The Settlements of the Celtic
   Saints in Wales*, University of Wales Press, Cardiff, 1956.

3. Notwithstanding the practicalities of the break between Rome
   and Constantinople, the fact that it resulted in two separate
   and independent Churches was not formalized by the denomi-
   nations concerned until 1945.

4. Anna Jameson, *Legends of the Madonna*, Houghton Mifflin,
   Boston, 1895.

5. Literature on the subject of this latter period of Merovingian
   history is fairly limited in the English language. Gregory of
   Tours' 6th-century *History of the Franks* does not extend to this
   era. It is covered, up to a point, in J. M. Wallace Hadrill, *The
   Long-Haired Kings*, but the best overview of the story of
   Dagobert II is recounted in various chapters of Baigent, Leigh

and Lincoln, *The Holy Blood and the Holy Grail*. There is also a
useful summary of the late Merovingian situation in Margaret
Deanesley, *A Medieval History of Europe 476 to 911*, Methuen,
London, 1956, ch. 15.

6. The transference of power from the Merovingians to the
   Carolingians is well narrated in R. H. C. Davis, *A History of
   Medieval Europe*, Longmans Green, London, 1957, ch. 6,
   pp. 120-53. Unlike the Dagobert intrigue, which is outside
   the scope of conventional history books, the rise of the
   Carolingians is widely documented as a historical subject
   in its own right.

7. The most comprehensive account to date of the Septimanian
   kingdom is in Arthur J. Zuckerman, *A Jewish Princedom in
   Feudal France*, Columbia University Press, New York, 1972.

8. The Jewish faith being represented here by the collective term
   (i.e., Torah) for the first five scriptural books of the Hebrew
   Bible.

Chapter 16: Temple of the Grail

1. See Chapter 12, *Merovingian Sorcerer Kings*.

2. Corbenic = Cors benicon = *Corpus benedictum* = 'Body
   blessed'—thus the Blessed Body. Accordingly, Château du
   Corbenic = Castle of the Blessed (or Consecrated) Body.

3. John Matthews, *The Grail: Quest for the Eternal*, Thames &
   Hudson, London, 1981, p. 8.

4. *Ibid.*, p. 9.

5. Harold Bayley, *The Lost Language of Symbolism*, Williams &
   Norgate, London, 1912, which contains comprehensive details
   of medieval watermarks in Provence.

6. Lionel Smithett Lewis, *Joseph of Arimathea at Glastonbury*, p. 35.

7. George F. Jowett, *The Drama of the Lost Disciples*, ch. 18, p. 212.

8. Gladys Taylor, *Our Neglected Heritage*, II, pp. 47-8.

Chapter 17: Guardians of the Grail

1. The original Order of Sion was established so that eligible
   Muslims, Jews and others could be allied to the Christian Order
   that became the Knights Templars.

2. Cistercian ideals were far removed from the concerns of the
   curia at the Vatican; they pertained to education, agriculture
   and the sacred arts.

3. The original Columban mission on Iona was destroyed by
   Norse pirates in 807. St. Bernard's new monastery on the site
   was Cistercian rather than Columban.

4. Ean Begg, *The Cult of the Black Virgin*, ch. 4, p. 103.

5. Louis Charpentier, *The Mysteries of Chartres Cathedral*, ch. 7,
   p. 55.

6. *Ibid.*, ch. 7, p. 56.

7. *Ibid.*, ch. 8, p. 69.

   Other selected works on the subject of the
   Templars and the Crusades are John C. Andressohn, *The
   Ancestry and Life of Godfrey de Bouillon*; Baigent and Leigh,
   The Temple and the Lodge; Desmond Seward, *The Monks of
   War*, and Steven Runciman, *A History of the Crusades*.

8. Louis Charpentier, *The Mysteries of Chartres Cathedral*, ch. 9,
   p. 70.

9. The *Notre Dame* ground plan made use of ley lines and Mother
   Earth locations in which the terrestrial forces were heightened
   by deep underground caverns or wells.

10. Louis Charpentier, *The Mysteries of Chartres Cathedral*, ch. 2,
    p. 29.

11. A dolmen usually consists of two upright stones with a horizontal capstone across the top, as at Stonehenge. From prehistoric times, dolmens were used as gigantic resonators (much like sound boxes used to amplify acoustic musical instruments) to boost the properties of the Earth's telluric current.

12. Laurence Gardner, *Genesis of the Grail Kings*, Bantam Press, London, 1999, ch. 14, p. 146.

13. The subject is well covered in Baigent, Leigh and Lincoln, *The Holy Blood and the Holy Grail*, ch. 2, pp. 19-34. Similarly, *The Temple and the Lodge* by Baignet and Leigh (ch 3, pp. 51-62 and ch. 4, pp. 63-76) is informative on the Inquisition of the Templars and the Templar Fleet.

14. A good overview of Provence as a 'cradle of awakening' is given in Margaret Starbird, *The Woman With the Alabaster Jar*, ch. 4, pp. 67-78.

15. Eleanor of Aquitaine (1122-1204) is a good example of female equality in the region. Her importance and influence were a constant embarrassment to the Roman Church bishops.

16. Selected works on the subject of the Albigensian Crusade are Zoe Oldenbourg, *Massacre at Montségur*, and J. Sumption, *The Albigensian Crusade*.

17. The excommunication of Scotland as a nation was not repealed until 1323. This followed Robert the Bruce's defeat of Edward II at Bannockburn in 1314 and the drawing up of the Scottish Constitution (the Declaration of Arbroath) in 1320. Subsequently, in 1328, the Treaty of Northampton confirmed Scotland's independence under King Robert I.

18. HRH Prince Michael of Albany, *The Forgotten Monarchy of Scotland*, Element Books, Shaftesbury, 1998, ch. 5, pp. 62-64.

CHAPTER 18: KINGDOM OF THE SCOTS

1. Although there were enclaves of celibate monks within the Celtic Church, the priests were permitted to marry. Their clerical ordination was strictly hereditary, passing from father to son. Crinan's ancestors had maintained the hereditary priesthood of Dull (Dule, near Aberfeldy, Perthshire) for more than five generations from around 850. By the late 900s Crinan was Seneschal (Steward) of the Isles, Abthane of Dull and Abbot of Dunkeld.

2. At the time of Malcolm III Canmore's installation, the Celtic Church prevailed. But this was destined to change. Malcolm's wife Margaret (the last Saxon heiress and a great-granddaughter of Aethelred the Unready) had been raised at the Roman Catholic Court of her grandfather King Stephen of Hungary. She also spent time at the court of Edward the Confessor in England. When she married Malcolm, Margaret had no knowledge of the Gaelic language used by the Celtic priests, but her son became King David I of Scots and, accordingly, head of the Sacred Kindred of St Columba. Margaret (later St. Margaret) ignored the Celtic heritage and pursued her Catholic endeavor, so that the two cultures became firmly integrated.

   The historical content of this section of the chapter derives from the family archives of the Royal House of Stewart and the records of the Sacred Kindred of Columba.

3. The monastery at Dol was founded by the Celtic saint, Samson, who first sailed to Brittany from Cornwall in the early 500s during the reign of the Merovingian King Childebert. Dol is on the Brittany coast near Dinan, not far from St. Michel. The spear-carrying Samson, with his long hair and druidic frontal tonsure, had been educated by the Welsh abbot Illtyd. He was installed as Bishop of Dol in about 530. The bishopric was elevated to become an archbishopric in 845. Later still, the ancient town of Dol (in which the main street was subsequently named

'la Grande Rue des Stuarts') became prominent in sovereign history. It was from here that the closely related major domos of the royal house (the Seneschals of Dol and Dinan) emerged through the female line to found the Royal House of Stewart in Scotland.

4. This error originated in *The History of Shropshire*, 1858.

5. This marriage is correctly recorded in Chalmers' *Caledonia*, 1807.

6. This error was an element of the 1895 book *The Isle of Bute in the Olden Time* by J. K. Hewison, in which he quite wrongly averred that 'Walter, the son of Fleadan, son of Banchu, is identical with Walter, son of Alan'.

   The historical content of this section of the chapter is extracted from the Jacobite Records of Saint Germain-en-Laye.

CHAPTER 19: THE AGE OF CHIVALRY

1. See Chapter 14, *The Historical Warlord*.

2. Brutus (d. *c.*1103 B.C.) was the grandson of Ascanius Julius, son of Aeneas and Creusa (daughter of King Priam of Troy.) After the fall of Troy in about 1184 B.C.E., the royal house of Dardanos was scattered. The Trojan Cycle, as listed by Proclus in the 2nd century C.E., records that Aeneas went to Italy with 88,000 Trojans in a fleet of 332 ships. Brutus led another party to Britain, where, as cited in Nennius' *Historia*, he founded London, calling it Trinovantium. The Brutus Stone, from which royal accessions were traditionally proclaimed, is at Totnes in Devon. See Gladys Taylor, *Our Neglected Heritage*, III, ch. 4, pp. 28-9.

3. Guanhumara of Ireland was the wife of Arthur of Dyfed, whereas Gwenhwyfar of Brittany married Arthur of Dalriada.

4. The historical Sword of Avallon was passed to Lancelot by his mother, Viviane del Acqs. He was to hold it in trust for Modred, Archpriest of the Celtic Kindred and son of the dynastic heiress, Morgaine. Instead, however, Lancelot gave the sword to Modred's father, Arthur—and this was reckoned to have caused the downfall of the kingdom. In the event, both Arthur and Lancelot were denounced by the Celtic Church.

5. Beryl Platts, *Scottish Hazard*, Proctor Press, London, 1985-90, *passim*.

6. See Chapter 16, *Persecution of the Knights Templars*.

7. Baigent and Leigh, *The Temple and the Lodge*, Jonathan Cape, London, 1989, ch. 8 p. 113.

8. Baigent, Leigh and Lincoln, *The Holy Blood and the Holy Grail*, ch. 6, p. 108.

9. Andrew Sinclair, *The Sword and the Grail*, ch. 7, pp. 77-8.

10. See Chapter 10, *Lordship of the Grail*.

CHAPTER 20: HERESY AND INQUISITION

1. Michael Howard, *The Occult Conspiracy*, ch. 3, p. 43.

2. The caduceus corresponds to the winged staff of Mercury, borne by him as a messenger of the gods.

3. Michael Howard, *The Occult Conspiracy*, ch. 4, pp. 73-4. Other selected works on the subject of the Rosicrucians are Frances A. Yates, *The Rosicrucian Enlightenment*, and Arthur E. Waite, *The Real History of the Rosicrucians*.

ART ACKNOWLEDGMENTS

Grateful acknowledgment is made for permission granted to reproduce images in the text:

Art Resource, New York: 188, 194; Bibliotheque National de France, Paris: 101; Birmingham Museum and Art Gallery: 93, 171; Bridgeman Art Library, London: 10, 24, 65, 139, 152, 162, 209; Britain on View / Stockwave, London: 142, 156, 185, 202; Britain on View / Stockwave, London © Barry Hicks: 137; Corbis, Los Angeles © Dave G. Houser: 186(rt.); Corbis, Los Angeles © Araldo de Luca: 163; Corbis, Los Angeles © Adam Woolfitt: 186(l); Entropic Fine Art Inc. <http://www.entropic-art.com/>: 68, 115, 222; E.T. Archive, London: 6, 15, 16, 23, 30, 31, 40, 48, 49, 77, 96, 97, 99(rt), 114, 118, 136, 157, 170, 184, 206, 213, 215, 216; Gemaldegalerie, Dresden: 44; Getty Images, London: 7; Images Color Library, London: 8(rt), 9, 11, 177(rt); Kunstistorisches Museum, Vienna: 2, 61; Louvre, Paris: 161; Mary Evans Picture Library, London: 2, 4, 8(l), 10, 19, 22, 25, 34, 35, 37, 38, 39, 53, 54, 55, 56, 57, 58, 60, 63, 64, 67, 71, 72, 74, 78, 81, 86, 88, 99(l), 105, 107, 117, 133, 148, 149, 150, 154, 165, 173, 177(rt), 178, 181, 182, 183, 191, 198, 200, 201, 204, 211, 212, 214; Mary Evans Picture Library, London / Edwin Wallace: 125, 134, 164, 203; Mary Evans Picture Library, London / Explorer: 12; Musee de la Chartreuse, Douai: 188; National Gallery of Art, Washington: 14, 159; National Gallery, London: Frontispiece, 26, 28, 29, 47, 62, 73, 90; Galleria Uffizi, Scala Museum, Florence: 79, 94; Royal Collection Enterprises, Windsor: 83; Tate Gallery, London: 43, 187, 205; The Ancient Art and Architecture Collection, Pinner: 18; The British Library, London: 5, 41, 84, 85, 102, 104, 126, 155, 189, 195, 210, ; The British Museum, London: 95, 113; The Detroit Institute of Arts: 61; The Royal Collection, Her Majesty Queen Elizabeth II, London: 66; Walker Art Gallery, Liverpool: 172; Werner Forman Archive, London: 116.

BIBLIOGRAPHY

BIBLICAL AND SCRIPTURAL

Aaron, Robert, *Jesus of Nazareth the Hidden Years* (trans. Frances Frenhaye), Hamish Hamilton, London, 1962.

Allegro, John M., *The Dead Sea Scrolls*, Penguin, Harmondsworth, 1964.

Anderson, Hugh, *Jesus and Christian Origins*, Oxford University Press, Oxford, 1964.

Baigent, M. and Leigh, R., *The Dead Sea Scrolls Deception*, Jonathan Cape, London, 1991.

Barclay, James, *The Mind of Jesus*, Harper & Row, New York, 1960.

Black, Matthew, *The Scrolls and Christian Origins*, Thomas Nelson, London, 1961.

Brandon, S.G.F., *The Fall of Jerusalem and the Christian Church*, SPCK, London, 1951.
Jesus and the Zealots, Charles Scribner's Sons, New York, 1967.

Brooke, G., *Temple Scroll Studies*, Sheffield Academic Press, Sheffield, 1989.

Catchpole, David R., *The Trial of Jesus*, E. J. Brill, Leiden, 1971.

Chase, Mary Ellen, *Life and Language in the Old Testament*, Collins, London, 1956.

Cranfield, CEB., *The Gospel According to St. Mark*, Cambridge University Press, Cambridge, 1959.

Danielou, Jean, *The Dead Sea Scrolls and Primitive Christianity* (trans. Salvator Attansio), New American Library, New York, 1962.

Dart, John, *The Laughing Savior*, Harper & Row, New York, 1976.

Dodd, C.H., *Historical Tradition in the Fourth Gospel*, Cambridge University Press, Cambridge, 1963.

Doresse, Jean, *The Secret Books of the Egyptian Gnostics* (trans. Philip Mairet), Hollis & Carter, London, 1960.

Dupont-Sommer, André, *The Essene Writings from Qumrân* (trans. G. Vermes), Basil Blackwell, Oxford, 1961.
The Jewish Sect of Qumrân and the Essenes, Vallentine Mitchell, London, 1954.

Eisenman, R.H., Maccabees, Zadokites, *Christians and Qumrân*, E.J. Brill, Leiden, 1983.
James the Just in the Habakkuk Pesher, E.J. Brill, Leiden, 1986.

Faber-Kaiser, Andraeus, *Jesus Died in Kashmir*, Abacus / Sphere, London, 1978.

Filliette, Edith, *Saint Mary Magdalene, Her Life and Times*, Society of St. Mary Magdalene, Newton Lower Falls, MA, 1983.

Fleetwood, Rev. John, *The Life of Our Lord and Savior Jesus Christ*, William Mackenzie, Glasgow, *c.*1900.

Finkel, A., *The Pharisees and the Teacher of Nazareth*, E.J. Brill, Leiden, 1964.

Gaster, T.H., *Samaritan Eschatology, Oral Law and Ancient Traditions*, Search, London, 1932.

Grant, M., *The Jews in the Roman World*, Weidenfeld & Nicolson, London, 1973.
Herod The Great, Weidenfeld & Nicolson, London, 1971.

James, Montague R. (ed.), *The Apocryphal New Testament*, Clarendon Press, Oxford, 1924.

Jeremias, J., *Jerusalem in the Time of Jesus*, SCM Press, London, 1969.

Josephus, Flavius, *The Jewish Wars* (trans. G.A. Williamson), Penguin, Harmondsworth, 1959.
Antiquities of the Jews and Wars of the Jews (trans. W. Whiston), Thomas Nelson, London, 1862. *The Works of Flavius Josephus*, Milner & Sowerby, London, 1870.

Joyce, Donovan, *The Jesus Scroll*, Angus & Robertson, London, 1973.

Kenyon, K.M., *Jerusalem: Excavating 3000 Years of History*, Thames & Hudson, London, 1967.

Kersten, Holger and Gruber, Elmar R., *The Jesus Conspiracy*, Barnes & Noble, New York, 1995.

Knox, Wilfred, *Sources of the Synoptic Gospels*, Cambridge University Press, Cambridge, 1959.

Lacordaire, Rev. Père, *Saint Mary Magdalene*, Thomas Richardson, Derby, 1880.

Lewis, Rev. Lionel Smithett, *St. Joseph of Arimathea at Glastonbury*, A.R. Mobray, London, 1927.

Malvern, Marjorie, *Venus in Sackcloth*, Southern Illinois University Press, 1975.

Mead, G.R.S., *The Gnostic John the Baptiser*, John M. Watkins, London, 1924.

Milik, J.T., *Ten Years of Discovery in the Wilderness of Judaea* (trans. J. Strugnell), SCM Press, London, 1959.

Osman, Ahmed, *Moses Pharaoh of Egypt*, Grafton/Collins, London, 1990.
The House of The Messiah, Harper Collins, London, 1992.

Pagels, Elaine, *The Gnostic Gospels*, Weidenfeld & Nicolson, London, 1980.

Patai, Raphael, *The Hebrew Goddess*, Wayne State University Press, Detroit, 1967.

Perowne, S., *The Life and Times of Herod the Great*, Hodder & Stoughton, London, 1956.
The Later Herods, Hodder & Stoughton, London, 1958.

Platt, Rutherford H. (ed.), *The Lost Books of the Bible*, World Publishing, New York, 1963.

Ringgren, Helmer, *The Faith of Qumran* (trans. Emile T. Sander), Fondress Press, Philadelphia, 1973.

Robinson, James M., *The Nag Hammadi Library*, Coptic Gnostic Library: Institute for Antiquity and Christianity at E.J. Brill, Leiden, 1977.

Schonfield, Hugh J., *The Authentic New Testament*, Denis Dobson, London, 1956.
The Essene Odyssey, Element Books, Shaftesbury,1984.
The Passover Plot, Element Books, Shaftesbury, 1985.

Smallwood. E.M., *The Jews Under Roman Rule*, E.J. Brill, Leiden, 1976.

Smith, Morton, *The Secret Gospel*, Victor Gollancz, London, 1974.

Stone, Merlin, *When God Was a Woman*, Dial Press, New York, 1976.

Thackery, H. St.John, *Josephus the Man and Historian*, KTAV, Hoboken, NJ, 1967.

Thiering, Barbara, *Jesus the Man*, Doubleday Transworld, London, 1992.

Times, The, *Atlas of the Bible*, Times Books, London, 1987.

Vermes, Geza, *The Dead Sea Scrolls in English*, Pelican, Harmondsworth, 1987.

Von Daniken, Erich, *Chariots of the Gods*, Souvenir Press, London, 1969.

Walker, Benjamin, *Gnosticism*, Aquarian Press, Wellingborough, 1983.

Williamson, G.A, *The World of Josephus*, Secker & Warburg, London, 1964.

Wilson, A.N., Jesus, *Sinclair Stevenson*, London, 1992.

Wilson, E., *The Dead Sea Scrolls*, Collins, London, 1971.

Yadin, Yigael, *Masada: Herod's Last Fortress*, Weidenfeld & Nicolson, London, 1966.

    The Temple Scroll: Hidden Law, Weidenfeld & Nicolson, London, 1985.

CULTS AND RELIGION

Adamnan, Saint, *A Life of Saint Columba* (trans. Wentworth Huyshe), George Routledge, London, 1908.

Aradi, Zsolt, *Shrines of Our Lady*, Farrar, Strauss & Young, New York, 1954.

Baigent, M., Leigh, R. and Lincoln, H., *The Messianic Legacy*, Jonathan Cape, London, 1986.

Baldock, John, *Christian Symbolism*, Element Books, Shaftesbury, 1990.

    The Alternative Gospel, Element Books, Shaftesbury, 1998.

Bander, P., *The Prophecies of St. Malachy and St. Columbkille*, Colin Smythe, Gerrards Cross, 1979.

Baring-Gould, S. and Fisher, J., *The Lives of the British Saints*, Cymmrodorion Society, London, 1907-1913.

Bede, The Venerable of Jarrow, *The Ecclesiastical History of the English Nation* (trans. J.A. Giles), Dent / Everyman, London, 1970.

Begg, Ean C.M., *The Cult of the Black Virgin*, Arkana, London, 1985.

Bernard de Clairvaux, *On the Song of Songs* (trans. Kilian Walsh), Cistercian Publishers, Michigan, 1976.

Bowen, E.G., *The Settlements of the Celtic Saints in Wales*, University of Wales Press, Cardiff, 1956.

Bull, Norman J., *The Rise of the Church*, Heinemann, London, 1967.

Bultmann, Rudolf, *Primitive Christianity in its Contemporary Setting* (trans. R.H. Fuller), Fontana / Collins, Glasgow, 1960.

Butterworth, G.W. (trans.), *Clement of Alexandria*, Heinemann, London, 1968.

Chadwick, H., *Priscillian of Avila*, Oxford University Press, Oxford, 1976.

    The Early Church, Penguin, Harmondsworth, 1978.

Chadwick, Nora K., *The Age of the Saints in the Early Celtic Church*, Oxford University Press, Oxford, 1961.

Clement, Saint of Alexandria, *Clementine Homilies and Apostolical Constitutions* (trans.), Ante-Nicene Library, T. & T. Clark, Edinburgh, 1870.

Constantinus of Lyons (*c.* 480 C.E.), *The Life of Saint Germanus of Auxerre* [in The Western Fathers] (ed. W. Levinson; trans. F.R. Hoare), Sheed & Ward, London, 1954.

Duncan, Anthony, *Celtic Christianity*, Element Books, Shaftesbury, 1992.

Eusebius of Caesaria, *History of the Church from Christ to Constantine* (trans. G.A. Williamson), Penguin Harmondsworth, 1981.

    Ecclesiastical History, (trans. C.F. Crusé), George Bell, London, 1874.

Farmer, D.H., *The Oxford Dictionary of Saints*, Clarendon Press, Oxford, 1978.

Gilson, Etienne, *The Mystical Theology of Saint Bernard*

(trans. A.H.C. Downes), Sheed & Ward, London, 1940.

Gimbutas, Marija, *The Gods and Goddesses of Old Europe*, Thames & Hudson, London, 1974.

Godwin, Joscelyn, *Mystery Religions in the Ancient World*, Thames & Hudson, London, 1981.

Gougaud, Dom Louis, *Christianity in Celtic Lands* (trans. Maud Joynt), Four Courts Press, Dublin, 1932.

Graves, Robert and Podro Joshua, *The Nazarene Gospel Restored*, Cassell, London, 1953.

Green, Miranda, *The Gods of the Celts*, Alan Sutton, Gloucester, 1986.

Halsberghe, G.S., *The Cult of Sol Invictus*, E.J. Brill, Leiden, 1972.

Herford, R. Travers, *Christianity in Talmud and Midrash*, Williams & Norgate, London, 1903.

Hewins, Prof. W.A.S., *The Royal Saints of Britain*, Chiswick Press, London, 1929.

Jacobus de Voragine, *The Golden Legend* (trans. William Caxton; ed. George V. O'Neill), Cambridge University Press, Cambridge, 1972.

James, B. S., *Saint Bernard of Clairvaux*, Harper, New York, 1957.

James, E.O., *The Cult of the Mother Goddess*, Thames & Hudson, London, 1959.

Jameson, Anna, *Legends of the Madonna*, Houghton Mifflin, Boston, 1895.

Johnston, Rev. Thomas J., *A History of the Church of Ireland*, APCK, Dublin, 1953.

Jonas, Hans, *The Gnostic Religion*, Routledge, London, 1992.

Jowett, George F., *The Drama of the Lost Disciples*, Covenant Books, London, 1961.

Knowles, David, *The Monastic Order in England*, Cambridge University Press, Cambridge, 1950.

Kramer, Samuel, *The Sacred Marriage Rite*, Indiana University Press, Bloomington, 1969.

Lewis, Rev. Lionel Smithett, *Glastonbury, the Mother of Saints*, St. Stephen's Press, Bristol, 1925.

Maclean, G.R.D., *Praying With the Highland Christians*, Triangle /SPCK, London, 1988.

Margoliouth, D.S., *Mohammed and the Rise of Islam*, Putnam, London, 1931.

Marsden, J., *The Illustrated Colmcille*, Macmillan, London, 1991.

Martin, Malachi, *The Decline and Fall of the Roman Church*, Secker & Warburg, London, 1982.

Nash-Williams, V.E., *The Early Christian Monuments of Wales*, University of Wales Press, Cardiff, 1950.

Piggot, Stuart, *The Druids, Penguin*, Harmondsworth ,1974.

Pope, Marvin H., *Song of Songs*, Garden City/Doubleday, New York, 1977.

Qualls-Corbett, Nancy, *The Sacred Prostitute*, Inner City Books, Toronto, 1988.

Rees, Rev. Rice, *An Essay on the Welsh Saints*, Longman, London, 1836.

Rees, Rev. W.J., *Lives of the Cambro-British Saints*, Welsh MSS Society/Longman, London, 1853.

Ross, Anne, *Pagan Celtic Britain*, Cardinal/Sphere Books, London, 1974.

Rutherford, Ward, *The Druids and Their Heritage*, Gordon & Cremonesi, London, 1978.

Scott, John, *The Early History of Glastonbury*, Boydell Press, London, 1981.

Taylor, Gladys, *Our Neglected Heritage*, Covenant Books, London, 1969-74.

Taylor, J.W., *The Coming of the Saints*, Covenant Books, London, 1969.

Wade-Evans, Arthur W., *Welsh Christian Origins*, Alden Press, Oxford, 1934.

Warren, F.E., *The Liturgy of the Celtic Church*, Oxford University Press, Oxford, 1881.

ANCIENT HISTORY AND PREHISTORY

Daniel, Glyn (ed.), *Encyclopedia of Archaeology*, Macmillan, London, 1978.
Guthrie, W.K.C., *The Greeks and Their Gods*, Methuen, London, 1950.
Kramer, Samuel, *History Begins at Sumer*, Thames & Hudson, London, 1958.
Rohl, David, *A Test of Time*, Century, London, 1995.
Roux, George, *Ancient Iraq*, George Allen & Unwin, London, 1964.
Woolley, C. Leonard, *Ur of the Chaldees*, Ernest Benn, London, 1930.

MYTHOLOGY AND FOLKLORE

Ames, Delano (trans.), *Greek Mythology* [from *Mythologie Générale Larousse*], Paul Hamlyn, London, 1963.
Bromwich, Rachel (trans.), *The Welsh Triads*, University of Wales Press, Cardiff, 1961.
Conran, Anthony, *The Penguin Book of Welsh Verse*, Penguin, Harmondsworth, 1967.
Crossley-Holland, Kevin, *British Folk Tales*, Macmillan, London, 1971.
Curtin, J., *Hero Tales of Ireland*, Macmillan, London, 1894.
Davidson, H.E., *Gods and Myths in Northern Europe*, Penguin, Harmondsworth, 1964.
Delaney, Frank, *Legends of the Celts*, Hodder & Stoughton, London, 1989.
Gantz, Jeffrey (trans.), *The Mabinogion*, Penguin, Harmondsworth, 1976.
Graves, Robert, *The White Goddess*, Faber & Faber, London, 1961.
Guest, Lady Charlotte (trans.), *The Mabinogion*, John Jones, Cardiff, 1977.
Hadas, Moses and Smith Morton, *Heroes and Gods*, Freeport, New York, 1965.
Matthews, C., *Mabon and the Mysteries of Britain*, Arkana, London, 1987.
O'Rahilly, Thomas, *Early Irish History and Mythology*, Dublin Institute for Advanced Studies, Dublin, 1946.
Price, Glanville (trans.), William, *Count of Orange* [French trad.], Dent, London, 1975.
Rhys, John, *Celtic Folklore*, Clarendon Press, Oxford, 1901.
Tatlock, J.S.P., *The Legendary History of Britain*, University of California, 1950.
Westwood, Jennifer, *A Guide to Legendary Britain*, Paladin, London, 1987.

CELTS, ROMANS AND THE DARK AGES

Chadwick, Nora K. (ed.), *Studies in Early British History*, Cambridge University Press, Cambridge, 1954.
Celtic Britain, Praeger, New York, 1963.
Celt and Saxon, Cambridge University Press, Cambridge, 1964.
The Celts, Penguin, Harmondsworth, 1970.
Cunliffe, Barry, *The Celtic World*, Bodley Head, London, 1979.
Delaney, Frank, *The Celts*, Grafton / Collins, London, 1989.
Dillon, Myles and Chadwick, Nora, *The Celtic Realms*, Weidenfeld & Nicolson, London, 1967.
Ellis, P.B., *The Celtic Empire*, Constable, London, 1990.
Gurney, Robert, *Celtic Heritage*, Chatto & Windus, London, 1969.
Herm, G., *The Celts*, Weidenfeld & Nicolson, London, 1976.
Hubert, Henry, *The Rise of the Celts*, Keegan Paul, London, 1934.
The Greatness and Decline of the Celts, Keegan Paul, London, 1934.
Markale, Jean, *Women of the Celts* (trans. A. Mygind, C. Hauch and P. Henry), Inner Traditions, Vermont, 1986.

Matthews, Caitlin, *The Celtic Tradition*, Element Books, Shaftesbury, 1989.
Nennius, *Historia Brittonium* (trans. John Morris), Phillimore, Chichester, 1980.
Rees, Alwyn and Brinley, *Celtic Heritage*, Thames & Hudson, London, 1961.
Thomas, Charles, *Celtic Britain*, Thames & Hudson, London, 1986.
Wood, Michael, *In Search of the Dark Ages*, BBC Books, London, 1981.

SCOTLAND

Albany, HRH Prince Michael of, *The Forgotten Monarchy of Scotland*, Element Books, Shaftesbury, 1998.
Anderson, Alan Orr, *Early Sources of Scottish History* (ed. Marjorie Anderson), Paul Watkins, London, 1990.
Anderson, Joseph, *Scotland in Early Christian Times*, David Douglas, Edinburgh, 1881.
Bain, J., *Calendar of Documents Relating to Scotland*, HM Stationery Office, Edinburgh, 1881-88.
Bain, Robert, *The Clans and Tartans of Scotland*, Fontana/Collins, Glasgow, 1981.
Barbour, John, *The Bruce*, William Mackenzie, Glasgow, 1909.
Barrow, G.W.S., *Robert Bruce and the Community of the Realm of Scotland*, Eyre & Spottiswoode, London, 1965. *The Kingdom of the Scots*, Edward Arnold, London, 1973.
Chadwick, Hector Munro, *Early Scotland, The Picts, Scots and Welsh of Southern Scotland*, Cambridge University Press, Cambridge, 1949.
Fairweather, Barbara, *Highland Heritage*, Glencoe and North Lorne Folk Museum, Argyll, 1984.
Harry, Rev. George Owen, *The Genealogy of the High and Mighty Monarch*, James, Simon Stafford, London, 1604.
Hewison, James King, *The Isle of Bute in the Olden Time*, William Blackwood, Edinburgh, 1895.
Kermack, William R., *Scottish Highlands: A Short History c.300-1746*, Johnston & Bacon, Edinburgh, 1957.
Maclain, R.R., *The Clans of the Scottish Highlands*, Webb & Bower, Exeter, 1983.
Mackie, J.D.A, *A History of Scotland*, Pelican, Harmondsworth, 1964.
Moncrieffe, Sir Iain of that Ilk, *The Highland Clans*, Barrie & Jenkins, London, 1982.
Murray, John, 7th Duke of Atholl, *Chronicles of Atholl and Tullibardine Families*, Ballantyne, London, 1908.
Platts, Beryl, *Scottish Hazard*, Proctor Press, London, 1985-1990.
Shaw, R. Cunliffe, *Post Roman Carlisle and the Kingdoms of the North-West*, Guardian Press, Preston, 1964.
Skene, William Forbes, *Chronicles of the Picts and Scots*, HM General Register, Edinburgh, 1867. *Celtic Scotland*, David Douglas, Edinburgh, 1886-1890.
Starforth, Michael, *Clan MacDougall*, Bell & Bain Press, Glasgow. 1960.
Stewart, Maj. John of Ardvorlich, *The Stewarts*, Johnston & Bacon, Edinburgh, 1954.
Watson, W.J., *The History of the Celtic Place Names of Scotland*, William Blackwood, Edinburgh, 1926.

IRELAND AND WALES

Bartrum, Peter C., *Early Welsh Genealogical Tracts*, University of Wales Press, Cardiff, 1966.
Charlsworth, M.P., *The Lost Province*, University of Wales Press, Cardiff, 1949.
Keating, Geoffrey, *The History of Ireland*, 1640 (trans. David Comyn and Rev. P.S. Dinneen), Irish Texts Society, London, 1902-1914.

Kenney, James F., *The Sources for the Early History of Ireland*, Four Courts Press, Dublin, 1966.

MacNeill, E., *Celtic Ireland*, Martin Lester, Dublin 1921, Academy Press, Dublin, 1981.

Morris, John (trans.), *Annales Cambriae: The Annals of Wales* [Nennius, British History and the Welsh Annals], Phillimore, Chichester, 1980.

Munch, P.A and Goss Rev. Dr., *The Chronicle of Man*, The Manx Society, Isle of Man, 1974.

O'Rahilly, Cecile, *Ireland and Wales*, Longmans Green, London, 1924.

Rhys, John and Brynmore-Jones D., *The Welsh People*, T. Fisher Unwin, London, 1900.

Skene, William Forbes, *The Four Ancient Books of Wales*, David Douglas, Edinburgh, 1868.

Simms, Katharine, *From Kings to Warlords*, Boydell Press, London, 1987.

Williams, A.H., *An Introduction to the History of Wales*, University of Wales Press, Cardiff, 1962.

ENGLAND AND BRITAIN GENERAL

Blair, P. Hunter, *The Origins of Northumbria*, Northumberland Press, Gateshead, 1948.

Copley, Gordon K., *The Conquest of Wessex in the Sixth Century*, Phoenix House, London, 1954.

Deacon, Richard, *A History of the British Secret Service*, Grafton/Collins, London, 1982.

Feiling, Keith, *A History of England*, Book Club Associates, London, 1972.

Garmonsway, G.N. (trans.), *The Anglo-Saxon Chronicle*, Dent/Everyman, London, 1967.

Geoffrey of Monmouth, *The History of the Kings of Britain* (ed. Lewis Thorpe), Penguin, Harmondsworth, 1966.

Gildas, *De Excidio et Conquestu Britanniae* (trans. Michael Winterbottom), Phillimore, Chichester, 1978.

Harvey, John, *The Plantagenets*, B.T. Batsford, London, 1959.

Hodgkin, R.H., *A History of the Anglo-Saxons*, Oxford University Press, Oxford, 1952.

Lloyd, Lewis C., *The Origins of Some Anglo-Norman Families* (ed. Charles Clay and David Douglas), Harleian Society, Leeds, 1951.

Lomax, Frank (trans.), *The Antiquities of Glastonbury*, Talbot /JMF Books, Llanerch, 1980.

Oman, Sir Charles, *England Before the Norman Conquest*, Methuen, London, 1938.

Stenton, F.M., *Anglo-Saxon England*, Oxford University Press, Oxford, 1950.

Thomas, Charles, *Britain and Ireland in Early Christian Times*, Thames & Hudson, London, 1971.

Whitelock, Dorothy, *English Historical Documents 500-1042 C.E.*, Eyre & Spottiswoode, London, 1955

William of Malmesbury, *Chronicles of the Kings of England*, Bell and Daldy, London, 1866.

EUROPEAN HISTORY

Castries, Duc de, *The Lives of the Kings and Queens of France* [for Académie Francaise] (trans. Anne Dobell), Weidenfeld & Nicolson, London, 1979.

Chadwick, Nora K., *Early Brittany*, University of Wales Press, Cardiff, 1969.

Davidson, Marshall B., *The Concise History of France*, American Heritage, New York, 1971.

Davis, R.H.C., *A History of Medieval Europe*, Longmans Green, London, 1957.

Deanesly, Margaret, *A History of Early Medieval Europe 476-911*, Methuen, London, 1956.

Dill, Sir Samuel, *Roman Society in Gaul in the Merovingian Age*, Macmillan, London, 1926.

Giot, P.R., *Brittany*, Thames and Hudson, London, 1960. *Gregory of Tours, A History of the Franks* (trans. Lewis Thorpe), Penguin, Harmondsworth, 1964.

Kendrick, T.D., *A History of the Vikings*, Frank Cass, London, 1930.

Lindsay, Jack, *The Normans and Their World*, Purnell, London, 1974.

McKendrick, Malvena, *A Concise History of Spain*, Cassell, London, 1972.

Meade, Marion, *Eleanor of Aquitaine*, Frederick Muller, London, 1978.

Painter, Sidney, *A History of the Middle Ages*, Macmillan, London, 1973.

Roget, F.F., *French History, Literature and Philology*, Williams & Norgate, London, 1904.

Round, J. Horace, *Calendar of Documents Preserved in France 918-1206*, Eyre & Spottiswoode, London, 1899. *Studies in Peerage and Family History*, Constable, London, 1901.

Sackville-West, V., *Saint Joan of Arc*, Michael Joseph, London, 1936.

Smith, George A., *The Historical Geography of the Holy Land*, Fontana/Collins, Glasgow, 1966.

Spence, Keith, *Brittany and the Bretons*, Victor Gollancz, London, 1978.

Stanley, John Edgcumbe, *King René d'Anjou and his Seven Queens*, John Long, London, 1912.

Tacitus, *The Annals of Imperial Rome* (trans Michael Grant), Cassell, London, 1963.

Thorpe, Lewis (trans.), *The Life of Charlemagne*, Penguin, Harmondsworth, 1979.

Ullman, W., *A History of Political Thought in the Middle Ages*, Penguin, Harmondsworth, 1970.

Wallace-Hadrill, J.M., *The Long Haired Kings*, Methuen, London, 1962.

Wells, H.G., *The Outline of History*, Cassell, London, 1920.

Zuckerman, Arthur J., *A Jewish Princedom in Feudal France*, Columbia University Press, New York, 1972.

KNIGHTS TEMPLARS AND CRUSADES

Andressohn, John C., *The Ancestry and Life of Godfrey of Bouillon*, University of Indiana Press, Bloomington, 1947.

Baigent, Michael and Leigh, Richard, *The Temple and the Lodge*, Jonathan Cape, London, 1989.

Barber, M., *The Trial of the Templars*, Cambridge University Press, Cambridge, 1978.

Birks, W. and Gilbert, R.A., *The Treasure of Montségur*, Crucible /Thorsons, London, 1987.

Delaforge, G., *The Templar Tradition in the Age of Aquarius*, Threshold, Vermont, 1987.

Durman, Edward, *The Templars, Knights of God*, Aquarian Press, Wellingborough, 1988.

Guilliame de Tyre, *A History of Deeds Done Beyond the Sea* (trans. Emily A. Babcock and A.C. Krey), Columbia University Press, New York, 1943.

Howarth, Stephen, *The Knights Templar*, Collins, London, 1982.

Joinville, Sire Jean de, *Chronicles of the Crusades* (trans. Margaret Shaw), Penguin, Harmondsworth, 1976.

McMahon, Norbert, *The Story of the Hospitallers of Saint John of God*, M.H. Gill, Dublin, 1958.

Oldenbourg, Zoé, *Massacre at Montségur* (trans. Peter Green), Pantheon, New York, 1961.

Runciman, Steven, *A History of the Crusades*, Cambridge University Press, Cambridge, 1951.

Seward, Desmond, *The Monks of War*, Paladin/Granada, St.Albans, 1974.

Smith, Jonathan Riley, *The Knights of Saint John of Jerusalem and Cyprus*, Macmillan, London, 1987.

FREEMASONRY AND THE ROSE CROSS

Gould, R.F., *Gould's History of Freemasonry*, Caxton, London, 1933.

Horne, Alexander, *King Solomon's Temple in the Masonic Tradition*, Aquarian Press, Wellingborough, 1972.

Jones, B.E., *Freemasons' Guide and Compendium*, Harrap, London, 1956
Freemasons' Book of the Royal Arch, Harrap, London, 1957.

Knight, S., *The Brotherhood, The Secret World of the Freemasons*, Granada, St. Albans, 1984.

Lawrence, J., *Freemasonry, a Religion*, Kingsway, Eastbourne, 1987.

Waite, Arthur E., *The New Encyclopedia of Freemasonry*, Weathervane, New York, 1970.

Ward, J.S.M., *Who Was Hiram Abiff?*, Baskerville, London 1925,
Freemasonry and the Ancient Gods, Baskerville, London, 1926.

Yates, Frances A., *The Rosicrucian Enlightenment*, Routledge & Kegan Paul, London, 1972.

ANCIENT AND ESOTERIC SCIENCE

Adams, Henry, *Mont Saint Michel and Chartres*, Houghton Mifflin, Boston, 1913.

Bayley, Harold, *The Lost Language of Symbolism*, Williams & Norgate, London, 1912.

Butler, E.M., *The Myth of the Magus*, Cambridge University Press, Cambridge, 1948.

Cavendish, Richard, *The Tarot*, Michael Joseph, London, 1975.

Charpentier, Louis, *The Mysteries of Chartres Cathedral*, Research into Lost Knowledge Organization/Thorsons, Wellingborough, 1972.

Harrison, Michael, *The Roots of Witchcraft*, Frederick Muller, London, 1973.

Howard, Michael, *The Occult Conspiracy*, Rider/Century Hutchinson, London, 1989.

Hulme, Edward F., *Symbolism in Christian Art*, Swann Sonnenschein, London, 1891.

Lincoln, Henry, *The Holy Place*, Jonathan Cape, London, 1991.

Lucie-Smith, Edward, *Symbolist Art*, Thames & Hudson, London, 1972.

Michell, John, *Ancient Metrology*, Pentacle Books, Bristol, 1981.
The Dimensions of Paradise, Thames & Hudson, London, 1988.

Pennick, Nigel, *Sacred Geometry*, Turnstone, Wellingborough, 1980.

Pincus-Witten, R., *Occult Symbolism in France*, Garland, London, 1976.

Richards, Steve, *Levitation*, Thorsons, Wellingborough, 1980

Rougemont, Denis de, *Love in the Western World* (trans. Montgomery Belgion), Princeton University Press, New Jersey, 1983.

Silberer, Herbert, *Hidden Symbolism of Alchemy and the Occult Arts*, Dover Publications, New York, 1971.

Steiner, R., *An Outline of Occult Science*, Anthroposophic Press, New York, 1972.

HERALDRY AND CHIVALRY

Aveling, S.T., *Heraldry, Ancient and Modern*, Frederick Warne, London, 1873.

Barber, Richard, *The Knight and Chivalry*, Longman, London, 1970.

Brook-Little, J.P., *Boutell's Heraldry*, Frederick Warne, London, 1969.

Capellanus, Andreas, *The Art of Courtly Love* (trans. J.J. Parry), Columbia University Press, New York, 1941.

Foster, Joseph, *The Dictionary of Heraldry*, Studio Editions, London, 1994.

Fox-Davies, Arthur C., *A Complete Guide to Heraldry*, T.C. & E.C. Jack, Edinburgh, 1929.

Hooke, S.H., *The Siege Perilous*, SCM Press, London, 1956.

Kennedy, B., *Knighthood in the Mort d'Arthur*, D.S. Brewer, Cambridge, 1986.

Platts, Beryl, *Origins of Heraldry*, Proctor Press, London, 1980.

ARTHURIAN HISTORY AND ROMANCE

Ashe, Geoffrey, *Camelot and the Vision of Albion*, Heinemann, London, 1971.
Avalonian Quest, Methuen, London, 1982.

Barber, Richard, *Arthur of Albion*, Boydell Press, London, 1971.
The Figure of Arthur, Longman, London, 1972.
King Arthur in Legend and History, Cardinal / Sphere, London, 1973.
The Arthurian Legends: An Illustrated Anthology, Barnes & Noble, New York, 1993.

Cavendish, Richard, *King Arthur and the Grail*, Weidenfeld & Nicolson, London, 1978.

Chambers, A.K., *Arthur of Britain*, Sidgwick & Jackson, London, 1966.

Chrétien de Troyes, *Arthurian Romances*, Dent, London, 1987.

Clarke, G. (ed.), *Life of Merlin*, University of Wales Press, Cardiff, 1973.

Comfort, W.W., *Arthurian Romances*, E.P. Dutton, New York, 1914.

Fife, Graham, *Arthur the King*, BBC Books, London, 1990.

Geoffrey of Monmouth, *The Life of Merlin* (ed. J. Parry), University of Illinois Press, 1925.

Goodrich, Norma, *Merlin*, Franklin Watts, New York, 1989.
Arthur, Franklin Watts, New York, 1989.

Jarman, A.O.H., *The Legend of Merlin*, University of Wales Press, Cardiff, 1960.

Knight, G., *The Secret Tradition in Arthurian Legend*, Aquarian Press, Wellingborough, 1983.

Layamon, *Arthurian Chronicles* (trans. Eugene Mason), Dent, London, 1972.

Loomis, Roger Sherman, *Celtic Myth and the Arthurian Romance*, Columbia University Press, New York, 1977.
Arthurian Literature in the Middle Ages, Clarendon Press, Oxford, 1979.

Malory, Sir Thomas, *Le Mort D'Arthur*, New York University Books, New York, 1961
Tales of King Arthur (ed. Michael Senior), Book Club Associates, London, 1980.

Markale, Jean, *King Arthur*, King of Kings (trans. Christine Hauch), Gordon & Cremonesi, London, 1977.

Matthews, Caitlin, *Arthur and the Sovereignty of Britain*, Arkana, London, 1989.

Matthews, John, *The Arthurian Tradition*, Element Books, Shaftesbury, 1989.

Morris, John, *The Age of Arthur*, Weidenfeld & Nicolson, London, 1973.

Newstead, Helaine., *Brân the Blessed in Arthurian Romance*, Columbia Univ. Press, New York, 1939

Phillips, Graham and Keatman, Martin, *King Arthur, the True Story*, Century, London, 1992.

Pollard, Alfred, *The Romance of King Arthur*, Macmillan, London, 1979.

Stewart, R.J., *The Mystic Life of Merlin*, Arkana, London, 1986.
Tolstoy, Count Nikolai, *The Quest for Merlin*, Hamish Hamilton, London, 1985.
Topsfield, L.T., *A Study of the Arthurian Romances of Chrétien de Troyes*, Cambridge University Press, Cambridge, 1981.
Wace, Robert, *Arthurian Chronicles* (trans. Eugene Mason), Dent, London, 1972.

THE HOLY GRAIL

Anderson, Flavia, *The Ancient Secret*, Research Into Lost Knowledge Organization/Thorsons, Wellingborough, 1953.
Baigent, M., Leigh, R. and Lincoln, H., *The Holy Blood and the Holy Grail*, Jonathan Cape, London, 1982.
Bogdanow, Fanni, *The Romance of the Grail*, Manchester University Press, Manchester, 1966.
Bryant, Nigel (trans.), *Perlesvaus*, D.S. Brewer, Cambridge, 1978.
Burns, Jane E. (ed.), *The Vulgate Cycle*, Ohio State University Press, 1985.
Chrétien de Troyes, *Le Conte del Graal: The Story of the Grail* (trans. Ruth Harwood Cline), University of Georgia Press, 1985.
The Story of the Grail (trans. R.W. Linker), North Carolina Press, Chapel Hill, 1952.
Currer-Briggs, N., *The Shroud and the Grail*, Weidenfeld & Nicolson, London, 1987.
Evans, Sebastian, *In Quest of the Holy Grail*, Dent, London, 1898.
The High History of the Holy Grail [*Perlesvaus*] (trans.), Dent/Everyman, London, 1912.
Frappier, Jean, *Chrétien de Troyes and his Work* (trans. Raymond Cormier), Ohio State University Press, 1982.
Furnival, Frederick J. (ed.), *The History of the Holy Grail* [from Roman l'Estoire dou Saint Graal by Sires Robert de Boron] (trans. Henry Lonelich Skynner), Early English Text Society / N. Turner, London, 1861.
Jung, Emma and Von Franz, Marie Louise, *The Grail Legends* (trans. Andrea Dykes), Hodder & Stoughton, London, 1971.
Loomis, Roger Sherman, *The Grail: From Celtic Myth to Christian Symbolism*, University of Wales Press, Cardiff, 1963.
Matarasso, P.M. (trans.), *The Quest of the Holy Grail* [from the Queste del Saint Graal], Penguin, Harmondsworth, 1976.
Matthews, John, *The Grail: Quest for the Eternal*, Thames & Hudson, London, 1981.
The Grail Tradition, Element Books, Shaftesbury, 1990.
Household of the Grail, Aquarian Press, Wellingborough, 1990.
Owen, D.D.R., *The Evolution of the Grail Legend*, Oliver & Boyd, London, 1968.
Richey, Margaret Fitzgerald, *Studies of Wolfram Von Eschenbach*, Oliver & Boyd, London, 1957.
Sinclair, Andrew, *The Sword and the Grail*, Crown, New York, 1992.
Skeels, Dell, *The Romance of Perceval*, University of Washington Press, 1966.
Starbird, Margaret, *The Woman With the Alabaster Jar*, Bear, Santa Fe, 1993.
Von Eschenbach, Wolfram, *Parzival* (ed. Hugh D. Sacker), Cambridge University Press, Cambridge, 1963.
Waite, Arthur E., *The Hidden Church of the Holy Grail*, Rebman, London, 1909.
Webster, K.G.T. (trans.), *Lanzelet*, Columbia University Press, New York, 1951.

PEERAGES AND FORMAL REGISTERS

Anderson, James, *Royal Genealogies*, 1732-1736.
Burke's *Peerage and Baronetage*, 1840.
Burke's *Landed Gentry*, 1848.
Burke's *Extinct and Dormant Peerages*, 1952.
Douglas, Sir Robert of Glenbervie, *The Peerage of Scotland*, 1764.
Douglas's *Baronage of Scotland*, 1798.
The Great Seal Register of Scotland.
Massue, Melville Henry, 9th Marquis of Ruvigny & Raineval, *The Royal Blood of Britain*, 1903.
The Jacobite Peerage, Baronage, Knightage and Grants of Honour, 1904.
The Titled Nobility of Europe, 1914.
Paul, Sir James Balfour, Lord Lyon, *Ordinary of Scottish Arms*, 1903.
The Scots Peerage, 1904-1914
The Privy Seal Register of Scotland

INDEX